A COMMENTARY

ON THE

New Testament Epistles of Peter, John, and Jude

BY

GUY N. WOODS

Other Books by the Same Author:
Commentary on John; Commentary on James; The Second Coming and Other Sermons; Questions and Answers—Open Forum; How to Read the Greek New Testament; Cogdill-Woods Debate; Woods-Franklin Debate; Woods-Griffin Debate; Britnell-Woods Debate

GOSPEL ADVOCATE COMPANY
NASHVILLE, TENN.
1991

COPYRIGHT BY
GUY N. WOODS

Complete Set ISBN 0-89225-000-3
This Volume ISBN 0-89225-013-5
Paperback ISBN 0-89225-445-9

To

B. C. GOODPASTURE

*An Esteemed Friend, A Beloved
Brother, and A Faithful
Co-laborer In The Lord*

A GENERAL INTRODUCTION

It is gratifying to have another Commentary on the Epistles of Peter, John, and Jude. The reference material on these Epistles is not extensive. By members of the churches of Christ little has been written on the General Epistles.

But this is not *just* another Commentary on the books of the New Testament in question. It is a scholarly and valuable work on some of the most practical and significant books of the Bible. By a careful study of this volume the reader will be led into a better understanding and a finer appreciation of these Epistles. Brother Woods has made frequent use of the original; but he has done so in such manner that those who have no knowledge of Greek can profit by his appeal to it.

This volume will rank with the best numbers in this series of New Testament Commentaries. This writer has carefully read it in manuscript form. He is glad to commend it to the diligent study of all. There are difficult passages in these Epistles—passages about the meaning of which scholars are not agreed. The reader may not always agree with the author, but he will always learn from him.

It is our hope and prediction that this book will enjoy a wide circulation.

B. C. Goodpasture

PREFACE

These notes represent the results of approximately eighteen months of the most intensive effort on the part of the author to explain the sacred text of the Epistles of Peter, John and Jude. In his effort to illumine the writings of these portions of the scripture every device available to this writer was utilized. Where such a vast variety of possible explanations obtain, it is not expected that all readers will always concur in every interpretation given, but it is hoped that the notes will prove to be thought-provoking, stimulative and prompting to further study. Though primarily designed for the ordinary English reader, it is thought that the critical notes which are interspersed may prove to be of value to those who are interested in the critical aspects of the study; and that they will not hinder or annoy any reader not interested therein. Those not concerned with the Greek words or phrases may simply skip them in their reading.

The author has refrained from a custom usually characteristic of commentators of parading a long list of authorities in support of the positions advocated. But few references will be found to what others have said; and these are, for the most part, limited to brief quotations from the so-called Church Fathers who lived near the apostolic age. It is believed that those who are interested in what others have written will prefer to consult them at their source; and those who look into this volume will do so to discover what it teaches and not some other. Neither is its pages burdened with a variety of interpretations which have accumulated through the years, only to refute them; those interested in such may read them from the pen of their authors. We have taken all the usual methods available to inform ourselves of what has been said with reference to these inspired books, and have then set out our considered judgment of the meaning in language, simple, concise, and clear.

It is remarkable that a commentary on the Epistles of Peter, John and Jude has never been written by a man whom we would regard as in fellowship with us today. Only two such works have appeared at all from men associated with the "Restoration movement," The People's New Testament with Notes, by B. W. Johnson; and, A Commentary on the Minor Epistles, by Judge Caton. Both of these men were members of what is now known as the

Christian Church. In order that these notes might be wholly independent of these works, and influenced in no fashion by them, we have refrained from consulting them in any particular.

The text followed has been that of the American Standard Version, copyrighted in 1901 by Thomas Nelson and Sons, on the whole, the most accurate and dependable translation in the English language.

The author makes this work available to the public fully aware of its imperfections, painfully conscious of its many defects, and with genuine regret that he is incapable of producing a better commentary on this marvelous portion of the Word of God. However, if it should, in some measure, cause fresh light to break out from the text, enable its readers to enter more fully into the mind of the Master as exhibited by these inspired penmen, and prompt any of us to greater faithfulness and fidelity in the Work of the Lord, we shall feel amply repaid for the almost unbelievable toil requisite to the production of such an effort.

PREFACE TO THE SECOND EDITION

This commentary, originally published in 1953, has been reprinted many times and is now offered in a slightly revised and enlarged edition. The author has had occasion often to review the positions advanced herein and is not aware of any he would now alter or reverse. We are grateful for the widespread acceptance it has enjoyed, and we believe that the additional material at the end will greatly enhance its value to serious and earnest students of the Word.

GUY N. WOODS
P.O. Box 150
Nashville, TN 37202

A COMMENTARY ON THE EPISTLES OF PETER

CONTENTS

INTRODUCTION

	Page
Biographical Sketch of the Author	11
Design and Characteristics of the Epistle	13
Genuineness of the Epistle	14
Time and Place of Writing	16

SECTION I (1: 1-12)

Introduction (1: 1-12)	19
Salutation (1: 1-12)	19
Eulogy and Thanksgiving (1: 3-5)	24
Joy in Affliction (1: 6-9)	28
Ministry of the Prophets (1: 10-12)	32

SECTION II (1: 13-2: 10)

Exhortations to Faithfulness	38
Soberness and Godliness Enjoined (1: 13-21)	38
Brotherly Love Enjoined (1: 22-25)	49
Means of Growth (2: 1-10)	52

SECTION III (2: 11-4: 5)

Special Duties Commanded	65
Conduct Before Unbelievers (2: 11, 12)	65
Submission to Civil Rulers (2: 13-17)	70
Duties of Servants to Masters (2: 18-25)	75
Duties of Wives to Husbands (3: 1-6)	86
Duties of Husbands to Wives (3: 7)	91
Duties of Christians to Each Other (3: 8-12)	93

Duties When Persecuted (3: 13-17) 96
Christ an Example of Suffering (3: 18-4: 6) 99
An Additional Note on 1 Pet. 3: 18-20 105

SECTION IV (4: 7-5: 9)

Admonitions to Christian Living 111
Faithfulness Enjoined (4: 7-11) 111
Suffering as Christians (4: 12-19) 116
Duties of Elders (5: 1-4) 122
Duties of the Young (5: 5a) 127
Humility and Watchfulness (5: 5b-9) 128

SECTION V (5: 10-14)

Conclusion 132
Benediction (5: 10-11) 132
Design and Bearer of the Epistle (5: 12) 133
Closing Salutations (5: 13, 14) 134
A COMMENTARY ON THE SECOND EPISTLE OF PETER ... 139
A COMMENTARY ON THE FIRST EPISTLE OF JOHN 195
A COMMENTARY ON THE SECOND EPISTLE OF JOHN 327
A COMMENTARY ON THE THIRD EPISTLE OF JOHN 353
A COMMENTARY ON THE EPISTLE OF JUDE 371

INTRODUCTION

AUTHOR OF THE EPISTLES OF PETER

Simon Peter, author of the epistles which bear his name (1 Pet. 1: 1; 2 Pet. 1: 1), was the son of Jonah (Matt. 16: 17), occasionally designated as John (John 21: 15-17), from a variant spelling of Joanes, the Greek name of his father. He was a brother of Andrew, with whom, along with James and John, the sons of Zebedee, he was engaged in the prosperous business of commercial fishing in the waters of the Sea of Galilee. His life, for the most part, was spent in that vicinity, first at Bethsaida (John 1: 44), and later at Capernaum, where it appears that he occupied a house in which his mother-in-law also lived. (Matt. 8: 14, 15.) He was of humble circumstances, and with little or no formal education, a fact noted by the Jewish Sanhedrin when, with John, he was arrested, brought before that tribunal, and straitly charged to speak no more in the name of Jesus. (Acts 4: 13.)

Peter was a married man, a fact to be gathered from references to his mother-in-law (Matt. 8: 14, 15); and it is implied that his wife accompanied him when at length he left his home to go forth preaching the gospel of the kingdom (1 Cor. 9: 5). Peter and his brother Andrew were first disciples of John the Baptist, from whom they received testimony regarding Jesus (John 1: 36); and shortly after, through the influence of Andrew, Peter was brought to Jesus, henceforth to be his disciple and servant (John 1: 40-42).

The author of the epistles of Peter was one of the original twelve appointed as apostles of the Lord (Mark 3: 13-19), and he was thereafter ever to occupy a most prominent and important place in the events of the Saviour's life. In all of the lists of apostles his name appears first. (Matt. 10: 4; Mark 3: 13-19; Luke 6: 12-16; Acts 1: 13.) With James and John, he enjoyed an intimacy with the Lord not vouchsafed to the other nine apostles. These three were privileged to be present when Jairus' daughter was raised (Mark 5: 22, 23, 35-43); to view the marvelous transformation scene (Matt. 17: 1ff.); and to witness the agony of dreadful Gethsemane (Matt. 26: 37.)

In a tragic moment, somberly described by the Lord as "the

hour and the power of darkness," the apostle, under the stress of great temptation, yielded shamefully to the flesh and three times denied, with oaths, the one for whom but a few short hours before he had so vigorously asserted his readiness to go to prison and to death. (Luke 22: 31-34, 54-60.) At the crowing of the cock, a token earlier announced, the sad, sorrowful eyes of the Saviour fell upon the wayward disciple, and he remembered his earlier protestations of undying faithfulness, and his heart broke under their steady gaze. As the full significance of his awful act dawned upon him, "he went out and wept bitterly." (Luke 22: 62.)

In consequence of his penitence, he was fully and freely forgiven, and restored to his position in the apostolic band. The women, to whom Jesus appeared following his resurrection, were instructed to bear the news to that disciple by name. (Mark 16: 7.) In an appearance to Peter, the apostle was led three times to express his love for the Lord, and as many times instructed to "feed my sheep." (John 21: 15-17.) He was privileged, on the day of Pentecost, to preach the gospel for the first time in the name of the risen Lord (Acts 2: 14ff.), and later at Caesarea, to "open the door of faith" to the Gentiles (Acts 10: 1-48), for which purpose the "keys of the kingdom of heaven" had been delivered unto him some months before (Matt. 16: 19).

Often, during the early days of the church, Peter was seized, imprisoned, beaten, and otherwise maltreated for his fidelity to the cause of Christ. Begotten again "unto a living hope by the resurrection of Jesus Christ from the dead" (1 Pet. 1: 3), he ever thereafter served his Lord with fortitude, zeal and faithfulness. He was impulsive, impetuous, warmhearted, disarming, sometimes vascillating, but always humble, devoted, courageous and true. The devotion which he felt to the cause to which he had dedicated his all is nowhere better evidenced than when, with John, he was forbidden to speak again the name of Jesus, he replied, "Whether it is right in the sight of God to hearken unto you rather than unto God, judge ye: for we cannot but speak the things which we saw and heard." (Acts 4: 13-20.)

The final mention of the apostle in Acts is in connection with the council held in Jerusalem (Acts 15), though later reference is made to him in Gal. 2: 11, when he was with Paul in Antioch.

Here, the curtain falls, and nothing more is certainly known of the colorful apostle other than the brief references to himself in his epistles. For the history of his subsequent labors we are dependent on tradition which, in this case, is most undependable. Of the time and place of his death, we have no reliable information. Clement of Rome, a hundred years following the last scriptural reference to Peter, says that he "through zeal undertook not one or two but numerous labors, and so having borne witness went to the place that was due to him." (Eph. 1: 4, 5.) There is a tradition that he was crucified head downward; and the prophecy regarding him in John 21: 18 implies a violent death. The claim of the Romanists, that the last years of his life were spent in Rome in a papal seat, are fanciful and false. There is no reliable evidence that Peter was ever in Rome.

DESIGN AND CHARACTERISTICS OF FIRST PETER

"I have written unto you briefly, exhorting, and testifying that this is the true grace of God: stand ye fast therein." (1 Pet. 5: 12.) The design of the epistle was thus (a) to exhort; (b) to testify with reference to "the true grace of God; and (c) to encourage the saints to greater stedfastness therein. Written to people who were then passing through a "fiery trial" of persecution, the purpose of the epistle was to confirm them in the faith of the gospel; strengthen them to greater endurance in the conflicts in which they struggled; and to comfort them with the assurance that in being "partakers of Christ's sufferings," they would, "at the revelation of his glory," be privileged "to rejoice with exceeding joy." (1 Pet. 4: 12, 13.) To this end many motives are advanced for the consolation of the saints and to encourage them to greater fortitude and patience in the "manifold trials" which beset them. Christ, as an example of patient resignation in suffering, is offered, and the readers urged to "follow" his steps. (1 Pet. 2: 21.) Helpless and alone before their cruel and bitter enemies Peter, a fellow sufferer, thus recalled for them the experiences of him who "when he was reviled, reviled not again; when he suffered, threatened not; but committed himself to him that judgeth righteously." (1 Pet. 2: 23.)

The key words of First Peter are, therefore, *patience* and *hope,*

—resignation in suffering, and an expectation of deliverance in the by and by. As grounds for such, the sufferings of Christ, the redemption thus obtained, the agony of the cross, the triumph of the resurrection, and the glory of the exaltation are often alluded to.

Knowing that those to whom he wrote were constantly being subjected to the evil influences of false and designing teachers who sought to lead the saints to use their freedom as "a cloak of wickedness" (1 Pet. 2: 16), he urged constant and unceasing vigilance against all such. Then, as now, there were those who sought to "turn the grace of God into lasciviousness," and who contended that when saved by grace one is released from the obligations of law and is no longer answerable for his conduct in the flesh; and these Peter wrote to refute, and to exhibit a true analysis of the grace of God.

There is little of a purely local or provincial character in First Peter, the themes treated being of general and universal application and therefore as applicable to us of this day as to those originally addressed. Penned by one far along in years and with the realization that he must soon put off his "earthly tabernacle" (2 Pet. 1: 12), Peter disregarded earthly and temporal matters and wrote vividly and feelingly of the eternal interests of the soul.

GENUINENESS OF FIRST PETER

The *genuineness* of a book or other literary production relates to the question of authorship—whether it actually proceeds from and was produced by the source or author to whom it is ascribed. Of many books this question is, at best, of secondary importance, such books being judged by the character of their contents, and not by the author whose name they bear. With reference to the books of the Bible, however, the question of *genuineness*—authorship—is, for many reasons, an exceedingly vital and important one. In many instances the authority of the book itself derives from the question of authorship; and in every case the reliability of the book is involved. Where a book is ascribed to a definite writer the historicity of the book depends on the truthfulness of the ascription. In every instance, therefore, the question of authorship is of the essence of the trustworthiness and credibility of the book itself.

INTRODUCTION 15

Proof of the genuineness of the first epistle of Peter is the most ancient and abundant of all the books of the New Testament. This evidence may be gathered up under three heads: (1) testimony of the letter itself; (2) internal evidence; (3) testimony of early writers.

(1) The epistle purports to be from the pen of Peter, his signature being affixed thereto, and appearing at the beginning: "Peter, an apostle of Jesus Christ. . . ." (1 Pet. 1: 1.) In view of the fact that the book claims to have been produced by that apostle, to attribute it to the authorship of another is to assign to the whole of it the character of a forged document, a spurious production. It is not possible to accept the book as a reliable and authentic production while denying that it was produced by him whose name it bears.

(2) Internal evidence of the Petrine authorship of First Peter is so abundant and overwhelming as to strike the reasonable mind with the force of a demonstration. Intimately interwoven into its very warf and woof are indications of genuineness impossible for a forger or an imitator to have achieved. A careful consideration of all the facts and a detailed examination of the text points irresistibly to Peter as the only possible author. In verse after verse of the book we see vividly portrayed the influence of events in the public ministry of our Lord in which Peter participated, or was present—an influence that could have been obtained in no other way. The evidence thus derived is all the stronger because it is undesigned. Without mentioning, or, for that matter, even hinting at the events which then occurred, the apostle, by the use of terms and modes of expression, reveals the indelible influence which the Lord wrought upon him in his public ministry.

For example, Jesus said to him, "Thou art Peter (*petros*) and upon this rock (*petra*) I will build my church." (Matt. 16: 18.) Why else but for the influence of this statement upon him should he later describe Christ as "a chief corner stone" of a spiritual house wherein his followers are "living stones"? (1 Pet. 1: 2, 4-8.) In the same context in which the Saviour referred to him as a rock, he called him an *offence*. The two references Peter took and joined together in the vivid and striking phrase, "a rock of offence." (1 Pet. 2: 8.) When the Lord bade him pay the temple tax (Matt. 17: 24), he reminded him that the children are free; and Peter was later to admonish those to whom he wrote that "though free" they were to be subject to every ordinance of man for the Lord's sake. When that disciple inquired of the Lord if it is sufficient to forgive seven times, and was told that it must be seventy times seven—that is, to infinity, he was later to write, "love covereth a multitude of sins." (Matt. 18: 22; 1 Pet. 4: 8.) In an object lesson in humility he had seen his Lord gird himself with a towel and wash the disciples' feet (John 13: 1-6); and he later bade Christians "to tie humility on them like a slave's apron" (1 Pet. 5: 5). Jesus often used the word "adversary" as an opposer (Matt. 5: 25; Luke 18: 3), a word which readily found its way into the apostle's vocabulary in the striking sentence, "Be sober, be watchful; your adversary the devil, as a roaring lion, walketh about, seeking whom he may devour" (1 Pet. 5: 8). He had seen—from afar—the Lord's submission to the shame of Pilate's Hall, and he therefore wrote with feeling of him "who, when he was reviled, reviled not again; when he suffered, threatened not; but committed himself to him that judgeth righteously." (1 Pet. 2: 23.) He had seen the ragged timber on which the Lord died, and to him it was a "tree" up to which the Saviour bore our sins. (1 Pet. 2: 24, margin.) Three times bidden to feed the flock of God (John 21: 15-17), he came to regard Christ as "the Shepherd and Bishop of souls, and his disciples as the flock of God (1 Pet. 2: 25; 5: 2). Many such allusions to events with which the apostle was perfectly familiar abound in the book, and constitute to the candid mind evidence of an irresistible nature touching the genuineness of First Peter.

TIME AND PLACE OF WRITING

While sufficient data from which to determine the exact time of the composition of the First Epistle of Peter does not exist, it is possible, from numerous incidental and inferential references in the book, to fix the date within reasonably well defined limits.

(1) There are numerous points of correspondence between the Ephesian letter of Paul and First Peter—similarities that can be accounted for on the hypothesis that the letter to the church in Ephesus was in the hands of Peter prior to the writing of his own

epistle. The following instances from the first chapter (and they are equally numerous in the other portions) will exhibit this dependence: 1 Pet. 1: 3, Eph. 1: 3; 1 Pet. 1: 1, Eph. 1: 4; 1 Pet. 1: 1, Eph. 5: 18; 1 Pet. 1: 15, Eph. 4: 1; 1 Pet. 1: 12, Eph. 3: 5, 10; 1 Pet. 1: 5, Eph. 1: 19; 1 Pet. 1: 14, Eph. 2: 3. It is now quite generally believed that the Ephesian letter was written near the close of the two years' imprisonment of Paul in Rome, A.D. 63. Inasmuch as the evidence tends to establish Peter's familiarity with that Epistle, it follows that First Peter was not written prior to A.D. 63.

(2) At the time Peter wrote the letter, John Mark was with him in Babylon. (1 Pet. 5: 13.) When the Colossian letter was written (A.D. 62, 63), Mark was with Paul in Rome, but was about to begin a journey into Asia Minor. (Col. 4: 10.) Four or five years later he was still in Asia Minor, but on the verge of returning to Rome with Timothy. (2 Tim. 4: 11.) It is, therefore, reasonable to conclude that within this interval, 63-67, Mark journeyed to Babylon and was in that city when the First Epistle of Peter was penned. The date of the epistle may then be confined between these limits.

(3) A time of trial was impending. The time had come for judgment to begin at the house of God. (1 Pet. 4: 17.) Persecution was not to be longer regarded as "a strange thing" (1 Pet. 4: 12), but as the "home portion" of the saints henceforth. It was the outbreak before the storm, advance persecution before the beginning of any determined and legalistic effort to exterminate Christianity. We may, therefore, with reasonable probability, fix the date of the epistle on the eve of the Neronian persecution— A.D. 65.

The *place* of composition, though designated by name, has occasioned much controversy. Near the close of the epistle, Peter wrote, "She that is in Babylon, elect together with you, saluteth you; and so doth Mark my son." (1 Pet. 5: 13.) The identity and location of the place styled "Babylon" in this message has been, and is, a matter of much dispute. Places suggested have been (a) Babylon in Egypt; (b) Jerusalem; (c) Rome; (d) Babylon on the Euphrates. Those who propose Jerusalem or Rome assign to the word "Babylon" a figurative meaning. There is, however, no evidence that Jerusalem was ever called Babylon; and it was long after Peter penned these words that such a designation was applied to Rome. We may, therefore, be reasonably certain that Peter referred to neither of these places in the foregoing passage. Babylon in Egypt was a small, unimportant, insignificant place; there were but few Jews there; and there is no evidence that a church was established there until long after the apostolic age. It is exceedingly unlikely that such was the "Babylon" to which the apostle alluded. There thus seems sufficient reason to conclude that the view that the epistle was written from the world famous Babylon on the Euphrates is the correct one, and it is accordingly adopted here. (For additional comments see note in the commentary on 1 Pet. 5: 13.)

A COMMENTARY ON THE FIRST EPISTLE OF PETER

SECTION ONE

THE INTRODUCTION
1: 1-12

1. SALUTATION
1: 1, 2

1 Peter, an apostle of Jesus Christ, to the elect who are sojourners of the Dispersion in Pontus, Galatia, Cappadocia, Asia, and Bithynia, 2 according

---

1 Peter,—The word "Peter" is the English translation of the Greek *petros*, a *rock* or *stone*. (See margin, American Standard Version.) The Greek lexicographers define it as "a detached but large fragment of rock." (Thayer, etc.) It was assigned as a proper name to the disciple by the Lord because of traits of character and habits of life he was later to exhibit. The Saviour saw, by anticipation, the enduring qualities of character which were to manifest themselves in his life, and hence said to him, "Thou art Simon the son of John: thou shalt be called Cephas (which is by interpretation, Peter). (John 1: 42.) The author thus began his epistle with the name which Jesus gave him instead of "Simon Bar-Jonah" (Simon *son* of Jonah) by which he was once known (Matt. 16: 18), an indication of the high regard he felt for the name which his Lord had assigned him. His two names occur in the New Testament in two forms, the fuller form of Simon being *Symeon,* appearing thus in the speech of James in Jerusalem (Acts 15: 14), the shorter and usual name Simon occurring often elsewhere. The other, Peter, occurs not only thus, but also in the Graecized form *Cephas,* from the Aramaic *Kepha*. (John 1: 42.) The Lord frequently addressed him as Simon, but the name Peter is that by which he is most often designated in the book of Acts, and by us today.

An apostle of Jesus Christ,—The words, "an apostle," are descriptive of the nature of Peter's work in the service of the Lord, and "of Jesus Christ," the source of the authority by which he exercised it. "Apostle" (*apo*—from, and *stello*,—to send), an envoy

to the foreknowledge of God the Father, in sanctification of the Spirit, unto

or ambassador, signifies one sent on a mission with proper credentials. The credentials of the apostles were the miracles they were enabled to perform in confirmation of their work (Mark 16: 20; Heb. 2: 1-4), and their mission was the proclamation of the gospel of Christ under the great commission (Mark 16: 15, 16; Acts 1: 8). Peter was one of the twelve chosen by the Lord to be apostles at the outset of his public ministry (Luke 6: 12-16), and his name appears first in all the lists thereof (Matt. 10: 4; Mark 3: 13; Luke 6: 12-16; Acts 1: 13). However, neither here nor elsewhere, did he claim, or seek to exercise, any superiority or distinction of rank over the other apostles, describing himself simply as *an* apostle (one among several) of Jesus Christ.

To the sojourners of the dispersion,—The word sojourners refers to people who have left their native land and are living temporarily on foreign soil, and among strangers. It is translated from *parepideemos*, compounded from *para*, beside, *epi*, upon, and *deemos* a strange people, thus, literally, to dwell alongside those of a strange land. The "Dispersion" was a technical term of common usage among the Jews to designate those of their race who were scattered among the Gentile nations. (John 7: 35.) It occurs in the Septuagint (a Greek translation of the Old Testament scriptures) in the passage, "Thou shalt be removed into all the kingdoms of the earth." (Deut. 25: 28.) In view of these facts, the temptation is strong to assign a literal significance to these terms here, and conclude that Peter wrote to Christian Jews away from Palestine, and in the provinces designated. An examination of the whole epistle, however, raises serious doubts as to the correctness of this conclusion. In 1 Pet. 2: 11, the author uses the word *parepideemos* (where it is translated *pilgrim*) in an obviously figurative sense (as does Paul in Heb. 11: 13), for Christians generally, without regard to former relationships or races; and it is therefore probable that in 1: 1 he intended to indicate by "sojourners" all people of God who were then sojourning on the earth among unbelievers, and therefore in a more comprehensive sense than the literal terms would signify. Other considerations suggest this conclusion: (a) From the narrative in Acts, we learn that the

obedience and sprinkling of the blood of Jesus Christ: Grace to you and peace be multiplied.

churches addressed—Pontus, Galatia, Cappadocia, Asia and Bithynia—were predominantly Gentile, and it appears unlikely that Peter would send such a missive to a minority among them. (b) Though the thoughts of the epistle are Jewish in background, and many quotations from the Old Testament occur, no reference is made to the law of Moses, as such; and the Greek word for law—*nomos*—does not occur in its vocabulary. (c) Statements occurring in 1: 14, 2: 10, 4: 3, and elsewhere seem to require a non-Jewish background for those particularly addressed. (d) It is unaccountable that Peter would have written to Jewish Christian women that they were (would become, *egeneetheete,* 2 per. plural, aor. 1 ind. pass. of *ginomai,* to become), daughters of Sarah "if ye do well." (1 Pet. 3: 6.) These premises lead to the conclusion that the apostle wrote to Christians, both Jew and Gentile, without regard to their religious or racial backgrounds, as composing the body in which there is "neither Greek nor Jew, circumcision and uncircumcision, barbarian, Scythian, bondman, freeman; but Christ is all and in all." (Col. 3: 11.)

In Pontus, Galatia, Cappadocia, Asia, and Bithynia,—The provinces designated were in that geographical subdivision known as "Asia Minor," north of the Mediterranean, and east of the Aegean Sea, in that country now known as Turkey.

1, 2 Elect . . . according to the foreknowledge of God the Father,—"Elect" is from *eklego,* a word signifying to choose or to select. A verb form of this word is translated "choose" in John 15: 16, "chose" in Eph. 1: 4, and "have chosen" in John 13: 18. "Foreknowledge" is from the Greek *"prognosis,"* previous determination, purpose. (Bagster.) These, therefore, to whom Peter wrote were chosen people, selected by an exercise of the divine will, and in keeping with a purpose earlier formed. Was this purpose or plan conditional or unconditional?

For centuries the religious world has been divided into two great camps, as this question has been answered affirmatively or negatively. Some maintain that the choice of the Father in the selection of those elected was sovereign and unconditional, and that it was made before the creation of the world. They also allege that it was done without regard to the worth or merit of those elected; that it was partial in nature and limited in application; and that the number is so fixed that it cannot be increased nor diminished. The theory was first formulated by Augustine, and adopted and popularized by Calvin during the Reformation.

Such a theory of election is palpably false for many reasons. (1) It is in conflict with the scriptures which positively assert the conditionality of salvation (Matt. 7: 21; Luke 13: 3; Acts 17: 30; 2 Thess. 1: 7-9; 1 John 2: 4; etc., etc.). (2) It represents God as a cruel and arbitrary sovereign acting by caprice and not by the principles of justice and right. (3) It cancels out all human responsibility, and reduces man to the status of a mere puppet manipulated by the Lord, unworthy of any commendation for good done, and deserving of no condemnation for any evil practiced. (2) All invitations, promises, warnings, threatenings and admonitions to faithfulness in the Word of God become meaningless and without significance. (5) It makes God a respecter of persons despite the definite declaration of scripture that he is not. (1 Pet. 1: 17.)

It should be observed that 1 Pet. 1: 1, 2 asserts the *fact* of election and its origin in the purpose and plan of God; the *manner* and *means* by which it is accomplished must be sought elsewhere. This information Paul supplies: "But we are bound to give thanks to God always for you, brethren beloved of the Lord, for that God chose you from the beginning unto salvation in sanctification of the Spirit and belief of the truth: whereunto he called you through our gospel, to the obtaining of the glory of our Lord Jesus Christ." (2 Thess. 2: 13, 14.) (1) God "chose." (2) He "chose from the beginning." (3) The choice was made "in sanctification of the Spirit and belief of the truth." (4) Those thus chosen were "called" through the gospel. The gospel is addressed to all men: "Go ye into all the world, and preach the gospel to the whole creation. He that believeth and is baptized shall be saved; but he that disbelieveth shall be condemned." (Mark 16: 15, 16.) Thus, (a) all are called by the gospel. (b) All who believe and obey the gospel are saved. (c) But God chooses (elects) those who are saved. (d) Therefore, God chooses or elects to salvation all who obey the gospel. Such is the true doctrine of election.

In sanctification of the Spirit,—The word "sanctification" is from the Greek *agiasmos,* the fundamental idea of which is derived from the Hebrew *kadosh,* separation. That which has been sanctified is set apart, separated to special purposes. We thus learn here that the function of the Spirit in election is to separate the sinner to the sphere where, through obedience and sprinkling of the blood of Christ he is made a chosen or elected one. This, the Spirit accomplishes by revealing, through the Word of truth, the means by which one obeys the Lord and is thereby enabled to appropriate to himself the benefits of the sprinkled blood.

Unto obedience and sprinkling of the blood of Jesus Christ. —The preposition "unto" *(eis)* indicates the design and end of the plan provided for man's salvation—to bring him to obedience, without which no election is available. In the "sprinkling of the blood of Jesus Christ," there is an allusion to the ceremonial of Ex. 24: 8, where Moses took the blood and sprinkled it on the people and said, "Behold, the blood of the covenant which the Lord hath made with you." In similar fashion, those who are chosen to salvation "in sanctification of the Spirit and belief of the truth" have had applied to them the precious blood of Jesus, by means of which they are cleansed from their sins, and made members of the new covenant. "Unto obedience" indicates the human, and "sprinkling the blood of Jesus Christ," the divine side of salvation. The prepositions of verses 1 and 2 are significant and revealing: Election is "according to" *(kata)* the purpose and plan of God; it is "in" *(en)* the sphere of the Spirit's influence; and it is "unto" *(eis),* i.e., designed to produce obedience. The work of the entire godhead in the salvation of man is evidenced in this remarkable passage. From it we learn that the Father elects, the Spirit sanctifies, and the Son, by his blood, redeems.

Grace to you, and peace be multiplied.—The author, in this salutation, joins the lovely and impressive greeting of the Greeks *(Chaire!* "grace") and the Hebrews *(shalom,* peace!), with which the people of these races were accustomed to hail one another. A similar salutation occurs often in Paul's epistles. (Rom. 1: 7; 1 Cor. 1: 3; Gal. 1: 3; Eph. 1: 2; Phil. 1: 2, etc.) See Matt. 10: 12, 13 for an example of the Hebrew usage (Acts 15: 23), for the usual formula of Greek missives. The grace Peter desired for his

3 Blessed *be* ¹the God and Father of our Lord Jesus Christ, who accord-

¹Or, *God and the Father* See Rom. 15. 6 marg.

readers was not, however, the mere favor of men and the earthly joy which the Greek greeting signified; nor was the peace no more than the tranquil and serene life desired by the Hebrews. The grace here contemplated embraced abundant spiritual blessing, and the peace was the peace of God and of Christ, as well as peace with one's brethren. Moreover, it included peace in one's soul, peace that influenced and sweetened the entire life. Such the apostle desired to abound (be multiplied) in the lives of those whom he had addressed.

2. EULOGY AND THANKSGIVING
1: 3-5

Preparatory to the introduction of the general theme of the epistle—patience in trial and hope for the future—Peter praised the Father for the re-establishment of their faith by the resurrection of Christ, for the living hope they now experienced through it, for the inheritance reserved in heaven for them, and for the promise of preservation that was theirs. Verses 3-5 emphasize the functions of the Father, verses 6-9 the activities of the Son, and verses 10-12 the participation of the Holy Spirit in these matters.

3 Blessed be the God and Father of our Lord Jesus Christ, —Here, as elsewhere in Peter's epistles, there is striking correspondence with sentiments expressed by Paul (2 Cor. 1: 3; Eph. 1: 3), indicating familiarity with Paul's writings. It is certain that Peter was acquainted with some of the epistles of Paul (2 Pet. 3: 15, 16), and his frequent reproduction of phrases characteristic of that apostle reveals that he was influence thereby.

"Blessed" is from the Greek *eulogetos* from which we derive our English words, "eulogy," "eulogize." The term occurs also in Rom. 1: 25; 9: 5; 2 Cor. 1: 3 and Eph. 1: 3. New Testament writers use it with reference to God only, though a participial form of it is sometimes applied to men. The word means to speak well of another; to praise. It is not the same word as that translated "blessed" in the beatitudes. (Matt. 5: 3-11.) There, the word is *makarios,* "spiritual prosperity."

ing to his great mercy begat us again unto a living hope by the resurrection

Who according to his great mercy begat us again unto a living hope by the resurrection of Jesus Christ from the dead, —The emphasis in this verse is on the word *again*. Peter and the other disciples of Jesus had been spiritually begotten before, but in the tragic hours of the Lord's condemnation and death their faith had failed and was not revived until the full impact and implications of the resurrection struck them with its irresistible force. The reference here is, therefore, to the re-establishment of the faith of the disciples by the resurrection of Jesus from the dead. Peter, along with all of the disciples, clung tenaciously to the view that Jesus would restore the Jewish political state and establish himself as an earthly ruler on the throne thereof, in Jerusalem. When he allowed himself to fall into the hands of the Romans and to die on the cross, the hope of the disciples was blasted and their faith failed. The attitude of all of them was feelingly expressed in the words of the two disciples on the road to Emmaus, when they sadly commented, "But we hoped that it was he who should redeem Israel." (Luke 23: 21.) Peter, his faith gone, returned to his nets. But, though his hopes died with Christ on the cross, and were buried with him in Joseph's tomb, they surged to new life, and to "a living hope" by the resurrection of the Lord from the dead. Peter describes this resurgence to hope by the word "living," in contrast to the temporal and perishable expectations of men which, however attractive and alluring, will, with all earthly things, inevitably fail. In the quickening to new faith and life, Peter saw an exhibition of God's "great mercy." Unbelievers all, and apostates from the faith, they were utterly unworthy of the rich provisions of grace so wondrously afforded them, and he attributed it all to the "great mercy of God."

The word "hope," or its equivalents, occurs often in Peter's phraseology. It was a sentiment especially precious to those who were suffering severe persecution (1 Pet. 4: 12), and it buoyed them up with the expectation of deliverance in the by and by. If it is proper to style John the apostle of *love*, and Paul the apostle of *faith*, it is eminently true that Peter may be regarded as the apostle of hope. It is significant that the word "hope" does not occur in the books of Matthew, Mark or Luke. In the classical writers the

of Jesus Christ from the dead, 4 unto an inheritance incorruptible, and undefiled, and that fadeth not away, reserved in heaven for you, 5 who by the

word here translated "hope" means no more than expectation, the element of desire being absent. It is through the influence of Christianity, and primarily the resurrection of Christ, that to the expectation a desire for better things was added to constitute Christian hope.

4 Unto an inheritance, incorruptible, and undefiled, and that fadeth not away,—While verse three deals primarily with the renewal of faith which the apostles and other disciples experienced as a result of the resurrection of Jesus, Peter's words appear to have an extended application and to apply in a secondary sense to all who have been born again. (John 3: 3-5; James 1: 18; 1 Cor. 4: 16; 1 Pet. 1: 23.) The new birth (John 3: 5), and the relationship of children which is implied in it, suggests an inheritance awaiting. In this relationship, his children are his heirs and joint heirs with the Lord Jesus Christ. (Rom. 8: 17.) The figure of an inheritance to indicate future blessings is a common one to New Testament writers. (Acts 20: 32; Gal. 3: 18; Eph. 1: 14, 18, and often elsewhere.)

(1) The inheritance which awaits the faithful children of God is "incorruptible" (*aphthartos*, immortal, imperishable, undying, enduring), and thus not affected by the lapse of ages. It is wholly unlike all earthly inheritances which, however attractive and satisfying for a time, must inevitably yield to dissolution and decay. Only the inheritance which we shall receive from the Father is incorruptible, for it alone is eternal.

(2) The inheritance is also "undefiled" (*amiantos*), unstained, unsoiled, therefore, pure and chaste. This word also appears in Heb. 7: 26, where it is used to describe the undefilement characteristic of Jesus, our High Priest. Being undefiled, the inheritance does not partake of the contamination characteristic of the inheritance of men. The earthly Canaan was not able to escape this defilement (Lev. 18: 27, 28), but into the heavenly Canaan nothing shall ever enter to defile or make it unclean (Rev. 21: 27).

(3) The inheritance is "unfading." The words, "that fadeth not away," are translated from the beautiful word *amarantos,* that which does not fade, or wither. The amaranth was a fabled flower

power of God are guarded through faith unto a salvation ready to be re-

whose bloom was perpetual, and whose loveliness never failed. The inheritance which awaits the children of God will not deteriorate, nor will passing ages render it less desirable or attractive. There is an assonance obtaining between the words translated "undefiled" and "that fadeth not away," which does not appear in English, but which may be reproduced by the English reader by pronouncing slowly the words, *am i an tos* and *am a ran tos*. The feebleness of conception characteristic of us with reference to that which awaits in the next world is indicated by the fact that the sacred writer, in describing some of its features, could only explain that *it is not like* the things wich which we are familiar *here*.

Reserved in heaven for you,—Hence, not available in this life. Eternal life—the inheritance of the people of God—is not a present possession, but a promise, the realization of which must await our entrance into the world to come. (Mark 10: 30; Tit. 1: 2; 1 John 2: 25.) This inheritance is "reserved" (*tereo*, to keep in watchful custody) "in heaven," and is, therefore, not a promise the enjoyment of which will be on earth, as premillennialists contend. The saint's future abode is in heaven, which Jesus has gone to prepare. (John 14: 2.)

5 **Who by the power of God are guarded through faith,**— The children of God are thus (a) guarded; (b) guarded by (literally *in*) the power of God; and (c) guarded through faith. "Guarded" is from *phrouomenous,* present participle of *phrouoreo*, to protect with a garrison, or military guard. The term thus has a military connotation, and as used here, metaphorically suggests a band of soldiers thrown about the faithful to protect and to guarantee their safety so long as theiy remain within the stockade of faith! The present tense indicates action in progress, and the guarding is, therefore, continuous and unfailing. It is exercised by (in) the power (*dunamis,* from which is derived our words, *dynamic, dynamo, dynamite*) of God, a statement reminiscent of Rom. 1: 16, where we are informed that the "gospel is the power of God unto salvation"; and the guarding is through faith, and not by an independent operation of God's power, apart from human participation or effort. It is possible for one's faith to fail (Luke

vealed in the last time. 6 Wherein ye greatly rejoice, though now for a little while, if need be, ye have been put to grief in manifold ²trials, 7 that

²Or, *temptations*

22: 31, 32), a fact with which Peter was painfully conscious; and there is an important sense in which one must keep himself in the love of God (Jude 21). Those whose faith endures are guarded effectively against the assaults of Satan, all others suffering defeat at his hands, as did Peter when his faith failed. This passage, far from teaching the impossibility of apostasy, establishes, by implication, its very definite possibility.

Unto a salvation ready to be revealed in the last time,— The salvation here contemplated is not that promised in Mark 16: 15, 16, that salvation being limited to past, or alien sins, but to the salvation of the soul in heaven. It is the equivalent of "the glory which shall be revealed to usward," at the revelation "of the sons of God." (Rom. 8: 18, 19.) This salvation is not available here, and cannot be enjoyed until the last day. Verse 5 contains a warning as well as a glorious and blessed assurance. While it assures us that the Father protects his heirs, even as he guards their inheritance, it also reveals that those who cease to believe will be excluded from the inheritance.

3. JOY IN AFFLICTION
1: 6-9

6 **Wherein ye greatly rejoice,**—Though "wherein" seems most naturally in our translation, to refer to the "salvation" of verse 5, actually the text will not bear this interpretation, for the word "herein" *(en ho)* is neuter gender, and thus requires a neuter antecedent. The word "salvation" is feminine. That which was in the apostle's mind was the whole of the blessings earlier enumerated—sonship, forgiveness of sins, the divine inheritance and the providential care of the Father. Notwithstanding the fact that these to whom Peter wrote were suffering severe persecution as Christians, he bade them to find occasion for rejoicing, in the midst of trial, in the contemplation of the present and the future blessings which were theirs as children of the heavenly Father. The adverb and verb "greatly rejoice" are translated from one Greek word *(angalliasthe,* to rejoice exceedingly, to exalt) which

the proof of your faith, *being* more precious than gold that perisheth though it is proved by fire, may be found unto praise and glory and honor at the

occurs also in the Sermon on the Mount when the Saviour said, "Blessed are ye when men shall reproach you, and persecute you, and say all manner of evil against you falsely, for my sake. Rejoice, *and be exceeding glad (angalliasthe):* for great is your reward in heaven: for so persecuted they the prophets that were before you." (Matt. 5: 11, 12.) Peter's use of the term in the same connection as that which characterized our Lord's use of it in that sermon is significant, being another indication (with which the epistles of Peter abound) of the profound influence the Lord wrote upon that disciple by his teaching during his public ministry.

Though now for a little while, if need be,—The "little while" is descriptive of the duration of suffering the saints were undergoing which, though it should extend through the whole of their life span would, in comparison with the endless ages of eternity, be slight. Similarly, Paul wrote, "For our light affliction, *which is for the moment,* worketh for us more and more exceeding an eternal weight of glory." (2 Cor. 4: 17.) "If need be" does not signify, as many commentators assert, that there is in these words an implication that the suffering of the saints was divinely sent; a view which seriously reflects on the goodness of God. The meaning is that if it should become necessary *(ei deon estin),* because of the circumstances characteristic of their time to be exposed to trials and hardships from without, they were not to despair, but to see in these difficulties an occasion for rejoicing in the test of their faith which such trials afforded.

7 That the proof of your faith, being more precious than gold that perisheth though it be proved by fire, may be found unto praise and glory and honor at the revelation of Jesus Christ.—The "manifold trials" in which they were being put to grief sum up the persecutions, deprivations, hardships and difficulties that they were experiencing as faithful children of God. The phrase "manifold trials" in Greek is the same as that translated "manifold temptations" in James 1: 2. The word "manifold" indicates that their trials had appeared in a variety of forms, suggesting diversity rather than number, though the number of them must also have been great.

revelation of Jesus Christ: 8 whom not having seen ye love; on whom, though now ye see him not, yet believing, ye rejoice greatly with joy un-

"Proof of your faith" is translated from the same phrase as "proving your faith" in James 1: 3. Here, as often elsewhere in the epistle, there is evidence of Peter's familiarity with the book of James and his dependence on it for many of his prominent ideas. The word "proof" from *dokimion*, suggests a trial or test for the purpose of determining the worthiness or character of that tested. As the assayer takes the gold ore and runs a test on it to determine the quality and quantity of the precious metal, so the trials through which the saints were passing constituted a crucible which tested their faith and revealed its true character. The Lexicographer Cremer says that the word *dokimion* signifies not only the "means of proof itself . . . but also the trace of the metal is left thereon."

This proof of faith is more precious than gold which perishes which, though proved by fire must, notwithstanding its enduring qualities, ultimately with all things worldly perish; whereas, "faith, hope and love" *abide,* such faith being unaffected by the corrupting and deteriorating influences of time.

The purpose for which this test is run is that the faith thus approved may be "found unto praise and glory and honor at the revelation of Jesus Christ," i.e., that it may show itself to be approved at the last day. The *praise* will consist of the benedictions of approval which shall come to those who have been good and faithful servants; the *glory* will be the tokens of triumph which shall then be bestowed; the crown and the robe and the palm; and the *honor* will be that which Jesus possessed before the world was, and which he will at length share with those who have followed him faithfully here. (John 17: 22.)

8 **Whom having not seen ye love:**—The saints to whom Peter wrote, being scattered through the provinces of Pontus, Galatia, Cappadocia, Asia, and Bithynia (1 Pet: 1), *had not seen* (literally, had not had so much as a glimpse of) the physical form of Jesus, and yet so vivid was their conception of him that they loved him as dearly as those disciples in Judaea who had been privileged to see his face. Their love did not depend, as human love ordinarily does, on outward, physical characteristics. In penning this statement, Peter was doubtless mindful of the words of the

speakable and ³full of glory: 9 receiving the end of your faith, *even the sal-*

³Gr. *glorified.*

Lord to the disciple Thomas: "Because thou hast seen me, thou hast believed: blessed are they that have not seen, and yet have believed." (John 20: 29.) Those who were acquainted with the fleshly characteristics of Jesus made no effort to retain them, allowing them to be replaced with the vision of the glorified Saviour. Said Paul, "Wherefore we henceforth know no man after the flesh: even though we have known Christ after the flesh, yet now we know him so no more." (2 Cor. 5: 16.) Jewish Christians, who had formerly placed so much confidence in fleshly descent, and he were at first attracted to Christ because he fulfilled the prophecies regarding fleshly descent from David, allowed these considerations, along with all the matters pertaining to the law, to pass from view, and henceforth regarded Jesus as the risen Son of God. The word "love" *(Agapao)* which the apostle uses in this passage is not a term which expresses affection between individuals on a human level, but one indicative of reverential awe and deep respect for the one loved. It is a type of love which is created and drawn out by the worthiness of the person which is its object.

On whom, though now ye see him not, yet believing, ye rejoice greatly with joy unspeakable and full of glory:— Though they had not seen the Lord with their physical eyes, they were nevertheless assured of his loveliness and attractiveness by faith; and in this consciousness they rejoiced (literally, *rejoiced exceedingly, exulted*). The verb is the same as in verse 6. Here, again, the contrast is between ordinary love and that which has as its object the Saviour. Love which has its origin and end in the flesh must depend on the presence of the one loved for the consummation of joy (2 John 12); whereas, this love rejoiced, amid the trials of life, in the unseen presence of the Lord. The joy which such emotion produces is "unspeakable," because it is far deeper than that which is common to human love.

9 Receiving the end of your faith, even the salvation of your souls,—The word "receiving," a participial form and in the middle voice, is used in 2 Cor. 5: 10, and in Eph. 6: 8, to indicate the reward which shall be vouchsafed to the saints in the judgment

vation of your souls. 10 Concerning which salvation the prophets sought and searched diligently, who prophesied of the grace that *should come* unto you:

day; and such is its meaning here. "End," from the Greek *telos,* signifies consummation or fulfillment; and thus the reference here is to the consummation and fulfillment of faith at the judgment day, this being the salvation of the soul. Salvation is the goal of faith, and its realization the end or design thereof. This consummation will be realized at the judgment day. As a matter of fact, salvation of the soul is the end and aim of all revelation. It has been said that there is not a book in the New Testament in which the word, either as a verb or concrete noun, does not appear. It is truly the fundamental idea of the Bible, the consummation of the divine plan for the redemption of the race. To accomplish it, Jesus came into the world. (Matt. 1: 21.)

4. MINISTRY OF THE PROPHETS
1: 10-12

10 **Concerning which salvation the prophets sought and searched diligently,**—To encourage the saints to bear patiently the trials through which they were passing (1 Pet. 4: 12), the apostle informed them that the salvation, referred to in verse 9, was not only the subject of prophecy, but that the prophets themselves had engaged in minute and detailed inquiry to determine, if possible, the nature and the time of the events which they had predicted. There is no article before the word "prophets" in the Greek text, and the reference is, therefore, to prophets as a class. These men "sought" (*ekzeteo,* to seek out, to engage in minute study, to scrutinize closely), and "searched diligently" *(exereunao,* to trace out in detail, to explore, as one carefully sifts ore to find the precious metal) their own writings in an effort to learn the time and the nature of the tokens by which these events would be ushered into the world. By prayer, by close study, by meditation, by the exercise of all their mental faculties they sought to learn the significance of the matters which had occasioned their prophecies.

Here is indisputable evidence of the verbal inspiration of the prophetical writings. These prophecies, far from being the productions of the prophets, unaided by inspiration, were so far above and beyond them, that they were dependent on others for instruc-

11 searching what *time* or what manner of time the Spirit of Christ which

tion enabling them to grasp the significance of their own writings. A remarkable example of this will be seen in the instance of Daniel inquiring of the angel the meaning of the matters revealed to him. (Dan. 7: 16.) See also Dan. 9: 2, 3. The Holy Spirit, by whose powers, and under whose influence they spoke, prompted them to give utterance to matters which were outside their apprehension, and which they sought, through patient scrutiny, to understand. They were not only *prophets,* they were *people,* and as such, had an absorbing interest in matters of such vital moment as that which occasioned their prophecies. Their primary purpose being consummated in the prophecies, they continued to pore over their predictions in an effort to learn what they signified.

Who prophesied of the grace that should come unto you.— Actually, "Who predicted the special grace intended for you alone." This does not mean that these disciples alone were the objects of the prophecy alluded to, or that the grace was not to be shared by others, but that those of this dispensation, of which they were a part, were the recipients of the blessings predicted. The word "grace" means unmerited favor, and the reference is, therefore, to the blessings which have come to the world in this dispensation through the manifestation of grace to men. This is the "grace and truth which came by Jesus Christ." (John 1: 17.) The word "grace" in this verse sums up the blessings of God vouchsafed to men under the present dispensation.

11 Searching what time or what manner of time the spirit of Christ which was in them did point unto, when it testified beforehand the sufferings of Christ, and the glories that should follow them.—Again, reference is made to the diligent and painstaking search the prophets instituted into their own writings, and the writings of other prophets to learn the significance of the matters predicted. The nature of their inquiry is said to have been with reference (a) to what time *(chronos)* and (b) what manner of time *(kairos)* "the Spirit of Christ which was in them did point unto." *Chronos,* time, is a simple term denoting duration, the lapse of moments; *kairos* describes the seasons, periods, epochs, etc., into which time is divided. Both of these words occur

was in them did point unto, when it testified beforehand the sufferings [1]of

[1]Gr. *unto*.

---

in our Lord's reply to the request of the disciples for information regarding the time of establishment of his kingdom, when he said, "It is not for you to know time *(chronos)* or seasons *(kairos)* which the Father has set within his own authority." (Acts 1: 6-8.) The prophets are thus represented as searching for the time when the events mentioned were to occur; or, if failing in that, the dispensation or age in which they could be expected. Thus, the matters about which they appear to have been especially concerned were the date and circumstances of the Lord's advent, and the consummation of the scheme of redemption from the salvation of man. Dan. 9: 25 was doubtless one of the passages particularly studied in an effort to determine the time of the Lord's appearance and the nature of the events described.

The prophets "testified" (bore witness) "beforehand of the sufferings of Christ, and the glory that should follow" by "the Spirit of Christ" which was "in them." The Spirit of Christ is the Holy Spirit, the third person of the Godhead. (Rom. 8: 9; Gal. 4: 6.) From this important truth several considerations follow: (1) The Holy Spirit dwelt in the prophets, directed their thoughts, and supplied the revelations which they delivered; (2) the same Spirit that influenced the apostles and inspired men of the New Testament period operated similarly in the Old Testament era (2 Pet. 1: 20, 21); (3) The Spirit *of Christ* having been in the prophets, it follows that Christ existed during the times of the prophets, and this verse thus becomes an important text in support of the deity and pre-existence of the Lord Jesus.

The Holy Spirit, in the prophets, led them to testify with reference to "the sufferings of Christ and the glory that should follow," or, more correctly, "the sufferings *appointed* or *destined* for Christ and the glories after these." That the expected Messiah should suffer was a matter clearly revealed by the Old Testament writers. (Isa. 53; Dan. 9: 25-27.) Numerous references to such predictions occur in the New Testament. "But the things which God foreshowed by the mouth of all the prophets, that his Christ should suffer, he thus fulfilled." (Acts 3: 18.) "Having therefore ob-

Christ, and the glories that should follow them. 12 To whom it was revealed, that not unto themselves, but unto you, did they minister these things, which now have been announced unto you through them that ⁵preached the gospel unto you ⁶by the Holy Spirit sent forth from heaven; which things angels desire to look into.

⁵Gr. *brought good tidings.* Comp. Mt. 11. 5.
⁶Gr. *in.*

---

tained the help that is from God, I stand unto this day testifying both to small and great, saying nothing but what the prophets and Moses did say should come: how that the Christ must suffer, and how that he first by the resurrection of the dead should proclaim light both to the people and to the Gentiles." (Acts 26: 23.) The Lord himself, in his famous interview with the two disciples on the road to Emmaus, gave utterance to the same sentiment: "O foolish men, and slow of heart to believe in all that the prophets have spoken! Behooved it not the Christ to suffer these things, and to enter into his glory? and beginning from Moses and from all the prophets, he interpreted to them in all the scriptures the things concerning himself." (Luke 24: 25-27.) The apostles and other inspired men entered into great detail regarding these matters, and gave much emphasis to them in an effort to overcome the repugnance the Jews felt to the idea of a suffering Messiah. Such a view many of them regarded as inconsistent with other prophecies which represent him as a triumphant and reigning Messiah. Such views continue to constitute a stumbling block in the way of the Jews today. They disregard the fact that Christ was *both*, i.e., a suffering Saviour, and a reigning Monarch; in him both lines of prophecy merge and find fulfillment.

The "glories after these," i.e., after the predicted sufferings, were the triumphs which came to the Saviour, including his resurrection, his ascension, his coronation, and reign at God's right hand.

12 **To whom it was revealed, that not unto themselves, but unto you, did they minister these things,**—By means of revelation, it was made known to these ancient seers that the matters which occasioned their prophecies would have their fulfillment, not in their day, or for their benefit, but in succeeding ages, and with reference to other people. To such ages and people they were ministering (serving), being instruments in the hand of God for

the deliverance of their message to the world. They were said to minister to the people to whom Peter wrote because these people lived within the period in which their prophecies converged. The benefit which the prophets derived from such activity was great; but it was nevertheless secondary and incidental to the functions designed for them in vouchsafing it to the world.

Which now have been announced unto you through them that preached the gospel unto you by the Holy Spirit sent forth from heaven;—The word "announced" points to the proclamation of the matters predicted by the prophets as having actually occurred; and the preaching of the gospel alluded to, included, and embraced the details thereof. This preaching was done by means of the Holy Spirit, the design of the apostle being to show that the same Spirit which motivated the prophets had led the apostles and others to preach the fulfillment of that which the prophets had predicted. Thus, the Spirit which had *predicted* the events, *preached* their fulfillment through the apostles. The Jews paid great deference to the prophets and regarded them as under the divine illumination; and Peter pointed out to them that the same Spirit effectively operated through the apostles to confirm and announce the fulfillment of the events which they regarded as divine predictions by holy men of old.

In directing attention to the fact that the Holy Spirit was sent down from heaven, it is entirely possible that it was his intention to indicate that whereas the prophets were merely influenced by the Spirit, the apostles were more powerfully directed by him, the Spirit having been sent down from heaven for this purpose.

Which things angels desire to look into.—"Which things" refer to, and include, the matters of prophecy and their fulfillment in the Christian dispensation, alluded to in verses 10-12. These things "angels," (heavenly messengers, inhabitants of the celestial abode), "ministering spirits, sent forth to do service for the sake of them that shall inherit salvation" (Heb. 1: 14), "desire to look into." "Desire" is from *epithumeo*, to set the heart on, to want passionately; a word indicative of the intensity of feeling characteristic of the angels as they contemplate the wonders of redemption; and the words, "look into," are from *parakupto*, to stoop down in order to look. It is used of Peter when he stooped down to look into the empty tomb of the risen Lord. (Luke 24: 12.) It is a picturesque word which suggests the act of leaning sideways to peer intently into a place or thing of interest. This passage thus vividly describes the angels as being possessed of a passionate desire to peer into the marvelous depths of redemption and discover its great and fundamental facts. The preposition *para* used in composition with the verb whose meaning is "beside" (from the outside), may be indicative of the fact that angels for whom no provision for salvation has been made, are outside the realm of redemption. "For verily not to angels doth he give help, but he giveth help to the seed of Abraham." (Heb. 2: 16.)

SECTION TWO

EXHORTATIONS TO FAITHFULNESS
1: 13-2: 10

1. SOBERNESS AND GODLINESS ENJOINED
1: 13-21

13 Wherefore girding up the loins of your mind, be sober and set your hope perfectly on the grace that ⁷is to be brought unto you at the revelation

---
⁷Gr. *is being brought.*

---

13 **Wherefore girding up the loins of your mind,**—"Wherefore" *(dio,* on which account, therefore) is a connective, introducing the inference which the apostle draws from considerations earlier presented. The meaning is, Notwithstanding the fact that you are now called upon to suffer a variety of trials (verse 6) because of your faithfulness to Christ and fidelity to his cause, and in view of the glorious and unfading inheritance which awaits, being reserved in heaven for you (verses 3-6), gird up "the loins of your mind. . . ." It is possible that the connection is even closer, and that Peter also connects this statement with that which had immediately preceded, viz., the reference to the participation of the prophets, the earlier evangelists, and the angels (verses 10-12), thus gathering up all matters mentioned earlier in the chapter, and on them basing the admonition which follows.

"Girding" *(anaxonnumi,* to gather up long, flowing garments by means of a belt or girdle) is a reference to the mode of dress characteristic of people in Oriental lands who, when they desired to run, set out on a trip, work, or otherwise engage in activity, gathered up their outer garment about them tightly so as not to be impeded or hindered in that which they sought to do. The usage here is, of course, figurative, and refers to the gathering up of all improper thoughts, feelings and activities of the mind and restraining them that they may not hinder one's progress toward heaven. There is a possible allusion in this to the instructions which Moses gave the Israelites in connection with the observance of the passover feast on the eve of their departure from the land of Egypt: "And thus shall ye eat it: with your loins girded, your shoes on your feet, and your staff in your hand; and ye shall eat it in haste. It is Jehovah's passover." (Ex. 12: 11.)

of Jesus Christ; 14 as children of obedience, not fashioning yourselves ac-

Be sober and set your hope perfectly on the grace that is to be brought unto you at the revelation of Jesus Christ;—Two exhortations are here given: (a) be sober; (b) set your hope perfectly on the grace that is to be brought. The sobriety enjoined is that which evidences itself in self-control; and is a soberness produced by continual calmness of mind and dispassionateness of spirit. One thus possessed exhibits great restraint of temper, controlled habits of thought and a calm and collected attitude toward irritations of whatever nature. The verb occurs in 1 Thess. 5: 6, 8 and in 1 Pet. 4: 7 and 5: 8. It is a grace which tempers enthusiasm and keeps it in proper bounds. When Paul was charged with fanaticism for preaching the gospel so fervently, he could reply: "I am not mad, most excellent Festus; but speak forth words of truth and soberness." (Acts 26: 25.)

The "hope" to which the apostle alludes, described as "perfectly" set, is composed of expectation and desire fused into an attitude that is unwavering, complete, lacking nothing in the assurances which it affords. This hope is directed toward *(epi,* with the accusative) grace indicating the constant reaching for of grace which should be characteristic of the faithful Christian. (Cf. James 4: 6: "He giveth more grace.") Grace is the unmerited favor of God; and it exhibits itself in the manifold blessings which are available to those who seek and serve him faithfully. The phrase, "that is to be brought," is translated from an article and a participle *(ten pheromenen)* in the present tense, indicative of the fact that the grace referred to is being brought now in a present revelation of Christ. Every gift of grace which the Christian receives is a further and additional revelation to him of Christ and what he means to the human soul.

14 **As children of obedience,**—This phrase is a Hebraism, a form of expression often occurring in Hebrew and other Oriental languages, in which matters closely and intimately related are presented under the figure of the relationship which exists between a child and his parents. Thus, "a child of obedience" is one who belongs to obedience and has partaken of its nature as a child belongs to, and has inherited the nature of, its parent. This is a mode of

cording to your former lusts in *the time* of your ignorance: 15 but ⁸like as he

⁸Or, *like the Holy One who called you*

---

expression often appearing in the scriptures, e.g.: "sons of disobedience" (Eph. 2: 3); "children of light" (Eph. 5: 8); "sons of this world" (Luke 16: 8); "son of perdition" (2 Thess. 2: 3); "children of cursing" (2 Pet. 2: 14). The figure originated in the Hebrew *ben-* "son," followed by a word indicative of quality, nature, characteristic, etc. The phrase emphasizes the essentiality of obedience to sonship, pointing to the fact that one becomes a child through obedience, and in obedience continues as a child. The blessings, hopes, joys and privileges of sonship cannot exist in the absence of obedience. (Matt. 7: 21; 1 John 2: 4; Rev. 22: 14; 2 Thess. 1: 7-9; Gal. 6: 5; James 2: 24.)

Not fashioning yourselves according to your former lusts in the time of your ignorance:—Here is evidence of the fact that Peter did not have solely in mind people of Jewish ancestry when he penned his epistle to "the elect who are sojourners of the Dispersion." (1 Pet. 1: 1.) See the Introduction to the Epistle. Reference to "former lusts" and "the time of your ignorance," while in some measure descriptive of the manner of life characteristic of the Jews before obedience to the gospel, are terms especially applicable to Gentiles, and often elsewhere applied to them. (Acts 17: 30.) The Jews regarded the Gentiles as ignorant, and frequently stigmatized them as such. As a matter of fact, the New Testament writers described the whole life of men, whether Jews or Gentiles, before the appearance of Christ, as a period of ignorance and to be considered as such in determining the relative guilt of those who then lived. Of the Gentiles Paul wrote, "This I say therefore, and testify in the Lord, that ye no longer walk as the Gentiles also walk, in the vanity of their mind, being darkened in their understanding, alienated from the life of God, because of the ignorance that is in them, because of the hardening of their heart." (Eph. 4: 17, 18). The Jews were similarly regarded as in spiritual darkness, though they were in possession of the "oracles of God." (Rom. 2: 1-29; 3: 1, 2.) The Jews had sinned against the light of truth and were in darkness; and the Gentiles, through long centuries of depravity, had lost the light they once had through the

who called you is holy, be ye yourselves also holy in all manner of living; 16

revelations of the patriarchal period. While there were notable exceptions to this on the part of both Jew and Gentile (Cornelius being a remarkable example of the latter; Nathaniel of the former) such was generally characteristic of the races as a whole. The ignorance of Jews and Gentiles differed in character, however; the ignorance of the Jew consisting of blindness with reference to the true character of the Messiah and his reign; and not of the moral law—the type of ignorance referred to by Peter. The Jews were in possession of the law and the prophets, and were thus acquainted with the will of God as revealed in the Old Testament scriptures. The ignorance contemplated by Peter, and such as was characteristic of Gentiles prior to their obedience to the gospel, was that with reference to moral conduct. In the ignorance which then possessed them and by which they were motivated, they indulged in "lusts." The word "lust" signifies passionate desire; and its contextual force here is descriptive of *evil* desire.

"Fashioning," a participial form of the verb which occurs in the familiar text, "And be not fashioned according to this world," refers to a common tendency of the race to affect the manner of speech, dress, mode and manner of life of those about us. In Rom. 12: 2, the warning is against conformity to the age, and here to the manner of life which these to whom Peter wrote had followed before they obeyed the gospel. The warning is an important one. The disposition to partake of the manners, morals, and modes of conduct of those about us is a common and dangerous one, and must be resisted. Compare the apostle's injunction with the edict of Moses: "Thou shalt not follow a multitude to do evil." (Ex. 23: 2.)

15, 16 **But like he who called you is holy, be ye yourselves also holy in all manner of living: because it is written, Ye shall be holy: for I am holy.**—In verse 1, those to whom Peter wrote are described as "elect"; here, as having been "called." God "called" through the gospel, "Whereunto he called you by our gospel (2 Thess. 2: 14); and inasmuch as the gospel is addressed to all nations and to every creature (Matt. 28: 18-20; Mark 16: 15, 16), it follows that all who heed the call become, through obedi-

because it is written, ⁹Ye shall be holy; for I am holy. 17 And if ye call on

⁹Lev. xi. 44 f.; xix. 2; xx. 7.

---

ence, the elect of God. The design of God's calling is holiness, the sanctification of the whole life to him: "For this is the will of God, even your sanctification, that ye abstain from fornication; . . . For God called us not for uncleanness, but in sanctification." (1 Thess. 4: 3, 7.) This holiness to which all are called is, essentially, separation from a life of habitual sin and all worldly defilement. Such is the meaning of the word translated "holiness" *(hagios.)* The words sanctify, sanctification, saint, holy and holiness all derive from this same root and thus bear related meanings. Here God, as a perfect pattern of holiness, is set forth for our emulation in "all manner of living."

The verb "be" is not the ordinary word for simple being, but one which means, literally, "to become." The tense of the verb (ingressive aorist) suggests the ushering in of one into a new state. This reveals that the holiness enjoined for the Christian is not such as is a necessary consequence of having obeyed the gospel, but a manner of life attained through a positive renunciation of the world by the individual himself. Sanctification is thus not some mysterious change wrought in the soul by an incomprehensible operation of the Holy Spirit, but a manner of life affected through godly conduct. In these words, there is an undoubted allusion to an admonition of the Lord in the sermon on the mount (Matt. 5: 48), another indication of the profound influence the Lord wrought upon the impulsive apostle during the public ministry.

The words, "Ye shall be holy; for I am holy," occur five times in the book of Leviticus from which they are cited. (Lev. 11: 44; 11: 45; 9: 2; 20: 7; 20: 26.) The words were, on some occasions, addressed to priests; at other times, to the whole nation of Israel. Peter regarded all Christians as priests (individuals qualified and empowered to engage in worship) and as constituting the "holy nation" of spiritual Israel, and thus worthy indeed to have the admonition applied to them. As the Israelites were required to be a holy nation and a peculiar people in the midst of the nations, so Christians who have succeeded to their spiritual status as the chosen people of the Lord must maintain the same separateness from the world about them. It is a characteristic of people to imitate

him as Father, who without respect of persons judgeth according to each man's work, pass the time of your sojourning in fear: 18 knowing that ye

the God whom they worship; and since he is wholly pure, followers of Jehovah have the perfect standard of excellence that is theirs to emulate. The word "I" in the quotation, "I am holy," is emphatic in the Greek text, signifying, "I, myself, apart from all others, am holy."

The quotation is introduced with the familiar formula, "it is written." The verb is in the perfect tense in Greek, thus indicating past action with existing results. Expanded, the phase means, It was written and now remains as a record. The phrase was used by the Lord in his encounter with Satan on the mount of temptation, and it constitutes a monument to the unchanging, inerrant and eternal word of God.

17 And if ye call on him as Father, who without respect of persons judgeth according to each man's work, pass the time of your sojourning in fear.—The word "if" is not to be taken as indicating doubt, but rather as the introduction of a condition which, being assumed, establishes a definite duty. It is nearly equivalent to "since." The meaning is "since (or, inasmuch), as ye call on God as Father. . . ." There is no article before the word Father in the Greek text, the implication of which is that those to whom Peter wrote were not worshiping a cruel and inhuman tyrant but one whose attributes and characteristics are those of a father. While the idea of the fatherhood of God was not advanced for the purpose of eliminating the idea of a judgment, it does reveal the comforting fact that our judge is also our Father!

We thus learn that (a) our heavenly Father is our judge; (b) the judgment is to be "according to every man's work"; and (c) it is to be conducted "without respect of persons," i.e., with complete fairness and impartiality. The phrase, "without respect of persons," is the translation of one Greek word, *aprosopoleptos,* an adverb indicating complete impartiality, meaning literally, "who does not receive face." (See Thayer.) God does not judge individuals on the basis of such outward characteristics as wealth, cultural background or social position, but with reference to their *work*. "The Lord seeth not as man seeth; for man looketh on the outward appearance, but the Lord looketh on the heart." (1 Sam.

were redeemed, not with corruptible things, with silver or gold, from your vain manner of life handed down from your fathers; 19 but with precious

16: 7 A.V.) the idea here expressed is a frequent one throughout the sacred writings. (Acts 10: 34; Matt. 22: 16; Rom. 2: 11; Gal. 2: 6.) "Work" in the text, is in the singular number, thus revealing the significant fact that the judgment alluded to is with reference to the life as a whole, and in its comprehensive aspect.

In an admonition based on these premises, those to whom Peter wrote were instructed to pass the time of their sojourning in fear. For the significance of the word "sojourning" see the comments on verse 1, and compare with 1 Pet. 2: 11, for an expansion of the same thought. In the word there is a continuation of the thought drawn from the relation of God as Father. In view of the fact that God is indeed the Father of his children, heaven—God's abiding place (John 14: 2)—thus becomes the children's permanent home, and they are but sojourners and pilgrims here. (See Eph. 2: 18, 19; Heb. 11: 13.)

The "fear that is to characterize those thus sojourning is not the terror of slaves, but the worshipful awe of obedient children toward their beloved parents. It is the fear of displeasing, the fear of causing pain on the part of those we love by conduct inconsistent with their wishes. It is such a fear as God approves, and which his faithful children feel. It is the fear of the Lord which is the beginning of wisdom. (Psalm 111: 10; Deut. 6: 2; Prov. 1: 7; 3: 13; 14: 26, 27.) Such fear is not the shrinking attitude of cowardice, but a courageous emotion which above all else dreads to displease God! "Be not afraid of them that kill the body, and after that have no more that they can do. But I will warn you whom ye should fear: Fear him, who, after he hath killed, hath power to cast into hell; yes, I say unto you, Fear him." (Luke 12: 4, 5.)

18 **Knowing that ye were redeemed, not with corruptible things, with silver or gold, from your vain manner of life handed down from your fathers,**—Verse 16 contains an admonition to holiness—godly living—founded on the example of God himself. Verse 17 is an exhortation to godly fear, based on the fact of a judgment conducted with impartiality and without respect of persons. Here, as in verse 18, there is an argument for

holiness from the premise of the redemption which has been obtained for us from the bondage of sin at such infinite cost.

The word "redeemed," from *lutroo*, means to set free by payment of a ransom, and was frequently used in the days of slavery to indicate the act of obtaining freedom for enslaved persons through the payment of a sum of money for their release. The noun form of the word occurs in the word *ransom* (which Peter heard from the lips of the Lord during his public ministry when he said, "Even as the Son of man came not to be ministered unto, but to minister, and to give his life *a ransom for many*" [Matt. 20: 28]). Peter's reference to these matters, and use of these terms is doubtless an echo of that which he received from the Lord on that and other occasions. Here, perhaps more clearly than anywhere else in the New Testament, there is revealed the chief purpose of redemption: the deliverance of us all from sin. It establishes, beyond reasonable controversy, the fact of vicarious suffering; that Jesus gave his life, not only in our behalf, but actually *instead of us*, and thus became the satisfaction for our sins. Even more, it teaches us that the liberty thus obtained is not only freedom from the penalty of sin, but from a sinful life itself. On this ground the apostle based his exhortation for a life of godliness and holy living. The central idea here is a common one in the New Testament: "For ye are bought with a price." (1 Cor. 6: 20.) "The master that bought them. . . ." (2 Pet. 2: 1.) "Christ redeemed us from the curse of the law, having become a curse for us." (Gal. 3: 13.)

The redemption was not obtained with "corruptible things," things subject to dissolution and decay, specifically here, silver and gold. The words, "silver" and "gold," in the text, are in diminutive form, the little things of the species, thus indicating that the ransom under consideration did not consist of the little silver and gold coins ordinarily used in obtaining the freedom of enslaved people. The medium, not mentioned in this verse, but described in the one which follows, was the "precious blood" of Christ.

The manner of life from which they had been delivered through the ransom which had been made for them is described as "vain" (a word used to describe idolatrous practices in Acts 14: 15), and as having been received by tradition from their fathers. Here, it appears that reference is made primarily to Gentiles who, before

blood, as of a lamb without blemish and without spot, *even the blood* of

their conversion to Christianity, had been disposed to engage in the heathen rites of idolatrous worship, a disposition which they had passed on to their children.

19 **But with precious blood, as of a lamb without blemish and without spot, even the blood of Christ**—The adjective "precious" *(timios)* is in contrast with the "corruptible things" of verse 18. The word is properly applied to that which is costly; hence, descriptive of anything regarded as highly valuable or precious. It occurs in the phrases, "most precious wood" (Rev. 18: 12), and "a stone most precious" (Rev. 21: 11). The blood, in contrast with the silver and gold alluded to in the verse preceding, is (a) intrinsically more valuable than such metals; and (b) accomplishes that which gold and silver cannot: ransom our souls from the slavery and guilt of sin.

In comparing the blood of Christ with that of a lamb "without blemish and without spot," the doctrine of atonement through the sacrifice of Christ and by means of his shed blood, is clearly and unmistakably taught. Peter had heard it earlier stated by John the Baptist, "Behold the Lamb of God that taketh away the sin of the world" (John 1: 29), and he repeats and gives emphasis to it here. The law of Moses required that all sacrifices be without blemish or spot (Lev. 4: 32; 22: 22-24; Num. 28: 3, 11), so that in them there should be no pollution or defilement whatsoever. In any atonement, it is necessary that the sacrifice should itself be free of the pollution it is designed to expiate; and Jesus, in the absolute sense, complied with this requirement, being utterly and wholly without sin. He was "without blemish," being perfect; and "without spot," undefiled by the world.

From the idea of redemption obtained by ransom (verse 18), there is a transition here to that of expiation, as in verse 19. Reference to gold and silver indicates the former; the blood and the lamb, the latter. The ransom effected man's deliverance from the power of sin; expiation from the guilt and pollution thereof. The blood of animals was powerless to remove sin (Heb. 10: 1-3), being typical and anticipatory in nature only, and foreshadowing the sacrifice of Christ on the cross.

Christ: 20 who was foreknown indeed before the foundation of the world, but was manifested at the end of the times for your sake, 21 who through

20 **Who was foreknown indeed before the foundation of the world, but was manifested at the end of the times for your sake.**—The antecedent of the pronoun "who" is Christ. As a lamb without spot and without blemish, Christ was "foreknown indeed before the foundation of the world." "Foreknown" means to *know before;* hence, Christ was so recognized from before "the foundation of the world." "Foundation" *(kataboles,* to throw down, thus, the first part of a building; the foundation) indicates here the beginning, and contextually, the beginning of the "world." The word "world" is from the Greek *kosmos,* an orderly system, hence age, or dispensation. Thus, Christ, as a lamb, was foreknown as such from before the beginning of the age or dispensation. What age? Creation, so some expositors affirm, thus projecting the time when Christ was ordained as a sacrifice into the period before creation of the universe. Though such a view is widely held, and many eminent commentators may be cited in support, the difficulties associated with it are, to this writer, insuperable. It is impossible to distinguish between the foreknowledge of God with reference to such a plan of redemption and the *will* that originated it. The two are in the nature of the case inseparable. To project a plan of redemption into the period prior to the fall of man raises immediately and inevitably the question of the free agency of Adam and Eve.

If God had already devised a plan for the redemption of man from a sin which was certain to be committed, how could Adam and Eve have avoided its commission? If Christ was a lamb for expiation of sin from before creation, how could the transgression have been other than inevitable since not only it, but the consequences therefor had been provided for in the councils of eternity. Since, in such a view of the case, our first parents were but passive actors in a drama written and stereotyped before they had existence, ought they not to be commended for *obedience* in dutifully furthering a plan ordained for them in eternity and which they could not possibly have altered without falsifying God's foreknowledge? Should they not, we repeat, be commended for obedience, rather

him are believers in God, that raised him from the dead, and gave him glory; so that your faith and hope might be in God.

---

than condemned for disobedience? Such must, in consequence, follow, if the popular view be true. The difficulties it entails are insurmountable.

The word "world," from the Greek *kosmos*, means an orderly system, an age or dispensation, and as such is often applied to the Mosaic age or dispensation. For examples of such see Luke 11: 50; Heb. 9: 26; Eph. 1: 4. Thus, Christ, before the beginnning of the Mosaic age, and before the intricate and detailed system of sacrifices which characterized it was originated, was ordained by the Father to suffer as a sacrificial lamb in expiation of the sins of the world; and the Mosaic age was arranged and its animal sacrifices provided as types and shadows of the redemption awaiting through Christ. For other references to the foreknowledge of God, see Acts 2: 23; 3: 18; 4: 28.

Christ, as a lamb, was foreknown as such from before the beginning of the sacrificial system originating on Sinai, and was manifested (made known, revealed) "at the end of the times," i.e., near the close of the age whose sacrifices typified and foreshadowed his own. Such provisions were, so the apostle declares, "for your sake," the revelation being for all men.

21 **Who through him are believers in God, that raised him from the dead, and gave him glory: so that your faith and hope might be in God.**—The pronoun "him" refers to Christ. Through Christ, these to whom Peter wrote became believers in God. These words apply with special force to the Gentile converts among them who, through the preaching of the gospel of Christ, were brought to God, though such is equally true of all Christians, both Jew and Gentile, since there is no saving knowledge of God apart from Christ. "And he came and preached peace to them that were far off, and peace to them that were nigh: for through him we both have our access in one Spirit unto the Father." (Eph. 2: 17, 18.) In the resurrection, ascension and consequent glorification at God's right hand we have the basis of our faith and hope in God. In Peter's speeches recorded in Acts much emphasis is given to this theme. (Acts 2: 32-36; 3: 15; 4: 10.)

2. BROTHERLY LOVE ENJOINED
1: 22-25

22 Seeing ye have purified your souls in your obedience to the truth unto unfeigned love of the brethren, love one another [1]from the heart fervently:

[1]Many ancient authorities read *from a clean heart.* Comp. 1 Tim. 1. 5.

22 Seeing ye have purified your souls in your obedience to the truth unto unfeigned love of the brethren,—"Have purified," is, literally, "having purified" from the perfect participle derived from *hagnizo*, to purify morally, to reform. The perfect tense places the action in the past, with existing results. Their souls had been, at some time in the past, purified; and they remained so. The manner in which such purification was accomplished was through obedience to the truth, and resulting from it was "unfeigned love of the brethren." Obedience to the truth thus became the ground of their godliness, and love of the brethren an effect of it. It is important to note the extent to which human agency is here made responsible for the purification of the soul. These words are reminiscent of those in the famous speech of Acts 2, when Peter, near the conclusion of that sermon, said, "Save yourselves from this crooked generation." (Acts 2: 40.) Their souls were purified by (a) hearing the truth, which is the word of God (John 17: 17; Rom. 10: 17); (b) obeying it (Matt. 7: 21; 1 John 2: 4; 2 Thess. 1: 7, 8); (c) the results were a pure heart; and (d) love of the brethren.

The love for the brethren which they thus experienced is described as "unfeigned" (literally, *not hypocritical* from *a*, not; and *hupocrites,* a play actor, one who exhibits the character of another, and in consequence, a hypocrite). Unfeigned love is, therefore, sincere affection, without admixture of deceit or affection. It is love which is not in word only, but also in deed, and in truth. (1 John 3: 18.) The words, "love of the brethren," are translated from one word—*philadelphia*—a term well known as the names of cities both ancient and modern. (Rev. 3: 7.) It is compounded from *philos,* love; and *adelphos,* a brother. The term is thus vividly descriptive of affection obtaining between brethren.

Love one another with a pure heart fervently:—Since their obedience had led to "unfeigned love" of the brethren, why did the apostle immediately admonish them to "love one another from the

23 having been begotten again, not of corruptible seed, but of incorruptible,

heart fervently"? The explanation is to be sought in the different words used for love in these clauses. In the expression, "love of the brethren," the word for love is *philos*, affection, fondness, human attachment or regard, friendship maintained because of the congeniality of the parties motivated by it; whereas, the word love in the second clause—"love one another from the heart fervently" —is from the Greek *agapao*, love which finds its origin, and is based on the worthiness or preciousness of the person loved. The two words and their difference in meaning may be seen in the Lord's query to Peter, "Simon, son of John, lovest (*agapao*) thou me more than these?" and the apostle's answer, "Yea, Lord; thou knowest that I love *(phileo)* thee." (John 21: 15.) Humbled by his recent experiences, Peter was unwilling to admit the greater love for the Lord, being content to use the humbler and more common term.

"Fervently," from *ektenos*, intensely, describes an emotion that is vivid and forceful, earnest and pointed. *Ektenos* originally had a musical significance, referring to the drawing out, or stretching, of a string. It thus signified to draw out; to stretch. Children of God are not to love one another indifferently, or loosely, as an unstrung instrument, but with the full tension of heartstrings drawn out fully. Such love does indeed for a symphony, the harmony of which rises to heaven, and falls pleasingly on the ears of our heavenly Father.

23 Having been begotten again, not of corruptible seed, but of incorruptible, through the word of God, which liveth and abideth.—"Having been begotten" is from the same verb as "begat" in verse 3. Reference to "love of the brethren," in verse 22, prompted Peter to recall for his readers the highest possible motive for such love, their common parenthood. Being children of the same Father, it was meet that they should indeed "be loving as brethren." (1 Pet. 3: 8.) Sonship and brotherhood are related terms; in becoming sons, we also become brothers, with all the duties and privileges belonging thereto. "Corruptible seed" is that by which the natural birth is produced; "incorruptible," the spiritual birth. The seed by which we are born into the world is

through the word of [2]God, which liveth and abideth. 24 For,
[3]All flesh is as grass,
And all the glory thereof as the flower of grass.
The grass withereth, and the flower falleth:

---

[2]Or, *God who liveth* Comp. Dan. 6. 26.
[3]Is. xi. 6ff.

---

the difference in the manner in which these births are accomplished. It is "of" (Greek, *ek*, out of) corruptible seed that we are born into the world of fleshly parents; but it is "through" *(dia)* the word of God that we are born spiritually. *Ek* (out of) indicates that the corruptible seed is the originating cause of the fleshly birth; *dia*, that the word of God is the instrumental cause of the spiritual birth. The seed by which we are born into the world is styled "corruptible" (subject to death) because mortality is a universal characteristic of that which pertains to the flesh. We are born into the world only to begin the journey which leads inevitably to the grave, and that which originates such life may therefore quite properly be styled corruptible. That by which we are born from above, however, is incorruptible, because the life which thus originates does not decay with the passing of the years. It is also incorruptible because the seed itself "liveth" *(zontos,* is possessed with life and vigor), and "abideth" *(menonto,* continues constant and unchanging). In Luke 8: 11, the "seed" is declared to be the word of God; here, there appears to be a verbal distinction between the "word" and the "seed," in that it is *through* the word of God that the seed begets, the word being the instrument of the begettal. The idea is parallel with that of John 3: 6, "That which is born (literally *begotten)* of the Spirit is spirit," the Holy Spirit there being made the germinal principle of life. This principle, however, finds expression only through the word, operating in no other fashion. Children of God become such by being begotten through the word, a word which is preached, believed, and obeyed. An example of the manner in which individuals are begotten and born again may be seen in the events of Pentecost when Peter, for the first time in the name of the risen Lord (Acts 2: 1-47), preached the conditions of salvation, and three thousand souls in obedience thereto were born of the Word. (Cf. James 1: 18; 1 Cor. 4: 15.)

24 **For, all flesh is as grass, and all the glory thereof as the**

25 But the ⁴word of the Lord abideth for ever. And this is the ⁴word of good tidings which was ⁵preached unto you.

⁴Gr. *saying*.
⁵See ver. 12.

---

flower of grass. The grass withereth, and the flower falleth, but the word of the Lord abideth for ever.—In proof of his assertion that the word of God is constant and unchanging, therefore abiding forever, Peter cites this statement from the prophet Isaiah. (Isa. 40: 6-8.) The quotation is from the Septuagint Version, slightly modified. In James 1: 10, 11, there is a reference to the same passage. All flesh, like grass *(chortos,* herbiage of the field, grass, hay, flowers), which withers and ultimately fades and perishes, will eventually go the way of all the earth; and the glory of man, like the flower of the grass which shrivels and falls, shall perish and fail and be forgotten, and the pride and the beauty and accomplishments attendant thereon vanish. In contrast with all such, "The word of the Lord abideth for ever."

25 **And this is the word of good tidings which was preached unto you.**—"Word" in verse 23 is *logos,* here it is *rhema,* a term more concrete, meaning an utterance, a thing said. The word which the apostles preached through the providence of Asia Minor Peter here declares to be the word *(logos)* which abides forever. It was the word of good tidings, because it brought to all who received it the knowledge of salvation through Christ. Here, again, emphasis is given to the fact that the means of their birth was the word preached unto them. Only where the word is preached is it possible for men to be born again.

3. MEANS OF GROWTH
2: 1-10

1 Putting away therefore all ⁶wickedness, and all guile, and hypocrisies,

⁶Or, *malice* 1 Cor. 14. 20.

---

1 **Putting away therefore all wickedness, and all guile, and hypocrisies, and envies, and all evil speakings,**—"Therefore" *(oun)* points to the logical inference drawn from the matters considered in the closing portions of the first chapter. The meaning, expanded, is, "In consequence of the fact that you have been regenerated to a new life by the word of God. (1: 23), lay aside, your

and envies, and all evil speakings, 2 as newborn babes, long for the [7]spiritual

[7]Gr. *belonging to the reason.* Comp. Rom. 12. 1.

---

former evil dispositions, and particularly that which is inconsistent with fervent love of the brethren" (1 : 22). The New Testament writers gave much emphasis to this theme, and much space to its elaboration. For a similar discussion of it by Paul, see Eph. 4 : 22-31, where most of the terms used by Peter here also occur.

"Putting away" *(apothemenoi,* aorist participle with imperative force) indicates a definite and decisive act with permanent results; and the preposition *(apo-,* from) in composition with the verb signifies separation. Thus, those to whom Peter wrote, in one decisive and positive act, and with results so pronounced as not to need repeating, were to separate themselves once for all from the sinful acts and dispositions mentioned, and henceforth to be free of their defilement. The verb *apotithemi* (from which the foregoing participle is derived) means literally to discard clothing; and as here figuratively used, signifies the putting away of the evils of one's former life as one would discard dirty and defiled linen. (Rom. 13 : 12; Col. 3 : 8, 10; James 1 : 21.) There is an interesting and significant tradition which comes down to us from the period of the early church that converts were accustomed to cast off forever their old clothing following their baptism into Christ, and to array themselves in new garments as a symbol of the new life upon which they had entered. The figure is a common one in the New Testament. (Rom. 13 : 14.) Christ is to be "put on" in baptism (Gal. 3 : 27), and the evils here designated are to be "put off."

Five terms are used by the apostle to designate the things that are to be put away. (1) "Wickedness *(kakian)* is evil of any kind, but here, particularly, an evil disposition and a malignant spirit; the desire to injure another. The word "malice" of the Authorized Version exactly represents the meaning here. (2) "Guile" *(dolon)* is translated from a term the verb of which means to catch with bait; thus, here, artifice, craftiness. (3) "Hypocrisies" are deceptive and deceitful actions and attitudes. (4) "Envies" are feelings of unhappiness because another has that which one desires for himself. (5) "Evil speakings" *(katalalias)* are slanderous and defamatory statements about others. The word is else-

milk which is without guile, that ye may grow thereby unto salvation; 3 if

where translated "backbitings" (2 Cor. 12: 20); and a verb form of it occurs in 1 Pet. 2: 12, where it is rendered "speak against." It should be observed that the sins designated in this catalog are such as operate to destroy the brotherly relationship which begets and maintains love, and to create an attitude of mind and disposition of heart where malice, bitterness and hate reign instead. These evils are closely related and develop from each other. A malicious disposition leads to deception, deceit, envy and defamation; and the effort to conceal such produces hypocrisy. All such attitudes are utterly foreign to the Spirit of Christ, and to the principles which governed and motivated his life. All such must be resolutely *put away* if we are to have his approval and commendation. "If a man say, I love God, and hateth his brother, he is a liar: for he that loveth not his brother whom he hath seen, cannot love God whom he hath not seen." (1 John 4: 20.)

2 **As newborn babes, long for the spiritual milk which is without guile,**—Twice before, in the epistle (1: 3, 23), the metaphor of a new birth and resultant entrance upon a new life has been used; and here, in the reference to "newborn babes," the figure is extended and repeated. It is a common one in the New Testament, being first used by the Lord in his teaching regarding the birth from above. (John 3: 3, 5.) Paul used it (1 Cor. 4: 15), as did John (1 John 5: 1); and Jesus often compared his disciples to little children (Matt. 18: 3; Mark 10: 14, 15.) The figure is applied in the Old Testament to those who, like children, are teachable and guileless. (Isa. 28: 9.) Babes (*brephe*) in the text signifies children of the earliest infancy; and the words "long for" (*epipotheo*) suggest great eagerness and an ever-recurring desire for the word of God such as is characteristic of infants in their passionate longing and yearning for the milk which alone constitutes their food. As babes instinctively turn to their mothers' breasts as the only source of their life, so are all children of God here admonished to desire the spiritual milk which is "without guile," and which alone can sustain their spiritual life. The appetite for spiritual food is not often as intense, alas, as that which prompts a baby to return again and again to its mother's breast.

ye have tasted that the Lord is gracious: 4 unto whom coming, a living

Infants do not have to be constantly urged and admonished to seek the source of their life!

The word "milk" in the text continues the figure of the new birth, and is used in opposition to the solid food (meat, 1 Cor. 3: 2; Heb. 5: 12), adaptable to the more mature. Under this figure reference is made to the simpler and more primary matters of the Christian life which are adaptable to the young and immature in Christ, in contrast to those matters which are profound and involved, and thus applicable only to the "full-grown." (Heb. 5: 14.) Here, as often elsewhere in the scriptures, emphasis is given to the fact that Christianity involves growth, such being comparable to that characteristic of an infant in its development from childhood to maturity, attained through feeding on the food especially adaptable to one's need.

The milk is described as spiritual *(logikon)*, rational, because it appeals to the reason, thus nourishing and sustaining it instead of performing the functions of ordinary milk in sustaining the body, the flesh. The word occurs only once elsewhere in the New Testament (Rom. 12: 1), where it describes the character of the service we are to render to God. There the Authorized, or King James Version renders it "reasonable," i.e., a service of the reason, one originating with, and performed by, the reason.

"Without guile" is, literally, "unadulterated." In ancient times milk was often adulterated with gypsum, a chalky-like substance to increase its volume, thus rendering it impure and contaminated. Such adulteration became a figure of the admixture of false doctrine with the pure word of God. Irenaeus, an early Christian writer, born between 120 and 140 A.D., said of the heretics of his time, "They mix gypsum with the milk, they taint the heavenly doctrine with the poison of their errors."

That ye may grow thereby unto salvation.—"That" introduces a purpose clause, meaning "in order that." "Thereby" is, actually, "therein." It is in feeding on the proper spiritual food that growth and development follow; and this is the purpose of the feeding. The salvation unto which one grows is the deliverance which awaits the faithful at the consummation of all things.

stone, rejected indeed of men, but with God elect, [8]precious, 5 ye also, as

[8]Or, *honorable*

"Grow" is, literally, to be nourished, such being the sole purpose of the milk which is "without guile." Such nourishment results in and produces salvation.

3 If ye have tasted that the Lord is gracious:—This is an exact quotation of Psalm 34: 8, as it appears in the Septuagint, a translation from Hebrew into Greek, made in 280 B.C., so the tradition runs, and used by Christ and the New Testament writers. The passage, in our text of the Old Testament, reads: "Oh taste and see that Jehovah is good." The conditional particle "if" with which the quotation begins does not imply doubt, but is a fulfilled condition, meaning "*since* you have tasted that the Lord is gracious." "Gracious," from *chrestos* in the Greek text, and *tobh* in the Hebrew, means "good," and is so translated in Psalm 34: 8 and Luke 5: 39. The metaphor of tasting that the Lord is good continues the figure suggested by reference to the milk beginning in verse 2. As an infant, once directed to the breast, continues to desire it, so their first experience in partaking of the delectable delights of the Lord should prompt them to return again and again to that feast.

4 Unto whom coming, a living stone rejected indeed of men, but with God, elect, precious.—From the figure of milk with which the apostle has been illustrating his teaching he now turns to that of a building, and particularly to the corner stone thereof, by which he represents Christ. There is a similar transition in Paul's writings when, in 1 Cor. 3, after asserting that he had fed the Corinthians with milk and not with meat, he resorts to the illustration of builders laying a foundation, and writes that "other foundation can no man lay than that which is laid, which is Jesus Christ." (1 Cor. 3: 1-11.)

"Unto whom coming" does not refer to the primary steps of salvation when the alien sinner first comes to Christ, but to the constant approaching of the Lord characteristic of all who find strength and support from the "living stone." It is only through continually reaching forth to Christ—the standard and ideal of Christianity—that the means and method of constructing the

Christian structure may be found. The approach is made by faith, and is constant and continuous if one is to realize the communion and union with the Lord without which all spiritual life must fail.

Christ is a "living stone," (1) because, unlike the inert, lifeless stones of the earth, he is a stone of energy, vitality, and life; and (2) having been raised from the dead, he *lives* to die no more. Being alive himself, he is thus the source of life to his followers. Though Peter was himself a stone *(petros)*, he was wholly unlike the stone *(lithos)* which he describes here. *Petros* is a fragment of native rock, unhewn; whereas, *lithos* is one shaped and fitted for the purpose designated.

"Rejected" is from *apodokimadzo,* to reject after trial and examination, as one casts aside worthless and spurious coins. The Jews examined the claims of Jesus, and because he did not conform to their expectations of a Messiah, nor establish the earthly kingdom they desired and expected, they rejected him as spurious. That men professedly religious could thus test and reject as worthless metal the Lord of glory is a measure of the appalling unbelief which obtained in that day, and which extends to our time on the part of those who still stumble after the same manner of unbelief. While this passage which Peter cities in support of his statement here (Psalm 118: 22) limits the rejection of the stone to the builders (see below under verses 7, 8), he extends it to embrace all of those who through unbelief repudiate and reject the Saviour.

The Stone was "with God elect," literally, "by the side of God *(para)* chosen." Though wicked men rejected him, God chose him, and sent him into the world a fitted and shaped stone *(lithos)* for the mission he was destined to fulfil. Moreover, God regarded him as "precious" *(entimos),* worthy of honor, in opposition to the attitude of repudiation and rejection characteristic of the "builders," the unbelieving Jews. "Precious" in 1 Pet. 1: 19, descriptive of the blood of Christ, is not the same in meaning as here. There it is translated from *timios,* that which has intrinsic value; here it is *entimos,* God's recognition of that intrinsic value. The contrast is further drawn out with reference to the manner in which God and men regarded Jesus. Though the Jews "rejected him," God "chose" him; though they counted him spurious and without value, God regarded him as worthy of great honor.

living stones, are built up ⁹a spiritual house, to be a holy priesthood, to offer up spiritual sacrifices, acceptable to God through Jesus Christ. 6 Because it

⁹Or, *a spiritual house for a holy priesthood*

5 **Ye also, as living stones, are built up a spiritual house, to be a holy priesthood, to offer up spiritual sacrifices, acceptable to God through Jesus Christ.**—Continuing the figure of a building in which Christ is the foundation stone, Peter declares that the followers of the Lord "as living stones" are built up into it so as to constitute a "spiritual house." In view of the fact that Christ is a "living stone" (verse 4), Christians are similarly described because they derive their life from his. In comparing believers to a building, Peter was doubtless recalling the famous words of the Lord to him in the coasts of Caesarea Philippi when he said to him, "And upon this rock I will build my church, and the gates of Hades shall not prevail against it." (Matt. 16: 18.) The "spiritual house" is the church. (1 Tim. 3: 14, 15.)

In this spiritual house—the church—there is a "holy priesthood." Here the figure changes from a building contemplated as a structure composed of many stones to a house occupied by servants. The servants are designated as priests. Under the law of Moses the priests constituted a special class empowered to officiate in worship. Inasmuch as all Christians are authorized to engage in the worship of God, all Christians are priests, and thus together constitute a priesthood of believers. This priesthood is "holy," because its members have been separated to the sacred purpose of worship before the altar of God. The word translated "holy" has, as its basic idea, separation for a special purpose. Derived from the same root are the words saint, sanctify, and sanctification.

The kind of sacrifices which this holy priesthood is to offer is described as "spiritual" to distinguish them in nature and character from the sacrifices required by the law of Moses. They are also spiritual to conform to the nature of the building (church) in which they are offered; to the priests which are to offer them; and to the God to whom they are to be offered. "Offer up," from *anaphero,* suggests the bearing up of sacrifices to the altar; and the aorist tense which occurs in the text here distinguishes between such acts contemplated as regular and habitual and a once-for-all dedication of the life on the altar of God, the meaning here.

is contained in ¹⁰scripture,
    ¹¹Behold, I lay in Zion a chief corner stone, elect, precious;
    And he that believeth on ¹²him shall not be put to shame.

---

¹⁰Or, *a scripture*
¹¹Is. xxviii. 16.
¹²Or, *it*

Prayer, praise, the contribution, indeed, all the items and acts of worship are thus figurativly included in the sacrifices which Christians, as priests officiating under Christ, the High Priest (Heb. 9: 11-28), are to offer in the spiritual temple, the church: "Through him then let us offer up a sacrifice of praise to God continually, that is, the fruit of lips which make confession to his name. But to do good and to communicate forget not: for with such sacrifices God is well pleased." (Heb. 13: 15, 16.)

The purpose of these sacrifices is to be pleasing to God "through Jesus Christ." "Acceptable" is from a word which means not only something received from another, but which, in addition, brings pleasure to the recipient *(euprosdektos)*. Such is "through Jesus Christ," because God is approachable in no other way. (John 14: 6.)

6 **Because it is contained in scripture, Behold, I lay in Zion a chief corner stone, elect, precious: and he that believeth on him shall not be put to shame.**—The prophecy to which Peter refers is recorded in Isa. 28: 16, though the quotation varies somewhat from both the Hebrew and the Greek Septuagint texts. It is a free rendering, such as one would make were he quoting the prophecy from memory. In Paul's citation of the same text (Rom. 9: 33), there is an even greater variation. Peter's quotation more nearly conforms to the Greek Septuagint text than to the original Hebrew. It does not include the words "a tried stone" and "a sure foundation," and for "shall not be in haste" it has "shall not be put to shame." For the meaning and significance of the phrases "a tried stone" and "a sure foundation," see comments under verses 4, 5.

The phrase "shall not be in haste," which Peter interprets to mean "shall not be put to shame," indicates an attitude of mind and disposition of heart enabling one to be calm and unflurried, hence not stampeded into fearful and hasty flight. Those whose

7 ¹³For you therefore that believe is the ¹⁴preciousness: but for such as disbelieve,
    ¹⁵The stone which the builders rejected,
    The same was made the head of the corner;

---

¹³Or, *In your sight*
¹⁴Or, *honor*
¹⁵Ps. cxviii. 22.

---

confidence is resolutely fixed on the Lord shall never have occasion to be ashamed thereof.

Christ is the "chief corner stone, elect precious," which has been laid in Zion. It is the function of a corner stone to unite and securely fasten the two walls of a building. Under the same figure, and in a passage which illustrates the meaning here, Paul wrote to the Ephesians: "For through him (Christ) we both (Jew and Gentile) have our access in one Spirit unto the Father. So then ye are no more strangers and sojourners, but we are fellow-citizens with the saints, and of the household of God, being built upon the foundation of the apostles and prophets, Christ Jesus himself being the chief corner stone; in whom each several building, fitly framed together, groweth into a holy temple in the Lord, in whom ye also are builded together for a habitation of God in the Spirit." (Eph. 2: 18-22.) Thus, in the joining of the Jew and Gentile into "one body"—the church—there is henceforth but one building, and in it Christ occupies the position of chief corner stone. The metaphor of the "chief corner stone" *(akrogoniaios lithos)* emphasizes the function Jesus performed in uniting Jews and Gentiles into the one body, the church. (Eph. 4: 4.)

The "Stone" is said to have been laid "in Zion" (Jerusalem, 1 Kings 8: 1), because there Jesus died; there he fulfilled the old law and removed it, nailing it to his cross; and there, on the first Pentecost following the resurrection, the Christian dispensation was inaugurated.

7 **For you therefore that believe is the preciousness: but for such as disbelieve, the stone which the builders rejected, the same was made the head of the corner.**—In view of the fact that the Stone (Christ) is precious (verse 6), its preciousness *(time,* literally honor), is transferred to those that believe. The preciousness of the stone of the foundation is acquired by the "living stones" (children of God) which rest upon it. This preciousness is available only to those that believe; those who disbelieve have

8 and, ¹⁶A stone of stumbling, and a rock of offence; ¹⁷for they ¹⁸stumble at the word, being disobedient: whereunto also they

---
¹⁶Is. viii. 14.
¹⁷Gr. *who.*
¹⁸Or, *stumble, being disobedient to the word*

---

rejected (cast aside as spurious) the living stone, Christ, and are in the same position of builders which have rejected a stone which they regarded as worthless but later discovered to be the head stone of the corner. The word "disbelieve" means more than the mere absence of faith; in it is the definite suggestion of positive disobedience. The words, "The stone which the builders rejected, the same was made the head of the corner," is a quotation from Psalm 118: 22. The builders were the Jewish teachers; the stone which they rejected was Christ.

8 And, a stone of stumbling, and a rock of offence; for they stumble at the word, being disobedient: whereunto also they were appointed.—Verses 7 and 8 contrast those who believe, and the honor that is theirs through believing, with those who disbelieve and the consequences attending such unbelief. The meaning, expanded, is, "For you who believe, there is the preciousness of the stone transferred to you; but to you who disbelieve, the stone, instead of being a source of preciousness (honor), becomes a stone *(lithos)* of stumbling, and a rock *(petra)* of offence." The words "stone of stumbling" and "rock of offence" are from Isa. 8: 14. Paul, in Rom. 9: 23, cites this passage and makes a similar application to that of Peter. It is interesting to observe that both Peter and Paul, in their reference to this prophecy, follow the Hebrew text rather than the Greek Septuagint.

"Stumbling" *(proskomma,* to collide with something, thus suffering hurt or injury), and "offence" *(skandalon,* a trap wherein with bait the unwary are caught), are terms suggestive of the ruin and utter calamity certain to overtake those who through unbelief are opposed to Christ. The passage means much more than mere vexation and mental annoyance at the claims of the Lord; it includes the ultimate consequence of unbelief and damnation awaiting those who have arrayed themselves against the "tried stone." The ruin awaiting such is put in contrast with the preciousness belonging to those who obey him. Peter, in his reference to the rock

were appointed. 9 But ye are an elect race, a royal priesthood, a holy nation, a people for *God's* own possession, that ye may show forth the excel-

of offence, must have recalled his own brief period of unbelief when the Lord addressed him as a "stumblingblock" *(skandalon).* (Matt. 16:23.)

Those who stumble at the word do so because they are disobedient; and this disobedience is the natural fruit of unbelief. The words, "Whereunto they were appointed," do not mean that they were predestined to such disobedience by arbitrary and immutable decree, but because such stumbling is the inevitable result of unbelief. Having given themselves over to unbelief, the fact that they stumbled was neither fortuitous nor accidental; it was simply the working out of the principle applicable in both the natural and the spiritual realms. "Be not deceived; God is not mocked: for whatsoever a man soweth, that shall he also reap." (Gal. 6:7.) God has ordained that to those who disbelieve Christ is a stone of stumbling and a rock of offence against which all such shall destroy themselves. These of whom Peter wrote were unbelievers. Hence, they were appointed to the destruction which is the inevitable lot of all such. It is idle to suppose that these individuals who deliberately repudiated Christ would have stood in the same relationship to God had they died in infancy. Had Judas been born a thousand years earlier he could not have sinned in the fashion he did. One may elect whether he will believe in Christ or not. If not, then through his own choice he places himself among those appointed to destruction. The word "appointed" *(tithemi)* means to set under certain and definite circumstances; to place, arrange, etc.; and God, in placing man under circumstances involving the possibility of great benefit as well as terrible dangers, expects man to seize the benefits and avoid the dangers; and if man refuses to do so, he cannot complain that God is unjust.

9 **But ye are an elect race, a royal priesthood, a holy nation, a people for God's own possession,**—"But *(de)* is a disjunctive, and the "ye" is emphatic, the meaning of which is, "But as for you, in contradistinction to the Jews who rejected Christ, you are an elect race, a royal priesthood, a holy nation, a people for God's own possession." The statement is designed to put in vivid contrast those who, through unbelief, were appointed to the

lencies of him who called you out of darkness into his marvellous light: 10 penalties of disobedience (verse 8), and those who, through obedience, became the recipients of blessings belonging only to the children of God. The phrases, and elect race, a royal priesthood, etc., were selected from various Old Testament passages originally applicable to the Israelite people, formerly regarded as the Lord's "chosen" (Isa. 43: 20, 21); but who, through their unbelief, were "broken off" (Rom. 11: 13-24), thus permitting the Gentiles, through Christ, to be "grafted in." It follows, therefore, that Christians are the true "Israel of God," today, the only Jews whom God recognizes! (Rom. 2: 28, 29.)

Peter describes the people of God as "an elect race," because they have been chosen *(eklekton)* to salvation, "in sanctification of the Spirit and belief of the truth" having been "called" by the gospel. Inasmuch as the gospel is addressed to all (Matt. 28: 18-20; Mark 16: 15, 16; Matt. 11: 28), all who believe and obey it are chosen to salvation, and thus comprise the elect race to which Peter refers. Such are also a priesthood, because empowered to officiate in worship (see comments under verse 5), and the priesthood is a "royal" one because of its relationship to the King. This portion of Peter's quotation is from Ex. 19: 6, where the Hebrew has "kingdom of priests" instead of "a royal priesthood." The ideas are very similar. Children of God constitute a "holy nation" (a) because the company to which they belong is a monarchy with Christ as King; and (b) it is "holy" because dedicated to a sacred purpose. The subjects of this holy nation are described as "a people for God's own possession," because they belong to him in a special and intimate sense characteristic of no other. This is cited from Deut. 7: 6. Mal. 3: 17 (Authorized Version) refers to them as the Lord's "jewels," i.e., a peculiar treasure belonging only to the Lord. The meaning of the words, "a people for God's own possession," literally suggests the idea of something acquired, gained, and includes the idea of preserving, keeping to one's self. It follows therefore that Christians are today the special, acquired treasure of God, precious jewels which he proposes to keep for himself. How we should rejoice that it is so!

That ye may show forth the excellencies of him who called you out of darkness into his marvellous light:—The words

who in time past were no people, but now are the people of God: who had not obtained mercy, but now have obtained mercy.

"show forth" mean, literally, to proclaim, to publish abroad, and the verse thus reveals the obligation of all children of God to herald abroad and give wide publicity to the excellencies (virtues, gracious dealings as exhibited in the plan of salvation) of him who called us from a sinful life into the marvelous light of truth. These words are especially applicable to those among Peter's readers who had formerly been idol worshipers; these, through the gospel, had been called from the darkness of heathenism to the glorious light of the truth. The words apply, however, to all, both Jew and Gentile, the state of sin being often described by the sacred writers as a condition of darkness, and Christianity as a world of light. (1 John 1: 5, 7, and often elsewhere, particularly in John's writings, and those of Paul, Eph. 5: 8.)

10 **Who in time past were no people, but now are the people of God: who had not obtained mercy, but now have obtained mercy.**—This is a quotation from Hos. 2: 23. Paul cites it in Rom. 9: 25, 26, and applies it to the Gentiles, as Peter apparently does here. Here, again, as often elsewhere in the epistle, it appears that the Gentiles were in the mind of the writer, and that the address to the "elect sojourners of the Dispersion" (verse 1 of the first chapter) is to be understood in a figurative sense as including children of God without regard to their racial origins. The Gentiles, before they obeyed the gospel, were "no people," being scattered through all the nations, with separate languages, governments, customs, etc., but through their obedience to the gospel were constituted into a holy nation with common interests, obligations, government and king. Formerly they had not "obtained mercy" *(eleemenoi,* perfect passive participle, literally, were up to a definite time *unpitied)* but now have "obtained mercy" *(eleethentes),* passive aoriest participle, obtained pity in a single act, and at a definite time, viz., at their conversion. Formerly unpitied and the objects of aversion and wrath, they had, by their conversion to Christ, become the objects of compassion and pity. This change in attitude on the part of God toward them was due to their renunciation of the evil which had characterized them, and to their acceptance of the truth in Christ.

SECTION THREE
SPECIAL DUTIES COMMANDED
2: 11-4: 5

1. CONDUCT BEFORE UNBELIEVERS
2: 11, 12

11 Beloved, I beseech you as sojourners and pilgrims, to abstain from fleshly lusts, which war against the soul; 12 having your behavior seemly

11 Beloved, I beseech you as sojourners and pilgrims, to abstain from fleshly lusts, which war against the soul;—Here, quite obviously, is the beginning of a new section of the epistle. Somewhat after the fashion of Paul who often ranged widely over the whole of the scheme of redemption, only to return to the starting point from which to launch a new survey, so here, Peter returns to that point in his letter when he addressed the "elect sojourners of the Dispersion" (verse 1 of the first chapter), from which to begin the practical portion of the epistle which follows. To this point Peter had given particular emphasis to the manner of life which should characterize his readers in view of their relationship to God; here he exhorts them to walk worthily and godly before unbelievers and their persecutors.

The section begins with a term of endearment. "Beloved," as a form of address, often occurs in the New Testament (1 Cor. 10: 14; 15: 58; 2 Cor. 7: 1; 1 John 3: 2 etc), though only once more elsewhere in the epistle. (4: 12.) The term reveals the warm affection Peter felt for his readers, his good will in their behalf, and the close and intimate relationship he sustained toward them.

The exhortations which follow take the form of an entreaty: "I beseech you. . . ." The word "beseech" *(parakaleo,* to call to one's side and tenderly admonish, thus, to entreat, to exhort, to plead with) suggests the tenderness which characterized the approach of the apostle to the matters to be discussed.

Those thus addressed were regarded as "sojourners and pilgrims." (A sojourner *(paroikos)* is one who lives as a foreigner in a strange land; a pilgrim *(parepidemos)* is one who remains in a place but a short while, as a traveler on a journey. Here, and in Eph. 2: 11, the meaning is metaphorical and describes the Chris-

among the Gentiles; that, wherein they speak against you as evil-doers, they

tian who, though resident on the earth, has his real and permanent home in heaven. Though sojourning on the earth, he dwells there as a temporary tenant only, his citizenship being in heaven (Phil. 3: 20), whence he derives his rights, privileges, laws, etc. The more nearly he conforms to the laws of the kingdom in which he has citizenship, the more apparent becomes the difference which obtains between himself and those of the land in which he sojourns; being a citizen of that, he is alien to this; and because his life is dedicated to him who reigns above, he must ever be on guard against the evil influences of him who is the prince of this world. (John 12: 31.) Such has ever been the attitude of God's faithful. Abraham "became a sojourner in the land of promise, as in a land not his own"; and the patriarchs "confessed that they were strangers and pilgrims on the earth." (Heb. 11: 9, 13.) Such a relationship sets up obligations and establishes responsibilities. Christians, being strangers in the world, are (a) not to partake of the customs and characteristics peculiar to it (1 John 2: 15; James 4: 4); and (b) not to offend unnecessarily those among whom they dwell; (c) in addition, they are to seek the good of those about them, and encourage them also to look "for the city which hath the foundations, whose builder and maker is God." (Heb. 11: 10.)

Because such a relationship obtains, Christians are to "abstain from fleshly lusts which war against the soul." "Abstain" *(apecho,* to hold back from), here, present, middle, infinitive thus to keep constantly holding one's self back from fleshly lusts, as a constant, ever-present duty. The fleshly lusts are all evil desires, the effect of which is to war against the soul, i.e., against the best interests of the soul; and the word "war (present, indicative middle of *strateuo)* does not mean merely a state of antagonism, but rather a constant, active, aggressive conflict which must be evermore resisted. See Gal. 5: 16-24 for a graphic description of this warfare by Paul. The "soul," in this passage, is man's higher nature, embracing the spirit, the immortal part of man directly derived from God. (Heb. 12: 9.)

may by your good works, which they behold, glorify God in the day of visitation.

12 Having your behavior seemly among the Gentiles;— This subdivision of the epistle, consisting of verses 11, 12, contains two general exhortations, the first negative, the second positive. Through abstinence from the fleshly lusts mentioned in verse 11, these addressed by Peter were, by their godly conduct, to silence the mouths of their accusers and prompt them to glorify God. Here, the word "gentiles" embraces the unconverted heathen resident in the provinces of Pontus, Galatia, Cappadocia, Asia and Bithynia (1: 1), and is figurativly used to designate the ungodly world in the midst of which the Christians of these provinces lived. "Seemly," sometimes translated *good,* and at other times *comely,* means more than mere moral rectitude. It also includes that which is beautiful, harmonious, lovely, and symmetrical. Works, in order to be good in God's sight, must also be beautiful; and it matters not how much one's life may conform to the laws of morality and right, it is imperfect unless it also measures to the law of beauty, i.e., to beautiful and lovely conduct. We are just as obligated to make our lives attractive and beautiful to others as we are to make them pure. He who exhibits a stern and unbending disposition, though his life be an exemplary one, is lacking in the qualities which are described in the Bible as good. (Matt. 5: 16; 26: 10.)

That, wherein they speak against you as evil-doers,— "Wherein," i.e., in the very matter in which they speak. The speaking designated is critical and adverse, literally "to speak down," and to find evil satisfaction in such criticism. In spite of such Peter admonished his readers to live so circumspectly that their accusers would be able to see in their conduct occasion not only to reverse their opinion, but actually to glorify God in so doing. It is worthy of note that the word "evil-doers" is the same as that which the chief priests applied to our Lord, and in thus being stigmatized, they were but suffering the same calumnies as the Saviour. (1 Pet. 2: 21.) The disciples of the period in which Peter wrote, and for many years afterward, were subjected to the most bitter calumny and the severest sort of persecution. They were charged with "turning the world upside down," with acting contrary to the decrees of Caesar, and with blaspheming the names of the popular gods and goddesses of the day. Unbelieving Gentiles, encouraged and led on by Jews, were most active in leveling false charges against the saints, charges based on numerous grounds. On political considerations they were charged with being enemies of the government (Acts 17: 6, 7); on religious considerations as opposed to the prevailing idolatry (Acts 19: 27-29); on business grounds as having interfered with the manufacture of idols; and on ethical considerations as having sought to abolish the customs and practices of the day. They were, by their enemies, held responsible for, and blamed with, all the national evils of the day. Wrote Tertullian (born about 160 A.D., died between 220 and 240 A.D.), "If the Tiber rises to the walls of the city, if the Nile does not irrigate the fields, if an earthquake takes place, if famine or the pestilence arise, they cry forthwith: Away with the Christians to the lions." Heathen writers, when not possessed of the bitterness of spirit and maliciousness of heart characteristic of those actively engaged in persecution of the church, were led by the popular feeling to speak of them in similar contemptuous vein, and to join in the condemnation which all but universally prevailed during the early years of Christianity. Tacitus, Suetonius, and Pliny—all prominent and well-known Roman authors and historians—imbibed the prevalent spirit and described the early Christians as being possessed of a perverse and excessive superstition, wicked and deadly in its nature. In suffering such the disciples were simply experiencing that which Jesus had predicted would come to pass, and were following in his own footsteps, in demonstration of the adage that the servant is not above his lord.

They may by your good works, which they behold, glorify God in the day of visitation.—"By your good works" is, literally "out of your beautiful deeds" *(ek ton kalon ergon)*. Here, again, it should be observed that the word translated "good" is that which is not only morally right, but beautiful, orderly, harmonious. These beautiful deeds their enemies "behold" *(epoptuontes,* present active participle of *epopteuo,* to scrutinize minutely, to examine carefully), *to keep on* examining until, though their original motive was to find occasion for further accusation, they are led from such minute scrutiny to reverse their attitude and glorify God "in the day of visitation." The design of beautiful conduct on the part of Christians is, therefore, that God should be glorified and his name made great in the earth. To this end Jesus taught the disciples, "Even so let your light shine before men; that they may see your good works, and glorify your Father who is in heaven." (Matt. 5: 16.) Thus, the ultimate design of such conduct is not to attract to oneself honor and praise, but that God may be honored and glorified among men. As praise bestowed on a child because of its pleasing manners and obedient conduct is, in reality, praise given to the parents for the training and instruction which produced such obedience, so when men praise the good works of Christians, they are actually praising and honoring the name of him who is the author of such works.

The phrase "day of visitation," with slight variation, occurs in Luke 19: 44. "Visitation" (Greek, *episkopes*) is derived from the same source from which our words bishop and overseer come. Peter's use of the phrase was doubtless prompted by his remembrance of the Lord's use thereof ("Because thou knewest not the time of thy visitation," Luke 19: 44), where it is applied to the time when God comes to oversee his people, not only to rebuke them, but to bring them, if possible, to repentance; and such appears to be its meaning here, expanded to include his coming in providence to all men, and in all the ways in which his gracious influence is wrought upon the world of mankind. It was thus the expressed hope of Peter that the godly conduct of the disciples to whom he wrote would be the means of influence for good in inducing many of the unbelievers who had formerly been their traducers and accusers to turn to God in penitence as they learned more and more of the salvation which had been vouchsafed to men. The context and the similarity which obtains between this phrase and the Lord's use of it prompts us to conclude that the "visitation" here was a coming in grace, rather than of judgment, as the term sometime means. Though God "visits" men with judgment, he also visits them with salvation. (Psalm 106: 4.)

13 Be subject to every [10]ordinance of man for the Lord's sake: whether to

[10]Gr. *creation*

2. SUBMISSION TO CIVIL RULERS

13 Be subject to every ordinance of man for the Lord's sake:—One of the most common slanders uttered against the early disciples by the enemies of Christianity was that they were disorderly in conduct, and disposed to disregard the edicts of civil authority. In Thessalonica, for example, it was charged that "they act contrary to the decrees of Caesar." (Acts 17: 7.) To refute such slanders, and to give special emphasis to those matters most likely to be observed by people in general, the apostle, from a discussion of general precepts dealing with conduct before unbelievers in general, passes to specific exhortation with reference to the conduct of Christians in relation to the secular authorities.

"Be subject" is from *hupotagete,* aorist passive of *hupotasso,* here used with the force of the middle, signifying to place one's self under subjection; to render one's self subordinate. The word occurs in Rom. 8: 20; 1 Cor. 14: 32; 15: 27; Luke 2: 51, and often elsewhere in the New Testament. Peter uses it again in 3: 22, in the phrase, "angels and authorities and powers being made subject unto him."

"Ordinance" *(ktisis),* literally "a creation," and so translated in Rom. 1: 20 and Col. 1: 15, denotes that which has been made, and the prepositional phrase "of man" indicates that the creation contemplated is human in origin. The Greeks and Romans were accustomed to describe the appointment of officers as the *creation* of them; and here, the reference is to the institution, which they administered—the civil government. Peter thus exhorted those to whom he wrote to put themselves in submission to the prevailing and secular power. It should be observed that neither here nor elsewhere in the scriptures do the sacred writers designate any special form of government to which Christians are to subject themselves, or attempt to determine the type of government best suited to their needs. Aware that the saints would have no choice in the nature of the secular power under which they lived, these writers concerned themselves solely with the conduct which should characterize them, regardless of the form of government to which they owed allegiance. Whether the government was monarchal,

2: 13.]   FIRST PETER   71

the king, as supreme; 14 or unto governors, as sent [20]by him for vengeance

[20]Gr. *through*.

democratic, or totalitarian, the obligation was the same. Christians under it were "to be subject to every ordinance of man." It is noteworthy that the form of government which then obtained was dictatorial, totalitarian, and tyrannical; and the men who dispensed the laws thereof were corrupt, depraved, and dissolute in the extreme. That the Christian's allegiance thereto was not unconditional, however, follows from the fact that the apostle who penned the words of this text himself disregarded the edicts of constituted authority when forbidden to preach in the name of Jesus. "But Peter and John answered and said unto them, Whether it is right in the sight of God to hearken unto you rather than unto God, judge ye: for we cannot but speak the things which we saw and heard." (Acts 4: 1-22.)

When the law of God and the edicts of men are not in conflict, the Christian is obligated to obey both. When conflict exists, he *must* disregard the secular for the divine. Peter announced the principles that must govern in all such cases when he said, "We must obey God rather than men." (Acts 5: 29.)

The submission here enjoined by the apostle was not to be from motives purely human, nor from the fear of punishment which follows disobedience, but because "the powers that be are ordained of God (Rom. 13: 1ff.), and to be in subjection to them is to be in subjection to God, who ordained them. The submission contemplated is to be "for the Lord's sake," i.e., because he commanded it (Matt. 17: 26, 27), and his name is honored as the leader of those rendering such submission.

Whether to the king, as supreme;—The king alluded to was the infamous Nero, emperor of Rome, and one of the most wicked, depraved and ungodly kings who ever reigned. Under him Paul suffered martyrdom; under him, multitudes of saints died rather than renounce the faith once delivered to the saints. These to whom Peter wrote were admonished to obey him, wicked though he was, since he derived his powers from God who ordains civil government. (Rom. 13: 1.) Because God does not determine the form of government under which his people live, or

on evil-doers and for praise to them that do well. 15 For so is the will of God, that by well-doing ye should put to silence the ignorance of foolish

arbitrarily select the ruler, wicked men are often elevated to positions of authority therein. An example will be seen in John 19: 11.

The word "supreme" is the same adjective as that translated "higher" in the phrase "higher powers" in Rom. 13: 1. It is used here to distinguish between the rulers in the highest position and those in more obscure places and who derived their powers through (verse 14) the king.

14 **Or unto governors, as sent by him for vengeance on evil-doers and for praise to them that do well.**—The "governors" were the proconsuls and magistrates of the provinces, subordinate officials variously designated as "Asiarchs," town clerks, proconsuls, etc. (Acts 19: 31, 35, 38.) The word "governors" means leaders (from *hegeomai,* to lead).

"By him" is, in the Greek text, literally "through him" *(di'autou),* the pronoun "him" referring to the king (verse 13), and not the Lord. Peter's design here was to show that these "governors" exercised their powers by virtue of the supreme authority of the king by whom they were sent. The purpose for which this was done—the design, incidentally, of all civil authority —was (a) to punish the wicked, and (b) encourage good works by protecting those engaged therein. It is significant that throughout this passage there is similarity in form and in meaning to that of Paul in the well-known passage in Rom. 13: 1-7.

The obligation of the Christian to conform to the laws of the land in which he lives, even though the government itself is corrupt, and the officials who administer the laws depraved, is here, and in the passage above alluded to by Paul, clearly taught. The test is simply this: is the edict in harmony with the law of God? If yes, it must be obeyed whatever the nature of the government, and despite the depravity of its officials; if no, it must be resisted, however worthy the government and benevolent its rulers in other respects. This principle admits of no exceptions. It is fatal to disregard it.

15 **For so is the will of God, that by well-doing ye should put to silence the ignorance of foolish men:**—Instead of indulging in vehement vindication of their character and conduct, the

men: 16 as free, and not [21]using your freedom for a cloak of wickedness, but

[21]Gr. *having*.

saints to whom Peter wrote were admonished to make their good deeds the most conspicuous feature of their lives, this being the most effective defence available to them against the false and malicious slanders which they were suffering at the hands of their enemies. "For so" *(outos esti),* "in this way," the will of God was discharged. This was the manner in which God wanted them to defend themselves against such attacks; and it is the way he wants us to meet such today. "Silence," in the text, is from *phimoun,* present infinitive active of *phimoo,* literally, to muzzle, to gag; thus, figuratively, to silence. Instances of its literal meaning, and where it is thus rendered are 1 Cor. 9: 9 and 1 Tim. 5: 18. Here, metaphorically, wicked men were to be muzzled, and the muzzle to be used was the saints' good deeds! As a muzzle renders even a vicious and ill-tempered dog harmless, so the godly behavior of Christians effectively muzzles their most malevolent foes.

The "ignorance" designated was not merely the lack of information characteristic of the uninformed *(agnoia),* but a type of ignorance that is willful, persistent, and disgraceful in nature *(agnosia).* It is the same as that which Paul regarded as shameful in 1 Cor. 15: 34. "Foolish" *(aphron),* senseless, indicates an evil condition not only of the mind but also of the heart, i.e., folly preceding not simply from lack of understanding, but from evil and corrupt motives also. The article appears before the word foolish in the text, thus designating these foolish men as a special class engaged in slandering the children of God, and not simply foolish men in general.

16 **As free, and not using your freedom for a cloak of wickedness, but as bondservants of God.**—Though they were free, the freedom which Peter's readers enjoyed was not license to ungodly indulgence. New Testament writers, and Paul particularly, gave much emphasis to the fact that children of God are free (Gal. 5: 1), free from the law, free from sin, free from fear, but with many cautions that this freedom must be kept within circumscribed bounds. Men were, in that day, especially disposed to allege their freedom as ground for disregarding the sanctions of the law, and as license to fleshly indulgence. Some Gentile sects, con-

as bondservants of God. 17 Honor all men. Love the brotherhood. Fear God. Honor the king.

fusing liberty with libertinism, maintained that grace meant deliverance from all law (a view likewise held today by those who subscribe to the doctrine of impossibility of apostasy), and the Jews, on the plea that they were in possession of the oracles of God, often claimed immunity from law originating with man.

To guard his readers against such wicked conclusions, Peter penned these words of caution. They were to remember that, though free, they were under definite obligation and with responsibilities not to be disregarded. These the apostle presented both negatively and positively. (a) This freedom they enjoyed was not to be used as a cloak (covering, veil) for wickedness; (b) instead, they were to live as "bondservants" of God. Free, they were, nevertheless, servants; the paradox being a well known Christian characteristic. There is indeed no such thing as absolute personal liberty. Liberty without restraint is license; and unrestrained license is abject bondage. The alcoholic, the dope addict, because they recognize no restraint, are in the most helpless slavery.

17 **Honor all men. Love the brotherhood. Fear God. Honor the king.**—Four rules of conduct are here designated. The first, "honor all men," being more general than the others, is in the aorist tense; the last three are present imperatives. As occasion arises, all men are to be honored; the brotherhood is to be continuously loved, God is evermore to be feared, and there is a constant, unceasing obligation to honor the king where such form of government exists. Inasmuch as all men have in them the image of God, however greatly marred it may be, they are to be accorded the respect that is their due. The "brotherhood" is the church of the Lord in its aggregate sense; the affection we are admonished to feel for it is the love which obtains between those of the same family with common parentage, common interests, and common aims. Though not as universal as the command of the Lord in Matt. 5: 44, "love your enemies," the special love which Christians are to feel for each other by no means excludes the love there enjoined for our enemies. The injunction to "fear God" and "honor the king," being so closely joined, suggests a relationship between them. To "fear God" is to show him holy, reverential

awe; and to "honor the king" is to accord him the respect that is due one in such a position of authority. The "fear" we are to feel for God is not dread nor terror; it is rather fear of offending, of causing pain through misconduct. "The fear (Hebrew *yirah,* reverence) of Jehovah is the beginning of knowledge." (Prov. 1: 7.) Though we do not live under a monarchy such as was characteristic of the saints to whom Peter wrote, the principle applies to the public servants empowered to administer the laws of the land, and these we are to honor.

3. DUTIES OF SERVANTS TO MASTERS
2: 18-25

18 [22]Servants, *be* in subjection to your masters with all fear; not only to

[22]Gr. *Household-servants.*

---

18 **Servants, be in subjection to your masters with all fear; not only to the good and gentle, but also to the froward.**—A common word for "servant," and that by which Paul often designated himself in the familiar phrase, "servant of Jesus Christ" (Rom. 1: 1; Phil. 1: 1; Titus 1: 1), is *doulos,* slave. Here, "servants" is from the milder *oiketes,* a domestic servant, a household slave. This class of servants, being more constantly in contact with their masters than would those slaves whose work was customarily in the fields and shops, would be subjected to greater provocation from evil masters, and are thus particularly addressed here. It is well known that many in the church during the apostolic age were in bondage; and instruction to those under such restraint is significantly large in the New Testament. (Eph. 6: 5-8; Col. 3: 22; 1 Tim. 6: 1, 2.) The reason is obvious. As Christians, they had learned of their equality with all men before God, and had come to recognize that in Christ Jesus all fleshly distinctions have been abolished. (Gal. 3: 28, 29.) There was thus grave danger that these considerations would prompt them to disregard their obligations, and to repudiate the relationship which subsisted between them and their earthly masters. The institution of slavery was opposed to the very spirit and genius of Christianity, and destined to perish as the influence thereof came to be dominantly felt; yet, so deeply rooted was it in the social and economic fabric of the time that a frontal attack upon it would have

the good and gentle, but also to the froward. 19 For this is [23]acceptable, if

[23]Gr. *grace*.

---

been disastrous to the cause of Christianity. The sacred writers thus tolerated it and regulated it until such time as it would disintegrate under the impact of the cross.

The relationship must have been an exceedingly trying one, particularly to those with heathen masters. In the first place it was difficult for them to reconcile subjection to men with spiritual liberty; and most difficult of all when these masters were evil men, and disposed to oppress and mistreat them. Yet, it was a relationship which, for the time, they could not escape; and these instructions were vitally essential to the progress and good name of Christianity among the heathen.

The "subjection" enjoined is to be related to that designated in verse 13, "be subject to every ordinance of man for the Lord's sake," the relationship of servants and masters being one of the ordinances of men there implied. It is also to be identified with the teaching of the entire context as another means by which to "silence" (muzzle) the mouths of their accusers and prompt those about them to "glorify God in the day of visitation."

The service commanded was to be rendered "with all fear." There are many kinds of fear: fear of punishment; fear of offending God; fear of bringing reproach on the name of Christ—all of which is to be included here. These to whom Peter wrote were not only to fear the displeasure of their earthly masters, but especially God, their highest Master. (Eph. 6: 5.) Moreover, their service was to be the same whether their masters were kind and benevolent or cruel and vindicative. It was to be given "not in the way of eye-service, as men-pleasers, but as servants of Christ, doing the will of God from the heart." (Eph. 6: 6.) The word "good," descriptive of humane masters, denotes inner goodness, kindness of heart; "gentle," that which is mild and considerate; "froward" is, literally, crooked, here figuratively used to indicate that disposition which is perverse, surly, opposed to gentle. Good and gentle masters were those who showed consideration for their servants; the froward were masters who oppressed and abused them.

for conscience [21]toward God a man endureth griefs, suffering wrongfully. 20 For what glory is it, if, when ye sin, and are buffeted *for it,* ye shall take it patiently? but if, when ye do well, and suffer *for it,* ye shall take it patiently,

[21]Gr. *of.*

---

19 For this is acceptable, if for conscience toward God a man endureth griefs, suffering wrongfully.—"This" *(touto,* neuter singular, this thing) refers to that immediately preceding—obedience to wicked and oppressive masters. "Acceptable" is translated from the same word *(charis)* as "thank" in the passage, "And if ye love them that love you, what *thank* have ye" (Luke 6: 32), where it signifies not only thanks, but also reward and praise. Here, as in that passage, such is contemplated as being witnessed by the Father, i.e., under his eye, and proceeding from his hand. The term is descriptive of the credit which belongs to those who exceed what might be ordinarily expected. Slaves of the world resent and rebel against the surly disposition and abusive condict of their wicked masters; but Christians, in the same relationship, suffer such uncomplainingly because of their consciousness of God's presence and approval. Peter is not to be understood as affirming here that suffering of itself is an occasion for commendation from God; it is only when such proceeds from one's determination to do that which is right that it is "acceptable" (thankworthy, A.V.) in God's sight.

20 For what glory is it, if, when ye sin, and are buffeted for it, ye take it patiently? but if, when ye do well, and suffer for it, ye shall take it patiently, this is acceptable with God.—"Glory" here is not that which affords occasion for boasting, but is that impression which, by worthy conduct, is made upon others. The word literally signifies renown, fame, praise earned by commendable achievement. Where punishment is suffered because of improper conduct, no praise accrues to the sufferer; good people feel that in such cases the culprit is merely receiving that which he deserved. "Buffeted" *(kolaphizo,* to strike with the fist, here present passive participle) means to be repeatedly pummelled, perhaps literally here to indicate the type and extent of the punishment slaves often received from their "froward" masters. When punishment is undeserved, and is administered because of the wickedness of the master, and Christian slaves endure it patiently because

this is [23]acceptable with God. 21 For hereunto were ye called: because Christ also suffered for you, leaving you an example, that ye should follow

---

they desire to do their duty to God, he approves and blesses. The word "acceptable" is similarly derived, and means the same as in verse 19. When men endure such treatment for conscience sake they are exceeding that which their fellows ordinarily do under such circumstances, and are therefore regarded as "thankworthy" in God's sight. The early Christians often found occasion to rejoice amidst the most severe persecution and trial. (Acts 5: 40-42; 16: 25.)

21 **For hereunto were ye called:**—Verses 18-20 deal with the *duty* of servants to continue in well doing, and to submit patiently to whatever trials it is their lot to bear; verses 21-25 establish the *motive* which should prompt to such manner of life. "Hereunto *(eis touto)* is, literally, "into this," i.e., into such a life as they were experiencing had they been called (by the gospel) to do good and to suffer patiently. While primarily applicable to Christian slaves, these words have a general application to all saints, for it is "through much tribulation" that we "enter into the kingdom of God" (Acts 14: 22), and Paul warned that all who would live godly in Christ Jesus shall "suffer persecution" (2 Tim. 3: 12). These saints to whom Peter wrote were "called" to such suffering, this being an inevitable consequence of their lot in life. Christianity is, itself, a calling (2 Thess. 2: 13, 14), and trials an invariable characteristic thereof. "Because to you it hath been granted in the behalf of Christ, not only to believe on him, but also to suffer in his behalf." (Phil. 1: 29.)

Because Christ also suffered for you, leaving you an example, that ye should follow in his steps:—The calling alluded to in the first clause of verse 21 is here explained: "because Christ also (literally, even Christ) suffered for you." Since the disciple is not above his master, nor the servant above his lord, such suffering was to be expected. Two ideas are here advanced: (1) Christ suffered; hence, you, his servants, must likewise suffer; (2) in suffering the Lord left an example for his disciples to imitate in enduring similar trials.

"Example," in the text, is from *hupogrammon,* accusative singular of *hupogrammos,* from the preposition *hupo-,* under, and

his steps: 22 who did no sin, neither was guile found in his mouth: 23 who,

gramma, to write; thus, literally, to write under; to copy, and here figuratively, a pattern or model for imitation. It is a figure suggested by the copy-book method of teaching penmanship. Christ thus becomes the copy-head, the beautiful writing at the top of the page. Implied in the figure is a copy-book, a perfect pattern of writing, a white, unblemished sheet of paper, the student's effort to transcribe the copy, the awkward attempts in the beginning, persistent determination, constant and unremitting practice; and then, eventually—success!

The purpose for which such an example has been provided is that we should "follow in his steps." "Steps" is from *ichnos,* the heel of a shoe; also, a footprint. At this point the figure changes from a copy-head to a guide who goes before and breaks out the path that others may safely and surely follow. The Lord thus becomes for us not only an example of patient resignation in suffering trial and hardship, he went before us marking out the path and leaving us footprints of meekness, gentleness, and fortitude. Christ's example was cited as a particular encouragement to the Christian slaves among those whom Peter wrote to bear patiently the unjust and undeserved reproaches which they received from their heathen masters. Suffering for evil conduct they might have accepted as that which should be expected under the circumstances; but to suffer unjustly and at the hands of unbelieving heathens was indeed a difficult trial to bear. Christ, as an example of an innocent sufferer, is offered to sustain them in bearing similar trials. Though he suffered, and suffered unjustly, this did not prompt him to sin, neither was guile found in his mouth. This pattern Peter's readers should strive to follow. The conduct of Christ under such great provocation is next alluded to by the apostle.

22 Who did no sin, neither was guile found in his mouth: —These words are cited, with slight variation, from the Septuagint translation of Isa. 53: 9, sin *(hamartia)* being substituted for violence *(anomia,* lawlessness) in our version of the Hebrew text. (See also, Zeph. 3: 13.) "Did" is from *epoiesen,* aorist tense of *poieo,* with the negative signifying that never in a single instance did Jesus commit sin. For the meaning of the word "guile," see

when he was reviled, reviled not again; when he suffered, threatened not;

comments on 1 Pet. 2: 1. "Found" is from a word *(eurisko)* which means to search diligently. No guile (deceit, deception) could be found in the words of our Lord, despite the fact that his enemies sought diligently and searched carefully to discover such. The Saviour's sincerity thus stood the test of hostile scrutiny. Peter may have cited this prophecy of Isaiah as especially significant to slaves because the Messiah is designated by that prophet as the *servant* of Jehovah (Isa. 52: 13), and an oppressed and afflicted one. (Isa. 53: 7, 8.) Other passages where the sinlessness of Jesus is expressly affirmed are Heb. 7: 26; 2 Cor. 5: 21; and 1 John 3: 5. He himself alluded to the fact in his challenge to his enemies, "Which of you convicteth me of sin?" (John 8: 46), a challenge infidels for twenty centuries have never accepted. Jesus *did* no sin, neither was guile found in his *mouth,* thus exhibiting perfect sinlessness, both in word and in deed. These words were especially relevant to slaves whose servitude and consequent oppression by evil masters laid them open to greater temptation to practice deception and deceit, and to resort to trickery and artifice in evading and avoiding the accusations of their masters. However great the provocation, Peter would have them remember, and imitate the Christ they followed. These words are as pertinent to us today as to those to whom they were originally penned.

23 Who, when he was reviled, reviled not again; when he suffered, threatened not; but committed himself to him that judgeth righteously:—The antecedent of "who" is Christ. (Verse 21.) The verbs "reviled" are translated from Greek imperfects, the force of which is to signify that when our Lord was being constantly reviled, he did not retaliate with railing for railing; while suffering the bitter taunts of his most determined enemies he did not utter vain and meaningless imprecations, but committed (Greek, *kept on committing*) himself to God with the assurance that, though being greatly wronged by man, he would receive righteous judgment at the hands of the Father.

The biographies of Jesus abound with instances of that to which Peter here alludes. The Jews charged him with being a devil, a winebibber, and a glutton, in league with Beelzebub, a blasphemer of God, and violator of the law. When on trial before the Sanhe-

but committed ¹*himself* to him that judgeth righteously: 24 who his own self

¹Or, his cause

drin—the supreme court of the Jews—the judges thereof ridiculed his claims, heaped scorn and contempt on his head, and spit in his face. Common soldiers, in further derision of his claims to royalty, placed a purple robe about his shoulders and did mock obeisance at his feet. While dying on the cross a bloodthirsty mob milled and surged about him, shouting, "He saved others; himself he cannot save." (Matt. 27: 39.) The stark tragedy of those fateful hours was deeply etched in Peter's consciousness, and he penned these words in vivid remembrance of scenes in which he himself had performed a disgraceful part.

Again, it should be noted that this instruction was especially pertinent to the Christian slaves to whom it was particularly addressed. (1 Pet. 2: 18.) They must often have been tempted to retaliate when reviled by their heartless masters. Even so, they were not to forget that their Master under circumstances even more trying had met such ungodly taunts with silent patience. In the indignation which they felt for undeserved and evil treatment incident to their position as slaves they were doubtless often sorely tempted to threaten dire vengeance against their oppressors. They must, in all such instances, remember that while the Lord could have brought to his side twelve legions of angels, he made no defense of himself, and gave utterance to no threats, quietly committing himself into the hands of his Father. As their master had done, so were his servants to do.

The pointed words of condemnation which Jesus sometimes hurled at the Pharisees and others (Matt. 7: 5; 16: 3; 22: 18; 23: 13; 23: 25-36) were not the bitter taunts of personal malice, nor the retaliatory retorts for insults received, but the probings of one capable of looking into the innermost recesses of the heart and exposing the corruption there, with the design of saving, if possible, the persons so possessed.

Our Saviour thus not only *taught* non-retaliation (Matt. 5: 38-48); he *practiced* it, and under the most trying circumstances possible to conceive. It is only when his disciples do likewise that they reflect his spirit and demonstrate in their lives his influence. Far from calling down upon his enemies the vengeance of his

²bare our sins in his body upon the tree, that we, having died unto sins, might live unto righteousness; by whose ³stripes ye were healed.

²Or, *carried up* . . . *to the tree* Comp. Col. 2. 14; 1 Macc. 4. 53 (Gr.).
³Gr. *bruise.*

Father, he prayed for and sought their conversion and salvation. "Say not, I will do so to him as he hath done to me; I will render to the man according to his work." (Prov. 4: 29.) "All things therefore whatsoever ye would that men should do unto you, even so do ye also unto them: for this is the law and the prophets." It is idle to claim the Spirit of Christ while disregarding, under any circumstances, the principles taught in this passage. They are universal in nature and applicable to every relationship possible to the Christian.

24 Who his own self bare our sins in his body upon the tree,—In the verses immediately preceding (21-23), the example of Christ, as a patient and uncomplaining sufferer under extreme provocation, was brought forth, and the Christian slaves, to whom Peter was particularly addressing this instruction, were admonished to "follow in his steps." Having thus had occasion to refer to the suffering and death of Christ on the cross, and unwilling to pass from this momentous theme when thus far he had pictured the Lord as merely a martyr courageously suffering and dying for a cherished cause, he here dwells on and considers his death in its relation to the redemption of man. Already, in the context, he had pointed out that Christ suffered "for you," and lest this should be interpreted as meaning no more than an example of patient endurance and an encouragement to holy living, he passes to the contemplation of his death in its atoning aspects and sharpens and extends the remarkable statement of verse 22. Not only had our Lord no sin, not only did he not sin himself, he also *bore our sins* in his body on the tree.

The word "bore" is translated from the Greek *anenegken*, second aorist active indicative of *anaphero*, the word used in the Greek Septuagint translation of the Old Testament of the bearing up on the altar of the sacrificial victim by the priest. Inherent in the word is thus the idea of sacrifice, and it is idle to attempt to weaken its meaning by its exclusion. The Lord not only died in our behalf; he also died in our stead. The vicarious aspect of the death of Christ is clearly taught here, as often elsewhere in the sacred writings. (Matt. 20: 28; Mark 10: 45; 1 Tim. 2: 6.) The position of the pronoun is emphatic; he, himself, bore our sins, he alone. This verse is an obvious allusion to the well-known prophecy of Isa. 53: "He shall see the travail of his soul, and shall be satisfied: by the knowledge of himself shall my righteous servant justify many; and he shall bear their iniquities. Therefore will I divide him a portion with the great, and he shall divide the spoil with the strong; because he poured out his soul unto death, and was numbered with the transgressors: yet he bare the sins of man, and made intercession for the transgressors." (Isa. 53: 11, 12.)

The Lord, in bearing the sins of the world, simply allowed the penalty of the law to fall upon him, the execution of which he suffered in our stead. Moreover, he bore our sins "in his own body." His body thus became the sacrificial victim, and the cross the altar on which it was offered. Christ in his death became both priest and victim; he bore our sins, thus making an offering for us; he bore our sins "in his own body," thus serving as the victim of sacrifice which he offered. (Heb. 9: 25-28.)

He bore our sins in his body "on the tree." For the cross the apostle uses here the word "tree" *(xulon),* the same term by which he designated the cross in his speeches in Acts. (Acts 5: 30; 10: 39.) Paul alluded to the cross in similar fashion (Gal. 3: 13), and both apostles were doubtless influenced to this end by Deut. 21: 23.

That we, having died unto sins, might live unto righteousness;—The two effects of Christ's death are here prominently exhibited: (1) by it our sins have been removed; (2) through its effects we are privileged to live unto righteousness. "Having died" is in the aorist tense, and thus refers to a definite and consummated act of renunciation of sin occurring in repentance and the reformation which follows; and the life of righteousness begins when one is raised from the baptismal grave. (Rom. 6: 1-6.) To live unto righteousness is simply to live in the service of righteousness. "Righteousness" is that state or condition existing when one keeps the commandments. (Psalm 119: 172.) The word "died" in this clause is an unusual one, occurring nowhere else in the

25 For ye were going astray like sheep; but are now returned unto the Shepherd and ⁴Bishop of your souls.

⁴Or, *Overseer*

scriptures. Its literal meaning is "having ceased to be." By virtue of the sacrificial atonement of Christ, when we turn from a life of sin the relationship which has thus far subsisted ceases to be, and when the "old man of sin" is buried in the watery grave, a new life unto righteousness ensues. (Rom. 6: 1-6.)

By whose stripes ye were healed.—These words are quoted from the Greek translation of Isa. 53: 5. "Stripes" is from the Greek *molops,* a bruised and swollen welt from which blood trickles, the livid mark on the quivering flesh, red and raw, from scourging. In the Greek the word is singular, as it also is in Isa. 53: 5, the body of Jesus being so bruised from the brutal beating he received that there was but one wound or stripe, and this covered his entire body. The instrument by which this punishment was inflicted—the scourge—was a leather whip of cords into which had been woven jagged bits of brass or iron. When these Christian slaves were beaten they were to remember that, however cruel and brutal such beatings were, none equalled that which the Lord suffered prior to his crucifixion.

By his stripes we "were healed." The word "healed" is here figuratively used for the salvation of the soul from sin, and may not properly be extended to include miraculous healing of the body from disease. The sickness implied in the word is of the soul, and the healing, redemption. An instance of such use by the Lord will be seen in Matt. 13: 15. Evidence that bodily healing as a part of the atonement is not taught here or elsewhere in the scriptures follows from the fact that (1) instances abound of individuals known to be saved who nevertheless suffered bodily affliction (Phil. 2: 27; 2 Tim. 4: 20; 2 Cor. 12: 7; 1 Tim. 5: 23); (2) were healing a part of the atonement, sickness in an individual would be proof that the soul is unsaved; (3) the context here clearly points to the fact that it is salvation from sin, and not physical healing of the body contemplated in this passage. So-called modern divine healers are guilty of a perversion of this text in extending it to include healing of the body from affliction and disease.

25 **For ye were going astray like sheep;**—The figure of sheep as representative of a people confused, bewildered, and without a leader is a common one in the scriptures. (Matt. 9: 36; Luke 15: 4; Num. 27: 17; 1 Kings 22: 17.) Wandering sheep, away from the fold, and exposed to the manifold dangers of the wilderness, are a fitting representation of those who have forsaken the right way and have gone astray. While the reference here is primarily to Isa. 53: 6 ("All we like sheep have gone astray"), Peter must have recalled the many allusions thereto by the Lord during his public ministry, and particularly the parable of the Good Shepherd. (John 10: 1-16.)

But are now returned unto the Shepherd and Bishop of your souls.—"Returned" is in the aorist tense, and thus indicates a single act, and a definite occasion when they returned—viz., at their conversion. The verb is also in the passive voice, often used as here with middle sense, to show that the subject acted upon itself to accomplish the desired result. Thus, these to whom Peter wrote, by their obedience to the gospel, were saved from the wandering life of sheep and the dangers incident thereto, and returned unto the "shepherd and bishop" of their souls. The Lord is presented here under two aspects (1) he is a shepherd, in that he feeds, guides, and protects his sheep; (2) he is a bishop (overseer) because he superintends, supervises, and directs their activity. Those whose duty it is to direct the affairs of the churches are undershepherds in feeding, guiding, and directing the work of the church; and they are bishops in overseeing, under Christ, the work committed into their hands. (Eph. 4: 11; Acts 20: 28.) The author of this epistle was an elder (1 Pet. 5: 1), and Christ is presented as the "chief shepherd" (1 Pet. 5: 4). There is perhaps significance in the fact that attention is drawn to Christ as shepherd and bishop of souls. Though these to whom Peter primarily wrote were in bondage in the flesh, their souls, their higher nature was free and answerable only to the Great Shepherd.

4. DUTIES OF WIVES TO HUSBANDS
3: 1-6

1 In like manner, ye wives, *be* in subjection to your own husbands; that, even if any obey not the word, they may without the word be gained by the

---

1 In like manner, ye wives, be in subjection to your own husbands;—From the consideration of duties derived from the relationship of servants and masters, discussed at length in the preceding chapter, the apostle passes to another element in the social life of the people involving, according to the concepts which then prevailed, an almost equal degree of subordination—that of wives to their husbands. Here, as elsewhere throughout the epistle, Peter's design appears to be to inculcate such principles as would enable the suffering saints to whom he wrote to bear patiently and worthily their burdens, however heavy and galling such should be.

The lot of women in non-Greek countries, particularly before the influence of the gospel began to be felt, was a deplorable one. Aristotle writes that among the barbarians (non-Greeks) women and slaves held the same rank; and though among the Greeks her position was not quite so degraded, they considered her as holding only an intermediate position between free persons and slaves, mother of her children, but not worthy to educate them, qualified to receive orders, but never to give them.

As the influence of Christianity began to exercise itself such barbarous ideas were destined to fail; slavery was to perish, and women to be elevated to their proper place in society; it was essential to the well-being of the cause which was to produce such effects, however, that these changes should be gradual and not violent; produced by instruction and not by revolution. Hence, the instructions given.

"In like manner" *(omoios,* in the same manner), i.e., in harmony with the principles taught as to the duty of Christian slaves to be subject to their masters, so wives are to be constantly submitting (present participle, middle voice) themselves to their own husbands. The word "own," in the text, is emphatic and significant. Christian women, with heathen husbands, might be tempted to despise their husbands and exhibit contempt for them, feeling obligated only to those Christian men with whom they were asso-

⁵behavior of their wives; 2 beholding your chaste ⁵behavior *coupled* with

⁵Or. *manner of life* ver. 16.

---

ciated in the church. The effect of such an attitude would be disastrous, not only to the church, but to the family and to society in general. Though Christians, and in an enviable position, they were not to forget the obligations that are fundamental and vital to the permanence of society.

That, even if any obey not the word, they may without the word be gained by the behavior of their wives;—In some instances both the husband and the wife would obey the gospel; in others, only the wife; and it is the latter with which the apostle deals here. "The word" in the phrase, "if any obey not the word," is the gospel. (Rom. 1: 16.) "Obey not" is translated from a term which denotes a degree of antagonism in addition to disobedience, plus an element of stubbornness. It means, literally, not to allow one's self to be persuaded. The text, as it runs in our translation, makes the apostle assert that such men may "without the word" be gained, i.e., they may be led to the word of truth without the word of truth! Such an idea is contradictory and does not correctly represent what the apostle actually said. The Greek article does not appear before the noun "word" in the phrase, "may without the word be gained. . . ." Here, "word" does not refer, as it does in the former phrase, to the word of truth—the gospel. Instead, it refers to the exhortations, the persuasions of the wives. These husbands had heard the gospel and were familiar with its demands. They had thus far been stubborn, rebellious, disobedient. Peter admonished the wives of such men to desist from further importunity, lest such should descend to nagging; and instead, by godly conduct and discreet behavior to encourage them to do that which they already understood to be their duty. Properly translated, the passage reads: "If any obey not the word, they may without *a word* (from the wife) be gained by her godly behavior." This is an instance when silent eloquence is more effective than vigorous and vehement debate. "Be gained" is a significant and important statement. Every soul saved is a gain to the Lord, to the church, and to itself. "Behavior" sums up the conduct of the wives addressed.

fear. 3 Whose *adorning* let it not be the outward adorning of braiding the

2 Beholding your chaste behavior coupled with fear.—The word "beholding" occurs also in 1 Pet. 2: 12, where see notes. It suggests the scrutiny of an eyewitness, and implies information from close and minute observation. From such examination, these unbelieving husbands would be able to form an evaluation of the chaste behavior of their wives and attribute such to the influence of Christianity. "Fear" in the text is reverence, awe, and is with reference to the husband, and not God. It is the same sort of fear as that designated by Paul in Eph. 5: 33. From Clement of Alexandria, born about the middle of the second century, comes this excellent comment: "The wise woman, then, will first choose to persuade her husband to be her associate in what is conducive to happiness. And should that be found impractical, let her by herself earnestly aim at virtue, gaining her husband's consent in everything, so as never to do anything against his will, with exception of what is reckoned as contributing to virtue and salvation." *(Ante-Nicene Fathers,* Vol. 2, page 432.)

3 Whose adorning let it not be the outward adorning of braiding the hair, and of wearing jewels of gold, or of putting on apparel;—The teaching of this verse is closely associated with that which immediately precedes it. Christian wives, far from following the tactics by which their worldly sisters attract and hold the attention of their husbands, are to give emphasis instead to "the hidden man of the heart," the "incorruptible apparel of a meek and quiet spirit which is in the sight of God of great price." (Verse 4.) Their adornment was thus not to be the (a) braiding of the hair; (b) wearing of jewels of gold; or (c) putting on of apparel. It is obvious from the mention of putting on apparel that the apostle's words are to be regarded as hortatory rather than unconditionally prohibitive. Taken literally, and without qualification, they would forbid not only the braiding of the hair and the wearing of jewels of gold, but also the putting on of clothing. It is, therefore, clear that Peter did not intend for his words to be interpreted as an unqualified and unconditional prohibition of the things mentioned, but as an exhortation to regard such as secondary and trivial in comparison with the inner adornment of character exhibited in the meek and quiet spirit composing

hair, and of wearing jewels of gold, or of putting on apparel; 4 but *let it be the hidden man of the heart, in the incorruptible apparel* of a meek and quiet

the incorruptible apparel which he enjoins. The form of exhortation here followed—sometimes styled a Hebraism—is a common one in the sacred writings. Jesus said, "Work not for the food which perisheth, but for the food which abideth unto eternal life." (John 6: 27.) Literally, these words forbid one to work for his daily bread; regarded as a Hebraism, which they are, they simply mean that one is not to place his chief emphasis on material things, but to give paramount attention to that which abideth unto eternal life. So here, the apostle does not forbid women to wear jewels, or to adorn themselves with modest apparel; he does admonish them to regard such as utterly worthless in comparison with the graces which adorn the Christian character, and which alone determine one's worth in God's sight.

Paul also gave attention to the vanity characteristic of worldly women in adorning themselves with "braided hair, gold or pearls or costly raiment" (1 Tim. 2: 9), and from the historians of the period in which Peter wrote, we learn that women were disposed to go to extreme lengths in braiding and plaiting their hair, often arranging massive whorls of it several inches above the head into which had been woven twisted strands of gold and chains of pearls which glistened and scintillated in the light, thus making an impression of great brilliance. Clement of Alexandria says that many women of his time dared not touch their heads for fear of disarranging their hair, and that they regarded sleep with terror lest during it they should destroy their waves. It is such vanity as this that the apostle condemns. Forbidden is any lavish display of artificial adornments and all gaudiness contributing to the vanity of those participating. Christians, whether men or women, should array themselves in modest and unassuming garments, befitting their station in life, and the cause which they have espoused.

4 But let it be the hidden man of the heart, in the incorruptible apparel of a meek and quiet spirit, which is in the sight of God of great price.—The "hidden man of the heart" is equivalent in meaning to that of the "inward man" of 2 Cor. 4: 16 and Rom. 7: 22, and the "new man" Col. 3: 10. "Of the heart" (genitive of apposition) indicates that the life of this "hid-

spirit, which is in the sight of God of great price. 5 For after this manner aforetime the holy women also, who hoped in God, adorned themselves, being in subjection to their own ⁶husbands: 6 as Sarah obeyed Abraham, calling him lord: whose children ye now are, if ye do well, and are not put in ⁷fear by any terror.

⁶Or, *husbands (as Sarah . . . ye are become), doing well, and not being afraid*
⁷Or, *afraid with*

---

den man" manifests itself in the realm of the heart, and not in ornamental display. It is said to be an "incorruptible apparel" because it is not perishable and worthless like the ornaments of gold and silver which the worldly minded use; and it consists of a meek and quiet spirit. A "meek spirit" is one not characterized by self-will, envy, pride, presumption or obstinacy; and a "quiet spirit" is one that is calm, tranquil, and at peace. The adjective "great" modifying "price" in the text *(poluteles)* is used in Mark 14: 3 to describe the value of the ointment ("pure nard very costly") which Mary used to anoint the Lord "beforehand" for his burying, thus indicating the preciousness with which God regards those women who adorn themselves in the manner which Peter admonishes.

5 **For after this manner aforetime the holy women also, who hoped in God, adorned themselves, being in subjection to their own husbands:**—To the precepts of the preceding verses, the apostle adds the example of faithful and godly women of old. These saintly sisters of the Old Testament period are styled "holy women" because they were set apart to a life of faithfulness to God and to their husbands; and they are said to have "hoped in God" because their expectations were grounded in him. The basis of their acceptance with God and their value to their husbands was not in the gaudy and spectacular ornaments of the thoughtless and vain, but in the worthy lives and submissive attitudes exhibited. For such they are imperishably inscribed in Inspiration's Hall of Fame. (Heb. 11: 11, 35.)

6 **As Sarah obeyed Abraham, calling him lord: whose children ye now are, if ye do well, and are not put in fear by any terror.**—Gen. 18: 12 is an instance of that to which Peter alludes in his reference to Sarah, the faithful wife of the patriarch Abraham. In referring to him as "lord" (a term which, as here used, is a title of honor addressed to one regarded as superior),

Sarah revealed an attitude of habitual and continuous subordination. Because she recognized the supremacy of her husband and gladly assumed her proper sphere in the home, she serves as an example for Christian wives today. "Whose children ye now are" is, literally, "whose daughters *you became*" *(hes egnethete tekna)*, i.e., by following the pattern of Sarah. By adorning themselves as Sarah did they became daughters of her to the extent that a child is like its parent. It is significant that this figure—a common one in the sacred writings—is used of those who follow in the steps of Abraham as believers: "Know therefore that they that are of faith, the same are the sons of Abraham." (Gal. 3: 7.) "And he (Abraham) received the sign of circumcision, a seal of the righteousness of the faith which he had while he was in uncircumcision: that he might be the father of all them that believe, though they be in uncircumcision, that righteousness might be reckoned unto them." (Rom. 4: 11.)

The words "if ye do well" contain the condition on which such a relationship to Sarah is obtained, and by which it is kept. Sarah earned her right to be regarded as the mother of those wives who do well by her own godly conduct; and her daughters are those who imitate her example. The "terror" against which the apostle warns in the final clause of the verse is not the "fear" *(phobos)* which he enjoins in verse 2, but the shrinking, shuddering fear *(ptoesis)* of one in the grip of extreme trepidation. In his admonition to Christian wives to avoid such an attitude, the writer appears to be guarding them from running out of one extreme into another. Those who had unbelieving husbands would often have heavy burdens to bear, and much abuse to hear, and if they exhibited terror in the presence of such husbands as if constantly expecting curses or blows, such an attitude might provoke the very thing they were seeking to avoid. Hence, Peter instructed them to "do well" and then to proceed with their daily tasks with calm, unruffled spirit, whatever might be the attitude of their husbands.

5. DUTIES OF HUSBANDS TO WIVES
3: 7

The exhortation of this portion of the epistle, like that of the two preceding sections—to Christian slaves (1 Pet. 2: 18-25), and to Christian wives of unbelieving husbands (1 Pet. 3: 1-16)—is

7 Ye husbands, in like manner, dwell with *your wives* according to knowledge, giving honor ⁸unto the woman, as unto the weaker vessel, as being also joint-heirs of the grace of life; to the end that your prayers be not hindered.

⁸Gr. *unto the female vessel, as weaker.*

closely connected with 1 Pet. 2: 11-17 in which the apostle admonishes godly conduct before the world as the most effective answer to the slanders evil men were disposed to utter against them. In discharging worthily and properly the duties of the relationship in which they lived they would demonstrate a worthy life, show honor to all men, and evidence reverence toward God.

The instruction to husbands is brief and appears to have been inserted parenthetically to guard against abuse to the wives just addressed. The general tenor of the epistle is to show the duty of submission and the obligation to recognize and accept the subordination characteristic of one's position in life; and lest the husbands should conclude that there were no mutual obligations and that, though the wives were bound, they were loosed with reference to any duties in the marriage state, these lines were penned. It is also significant that while the apostle particularly addressed himself to the wives of unbelieving husbands, the implication here is that the wives of these believers were also Christians. This was a logical conclusion from the nature of the society then existing. Wives might occasionally obey the gospel without their husbands, but not likely would husbands become Christians without their wives.

7 **Ye husbands, in like manner, dwell with your wives according to knowledge,**—"Dwell," translated from a term which denotes domestic association, sums up the relationships of the marriage state. Such association is to be "according to knowledge," i.e., with due understanding of the nature of the marital relation, each showing proper regard for the other, and both discharging the duties peculiarly theirs.

Giving honor unto the woman, as unto the weaker vessel, as being also joint-heirs of the grace of life;—The word "giving," translated from a term which occurs nowhere else in the scriptures *(aponemo),* means to assign; to apportion; and "honor" in the text is the rendering of the same word translated "precious" in 1 Pet. 1: 19. Christian husbands are to regard their faithful wives as precious and to assign to them the honor that is their due. The woman is called a "weaker vessel" not because of moral or intellectual weaknesses, but solely from the fact that she lacks the physical prowess commonly characteristic of man. The husband is exhorted to dwell with his wife in due consideration of the fact that she is physically weaker; and to regard her always as a fellow heir of the grace of life—life eternal—which awaits all of the faithful. (John 17: 3.) In styling the wife as the *weaker* vessel the implication is that man is also a vessel—both the husband and wife being instruments which God uses in his service.

To the end that your prayers be not hindered.—The word "hindered" is the rendering of a word which means literally to cut in, to interrupt. Where strife and discord obtain in a home, prayer is cut into and interrupted—the message to heaven is short-circuited! Bitterness, division, and bickering are opposed to the spirit of prayer and operate to terminate all efforts in that respect. Only where peace and harmony prevail can the husband and wife join their efforts in united prayer to the throne of grace.

6. DUTIES OF CHRISTIANS TO ONE ANOTHER
3: 8-12

8 Finally, *be* ye all likeminded, ⁰compassionate, loving as brethren, tender-

---
⁰Gr. *sympathetic*.

---

8 Finally, be ye all likeminded, compassionate, loving as brethren, tenderhearted, humbleminded:—"Finally" *(to telos, the end)* does not, of course, indicate the end of the epistle, but the conclusion of the special addresses to the various classes. Having addressed slaves, Christian wives, and husbands, this portion of the epistle is concluded with an exhortation to Christians generally in their relations with each other. These duties are embraced in five Greek words, three of which occur nowhere else in the New Testament. "Likeminded" is unity of mind and purpose, agreement in all the major details of Christian life and activity; "compassionate" derived from the Greek *sumpatheis,* from which we get our word sympathy, is that attitude of mind which leads one to rejoice when others rejoice, and to weep when others weep; "loving as brethren"

hearted, humbleminded: 9 not rendering evil for evil, or reviling for reviling; but contrariwise blessing; for hereunto were ye called, that ye should inherit a blessing. 10 For,

(literally, brother lovers) is the special feeling which brothers of a common parentage have for each other; "tenderhearted" (literally, goodhearted) is an attitude which manifests itself in pity and affection; and "humbleminded" is the opposite of arrogance and pride. These are fundamental Christian principles and must be characteristic of all who desire to follow in the footsteps of the Master.

9 **Not rendering evil for evil, or reviling for reviling; but contrariwise blessing; for hereunto were ye called, that ye should inherit a blessing.**—Here Peter (as did Paul in Rom. 12: 17 and 1 Thess. 5: 15) echoes the spirit of the sermon on the mount in those significant words of our Lord: "But I say unto you, Resist not him that is evil: but whosoever smiteth thee on thy right cheek, turn to him the other also." (Matt. 5: 39.) "Not rendering" is, literally *not giving back;* and the preposition "for" as here used denotes something given in exchange. Christians are, under no circumstances, to give back evil in exchange for evil done them, or to engage in reviling though reviled themselves. This verse was designed to forbid all retaliation, whether in word or in deed.

In the phrase, "but contrariwise blessing," the word "blessing" is not a noun, but a present participle. The meaning is, "Instead of giving back evil in exchange for evil, or reviling when reviled, be continually blessing!" This, too, is in harmony with what the Lord taught in the mountain instruction when he said, "Love your enemies and pray for (bless, King James translation) them that persecute you." (Matt. 5: 24.) Christianity is, itself, a blessing; and those who are Christians are called to receive the blessing which it offers and thus should ever be blessing others themselves. Our Father blesses us; we must, then, bless others; from him we receive forgiveness for our sins; therefore we must be constantly forgiving others. Retaliation for evil done us operates to deprive us of the blessing to which we, as Christians, have been called.

¹⁰He that would love life,
And see good days,
Let him refrain his tongue from evil,
And his lips that they speak no guile:
11 And let him turn away from evil, and do good;
Let him seek peace, and pursue it.
12 For the eyes of the Lord are upon the righteous,

---

¹⁰Ps. xxxiv. 12 ff.

---

10 **For, he that would love life, and see good days, let him refrain his tongue from evil, and his lips that they speak no guile:**—To support his argument that Christians should refrain from all wrongdoing and evil speaking, in order to be assured of the protection, approbation and blessing of God, the apostle cites a statement from Psalm 34: 12-16. The quotation extends from verse 10 through 12 and follows the Greek Septuagint translation of the Old Testament with slight variation. "He that would love life" is, literally, "he that willeth to love life," that is, who now loves life and wishes to continue to do so. The "good days" are days of happiness, usefully and worthily spent. To enjoy such one must "refrain" his tongue from evil and his lips from speaking guile. "Refrain" is translated from a term *(pauo)* which means to cease, and implies a natural unruliness on the part of the tongue to utter evil things. The evil to be refrained from includes all perverse speaking, and the guile is deceit and all deception. (See the word defined more particularly in the comments on 1 Pet. 2: 1.) In each of these verses which Peter cites from the Psalms, we have excellent examples of the parallelism in Hebrew poetry, in which the movement and rhythm are obtained by a repetition of the idea in slightly different form.

11 **And let him turn away from evil, and do good; let him seek peace, and pursue it.**—"Turn away" is from *ekklino,* to bend away from, as one inclines himself in a narrow path to let another pass. The Christian must, therefore, shun, avoid, and turn aside from all appearance of evil (1 Thess. 5: 22) and do only that which is good. He is to "seek peace" because in a world of war and strife it is not always apparent, and, when seen, may be seized and possessed only by diligent pursuit.

12 **For the eyes of the Lord are upon the righteous, and his ears unto their supplication: but the face of the Lord is**

And his ears unto their supplication:
But the face of the Lord is upon them that do evil.

upon them that do evil.—The preposition "upon" in this passage is from the Greek word *(epi)*. The eyes of the Lord are *upon* the righteous *and* the evil. His eyes are upon the righteous with approval, and his ears are tuned to their supplications, but his face is upon those who do evil with extreme displeasure. (Isa. 59: 1, 2; John 9: 31.) "He that turneth away his ear from hearing the law, even his prayer is an abomination." (Prov. 28: 9.)

7. WHEN PERSECUTED
3: 13-17

13 And who is he that will harm you, if ye be zealous of that which is good? 14 But even if ye should suffer for righteousness' sake, blessed *are*

13 And who is he that will harm you, if ye be zealous of that which is good?—These words contain an inference drawn by the apostle from the teaching of the passage which he had just cited from David and the Psalms. Since the Lord watches for the righteous, and his ears are ever open to their prayers, who can harm them? The word "harm" means to do one real and permanent evil, and is emphatic. It will be observed that the apostle does not affirm that men will not seek to injure them; or, that they will not succeed in such injury; he teaches that with God's continual watchfulness over them though men do persecute them, eventually all matters will result in their good, and no permanent and real harm will befall them. (See Matt. 10: 28; Mark 10: 29, 30; Rom. 8: 28.) "Zealous" means to be full of zeal, to devote oneself earnestly to the cause espoused. These words, addressed to suffering saints, were a glorious and heart-warming assurance of ultimate triumph over the difficulties and hardships through which they were even then passing. They offer similar hope for our time.

14 But even if ye should suffer for righteousness' sake, blessed are ye: and fear not their fear, neither be troubled;— To clarify his statement in verse 13, and to guard his readers against the erroneous conclusion that they need expect no difficulties of any nature, these words were penned. They mean, "But if it should happen that sufferings come to you because of your

ye: and fear not their fear, neither be troubled; 15 but sanctify in your hearts Christ as Lord: *being* ready always to give answer to every man that asketh you a reason concerning the hope that is in you, yet with meekness

obedience to the Lord, regard this as a blessing, because Jesus said, Blessed are they that have been persecuted for righteousness' sake: for theirs is the kingdom of heaven." (Matt. 5: 10.) The word "blessed" means happy, prosperous, and denotes an inner, spiritual form of prosperity. To suffer for righteousness' sake is to suffer on account of righteousness, i.e., because of the godly life and holy conduct characteristic of the righteous. The final clause, "and fear not their fear, neither be troubled," is quoted from Isa. 8: 12 and means, "be not influenced by the terror which your persecutors would instill in you, neither be agitated." It is an injunction to complete composure in the face of bitter and determined enemies.

15 But sanctify in your hearts Christ as Lord:—This clause, with variations, from Isa. 8: 13. To sanctify is to set apart; and to sanctify in one's heart Christ the Lord is to regard him with that reverence and awe befitting the Lord of glory. "But" (*de,* adversative) suggests "nay, rather," i.e., instead of being tormented with the fear which your enemies would instill in you, be concerned only with the enthronement of Christ in your hearts as Lord. This done, you may be sure that nothing can disturb you. "Christ" (Hebrew *Messiah*) means the "anointed one"; "Lord" *(kurios),* literally a master or owner, here designates him who has authority over all things, both in heaven and on earth (Matt. 28: 18-20), the Saviour of the world. Peter offers here direct and unequivocal testimony of the deity of the Lord Jesus, and to his relationship to the God of the universe.

Being ready always to give answer to every man that asketh you a reason concerning the hope that is in you, yet with meekness and fear:—This readiness to "give answer" (literally, to make defence, *apologia*), is to be constant: "being ready always...." It is to be given "to every man that asketh ... a reason," not necessarily to every scoffer and captious person who lacks the sincerity of honest inquirers. Our Lord often met such inquiries with the dignity of complete silence. It is significant that the words "answer" and "reason" in the text are closely related in

and fear: 16 having a good conscience; that, wherein ye are spoken against, they may be put to shame who revile your good manner of life in Christ. 17 For it is better, if the will of God should so will, that ye suffer for well-

meaning: To every one who asks an *account* we are to give an *account*. The answer is to be given with reference to the hope entertained, i.e., with respect to the grounds on which the hope is based. This obligation implies sufficient acquaintance with the word of God to substantiate one's hope therewith, and godliness of life consistent with its teaching. It is said that every citizen in Athens was expected to keep himself sufficiently informed in civic affairs to be able to participate intelligently in any discussion thereof. Christians should be equally well informed in the things of God and as skillful in their presentation.

The defence is to be made with "meekness and fear." When called on to justify their position, Christians are to do so with reason and logic; but not with bold defiance nor arrogance and pride; the "answer" is to be made with "meekness," i.e., an attitude free of scorn, haughtiness and bitterness; and "in fear," fear of God and the judgment.

16 Having a good conscience; that, wherein ye are spoken against, they may be put to shame who revile your good manner of life in Christ.—In addition to the attitude of "meekness and fear" enjoined in the preceding verse, he who would successfully defend his faith must have a good conscience, i.e., a firm conviction of the righteousness of his cause, and his worthiness to represent it. However skillful he may be in debate, his work must fail if his life is inconsistent with that for what he contends. Only when the two harmonize—skillfulness of speech, and godliness of life—is the answer effective and convincing.

When the conscience is clear, the spirit meek and the heart filled with the knowledge and holy fear of God, the false accusers of the righteous will be put to shame. The word "revile" in this passage does not designate formal accusations, but wild, unfounded charges. Those who indulge in such will eventually be put to shame because they will be exposed as liars, slanderers and calumniators of those who are good.

17 For it is better, if the will of God should so will, that ye suffer for well-doing than for evil-doing.—See a similar statement from the writer earlier in the epistle in 1 Pet. 2: 20. These words were penned in further confirmation of that which he had said in the preceding verses. The value of suffering for righteousness' sake is often emphasized in the epistle. To endure patiently and uncomplainingly silences false accusers (verse 16); it is in imitation of Christ's own example (verse 18); and is "better" because there is the possibility that such is the "will of God" (verse 17). The words, "if the will of God should so will," are in a construction signifying, not a probability, but merely a possibility: "If it should happen to be the will of God...."

8. CHRIST AN EXAMPLE OF SUFFERING
3: 18-4: 6

doing than for evil-doing. 18 Because Christ also [11]suffered for sins once, the righteous for the unrighteous, that he might bring us to God; being put

---
[11]Many ancient authorities read *died*.

---

18 Because Christ also suffered for sins once, the righteous for the unrighteous, that he might bring us to God:—One cannot escape the conclusion that the apostles of our Lord were Christ-intoxicated men! It is highly significant that they did not write on any theme associated with redemption without being immediately reminded of, and alluding to, their matchless leader and guide. Peter's reference to suffering wrongfully for righteousness' sake brought immediately to his mind the one who, above all others, suffered in this manner; and he is offered, as in 1 Pet. 2: 21-25, as a pattern for other innocent suffers. Here, as there, the apostle appeared to be unwilling to quit the subject with Christ presented as no more than an example of suffering; and he therefore proceeds to present the higher aspects of the Lord's suffering and death in relation to the redemption and salvation of man. To this end, the writer sets forth the reason why it is blessed to suffer for righteousness' sake. Christ suffered in this manner; Christ is our example; hence, he who suffers as the Lord did, more nearly identifies himself with Christ.

Each word in this text is vitally significant. Christ "suffered"; he suffered "for" *(peri,* concerning) our sins; he suffered concerning our sins once for all *(apax),* it not being necessary to make continual offerings as under the old order; and the design of his offering was "that he might bring us to God." Through his suf-

to death in the flesh, but made alive in the spirit; 19 in which also he went

fering we now have access to God (Rom. 5: 2), and are privileged to come boldly to the throne of grace (Heb. 10: 19) ; though once afar off (Eph. 2: 17), we have been brought near by the blood of Christ (Eph. 2: 13). It is significant that there is no article before the words "righteous" and "unrighteous" in the original text. The meaning is, A righteous person suffering for *(huper,* on behalf of) unrighteous persons, a fact without which the blood of Jesus would have been no more efficacious than that of any other man.

Being put to death in the flesh, but made alive in the spirit;—Two things are affirmed of the Lord in this statement: (1) he was put to death in flesh (there is no article before either "flesh" or "spirit" in this affirmation) ; (2) he was made alive in spirit. "In flesh" *(sarki)* and "in spirit" *(Pneumati)* are locatives, indicative of the sphere in which the action occurred. "Put to death" and "made alive" are aorist passive participles, thus pointing to a definite occasion when these events happened. The meaning is, the sphere of death, for our Lord, was in the flesh; the sphere in which he was made alive (quickened, A.V.) was in the spirit. Death affected only his flesh; for from dying in spirit, here he was quickened, made alive. In what spirit? "In flesh" and "in spirit" are exactly balanced in the text; it is not likely that one is locative and the other instrumental; each is to be regarded as measuring the extent of the participles to which they are attached. "Flesh" and "spirit" are often opposed to each other in the sacred writings: "Manifested in the flesh, justified in the spirit" (1 Tim. 3: 16) ; judged according to men in the flesh, but live according to God in the spirit. The "spirit" alluded to in this verse is, therefore, that inner principle which stands in contrast with the flesh—the divine spirit which Jesus possessed in common with all men, and which was not affected by the death which he suffered. Why should it be asserted that in this spirit he was made alive? It should be remembered that it was Peter's purpose to show that though Christ suffered death this, far from terminating his existence or destroying his influence, merely enabled him to be energized, brought to active life in the realm of the spirit. His spirit, instead of perishing in death, was clothed with renewed and en-

and preached unto the spirits in prison, 20 that aforetime were disobedient, when the longsuffering of God waited in the days of Noah, while the ark was a preparing, ¹²wherein few, that is, eight souls, were saved through

¹²Or, *into which few, that is, eight souls, were brought safely through water*

hanced powers of life. At death, this spirit passed into a new sphere of existence, hence was said to have been made alive.

19 In which also he went and preached unto the spirits in prison,—"In which"*(en hoi)*, i.e., in which spirit—the spirit referred to in the preceding verse—the inner principle of life not subject to death. In this spirit he preached. "Preached" *(ekeruxen,* aorist indicative of *kerusso,* to herald abroad, to proclaim), is a general term denoting a public proclamation or announcement. What was preached is not stated. This preaching was done to "spirits in prison." They are called "spirits" because they were in a disembodied state when Peter wrote; and they were "in prison" i.e., under restraint as wicked beings. "In prison" is of frequent usage to denote the state or condition of those spirits which because of disobedience await condemnation at the last day. (2 Pet. 2: 4; Jude 6; Rev. 20: 7.) It should be noted that Peter does not declare that these who were the objects of this preaching were in a disembodied state and in prison *when the preaching was done*; such was their condition *when he wrote.* The period in which such lived in the flesh, and the time when this preaching was done is clearly stated in the verse which follows.

That aforetime were disobedient, when the longsuffering of God waited in the days of Noah, while the ark was a preparing,—These "spirits" were once in the flesh; they were once upon a time *(hote)* disobedient; the period of their disobedience was "while the ark was a preparing"; and during this period Christ preached to them. What one does through an authorized agent, he is said to do himself (1 John 4: 1), hence Christ, in the person of Noah, preached to the antediluvians during the period in which the ark was being constructed; and these, having rejected this preaching, died in disobedience, and were under restraint in the spirit realm when Peter wrote. The meaning of the passage, simply and briefly put, is this: Christ preached; he preached "in spirit" to "spirits in prison." These spirits in prison were wicked persons who lived while the ark was "a preparing." The preach-

water: 21 which also [13] after a true likeness doth now save you, *even* baptism, not the putting away of the filth of the flesh, but the [14]interrogation of

[13]Or, *in the antitype*
[14]Or, *inquiry* Or, *appeal*

ing which Christ did was through Noah. Those to whom the preaching was done were bound in the prison house of disobedient spirits at the time the letter Peter wrote was penned. (See additional note on these verses at the end of the chapter.)

Demonstrated in the events associated with the ark and the flood was the "longsuffering of God." One hundred and twenty years were especially designated as the probationary period afforded man. (Gen. 6: 3.) During this period there must have been many opportunities afforded the antediluvian world to turn in penitence to the Lord. These were, for the most part, rejected.

Wherein few, that is, eight souls, were saved through water:—"Wherein" is, literally, "into which" *(eis hen)*, i.e., into the ark in order to be saved the eight souls went, being saved in it through *(dia,* by) means of the water. They were saved in the ark, and by the water; the ark protected them from the flood, and the water bore up the ark, the means of their salvation from the old world. The eight souls saved were Noah and his wife, Shem, Ham, and Japheth, the sons of Noah, and their wives. (Gen. 7: 13.) Noah was a preacher of righteousness. (2 Pet. 2: 5.) Though he continued his preaching through the period in which the ark was being constructed, only those of his family were finally induced to avail themselves of the protection it afforded. The vast world of unbelievers about him perished. Those saved in the ark were "saved through water."

21 **Which also after a true likeness doth now save you, even baptism,**—The antecedent of "which" is the "water" alluded to in verse 20, not, however, the water of the flood, but water generally, and in this clause identified as the water of baptism. The apostle thus affirms that water, utilized in baptism, "after a true likeness," of that characteristic of the deliverance of Noah and his family from the old world, now saves. "After a true likeness doth now save you, even baptism" is, literally, in the Greek text, "which antetype is now saving you, even baptism." The salvation of Noah and those with him is thus made a type of

a good conscience toward God, through the resurrection of Jesus Christ; 22

the deliverance which the sinner receives in passing through the waters of baptism. The "likeness" obtains in the following manner: (1) the waters of the flood bore up the ark and delivered its occupants from the destruction of the antediluvian world; (2) these waters separated those who were saved from those who drowned in them; (3) the flood destroyed the evils of the old world and enabled Noah and his family to emerge into a new existence. In like fashion, (1) baptism is the final condition in a plan through obedience to which one is enabled to escape the condemnation of the lost. (Mark 15: 15, 16.) (2) Baptism designates the line of demarcation between the saved and the lost. (3) In baptism the "old man of sin" is buried, and from its watery grave one comes forth to "walk in newness of life." (Rom. 6: 4.)

It should be noted: (1) The baptism which is here declared to *save* is water baptism—baptism being the antetype of the water of deliverance in the flood. "Which also. . . ." is a reference to water, ordinary water, the same kind of water in the flood. The baptism which saves is, therefore, water baptism. (2) The salvation contemplated is not deliverance from persecution, affliction, sickness, or death; all of these embraced in Peter's statement suffered such. Neither is the salvation future; baptism is said to save *now*. Inasmuch as the salvation promised is not deliverance from earthly suffering or trial, and is declared to be "now," the conclusion is inescapable that the deliverance promised is salvation from past, or alien, sins; and the statement is thus in exact harmony with one earlier made by the same apostle when, in response to the query, "Brethren, what shall we do?" answered, "Repent ye, and be baptized every one of you in the name of Jesus Christ unto the remission of your sins; and ye shall receive the gift of the Holy Spirit." (Acts 2: 37, 38.)

The mention of water in connection with Noah's deliverance from the old world immediately suggested to Peter a resemblance which exists in the water of our salvation, "even baptism." It should be noted that Peter does not affirm that Noah and his family were saved *by* water, nor *in* water, nor *from* water; they were saved *through* water, i.e., the water was the means through which

who is on the right hand of God, having gone into heaven; angels and au-

God exercised his saving power. Following "a true likeness" baptism saves *now,* not of course as a *Saviour,* but as an instrument through which God exerts saving power. When Naaman was led finally to dip in the river Jordan to be cleansed of his leprosy, he did not attribute miraculous efficacy to its muddy waters; this power resided only in God. Yet it was not until *he dipped* that he was cleansed. (2 Kings 5: 14.) Similarly, when one is properly and intelligently baptized today, he does not understand that the power of forgiveness resides in the water, but in God; and that the baptism is a condition precedent to receiving salvation from God's hand.

Not the putting away of the filth of the flesh, but the interrogation of a good conscience toward God, through the resurrection of Jesus Christ;—To guard against any misunderstanding that should arise as a result of a misinterpretation of the first clause of this verse, Peter explains that baptism does not put away "the filth of the flesh." "Filth" *(rupos)* refers to that which is dirty, physically defiled. Baptism does not wash sin from the skin, and is not to be confused with a bath for the body or a ceremonial cleansing of the flesh. It is a condition precedent to the forgiveness which God alone exercises. (Mark 16: 15, 16; Rom. 6: 3, 4.)

Having explained what baptism is *not,* Peter tells what it *is:* "the interrogation of a good conscience toward God." An "interrogation" is a question, an inquiry; baptism thus becomes an act through which an individual seeks to manifest a good conscience. One submitting sincerely to baptism follows the promptings of a good conscience; indicates thereby that his conscience is sensitive, and that he is desirous of doing exactly what the Lord has commanded. That the conscience is here declared to be good prior to baptism is no objection to the conclusion that baptism is essential to salvation. Saul of Tarsus possessed a good conscience while in unbelief and a persecutor of the church. (Acts 23: 1.)

Baptism derives its benefits "through the resurrection of Jesus Christ" which it symbolizes. Baptism "doth now save" only because Jesus was raised from the dead.

thorities and powers being made subject unto him.

22 **Who is on the right hand of God, having gone into heaven; angels and authorities and powers being made subject unto him.**—Jesus is often said to be at the right hand of God. (Psalm 110: 1; Rom. 8: 34; Eph. 1: 20; Heb. 1: 3.) It is a position of eminence, honor, dignity, and power to which he was elevated following his ascension. In the announcement of the great commission (Matt. 28: 18-21), Jesus declared that all authority had been delivered into his hands; and here, the lesser authorities of the universe are said to be under subjection to him. For a similar declaration of Christ's authority, see Eph. 1: 19-23. "Angels and authorities and powers" embrace the hierarchy of heaven. (Col. 2: 10-15.) The words include not only the good angels, but also the bad; and "authorities and powers" are comprehensive terms designed to embrace all of every class of beings under God.

AN ADDITIONAL NOTE ON 1 PETER
3: 18-20

Many matters mentioned and otherwise alluded to in this remarkable passage have long been a source of much controversy and disagreement among scholars. Many distinguished commentators have advocated the view that Christ in his own person (and not through the agency of Noah) during the three days' interval between his death and resurrection and while he was in the spirit realm *(Hades),* actually and literally preached to the disembodied spirits who lived while the ark was being constructed but who were dead and incarcerated in the prison house of *Hades* at the time the preaching occurred.

Objections to this view are, in the opinion of this writer, numerous and insuperable: (1) Those subscribing to this view are unable to explain why the preaching was limited to the spirits of those who lived just prior to the flood. Since God is no respecter of persons, why were these spirits afforded opportunities not vouchsafed to others? (2) What was the nature of the message proclaimed to spirits who died in disobedience? (a) If the offer was one of salvation, what of the many passages in the scriptures which clearly teach that at death one's destiny is sealed; that the judgment will be based on the manner of life here; and that between the abode of the righteous and the wicked an impassable gulf stretches? (b) If the offer was not of salvation, why was the preaching done? To inform the faithful that redemption through his death had been accomplished? The preaching was not to the faithful, but to those who died in disobedience.

The simple and obvious import of the words of the text is that of the explanation offered in the comments thereon. (1) A reasonable interpretation of the passage leads to this conclusion. (2) The conclusion harmonizes with the general teaching of the scriptures regarding the state of the dead. (3) The interpretation is in keeping with the earlier teaching of the epistle in which it is declared that the Holy Spirit preached through the prophets. (1 Pet. 1: 11.) (4) Noah was "a preacher of righteousness" (2 Pet. 2: 5), and was directed by the Spirit in his preaching (Gen. 6: 3). What impropriety is there then in asserting that in such preaching he was the agent or instrument of Christ?

It is alleged that since it is said that Christ *went* and preached he must therefore have actually and literally gone in his own person. The objection is invalid because no special significance is to be attached to the repetition of the idea involved. It is a simple pleonism for "he preached" of which many examples may be produced. It is, for example, said of Christ that "he came and preached peace to you that were afar off (Gentiles), and to them that were nigh" (Jews). (Eph. 2: 17.) Certainly our Lord never, at any time following his resurrection, preached to the Gentiles in his own person. Such preaching as is here alluded to was done through the apostles, principally by Paul. If Christ could preach to the Gentiles through Paul, why not to the people before the flood through Noah? As a matter of historic fact such he did, and such these passages affirm, Paul and Noah being the agents or instruments through which the preaching was accomplished.

The interpretation set forth in the comments on the passage avoids the difficulties in the way of the view considered above, and accords with the simple and obvious import of the words used. Rightly interpreted this passage yields no support to the Roman Catholic doctrine of purgatory. This dogma, whether advocated by so-called Protestant scholars or Catholic theologians, is utterly and palpably false.

1 Forasmuch then as Christ suffered in the flesh, arm ye yourselves also with the same [15]mind; for he that hath suffered in the flesh hath ceased [16]from sin; 2 that [17]ye no longer should live the rest of your time in the flesh

[15]Or, *thought*
[16]Some ancient authorities read *unto sins.*
[17]Or, *he no longer . . . his time*

1 Forasmuch then as Christ suffered in the flesh, arm ye yourselves also with the same mind;—"Forasmuch then" establishes a logical connection with matters earlier mentioned by the apostle, and, in particular, Christ's sufferings. (1 Pet. 3: 18.) Peter exhorted his readers, in imitation of the motives which influenced the Lord to "arm" themselves with the "same mind." "Mind" *(ennoia)* refers to the thoughts, the will; and the meaning is that Christians are to be influenced by the same purposes, thoughts, and intentions which characterized the Saviour in the sufferings which he endured. In view of the fact that Peter was addressing saints who were soon to pass through the fiery ordeal of persecution they were to protect themselves in the fray with the only effective armor available to them, the purposes which motivated Christ under similar trials. This armor consisted in an unwavering faith in the righteousness of his cause and patient resignation in whatever might befall him here.

For he that hath suffered in the flesh hath ceased from sin; —Of similar import is Paul's statement: "For he that hath died is justified from sin." (Rom. 6: 7.) To indicate that suffering is not an unmitigated evil, Peter directed attention to the fact that one who suffers in the flesh is made to cease from sin. Obviously this does not include all suffering, or suffering by all people; the contectual limits indicate that it is the suffering of righteous people in imitation of Christ that is here contemplated. One who has embraced the mind of Christ, and whose life is so influenced by him that he suffers persecution is not in danger of succumbing to the weaker temptations of the flesh. To such an individual these allurements lose their appeal. Martyrs, in the hour of persecution and death, do not toy with temptation or surrender to the seductions of the world!

2 That ye no longer should live the rest of your time in the flesh to the lusts of men, but to the will of God.—"That" introduced the purpose clause which follows, and which is closely

to the lusts of men, but to the will of God. 3 For the time past may suffice to have wrought the desire of the Gentiles, and to have walked in lasciviousness, lusts, winebibbings, revellings, carousings and abominable idolatries: 4

connected with the verb "arm" in the preceding verse. The meaning is, "Arm yourselves with the mind of Christ in order that ye may no longer live in the flesh to the lusts of men, but to the will of God." "In the flesh" refers to the period of bodily existence in the world, and "the rest of your time" to that portion of it remaining for such sojourn. "Lusts" denotes passionate desires and is here used to indicate those that are evil. "Lusts of men" is put in contrast with "the will of God," which will, when followed, becomes the only effective defence against such desires. "For this is the will of God, even your sanctification, that ye abstain from fornication . . . not in the passion of lust, even as the Gentiles who know not God." (1 Thess. 4: 3, 5.)

3 For the time past may suffice to have wrought the desire of the Gentiles,—The tense of the verbs in this verse is significant. "Past" is, in the Greek, a perfect participle, and "have wrought" a perfect infinitive, indicating that the period under consideration had been terminated and closed. The statement is one of irony, and means that enough time, and more than enough, had already been given to ungodly living such as was generally characteristic of the Gentiles of that period. For a similar admonition from Paul, see Rom. 13: 11, 12.

And to have walked in lasciviousness, lusts, winebibbings, revellings, carousings, and abominable idolatries:—The Gentiles (a figurative term indicative of the great unregenerate and heathen world) are said to have "walked" in the sins enumerated, not only because life itself is a journey, but because there is a disposition for those engaging in such to go on from sin to sin, each departure leading to deeper degradation. "Lasciviousness" *(aselgeia),* a plural term in the Greek text, embraces the unbridled lusts and excesses of the age—outward actions and overt deeds as distinguished from the "lusts" *(epithumia,* desires) which are inwardly entertained. "Winebibbings" *(oinophlugia)* from *oinos,* wine, and *phluo,* to bubble up, to overflow, is a vivid picture of drunkenness; "revellings" *(komos)* was first used innocently of village merrymaking, but later came to be applied to rioting, drink-

wherein they think it strange that ye run not with *them* into the same
¹excess of riot, speaking evil of *you*: 5 who shall give account to him that is

---

¹Or, *flood*

---

ing parties, and is so used here; "carousings" *(potos)* were drinking matches in which each participant sought to outdo all others engaging; and the "abominable idolatries" were licentious and drunken parties in which not only fleshly sins were engaged in, but also idolatrous worship. The first three sins designated by the apostle are primarily personal sins; the last three are social evils, and all common to the unregenerate world of the first century.

4 **Wherein they think it strange that ye run not with them into the same excess of riot, speaking evil of you:**—Because the unconverted people of that period were utterly unrestrained in their conduct and did not regard the acts enumerated in the foregoing verse as objectionable, they looked with astonishment on the refusal of Christians to participate with them, considering them anti-social, unfriendly, and bigoted. The words "run not with them into the same excess of riot" are significant and impressive. "Run" denotes more than mere association; it indicates eagerness of participation and fellowship in the vices mentioned. "Excess" is from a term which means, literally, an overflowing, and in classical Greek referred to gutters suddenly swollen from rains which poured their contents into common sewers. The picture is one of depraved and abandoned groups wildly rushing into filthy and ungodly excesses in a whirlpool of sin. Those thus engaged "speak evil" (literally, *blaspheme*) Christians for their refusal to engage with them in such.

5 **Who shall give account to him that is ready to judge the living and the dead.**—"Who" is in apposition to the participle translated "speaking evil" and establishes what is taught clearly elsewhere (Matt. 25: 31-46), that the wicked will eventually answer in judgment for their evil conduct here. These who demanded an accounting for the conduct of Christians about them would themselves be required one day to render an accounting for their own lives. The "living and the dead" is a comprehensive statement embracing all men, whether alive or in the tomb, and

ready to judge the living and the dead. 6 For unto this end ²was the gospel preached even to the dead, that they might be judged indeed according to men in the flesh, but live according to God in the spirit.

---

²Or, *were the good tidings preached*

---

was designed to indicate the universality of the judgment. (2 Cor. 5: 10.)

6 **For unto this end was the gospel preached even to the dead, that they might be judged indeed according to men in the flesh, but live according to God in the spirit.**—The words "for unto this end" indicate the purpose or object for which the gospel was preached to the dead, viz., that they might be judged according to men in the flesh, but live according to God in the spirit. That which was preached was the "gospel," God's power to save (Rom. 1: 16); and the preaching thereof was to "the dead," dead and in the spirit land *when Peter wrote,* but alive and in the world when the gospel was preached to them. As a result of having heard this preaching, they obeyed the gospel and became Christians; but they had since died, and were thus dead when the epistle was written. While they lived they too were subjected to the evil speaking which Peter's readers were then suffering; and they, although judged and condemned by "men in the flesh" because of their faithfulness and fidelity to the cause, lived according to God in the spirit, i.e., in the higher, nobler life of the spirit. Such we conceive to be the meaning of what is doubtless one of the most controversial and difficult passages in the Bible. That these to whom the gospel was preached were not the same as those contemplated in 1 Pet. 3: 19, 20, follows from the fact that those who were the objects of Noah's preaching rejected that patriarch's warnings and perished in disobedience in the flood; whereas, these who were the objects of the preaching to which Peter refers had accepted the gospel, and, though dead, had the approbation of God in the spirit realm.

SECTION FOUR

ADMONITIONS TO CHRISTIAN LIVING
4:7-5:9

1. FAITHFULNESS ENJOINED
4:7-11

7 But the end of all things is at hand: be ye therefore of sound mind, and

7 But the end of all things is at hand:—"Of all things" is from a word which appears first in the text *(panton)* and is thus emphatic: "Of all things the end is at hand." "At hand" *(eggidzo)* means literally "to draw near," and is the word used by John the Baptist to announce the near approach of the kingdom of Christ. (Matt. 3:1.) "Of all things the end draws near." What end? The consummation of the age, and the judgment day, so many commentators contend; and to the objection that these matters *were not at hand* when Peter wrote, two thousand years having elapsed, and the end not yet, it is alleged that Peter, in common with all the apostles, held, and here gives expression to the erroneous view that the return of Christ was, at the time he wrote, imminent and pending and would occur in his lifetime! Those who hesitate to impute error to the apostle in this bold fashion nevertheless weaken his words with the assertion that the time clock of God in the grand sweep of eternity is little concerned with the passage of time, "a thousand years being as one day." (2 Pet. 3:8.) The first objection is a denial of the inerrancy of the scriptures, imputing error to the writers; and the second is based on a misconception of 2 Pet. 3:8. (See comments on this passage.) Moreover, the words of the text served as a basis and ground for the exhortation which follows, and hence must be determined in harmony with man's relation to time, and not God's.

It thus follows that the "end" was not the judgment day and the consummation of the age. It should be remembered that these words of the apostle were written on the eve of the destruction of the Jewish state. Already terminated as a system of acceptable worship, its forms and ceremonies had persisted through the efforts of unbelieving Jews who had desperately resisted the march of Christianity. Soon, the temple, the Levitical system, and the Jewish economy were to perish in the fearful destruction about to

be sober unto ³prayer: 8 above all things being fervent in your love among

³Gr. *prayers.*

---

fall upon Jerusalem. For these relics of a former system of worship the end approached, and with it would come times of trial and difficulty for all and particularly those who had espoused a religion traceable to Jews. Aware that Christianity had its origin with a Jew—Christ—the persecutors of the Jews would not distinguish between them and Christians. It was inevitable that they should suffer in consequence of the doom soon to befall the Jewish state. Hence, the occasion of the admonition which follows.

Be ye therefore of sound mind, and be sober unto prayer: —An injunction to sobriety was especially pertinent in view of the fearful trials soon to come. A sound mind and a sober disposition prompting to regular and persistent prayer would best avail them in the midst of the dangers with which they were soon to be assailed.

8 Above all things being fervent in your love among yourselves; for love covereth a multitude of sins:—"Fervent" *(ektenes,* to stretch out, as of a string drawn taut on an instrument; see comments on 1 Pet. 1: 22) suggests the intensity which should characterize Christians in their love for one another. In view of the fact that love is the badge of their discipleship (John 13: 35), it behooves them to exhibit intense affection for each other. It is possible that Peter, having just referred to a love which stretches itself on behalf of the brethren, should think of it as having extended itself in its fervency to cover the sins of the brethren. When one loves another he forgives; and thus the way to peace and harmony in the church is through fervent love. In recognition of its potency Peter admonished that this be "above all things," i.e., before all other things in the order of importance. The words "love covers a multitude of sins" are reminiscent of James 5: 20 where, however, the meaning is different from this. There, it appears to be the design of the writer to point out that the love we have for our brethren prompts us to busy ourselves in their behalf in restoring them to the truth so that God may forgive them and thus cover their sins. Both Peter and James were doubtless influenced in their use of the phrase by Solomon in Prov. 10: 12.

yourselves; for love covereth a multitude of sins; 9 using hospitality one to another without murmuring: 10 according as each hath received a gift, ministering it among yourselves, as good stewards of the manifold grace of God;

9 **Using hospitality one to another without murmuring:—** The word "hospitality" is translated from a term which means "friendly to strangers." This duty is given much emphasis in the New Testament. (Rom. 12: 13; Heb. 12: 2; 1 Tim. 3: 2.) Christian travelers of the period in which Peter wrote were often under considerable difficulty in finding proper accommodations. The inns—hotels—of the time were places of gross sin and corruption; and the homes of heathen friends if open to them would often subject them to ridicule for their espousal of Christianity or what was worse, temptation to resume their former manner of life. Hence, only the private homes of Christians provided suitable association for those whose travels took them away from their homes. To guard the hospitality-minded against imposition by unworthy people, the letters of commendation mentioned by Paul (2 Cor. 3: 1) came into use.

The hospitality thus enjoyed was to be rendered "without murmuring," i.e., without giving vent to expressions of displeasure either secretly or otherwise, because of the responsibility involved. The bestowal of such hospitality would necessitate some expense; occasionally it would be attended by considerable inconvenience and the duty at other times might become somewhat of a nuisance; yet, the obligation was clear and the responsibility certain. It was to be discharged without complaint. Here, as also in the formal contributions of the saints, God loves a cheerful giver. (2 Cor. 9: 7.)

10 **According as each hath received a gift, ministering it among yourselves, as good stewards of the manifold grace of God:**—"Gift" *(charisma)* here is the same as those under consideration in 1 Cor. 12. The word "received" is in the aorist tense *(lambano)* and points to a definite time when the gift was received, either when they were baptized (Acts 2: 38) or through imposition of an apostle's hands (Acts 8: 16). Whatever the nature of the gift—means by which to identify it not being available —it was a gift of grace and designed to be used in the interests of others. In the administration of such gifts the saints were to be

11 if any man speaketh, *speaking* as it were oracles of God; if any man ministereth, *ministering* as of the strength which God supplieth: that in all

---

"good stewards" (literally, beautiful stewards, *kalos*) of the manifold grace of God. The word "manifold" *(poikile)*, here descriptive of the grace of God, signifies that which exists in varied content, and suggests that widespread bestowal of such gifts in the apostolic age.

11 **If any man speaketh, speaking as it were oracles of God;**—In verse 10 the apostle had alluded to the reception and administration of gifts characteristic of the apostolic age. Here, he proceeds to instruct his readers concerning two classes of such gifts—those in which one *speaks* and those requiring *doing*. The word "oracle" *(logia)* was used in classical Greek of the alleged sayings of heathen deities; and it occurs in the New Testament in Acts 7: 38; Rom. 3: 2; and Heb. 5: 12 with no trace, of course, of its former significance. The oracles here referred to were divine utterances delivered through the recognized agencies of the early church—the apostles, prophets, and inspired teachers. The meaning is that these gifts were properly exercised only when that which was said was in harmony with the oracles of God. When one allegedly spoke by inspiration it was to be done in such fashion that the utterance was to be readily recognizable as of divine origin. In this, as in all matters pertaining to the "manifold grace of God," the speaker was to discharge his obligation as a "good steward."

If any man ministereth, ministering as of the strength which God supplieth:—The "ministering" (serving) under consideration was such as required the exercise of the gifts of the apostolic period requiring doing as distinguished from those in the foregoing clause involving speaking alone. Those thus exercised were to be mindful of the fact that they served with strength not their own, and with that which God alone supplies. "Ministereth" is derived from the same word translated "deacon" in the New Testament (e.g., Phil. 1: 1), though here, as often in the sacred writings, it does not designate those appointed to this work, but simply those who serve. The verb "supplieth" *(choregeo)*, translated "giveth" in the King James Version, meant in classical

things God may be glorified through Jesus Christ, whose is the glory and the dominion ⁴for ever and ever. Amen.

⁴Gr. *unto the ages of the ages.*

Greek to supply the expenses of a chorus in public performances, and then came to indicate any liberal bestowal of whatever nature. It occurs in this latter sense in 2 Cor. 9: 10.

That in all things God may be glorified through Jesus Christ, whose is the glory and the dominion for ever and ever. Amen.—These words designate the design of the proper exercise of the gifts mentioned: that God may be glorified through Jesus Christ. Such is the first and paramount duty of man; and in so teaching Peter was but echoing the words of the Lord when he said, "Even so let your light shine before men; that they may see your good works, and glorify your Father who is in heaven" (Matt. 5: 16), as also Paul: "Whether therefore ye eat, or drink, or whatsoever ye do, do all to the glory of God" (1 Cor. 10: 31). There is a possibility that the words "whose is the glory and the dominion for ever and ever. Amen," were a portion of some ancient prayer, and are appended here as a doxology. It is not clear from the construction of the passage what the antecedent of "whose" is, whether God, the Father, or Jesus Christ, the Son, though the probability is that the reference is to God. "For ever and ever" is, literally, "unto the ages of the ages." It is a phrase indicative of eternity, and is so used with frequency in the New Testament. "Amen," with which the ascription of praise concludes, occurs many times in the scriptures and with a variety of uses. It was often on the lips of the Lord, occurring in the familiar phrase, "verily, verily" (actually *amen, amen*) about twenty-five times in the book of John. The word occurs in the phraseology of the Lord—though variously rendered—about a hundred times. It is derived from a Hebrew verb which means to support; and when passive, to be a support, trustworthy, sure. It is sometimes an endorsement of what is said—as in the foregoing instance from Peter —in which case it means "so it is"; in others a petition meaning "be it so," the use made of it at the conclusion of our prayers.

2. SUFFERING AS CHRISTIANS
4: 12-19

12 Beloved, think it not strange concerning the fiery trial among you, which cometh upon you to prove you, as though a strange thing happened unto you: 13 but insomuch as ye are partakers of Christ's sufferings, rejoice; that at the revelation of his glory also ye may rejoice with exceeding joy.

12 Beloved, think it not strange concerning the fiery trial among you, which cometh upon you to prove you, as though a strange thing happened unto you:—Here the writer reverts to a subject with which he has intermittently dealt from the beginning of the epistle: the occasion and design of suffering by the saints. (1 Pet. 1: 3-9.) "Beloved" is plural, thus "beloved ones," a term of endearment indicative of the vast sympathy which Peter entertained for the embattled saints. The word "strange," occurring also in 1 Pet. 4: 4, suggests that which is foreign, alien; these suffering disciples were not to regard their trials as foreign to the cause they had espoused, but as common to it and characteristic of it. (2 Tim. 3: 12.) The fiery trial of persecution was not a thing alien to their profession; it was their home portion in this life, its design being to prove (test) them. The figure here used is that of gold ore cast into a crucible for the purpose of separating the worthless dross from the precious metal. The illustration is a frequent one in the Bible. (Psalm 66: 20; Prov. 27: 31.)

13 But insomuch as ye are partakers of Christ's sufferings, rejoice;—These words are remindful of those which Peter must have often heard from the lips of the Lord: "Blessed are ye when men shall reproach you, and persecute you, and say all manner of evil against you falsely, for my sake. Rejoice, and be exceeding glad." (Matt. 5: 11, 12.) "Insomuch" signifies "to the extent in which." Thus, so far as the sufferings of Christians are of the same kind, originate in the same causes and are prompted by the same motives as those the Saviour suffered, they have occasion to rejoice in the assurance that such suffering will secure for them participation in his glory in the by and by.

That at the revelation of his glory also ye may rejoice with exceeding joy.—The "revelation of his glory" designates the time of his return to judge the world. (Luke 17: 30.) The "joy" the saints are to experience in the suffering they must undergo

14 If ye are reproached ⁵for the name of Christ, blessed *are ye*; because the *Spirit* of glory and the Spirit of God resteth upon you. 15 For let none of you suffer as a murderer, or a thief, or an evil-doer, or as a meddler in other

⁵Gr. *in.*

here is to be regarded as a token and earnest of the "exceeding joy" which will be theirs in that day.

14 If ye are reproached for the name of Christ, blessed are ye; because the Spirit of glory and the Spirit of God resteth upon you.—The particle "if" with which this verse begins does not denote a contingency, but declares a fact. As used here, it corresponds roughly to the word "when." The verb *reproached* describes the nature of the persecution here particularly dealt with. The word means to revile, to slander, to blaspheme; to speak evil of another. "For the name of Christ" is, literally, "in the name of Christ," i.e., because of their adoption of the name of Christ—the name Christian—and their loyalty to it. Thus, "When you are reviled because of your loyalty to Christ, blessed are you." The word "blessed" is the same, and means the same here as in the beatitudes. (Matt. 5: 1-12.) It is blessed to be thus reproached because it identifies one with his Lord; it shows one's willingness to suffer in his behalf; and it is such suffering as will be rewarded in heaven. (Matt. 5: 11, 12.) As evidence of the blessedness of those thus persecuted, the apostle declares that the "Spirit of glory and the Spirit of God resteth upon" them. The "Spirit of glory" and the "Spirit of God" are the same, and refer to the Holy Spirit —the third person in the godhead. Since the Spirit is promised to those who are faithful, and abides with those who are persecuted, his presence is a token of the blessedness of those who suffer for righteousness' sake. The verb "resteth" is of special significance here, being translated from the same word as thus used in the Greek version of the Old Testament of the abiding presence of the Lord. (Isa. 11: 2.)

15 For let none of you suffer as a murderer, or a thief, or an evil-doer, or as a meddler in other men's matters:—See the comments on 1 Pet. 3: 14-17. Only such suffering as is for righteousness' sake is blessed; the blessing being dependent not on the *fact* of suffering, but the *occasion* or the *cause* which prompts it. This fundamental principle is taught negatively in this verse, and

men's matters: 16 but if *a man suffer* as a Christian, let him not be ashamed; but let him glorify God in this name. 17 For the time *is come* for

positively in the verse which follows. Human life was lightly regarded in that period and murder was common. Thievery was an especially frequent crime, particularly among slaves. The word "evil-doer," a term equivalent to law-violater, or criminal, sums up all infraction of law; and "a meddler in other men's matters" is one who concerns himself improperly with the affairs of others. This entire phrase—"a meddler in other men's matters"—is translated from the Greek word, *allotrioepiskopos,* compounded from *allotrios,* belonging to another, and *episkopos,* the usual word for bishop or overseer in the New Testament; thus, literally, *a bishop or overseer over other men's matters!* The word forbids all intrusion into those things which do not concern us, all interference in the affairs of others. For an illustration of the principle taught here, see John 21: 21, 22. The lesson is one needing emphasis at all times and places.

16 **But if a man suffer as a Christian, let him not be ashamed; but let him glorify God in this name.**—To suffer "as a Christian" is to suffer persecution for *being* a Christian; and those thus suffering are not to be ashamed (because they suffer for this reason) but are to "glorify God" (praise and honor him) "in this name" (i.e., in the name Christian). A thrilling example of such will be seen in the conduct of Peter and John in Jerusalem when persecuted for preaching in the name of Christ, and their consequent "rejoicing that they were counted worthy to suffer dishonor for the Name." (Acts 5: 41.)

The name "Christian" *(christianos,* a follower of Christ) occurs three times in the New Testament. (Acts 11: 26; 26: 28; 1 Pet. 4: 16.) It was given, by divine origin, for the first time to the disciples in Antioch (Acts 11: 26), being the "new name" which the "mouth of the Lord would name" (Isa. 62: 2.) The etymology and derivation of the word "Christian" contain an amazing epitome of the root, the growth, and the spread of the religion which he whom the name honors established. The meaning is of Hebrew origin; it appears in the New Testament in Greek form, with a Latin termination; and points, like the inscription which Pi-

judgment to begin at the house of God: and if *it begin* first at us, what *shall be* the end of them that obey not the [6]gospel of God? 18 And if the righteous is scarcely saved, where shall the ungodly and sinner appear? 19

[6]Gr. *good tidings.* See Mt. 4. 23 marg.

---

late caused to be placed on the cross to the world-wide empire which he established.

17 For the time is come for judgment to begin at the house of God:—"For the time" is translated from a phrase which means "it is the season." Thus the period designated by the apostles was already upon his readers. "Judgment" *(krima),* as used here, denotes severe trial. The house of God is the family of God, the church. (1 Tim. 3: 15.) The meaning is that the time when severe trial would fall upon the church was at hand. That the "judgment" here contemplated is not the day when all the nations shall be gathered before the judgment bar of God (2 Cor. 5: 10; Matt. 25: 31-46), follows from the fact that this day was at least 1,900 years distant when Peter wrote; whereas, the "judgment" to which he alludes was at hand and impending. What that "judgment" was, and the "time" when it would appear, is indicated in the verses which follow.

And if it begin first at us, what shall be the end of them that obey not the gospel of God?—This is an *a fortiori* argument—from the less to the greater—similar to that of Paul in Rom. 11: 21, "For if God spared not the natural branches, neither will he spare thee." "End" *(telos)* denotes the doom awaiting those to whom Peter referred as not having obeyed the gospel. The significance is, If the church, which is ever the object of God's care, is soon to fall into trial and sore persecution, how much greater must be the misery and wretchedness of those who do not rely on the Lord, and are thus without the comforting assurances of the gospel?

18 And if the righteous is scarcely saved, where shall the ungodly and sinner appear?—This is a quotation from the Greek translation of Prov. 11: 31. It is cited to illustrate and enforce the teaching of verse 17. If, in the affliction which then loomed large on the horizon, the righteous man was scarcely saved, how infinitely worse the lot of the lost, and impossible the salvation of the ungodly and sinner. "Scarcely" *(molis)* denotes that which

Wherefore let them also that suffer according to the will of God commit their souls in well-doing unto a faithful Creator.

is accomplished only with great difficulty. It does not suggest doubt as to the outcome; only wonder that such a thing is possible! The "righteous" man is one who is upright, virtuous, and good; one who keeps the commandments of God. (Matt. 7: 21; 1 John 2: 4.) The "judgment" (verse 17) which drew near would be so severe that even the pure and good would with great difficulty escape the destruction which it threatened. If such were so with reference to the righteous, what of the "ungodly" and "sinner"? The "ungodly" man *(asebes)* is a man destitute of reverential awe toward God; an impious, irreligious character; and the "sinner" *(hamartolos)* is one whose life is devoted to sin. In the Greek text the article appears before the word "ungodly" only, thus indicating that the term "sinner" is to be understood as an additional description of the "ungodly" man, and that both terms refer to the same individual. Impiety, irreverence, leads irresistibly into positive sin.

What, then, was the "judgment" (verse 17) soon to begin? Not the general judgment, for (a) it was then (and may still be) in the distant future; (b) in it the "righteous" will scarcely (with great difficulty) be saved; whereas, the deliverance of the righteous in the last day and their entrance into the heavenly kingdom will be "richly supplied": "Wherefore, brethren, give the more diligence to make your calling and election sure: *for if ye do these things, ye shall never stumble: for thus shall be richly supplied unto you the entrance into the eternal kingdom of our Lord and Saviour Jesus Christ."* (2 Pet. 1: 10, 11.) Inasmuch as it was the same apostle who declared that the "righteous shall scarcely be saved" and the faithful shall be "richly supplied" with an entrance, it must follow that he does not refer in these passages to the same salvation. The verb "supplied" *(epichoregeo)* is derived similarly to that which occurs in 1 Pet. 4: 11, compounded with the preposition *epi,* and with the adverb "richly" added. The ultimate salvation thus promised is not only freely supplied; its abundance is enhanced by the word "richly." But if such is to be the manner of entrance into final bliss by the righteous, how can it be said that the "righteous" shall scarcely (i.e., with great difficulty) be saved? It is obvious that two different "salvations" are contemplated by the apostle in these passages. To what salvation does he refer in our text?

Intimations of imminent trial and extreme suffering in the epistle are frequent. A fiery trial is soon to come upon the saints (1 Pet. 4: 12); they are to suffer as Christians (verse 16); there was an "end" approaching necessitating a "sound mind" and that the saints be "sober unto prayer" (verse 7). In the disaster which was then threatening, they would "scarcely" be saved. The words of this epistle were penned shortly before the destruction of Jerusalem by the Romans. The effects of this terrible disaster extended into the remotest sections of the earth. Conducted by heathens who, in many instances, made no effort to distinguish between Jewish Christians and Gentile Christians, it was impossible that the effects of this mighty pogrom should not be felt by Gentile Christians also. There is a remarkable similarity between these words of the apostle and those of the Lord in describing the end of the Jewish state. (Matt. 24: 1-28.) Particularly is this true of the following: "And except those days had been shortened, no flesh would have been saved; *but for the elect's sake those days shall be shortened."* (Matt. 24: 22.) The "elect" were the saints; the "shortening" referred to was the termination of the terrible siege in Jerusalem; and the salvation of the "flesh" mentioned was physical deliverance from the trials and ordeals of that event.

We hence conclude that the salvation of the "righteous" alluded to by Peter and to be accomplished with such difficulty as to be a matter of wonder was deliverance from complete destruction in the persecution which swept over the world in connection with the destruction of the temple and annihilation of the Jewish state in Jerusalem.

19 **Wherefore let them also that suffer according to the will of God commit their souls in well-doing unto a faithful Creator.**—"Wherefore" is a logical term pointing to the conclusion to be drawn from the foregoing premises. The Christian who suffers persecution for faithfulness suffers according to the will of God, and thus in keeping with a wise and holy purpose. In view of this he is to "commit" (deliver as a deposit) his soul into the hands of God who as a faithful Creator will preserve inviolate the trust imposed.

3. DUTIES OF ELDERS
5: 1-4

1 The elders therefore among you I exhort, who am a fellow-elder, and a witness of the sufferings of Christ, who am also a partaker of the glory that

1 **The elders therefore among you I exhort,**—"Therefore" logically associates the present exhortation with the sequence of thought at the end of the preceding chapter. There, the saints were admonished to continue in "well-doing" and to prepare themselves for the "judgment" impending (1 Pet. 4: 17, 19); and here, the elders are instructed to encourage them in the one, and to assist them in preparing for the other.

The word "elder" is translated from the Greek *presbuteros,* a presbyter. Originally, it had reference to age, but it later came to be the most common designation of those empowered by the Holy Spirit to exercise oversight of the churches. (Acts 20: 28.) Each congregation of the apostolic age had a plurality of men so functioning, their duties being to feed the flock (Acts 20: 28), to administer discipline (1 Thess. 5: 12), and to watch for the souls of the saints committed to their care (Heb. 13: 17). They are thus variously styled "bishops" (Acts 20: 28), "pastors" (Eph. 4: 11), "teachers" (Eph. 4: 11), and "presbyters" (1 Tim. 4: 14), in keeping with the functions required of them. Their activities, in the functional capacities above designated, were limited to the congregations in which they held membership, and the foregoing designations are descriptive of the same men—the distinctions between elders, bishops and pastors which later developed and which are currently used in the denominational world being without New Testament sanction. Qualifications of elders are listed in 1 Tim. 3: 1-7; Tit. 1: 5-16.

The word "exhort" is a term of persuasion; and far from supporting the Romish view that Peter exercised supremacy over the other apostles, the word is a common one to the sacred writers and the duty involved a fitting one for all saints. (Heb. 3: 13; 10: 25.) The exhortation to the elders was based on three considerations: (1) Peter was also an elder; (2) he was a witness of the sufferings of Christ; and (3) he shared with the saints to whom he wrote the hope of ultimate glory.

shall be revealed: 2 Tend the flock of God which is among you, ⁷exercising

_{⁷Some ancient authorities omit *exercising the oversight*.}

Who am a fellow-elder,—*(ho sumprebuteros,* the fellow-elder). Though one of the apostles, he chose to base his exhortation on the fact that he, too, was an elder, and thus on the same level in this respect as those to whom he wrote.

And a witness of the sufferings of Christ, who am also a partaker of the glory that shall be revealed:—Though Peter had seen—from afar—the agony of Christ on the cross, and was, in this manner, a "witness" of the suffering of Christ, the word "witness" here *(martus)* signifies "testimony," and the meaning is that Peter was chosen to testify regarding the sufferings he had seen. The Lord had said he was to do this (Acts 1: 8), and Peter, on more than one occasion, alluded thereto (Acts 3: 15; 10: 39). Here, as in 1 Pet. 1: 11 and 4: 13, the thought of these sufferings led the apostle to make mention of the glory which awaits those who patiently and faithfully endure.

2 Tend the flock of God which is among you,—The verb "tend" *(poimaino,* to shepherd; to care for sheep) points to the similarity which obtains between the work of a shepherd and the duty of elders in the church. The word includes more than simply preaching or teaching; in it are all the varied duties which we sometimes, and properly so, style the "pastoral" office. The noun form of the verb "tend" is translated "pastors" in Eph. 4: 11. A shepherd and his sheep have long served as a figure of teachers and those committed to their care. When David was taken from the sheepfolds of his father it was that he might feed Israel, "the flock of Jehovah." "So he was their shepherd according to the integrity of his heart, and guided them by the skillfulness of his hands." (Psalm 78: 70-72.) One of the many charges leveled against the disobedient kings and rulers of Judah was that they did not tend the flock but scattered and destroyed it. (Jer. 23: 1-4.) It is the flock *of God,* and not of the shepherds; a reminder that elders serve under the "Chief Shepherd" to whom they, also, must some day give an account. The words "which are among you" identify the ones for whom the shepherds are responsible: those of their own flock, or congregation.

the oversight, not of constraint but willingly, [8]according to *the will of* God;

[8]Some ancient authorities omit *according to* the will of *God.*

Exercising the oversight, not of constraint, but willingly, according to the will of God;—The words "exercising the oversight" translate the Greek participle *episkopountes,* derived from *episkopos,* the usual word for "bishop" or "overseer." (Acts 20: 28.) An *episkopos* is a superintendent, or overseer; and in exercising oversight of the flock of God, bishops or elders are obligated to superintend and direct the affairs of the congregation committed to their care. (Heb. 13: 17.) To fail to do so is to be remiss in duty and recreant to the trust imposed; and for the congregation to refuse to recognize this oversight when properly exercised and by duly qualified and appointed elders, is to be in rebellion against God himself.

This oversight the elders are to exercise "not of restraint," i.e., not in forced service and through a burdened sense of duty, but "willingly," and in harmony with the will of God who requires it.

Nor yet for filthy lucre, but of a ready mind;—"Filthy lucre" is from the compound adverb *aischrokerdes,* and occurs only here, though an adjectival form of the word is in 1 Tim. 3: 8 and Tit. 1: 7. The word describes gain that is base and dishonorable. This statement is significant beyond the instruction which it contains in revealing that in the apostolic age elders were supported financially by the congregation in the work in which they were engaged. Despite the troublous times which then prevailed and the comparative poverty of the congregations in most parts of the world, there was sufficient money available to make the work lucrative. Paul provided that the elders who ruled well should be accorded a double stipend—"especially those who labor in the word and in teaching." (1 Tim. 5: 17.) The duties of elders are so varied and pressing that the church will never make the growth it should until this practice—of supporting elders fully that they may devote their entire time to the work of the church—is adopted. These words of warning were necessary because there was always the possibility that some would be tempted to use their position in the church for base ends and personal gain. It is noteworthy that the term used to describe the character of money obtained in this manner is that which the Greek writers commonly

nor yet for filthy lucre, but of a ready mind; 3 neither as lording it over the charge allotted to you, but making yourselves ensamples to the flock. 4 And

used of one who sought gain in a sordid way. Thus an elder (or, for that matter, any spiritual teacher) who obtains money as the result of the misuse of his position is as base and disreputable as the extortioner, the trafficker in the bodies of women, and the seller of slaves. Then, as now, some turned religion into a trade and commercialized the gospel of Christ, "supposing that godliness is a way of gain." (1 Tim. 5: 5.) In contrast with all such is the faithful elder who serves with a "ready mind," his service being a willing one, i.e., eagerly and with earnest desire to please the Father.

3 Neither as lording it over the charge allotted to you, but making yourselves ensamples to the flock.—In verse 2, Peter forbade the elders to exercise their functions from base and sordid motives of avarice and greed; here, he warns them against the unseemly ambition and abuse of power in the same work. Such ambition and abuse of power was, in the apostle's view, as wrong as that condemned in the preceding verse; and the history of religion from the apostolic age to the present is a demonstration of the correctness of this claim. Warnings against such a disposition recur in our Saviour's teaching. (Matt. 20: 25-28; Luke 22: 24-26; Mark 9: 34, 35.) The words "lording it over" (from *katakurieuo*, to rule over others highhandedly and autocratically) suggests an arrogant, domineering spirit, and is here positively forbidden to those who would serve acceptably as elders or bishops. That such a spirit early manifested itself in the church may be seen from 3 John 9.

The "charge allotted" to the elders was the congregation in which they served. These words are translated from *kleron*, plural of *kleros*, a lot or portion. In the Greek Septuagint, the word designated a portion assigned by lot. (Deut. 10: 9; 12: 12.) Jehovah is there declared to be the "portion" or "lot" of the Levites, the priestly tribe. The word as here used is applied to that portion of the church which the elders have assigned to them as their lot or portion over which to exercise superintendency—i.e., the congregations in which they hold membership. It is significant that our English word *clergy* derives from *kleros,* the lot or portion over which elders are to exercise watchful care. In this, as in many other instances, the denominational world has abandoned the New Testament usage; and instead of applying the word to the members of the church as Peter did, they use it as a special designation for preachers!

Elders, far from manifesting a spirit of arrogance and autocracy in their work, are to serve as "ensamples" to the flock, the church. The word "ensample" is from *tupos,* type; the print or mark left from the impression; thus, an example or pattern. Elders are to serve therefore as patterns or models from the emulation of those committed to their care, even as they follow the pattern of Christ, the "chief shepherd." (Verse 4.) It is important to note that in the foregoing verse that which Peter forbids is the *abuse* of authority and not its proper *use*. To cite this passage as proof that elders are vested with no authority in directing the affairs of the congregation is utterly to misapprehend the apostle's teaching. It is not the exercise of spiritual authority as such which is here condemned; it is its excesses and abuses; and in doing this, the apostle directed attention to the fact that the power of a good example is much more effective than the mere exercise of authority, and that to seek for such influence is the best guarantee against its improper use. It is not to be forgotten that to deny to elders the proper exercise of authority in the oversight of the church is as much a perversion of New Testament teaching as it is for the elders to abuse their rights and privileges through improper seizure of authority. There is in the church today tendencies toward both extremes; each of them should be, and must be, strictly curbed.

4 **And when the chief Shepherd shall be manifested, ye shall receive the crown of glory that fadeth not away.**—The words "chief Shepherd" occur nowhere else in the New Testament, and were, therefore, coined by Peter, perhaps in memory of the Lord's allusion to himself as the Good Shepherd in the parable of the sheepfold. (John 10: 14.) The Hebrew writer in similar fashion referred to "the great shepherd of the sheep." (Heb. 13: 20.) Elders are thus to regard themselves as under-shepherds, deriving their powers and exercising their functions by the will of the

"Chief Shepherd," Christ. The manifestation of Christ will be at his second coming, at which time the under-shepherds, here particularly addressed, will "receive the crown of glory that fadeth not away." Instead of striving for material gain or popular applause elders are to serve in such fashion that the unfading crown of glory reserved for such will be there. The words "that fadeth not away" are from *amarantinos*, not subject to withering; a flower that never fades, hence, the symbol of perpetuity and immortality. See a similar use and further explanation of the term in 1 Pet. 1: 4. "Of glory" is in apposition to "crown" and it is, therefore a glorious crown. The crown *(stephanos)* is the wreath or chaplet worn by heroes or conquerors, and not the *diadema* of sovereignty or royalty. It designates the reward which is bestowed for faithful and valued service. And it is an amaranthine wreath, not subject to fading as were the wreaths fashioned for, and bestowed on, the popular heroes of the day. The thought and word occur in one of Milton's finest passages:

> "Immortal *Amaranth,* a flower which once
> In Paradise, hard by the tree of life,
> Began to bloom, but soon, for man's offence
> To heaven removed, where first it grew, there grows
> And flowers aloft, shading the fount of life;
> And where the river of bliss through midst of heaven
> Rolls o'er Elysian flowers her amber stream
> With these, that never fade, the spirits elect
> Bind their resplendent locks, inwreathed with beams."
> —*Paradise Lost, III, 353-361.*

4. DUTIES OF THE YOUNG
5: 5a

glory that fadeth not away. 5 ⁹Likewise, ye younger, be subject unto the elder. Yea, all of you gird yourselves with humility, to serve one another: for God resisteth the proud, but giveth grace to the humble. 6 Humble

⁹Or, *Likewise . . . elder; yea, all of you to another. Gird yourselves with humility*

5a Likewise, ye younger, be subject unto the elder.—"Likewise" (*homoios,* as in 1 Pet. 3: 7, in like manner, in your turn), points to the corresponding obligations of the younger members of the church. "Be subject (*hupotasso,* cf. 1 Pet. 2: 13, 18; 3: 1) is an injunction to these younger members to be subject to the older members of the congregation. "Elder" in the text is plural *(presbuterio)* as is the word younger *(neoteroi).* Does the word "elder" here refer to age alone, or to the functional position designated by the term in verse 1? It is not possible to know definitely. In support of the view that it refers to men who serve as elders in the church is the fact that in the verses immediately preceding such are unmistakably designed by the word. It would be unusual for a word to be used in two different senses in such close connection. On the other hand, it seems natural to regard the words "younger" and "elder" as opposed to each other, and hence in natural antithesis, the first of the younger people, and the second of the older people in the congregation. Paul, in 1 Tim. 5: 1, uses the word in this ordinary signification; and such seems the more probable meaning here. But, whether the word be taken in its functional or its ordinary sense, the obligation of the younger to the older people remains. All such are, of course, to be in subjection to the elders of the church, and in addition to render that deference and respect owed by the young to the aged.

5. HUMILITY AND WATCHFULNESS
5: 5b-9

yourselves therefore under the mighty hand of God, that he may exalt you in

5b Yea, all of you gird yourselves with humility, to serve one another: for God resisteth the proud, but giveth grace to the humble.—Here, the effort to designate obligations of specific classes is dropped and the duty of all declared. It is as if the apostle had said, "Why should I attempt to specify particular duties for each class when one injunction will cover them all." "All of you gird yourselves with humility to serve one another." "Gird yourselves" is translated from the Greek verb *egkomboomai,* a term of exceeding interest and significance. The noun from which it is derived *(kombos)* signifies a knot; and the noun form means to tie with a knot. From this noun, the verb of our text, denoting the garment thus tied on, is derived. It was used at the beginning of the Christian era of the white scarf or apron which slaves wore

due time; 7 casting all your anxiety upon him, because he careth for you. 8

tightly fastened around the waist to distinguish them from freemen. Used figuratively here, the meaning is, "Tie on humility like a slave's apron." The saints were thus to array themselves in humility; to tie it on securely like a garment so that it might never fall away. So arrayed, they were to regard no service as too menial or lowly, no task too small for them to perform. Peter must have had a vivid mental picture of the Lord's action when he tied a towel about him and washed the disciples' feet, when these words were penned. (John 13: 10-17.)

The phrase, "for God resisteth the proud, but giveth grace to the humble," is a quotation from the Greek translation of the Old Testament, occurring in Prov. 3: 34. The verb "resisteth" is a military term, as of an army marshaled for battle. Spiritual forces are thus arrayed against the proud. These words of Solomon are cited by Peter as an additional reason why saints should clothe themselves in the garment of humility. "Grace" is favor unmerited; God sheds his favor only upon those who humble themselves in his sight.

6 **Humble yourselves therefore under the mighty hand of God, that he may exalt you in due time;**—The "hand of God" is mighty because it is all-powerful and irresistible in its operations. Inasmuch as it is sheer folly for man to resist God, the wise course is for one to humble himself under the Lord's hand, with the assurance that he will be exalted in due time. The Saviour's words, "And whosoever shall exalt himself shall be humbled; and whosoever shall humble himself shall be exalted" (Matt. 23: 12), must have been in Peter's thoughts when he wrote these words.

7 **Casting all your anxiety upon him, because he careth for you.**—The word "casting" is derived from a term which means to *deposit,* and is in the aorist tense here, thus signifying a once-for-all act by which one rids himself forevermore of all anxious care by depositing it with the Lord! "Be not therefore anxious, saying, What shall we eat, or What shall we drink? or, Wherewithal shall we be clothed. . . . For your heavenly Father knoweth that ye have need of all these things." One may, with complete confidence, cast his anxiety on the Lord for the reason that he

Be sober, be watchful; your adversary the devil, as a roaring lion, walketh about, seeking whom he may devour: 9 whom withstand stedfast in [10]your faith, knowing that the same sufferings are [11]accomplished in your [12]brethren

[10]Or, *the*
[11]Gr. *being accomplished.*
[12]Gr. *brotherhood.*

---

cares for his saints, and will not forsake them in their time of need. (Psalm 55: 22.)

8 **Be sober, be watchful: your adversary the devil, as a roaring lion, walketh about, seeking whom he may devour:**—"Be sober" is an admonition to calmness of mind; mental self-control. The verb occurs in 1 Pet. 4: 7. "Be watchful" is translated from a word often used by the Lord. (Mark 13: 35, 37; Matt. 26: 40, 41.) An "adversary" is, technically, an opponent in a lawsuit; here, it is used to identify Satan as the one on the opposite side of a trial for life or death. He is the "devil," because he is a calumniator, one who deliberately and knowingly makes false charges against the saints of God; and he is called "a roaring lion," because of the fierceness with which he stalks, and if possible, runs down the saints. The word "roar" describes the howl of the lion or wolf in hunger. He is a *serpent* because of his subtlety (2 Cor. 11: 1-4); a *lion* because of his strength and ferocity. The verb "walketh about" indicates his restless energy; and "seeking" the persistence with which he searched out his victims. "Walketh about" is translated from a word which means, literally, to prowl about, not daring to enter the fold where the sheep are, but ready to spring upon, and devour any wanderer outside. The word "devour" is, in the Greek, to gulp down, or swallow, thus utterly to destroy.

9 **Whom withstand stedfast in your faith, knowing that the same sufferings are accomplished in your brethren who are in the world.**—"Withstand" *(anthistemi)* is translated from the same word as "resist" in the familiar passage in James, "But resist the devil and he will flee from you." (James 4: 7.) The verb means to stand firmly against attack; to be unwavering in resistance. The word "stedfast" *(stereos)* indicates rock-like stability, a solidity and firmness originating in faith; not, however, objective faith—unwavering orthodoxy—but an immovable trust in God.

The means by which to withstand Satan are, (1) stedfastness in faith; (2) recognition that the suffering to which the saints are subjected is not peculiar to them; and (3) that the same suffering has been undergone by the brethren before them. Not alone in their trials, they were to remember that they formed a community of believers who were all suffering for the Name they so proudly wore. "Brethren" in the text is a collective term, properly, "brotherhood," and is so translated in 1 Pet. 2: 17. "In the world" is a comprehensive term, meaning in all parts of the world.

SECTION FIVE

CONCLUSION, 5: 10-14

1. BENEDICTION
5: 10, 11

who are in the world. 10 And the God of all grace, who called you unto his eternal glory in Christ, after that ye have suffered a little while, shall himself [13]perfect, establish, strengthen [14]you. 11 To him *be* the dominion [4]for ever and ever. Amen.

[13]Or, *restore*
[14]Many ancient authorities add *settle*.

10 **And the God of all grace, who called you unto his eternal glory in Christ, after that ye have suffered a little while, shall himself perfect, establish, strengthen you.**—"Grace" is the unmerited favor of God. He is the God of "all grace" as he is the God of "all comfort" (2 Cor. 1: 3), because he is the sole source and giver of the grace and comfort the saints so sorely need. These to whom Peter wrote had been "called"; this calling had been accomplished by means of the gospel (2 Thess. 2: 13, 14); the calling was to a share of God's eternal glory; and the sphere was Christ.

Compared with the glories that are to be revealed they were to know that, however severe the trials of the moment, it was for "a little while," working for them "more and more exceedingly an eternal weight of glory." (2 Cor. 4: 17.)

"Perfect," "establish," and "strengthen" are verbs in the future tense. "Perfect" *(katartidzo,* to mend, repair, used of fishermen repairing their nets, Mark 4: 21) indicates the action of God in eliminating the deficiencies of the saints and bringing them to a standard of usefulness in his service; "establish" *(sterizo,* to make fast, to support that which totters) refers to the fixity and immobility of those who rely on the Lord, the term being used by the Lord in his admonition to Peter, "When thou hast turned again, establish *(sterizo)* thy brethren." (Luke 22: 32.) "Strengthen" *(sthenoo,* to impart strength), a word meaning to supply strength to resist attack, occurs nowhere else in the New Testament.

11 To him be the dominion for ever and ever. Amen.— See the comments on 1 Pet. 4: 11. One who has been perfected, established, and strengthened will rejoice to ascribe to him who is the source of all grace, and the supplier of all strength "dominion for ever and ever," and with fervency and adoration indeed exclaim, "Amen!"

2. DESIGN AND BEARER OF THE EPISTLE
5: 12

12 By Silvanus, [15]our faithful brother, as I account *him*, I have written unto you briefly, exhorting, and testifying that this is the true grace of God:

---

[15]Gr. *the*.

---

12 By Silvanus, our faithful brother, as I account him, I have written unto you briefly, exhorting, and testifying that this is the true grace of God: stand ye fast therein.—The epistle was "by" Silvanus, either as the bearer of the letter, or the one to whom Peter dictated it (Rom. 16: 22), or both. It is possible that Peter wrote with his own hand these words, following a practice of Paul, in attestation of the letter itself. (Gal. 6: 11.) It appears that such was a common practice of the New Testament writers as a guarantee of the genuineness thereof.

Silvanus is the same as the Silas of Acts 15: 22, 32, 40, and the Silvanus of 1 Thess. 1: 1; 2 Cor. 1: 19. He accompanied Paul on the second of the great missionary tours recorded in Acts, and was with him in Corinth in A.D. 53. (Acts 18: 5.) He was very active in the church in Jerusalem, and was possessed of prophetic gifts. (Acts 15: 32.) It was characteristic of the Jews who traveled extensively in Gentile lands to change the form of their names (e.g., Saul to Paul, Joshua to Jason, John surnamed Mark, etc.). Silvanus was "a faithful brother," known as such to the brethren for whom the epistle was intended, and declared to be such by Peter. The apostle wrote "briefly," literally, by a few words *(di' oligon)*, both with reference to the length of the letter and the importance of the subjects treated. Its design was to exhort and testify regarding the true grace of God. The exhortation was therefore earnest persuasion; the testimony strong confirmation of the matters presented. The purpose of the apostle was to supply indisputable evidence of the soundness of the faith which they possessed. This was the true grace of God which had been bestowed upon them, and in it they were to continue. It was theirs; they were experiencing and enjoying its blessings; hence, their obligation to "stand fast therein." The construction in the Greek text is significant: *eis hen hestekate,* "into which (having entered) stand!"

3. CLOSING SALUTATIONS
5: 13, 14

stand ye fast therein. 13 [1]She that is in Babylon, elect together with *you,*

---
[1]That is, The church, or, The sister.

---

13 She that is in Babylon, elect together with you, saluteth you; and so doth Mark my son.—For "She that is in Babylon," the King James translation has "The church that is in Babylon, . . ." The American Standard version adds the marginal reading, "That is, The church, or The sister." There is, however, no noun in the Greek text corresponding to the word "church," and it is therefore not properly inserted in this passage. The words, "she . . . elect together with you," are from *he suneklekte,* nominative feminine form of *sunekiklektos,* elect with others, thus, actually, "the co-elect woman." What woman? Some expositors regard the word woman as figurative, and understand the reference to be the church in Babylon, supporting such a view by citing 2 John 1. The "elect lady" there, however, does not refer to a church, but to an individual; and in the light of the fact that Mark—an individual—is joined with the "co-elect woman," it is unaccountable that a *figure of speech* and *a person* would be joined in the salutation in such fashion; and we therefore conclude that the reference is to a sister in the church in Babylon. To what sister? She was then in Babylon; she had traveled among the saints in Asia Minor; and she was known to the people to whom the epistle was addressed. What sister could so well meet these conditions as Peter's *wife?* She was a "sister-wife" *(adelphe gune,* a wife who was also a sister in Christ), and she accompanied Peter on his travels at least a portion of the time. (1 Cor. 9: 5.) There was an especial appropriateness in sending a greeting from her to saints with whom she had been formerly associated and whom she well knew, in an epistle that had dealt so specifically with the duties and **responsibilities** of women. (1 Pet. 3: 1-7.)

saluteth you; and *so doth* Mark my son. 14 Salute one another with a kiss of love.
Peace be unto you all that are in Christ.

Mark, styled the "son" of Peter, was John Mark, the disciple who incurred the extreme displeasure of Paul because of his defection at Perga on the first missionary journey (Acts 13: 5, 13; 15: 36-41), but who was later restored to the good graces of that apostle by subsequent faithfulness and fidelity to duty (Col. 4: 10; 2 Tim. 4: 11). He was the "son" of Peter, as Timothy was the "child" of Paul (Phil. 2: 22; 1 Tim. 1: 1, 2), a spiritual relationship, and not a fleshly one. Mark composed one of the biographies of Jesus, "The Gospel According to Mark," and was, traditionally, "'the interpreter of Peter." His mother's name was Mary; and he was a cousin of Barnabas. (Acts 12: 2; Col. 4: 10.)

The reference to "Babylon" as the place from which these salutations were sent raises again the question, already considered in the Introduction, From what place did Peter write the epistle? Because Rome is referred to as "Babylon" in the Revelation (Rev. 14: 8; 17: 6, 18; 18: 2, 10), all Catholic theologians and many Protestant commentators maintain that reference thereto is to be regarded as mystical and figurative; and that Peter was in Rome when the letter was penned. Opposed to this view, however, are the following weighty considerations: (1) Internal evidence leads irresistibly to the conclusion that First Peter was written *before* the destruction of Jerusalem. (According to eminent Talmudic authorities, the Jews did not begin to designate Rome by the figurative term "Babylon" until after that event.) (2) In the foregoing references in the Revelation Rome is never referred to as "Babylon" by this designation alone, but always as "Babylon, the great," "Babylon, the strong city," etc. (3) The fact that the word "Babylon" is used thus mystically in a highly symbolic and figurative book such as the Revelation does not argue that reference thereto is the same in a book of an entirely different character such as First Peter. (4) Other geographical references in First Peter are admittedly literal. Why, then, should it be concluded that "Babylon" is the sole exception? (5) Peter wrote long before John penned the Revelation, and thus could not have been following John's use of the term. (6) The name "Babylon," when figuratively used, is the symbol of confusion, corruption, apostasy. What possible reason could Peter have had in using the term in this fashion in an epistle designed to protect the ones addressed from just such a manner of life which it typified? A candid consideration of all the facts leads to the conclusion that the word "Babylon" is to be taken in its ordinary, geographical sense; and that Peter was in the well-known city by that name on the Euphrates when he wrote the epistle which bears his name.

14 **Salute one another with a kiss of love.**—Greeting, by means of a kiss, appears to have been a common practice in the early church, and to have been followed for some centuries after the beginning of the Christian era. The custom is mentioned by Justin Martyr, Tertullian, Chrysostom, Augustine, and numerous other early writers; and references thereto are frequent in the New Testament. (Rom. 16: 16; 1 Cor. 16: 20; 2 Cor. 13: 12; 1 Thess. 5: 26.) According to the historians of the early church, the abuses to which the practice would ordinarily lead were avoided by the separation of the sexes when the church assembled for worship—an arrangement inherited from the synagogue. The "constitutions of the Holy Apostles," believed to have been written between A.D. 300 and 400, contain the following injunction: "Then let the men give the men, and the women give the women, the Lord's kiss. But let no one do it with deceit, as Judas betrayed the Lord with a kiss." (Book 2, 57, page 422, Vol. 7, *The Ante-Nicene Fathers.*) Clement of Alexandria, who died about A.D. 220, wrote, under the heading, "Love and the Kiss of Charity," these words: "And if we are called to the kingdom of God, let us walk worthy of the kingdom, loving God and our neighbor. But love is not proved by a kiss, but by kindly feeling. But there are those that do nothing but make the churches resound with a kiss, not having love itself within. For this very thing, the shameless use of a kiss, which ought to be mystic, occasions foul suspicions and evil reports. The apostle calls the kiss holy." ("The Instructor," Ch. 12, *Ante-Nicene Fathers,* Vol. 2, page 291.)

It should be noted that the apostle did not enjoin kissing as a method of greeting; the custom already prevailed. His words were designed to insure that the custom would be observed in keeping with the morality and chastity characteristic of the high calling of Christianity. Kissing, as a mode of salutation, was no more sanctioned than the handshake is today, both methods being customs of the times. But, as Christianity requires complete sincerity in this manner of greeting today, so it enjoined it in the kiss of that day. The kiss was to be one "of love," i.e., prompted by love, and in exhibition of it.

Peace be unto you all that are in Christ.—It is significant that Paul, the apostle to the Gentiles, chose to use as his benediction the Greek word of greeting, *charis* ("Grace be with you all, 1 Cor. 16: 23; Rom. 16: 24), while Peter, the apostle to the Circumcision, followed the Hebrew greeting, *shalom*, peace. (Matt. 10: 13.) This blessing is available only in Christ, who is "our peace." (Eph. 2: 14.) Thus, only those who have been "baptized into Christ" (Gal. 3: 27) have entered the sphere where this peace is enjoyed.

A COMMENTARY ON THE SECOND EPISTLE OF PETER

CONTENTS

Page

INTRODUCTION

The Author 143

Design and Occasion of the Epistle 144

Persons to Whom Written 144

Time and Place of Writing 145

SECTION ONE (1: 1-21)

Introduction (1: 1, 2) 147

Exhortation to Growth in Grace (1: 3-11) 148

Source of Their Knowledge (1: 12-21) 155

SECTION TWO (2: 1-22)

Warning Against False Teachers (1: 1-11) 163

Characteristics and Final Destiny of False Teachers (2: 12-22) 171

SECTION THREE (3: 1-18)

The Second Coming of the Lord and End of the World (3: 1-13) 179

Concluding Exhortations and Doxology (3: 14-18) 189

INTRODUCTION TO THE SECOND EPISTLE OF PETER

THE AUTHOR

The name of the author is affixed to the epistle itself. "Simon Peter, a servant and apostle of Jesus Christ. . . ." (2 Pet. 1: 1.) Despite this, more serious doubts have been raised regarding the genuineness of the epistle of Second Peter than any other portion of the New Testament. The uncertainty which attaches to the matter of authorship has existed from an early age. Eusebius, sometimes styled the "Father of Church History," placed it among the *antilegoma,* books not universally admitted to be genuine, "disputed, indeed, but known to most men." (Ecclesiastical History, book iii, 25.) This history was written, it is believed, about A.D. 325. Jerome, born A.D. 350, wrote that "Peter wrote two epistles called catholic; the second of which is denied by many to be his, because of differences of style from the former." Origen (who died A.D. 253) said, "Peter has left one acknowledged epistle: let it be granted that he left a second, for this is disputed."

By the end of the fourth century the epistle had come to be regarded as genuine by all except the Syrians. It was recognized as canonical (entitled to a place in the canon of scripture) by the councils of Laodicea (A.D. 366), Hippo (A.D. 393), and Carthage (A.D. 397). Though excluded from the Old Syrian Version, it was included in the Philoxenian, or Later Syriac, and eventually came to be regarded as genuine by the majority of conservative scholars.

It should be observed that Eusebius, Jerome, and Origen did not themselves express doubts regarding its genuineness; they merely noted that *some* in their time had questioned it. The doubts were with reference to its authorship, and these appear to have gradually disappeared following its acceptance by Jerome who included it in his Latin Version of the scriptures. The alleged differences in style are doubtless due to the difference in the nature of the subjects treated, and are more than offset by the many points of resemblance discernible between the first and second epistles and the author's recorded speeches in the Book of Acts. (1) The epistle

144   INTRODUCTION

claims to have been written by Peter. (2 Pet. 1: 1.) (2) There are numerous references in it to incidents which are applicable to Peter: (a) a warning of sudden death (2 Pet. 1: 14; John 21: 18, 19); (b) the experience of the transfiguration (1: 16-18; Matt. 17: 1ff). (3) The first epistle is universally admitted to be genuine, and the second affects to be addressed by the same author to the same readers (3: 1). (4) Its reliability and authenticity depend on the Petrine authorship; it is either a production of the author whose name it bears, or it is a spurious document and thus unworthy of consideration. A candid consideration of all the facts leads to the conclusion that Peter was its author; that it was addressed to the same persons as the first epistle; and that it is as authoritative and true as any portion of the sacred writings.

DESIGN AND OCCASION OF THE EPISTLE

The keynote of the first epistle of Peter is *hope;* in the *second*, it is *knowledge*. The first epistle was written to sustain the saints in the severe trials through which they were passing; the second was designed to guard them against the errors being industriously propagated by false teachers. The only safeguard against their deductions was knowledge—the full knowledge *(epignosis)* of Jesus Christ. The epistle is, therefore, largely devoted to the description of the false teachers then active, and to a refutation of their specious and false doctrines. As it was necessary, in the first epistle, to warn the saints of the dangers of discouragement in the face of trial, so here, he thought it wise to admonish them to avoid the errors of doctrine with which they were certain to come in contact. Among the false doctrines dealt with in the epistle are: (a) the denial of the deity of Jesus (2: 1); (b) sensuality in the name of religion (2: 1ff.); (c) a disposition to be disrespectful of dignitaries (2: 10-12); (d) a repudiation of the teaching of the apostles regarding the judgment, the end of the world, and the dissolution of the heavens and the earth.

PERSONS TO WHOM WRITTEN

Both epistles of Peter were addressed to the same persons: "This is now, beloved, the second epistle that I write unto you; and in both of them I stir up your sincere mind by putting you in remembrance." (2 Pet. 3: 1.) The first epistle was written to saints sojourning in Asia Minor: "Peter, an apostle of Jesus Christ, to the elect who are sojourners of the Dispersion in Pontus, Galatia, Cappadocia, Asia, and Bithynia. . . ." (1 Pet. 1: 1, 2.)

TIME AND PLACE OF WRITING

It is not possible to determine, with any degree of certainty, either *when,* or *where,* the second epistle of Peter was written. The letter itself contains no data sufficient to reach a definite conclusion regarding these matters; and the effort is, therefore, speculative. From the fact that the King James Version has the apostle saying that he must shortly put off his tabernacle (2 Pet. 1: 14), it has led to the assumption that it was written very near his death. A correct translation of the word *tachine* (swiftly, rather than shortly), however, points to the suddenness with which death would descend upon the apostle, rather than the nearness of its approach. It is, on the other hand, certain that Peter was advanced in years when he penned these words, and realized that death, in the natural order of events, could not be far distant. We may therefore assume that the epistle was written soon after the first, perhaps A.D. 64 or 65. From the fact that no reference is made to the place from which it was written, and that the apostle was in Babylon when he wrote the first letter, it is proper to assume that he was still in that city. The traditions of the Roman church are, on the question, biased and thus utterly unreliable. Evidence that Peter was ever in Rome does not exist; and the claims of Catholics in this matter are as unjustifiable as their assumption that Peter founded the See of Rome and was its first occupant.

A COMMENTARY ON THE SECOND EPISTLE OF PETER

SECTION ONE

INTRODUCTION
1: 1, 2

1 [1]Simon Peter, a [2]servant and apostle of Jesus Christ, to them that have obtained [3]a like precious faith with us in the righteousness of [4]our God and

---
[1]Many ancient authorities read *Symeon.* See Acts 15. 14.
[2]Gr. *bondservant.*
[3]Gr. *an equally precious.*
[4]Or, *our God and Saviour* Comp. ver. 11; 2. 20; 3. 18; Tit. 2. 13.

---

1 Simon Peter,—In the first epistle, the author designates himself by the name "Peter" only; here, he joins to that designation the Jewish name Simon by which he was known when called into the service of the Lord. See 1 Pet. 1: 1 and comments thereunder on the significance and origin of the names of the apostle.

A servant and apostle of Jesus Christ,—While this precise reference is peculiar to Peter, Paul uses a similar one in Titus 1: 1. "Servant" is, literally, "bond-slave" *(doulos)*, one who "gives himself up wholly to another's will" (Thayer), i.e., devotion to the utter disregard of one's own interests. The word "apostle" indicates the sphere of service into which the devotion led him. See the word fully explained in the comments on 1 Pet. 1: 1.

To them that have obtained a like precious faith with us—"With us" embraces the Jewish Christians; "to them," the Gentile Christians. "Like precious" is, more accurately, "equally precious," thus indicating that the "faith" which had been made available to the Gentiles admitted them to the same precious privileges vouchsafed to the Jews. "Faith" in this passage is not subjective; it does not refer to belief; it is objective, being synonymous with *the gospel.* It is used here in the same sense as in Gal. 1: 23, where it is said that Paul preached "the faith" he once destroyed. This conclusion follows from the fact that the verb "obtained" *(lagchano)* denotes that which is received by lot, by fortune, by divine appointment, and not through human exertion or merit. The word is translated "lot" in Luke 1: 9, "portion" in Acts 1: 17.

the Saviour Jesus Christ: 2 Grace to you and peace be multiplied in the knowledge of God and of Jesus our Lord; 3 seeing that his divine power hath granted unto us all things that pertain unto life and godliness, through the knowledge of him that called us [5]by his own glory and virtue; 4 whereby

[5]Some ancient authorities read *through glory and virtue.*

In the righteousness of our God and the Saviour Jesus Christ:—"Righteousness" here is the righteous dealing of God in providing equal blessings for both Jew and Gentile in Christ. (Acts 15: 9.) Righteousness is an essential attribute of God; whatever he does is right. (Acts 10: 34.)

2 Grace to you and peace be multiplied in the knowledge of God and of Jesus our Lord;—See comments under 1 Pet. 1: 2. "Knowledge" in the text is not translated from the ordinary Greek word for knowledge—*gnosis*—but is from *epignosis*, knowledge toward an object, ever maturing, but never matured. Grace and peace are multiplied—made to abound—in this knowledge. It involves much more than the possession of facts; it includes the idea of deep and loving contemplation of matters too profound for complete mastery. The word often occurs in the New Testament.

EXHORTATION TO GROWTH IN GRACE
1: 3-11

3 Seeing that his divine power hath granted unto us all things that pertain to life and godliness,—These words are to be closely construed with verse 2. On our part there is no occasion for alarm that we will not be properly supplied seeing that all things pertaining to life and godliness have been granted us. "Life" refers to the spiritual vigor which the soul possesses; "godliness" to the conduct necessary to preserve and maintain it. This verse is a clear affirmation of the sufficiency of God's revelation to man, as well as an unmistakable assurance that every need of every kind will be supplied.

Through the knowledge of him that called us by his own glory and virtue;—"Knowledge" here is from the same word as in verse 2. This grant of all things needful is supplied through this knowledge. (John 17: 3.) The manner in which Christians are called by his glory and virtue is explained by Paul in Eph. 1: 17ff.

he hath granted unto us his precious and exceeding great promises; that through these ye may become partakers of ᵃthe divine nature, having escaped from the corruption that is in the world by lust. 5 Yea, and for this very cause adding on your part all diligence, in your faith supply virtue; and in

ᵃOr, a

4 Whereby he hath granted unto us his precious and exceeding great promises;—It is through the glory and the virtue mentioned in the preceding verse that these precious and exceeding great promises have been vouchsafed to man. The promises are precious because of what they mean to the human soul; and they are exceeding great because they include forgiveness, peace, the promise of eternal life and a share in the divine nature.

That through these ye may become partakers of the divine nature, having escaped from the corruption that is in the world by lusts.—The word for "partakers" *(koinonoi)* is, literally, "sharers," "partners," and points to the relationship which Christians sustain to the Lord. By availing themselves of these precious and exceeding great promises they are privileged to share in the divine nature—the holy character which God possesses. The chastening and disciplining to which children of God are subjected in this life is for the purpose of enabling them to be "partakers of his holiness." (Heb. 12: 10.) Man was originally created in the image, and after the likeness, of God (Gen. 1: 26); but this image and rational likeness was lost in the fall. It is restored to man in the transformation which occurs in conversion. (2 Cor. 3: 18; Col. 3: 10.) "Having escaped the corruption that is in the world through lust," is, in the Greek text, "having escaped from the corruption that is *in* the world *in* lust." The meaning is, that corruption is in the world; it operates through lust; and only those who are partakers of the divine nature escape its ravages. The second clause of the verse sets forth the positive side of Christianity; the third, the negative side.

5 Yea, and for this very cause adding on your part all diligence,—An exhortation based on premises drawn from verse 4. "Because of the precious and exceeding great promises which are yours, be adding on your part all diligence." "Adding on your part" translates a remarkable word *(pareisenegkantes)* occurring nowhere else in the Greek Testament, and meaning, literally,

your virtue knowledge; 6 and in *your* knowledge self-control; and in *your*

"bringing in by the side of." The term indicates the comparative unimportance of man's participation in his salvation by suggesting that his part is merely contributory, "brought in by the side of what God does," and yet is absolutely essential, since God's part is done only on condition that man complies with his. In view of the absolute necessity of man's contribution by the side of what God does, Peter admonishes "all diligence." "Diligence" is from *spoude,* to hasten. All children of God are thus exhorted to hasten to bring in their part, though small and insigificant compared with what God does for us, in order that they may avail themselves of the blessings which the Father has made available to them. That in which diligence is particularly enjoined follows.

In your faith supply virtue;—"Without faith it is impossible to please God" (Heb. 11: 6); hence, it is the foundation and the source from which all other duties spring. The word "supply" (from the Greek *epichoregeo*) is highly suggestive and interesting in the implications which follow from its origin. Originally it meant to found and support a chorus, to lead a choir, to keep in tune, and then, to supply or provide. As here used, the graces which adorn the Christian's character are to be chorused into a grand symphony to the delight and pleasure of him who fashioned and made us for his own good pleasure. It will be seen that there are eight of the graces, and that they thus form an octave of soul tones, the first being faith, the last love, an octave higher. When these are harmonized and played on by the divine Spirit, disharmony disappears and life's discords vanish. How we should rejoice that we have been privileged to provide such an instrument in the hand of our God!

"Virtue" *(arete)* which faith supplies is courage and soul vigor, the manliness and the determination to do that which is right.

And in your virtue knowledge;—As faith is to supply virtue, virtue is to supply knowledge, knowledge is to supply self-control, and so through the entire list of graces mentioned. Each thus becomes an instrument by which that which follows is to be wrought out and perfected. "Knowledge" *(gnosis)* is the discrimination indicated in Eph. 5: 17 and Heb. 5: 14. This knowledge is gained by, and grows out of, the practice of virtue.

self-control ⁷patience; and in *your* ⁷patience godliness; 7 and in *your* godliness ⁸*brotherly* kindness; and in *your* ⁸brotherly kindness love. 8 For if

⁷Or, *stedfastness*
⁸Gr. *love of the brethren.*

6 And in your knowledge self-control;—The familiar "temperance" of the King James Version has properly given way to the more accurate rendering "self-control." The word is derived from *en* and *krates,* "one who holds himself in." It denotes self-government, discipline, the ability of one to control his own life. It is acquired through the exercise of discernment, the knowledge by which one differentiates between right and wrong, and thus develops from it. One possessed of such knowledge and being thus equipped to identify evil is able to avoid it.

And in your self-control patience;—The word translated patience here is more nearly endurance, inasmuch as it suggests somewhat more than mere resignation to life's difficulties. It includes the idea of positive resistance of evils and a stedfast bearing up under them. Self-control leads to and perfects patient endurance, because only those who discipline themselves are able to endure patiently the trials of life.

And in your patience godliness;—"Godliness" *(eusebeia)* is humble reverence and deep piety toward God. Often unbelievers manifest a stoical patience toward the adversities of life, but without the motive which springs from respect and devotion toward God. Patience is approved only when it results in submission to the burdens of life for the sake of pleasing the Father. The desire to be godlike is the motive from which all our actions should originate, and without which there can be no acceptable service rendered to God.

7 And in your godliness brotherly kindness;—"Brotherly kindness" is from the Greek word *philadelphia,* literally, love of the brethren. As God is our Father, his children are our brethren, and the obligation to love them is clear and explicit: "And whosoever loveth him that begat loveth him also that is begotten of him." (1 John 5: 1.)

And in your brotherly kindness love.—A warmhearted affection for the brethren is to lead to love, love not only for the brethren, but all men, love—the crown and jewel of all graces. "And the greatest of these is love." (1 Cor. 13: 13.) Its right to occupy this foremost position among all the graces is further evidenced by Paul to the Colossians: "And above all these things put on love, which is the bond of perfectness." (Col. 3: 14.)

It is important to observe that it was the apostle's intention to indicate that each of these graces grows out of, and is produced by, the one which precedes it. Before each grace mentioned, the verb "supply" is to be understood. Each creates and makes possible the next; each tempers and makes perfect that which goes before it. The preposition *in* which he attaches to each indicates that the grace which follows is included in the one which precedes it, and is thus produced by it. The list of graces enumerated may be analyzed as follows: (1) Those which are necessary to form the Christian character: virtue, knowledge, self-control, patience; (2) that which reveals the follower of Christ to be a servant of God (godliness), a member of the family of God (brotherly kindness), and well disposed toward all men (love). From this we learn that no grace can stand alone; each is possessed only as it is able to produce and make permanent in the life of others without which the Christian character cannot exist.

8 For if these things are yours and abound, they make you to be not idle nor unfruitful unto the knowledge of our Lord Jesus Christ.—"Are yours" is a better translation than the "in you" of the King James Version, since the verb conveys the idea of a permanent possession rather than a mere indwelling of the graces designated. These graces are to become an integral part of Christian character and to reproduce themselves in the manifold acts of the Christian life as they "abound" (better, *multiply)* to that end. Thus activated, one is neither idle nor unfruitful; the trend of his life is toward the "full knowledge" *(epignosis)* of the higher life of the spirit. Thus full, or complete, knowledge is the goal toward which all Christian service tends, and which may be reached in no other way. Either one abounds in good works, or his life is idle and fruitless. There is no alternative.

9 For he that lacketh these things is blind, seeing only what is near, having forgotten the cleansing from his old sins.

eth these things is blind, ⁹seeing only what is near, having forgotten the cleansing from his old sins. 10 Wherefore, brethren, give the more diligence to make your calling and election sure: for if ye do these things, ye shall

⁹Or, *closing his eyes*

—"For" is causal and indicates the sequence of thought intended by the apostle. We are to possess the Christian graces and allow them to multiply in good works unto the knowledge of Christ, *for* if we do not do so we suffer an impairment of sight making it impossible for us to discern the most elementary matters of the Christian life. The words "seeing only what is near" are from the Greek *muopadzo,* and used of one who is able to see only by constantly blinking his eyes and keeping them partially closed. One so afflicted closes his eyes, not to keep from seeing, but in order that he may be able to see, his myoptic condition rendering him unable to look directly into the light. Thus hindered in his vision, distant objects are to him indistinct, and he sees only that which is near. In this figurative fashion Peter pictures for us the man deficient spiritually and hence able to see only the things about him—the world and its affairs—having lost the power to look into the future and see by faith beyond the gate of life eternal.

Such a one has forgotten the cleansing he received from his old sins when he was baptized (Acts 2: 38; 22: 16; 1 Pet. 3: 21), because he is no longer influenced by such recollection. His attitude is so much the same as before he was baptized that he regards himself as in his original condition of sin. The words "having forgotten" are from an unusual phrase, occurring only here in the New Testament, *lethen labon,* signifying "having received or accepted forgetfulness." By a voluntary act such a one has adopted an attitude of forgetfulness toward his former obedience. The meaning is that one who does not supply in his faith the graces mentioned accepts a situation in life wherein he disregards the fact that he was once purged (cleansed, forgiven) of his sins.

10 **Wherefore, brethren, give the more diligence to make your calling and election sure:**—"Wherefore," i.e., in view of the matters set forth in verses 5-9, "give the more diligence. . . ." "Diligence" here, as in verse 5, means "to hasten," and the exhortation is to more *(mallon)* haste, greater zeal and earnestness in the pursuit of those qualities essential to the Christian life. The

infinitive *to make* is significant, and is translated, not from *poiein*, absolutely to make or do a thing man is incapable of, respecting his salvation, but from *poiesthai*, present middle infinitive, to make or to do for one's self. Unable to fashion a plan by which to save himself, man may and must comply with God's plan in order to his salvation. Salvation is indeed a "calling" and an "election"; it is God who calls and elects; but he calls by his gospel (2 Thess. 2: 13, 14), and he elects only those who place themselves in the way of salvation through obedience to his will (Matt. 7: 21). Election and calling never operate to destroy the free agency of man. God's grace is not irresistible; man may make it void (Gal. 2: 21) and receive it in vain (2 Cor. 6: 1). God's calling is the invitation *(klesis)*; the election *(ekloge)* is man's acceptance. This calling and election is to be made sure (actually, *secure*), and this is done through human instrumentality. Here is a thorough and decisive refutation of the doctrine of the impossibility of apostasy. It is impossible to make secure that which has never been in doubt.

For if ye do these things, ye shall never stumble:—"If," i.e., on condition that you do these things—supply in your faith the graces hereinbefore enumerated. Those who thus do have an effective defence against falling; they shall never stumble *(ptaio*, to strike one's foot against an object and fall).

11 For thus shall be richly supplied unto you the entrance into the eternal kingdom of our Lord and Saviour Jesus Christ. —The verb "supplied" is translated from the same word as "supply" in verse 5, where see comments. There is a designed correspondence between the words "supply" and "abound" in verses 5 and 8 and the words "supplied" and "richly" here. We are to supply the virtues mentioned, and God will supply the entrance into the eternal kingdom; we are to abound in these graces and he will richly provide his part. The kingdom is styled "eternal" because it will never end. The blessings which it contains will never fail. Because it is described as the kingdom "of our Lord and Saviour Jesus Christ," we are not to conclude that Christ will reign as king over it after the second coming. At the end of this, the Christian dispensation, and following the resurrection and the general judgment he will abdicate in favor of his Father: "But each in his own order: Christ the firstfruits; then they that are Christ's at his coming. Then cometh the end, when he shall deliver up the kingdom to God, even the Father; when he shall have abolished all rule and all authority and power." (1 Cor. 15: 23, 24.) "Kingdom of our Lord. . . ." is genitive of the agent, and not of possession, and it designates the kingdom which was established through his direction on the first Pentecost following his resurrection. It is styled "eternal" because it shall stand forever.

SOURCE OF THEIR KNOWLEDGE
1: 12-21

12 Wherefore I shall be ready always to put you in remembrance of these things, though ye know them, and are established in the truth which is with *you*. 13 And I think it right, as long as I am in this tabernacle, to stir you

12 Wherefore I shall be ready always to put you in remembrance of these things, though ye know them, and are established in the truth which is in you.—The meaning, in the light of the connection in which the verse appears, is, In order that the blessings and privileges of Christ's kingdom may be yours, I shall not fail to exhort you with reference to those duties and responsibilities which you sustain, though you are aware of them and are established in the truth. There are two distinct phases in the Christian ministry: (1) preaching the gospel to the untaught and (2) exhorting those who have been taught to greater faithfulness and zeal in the matters which they have received. Man is by nature very prone to forget the lessons of the past, and truth once received may become dim and indistinct to those whose hearts incline toward the world. There is therefore a weighty responsibility upon those who preach and teach the word to be tireless in exhorting to greater fidelity and devotion to the cause which they have espoused. The only guarantee against apostasy is ceaseless vigilance against error and constant instruction of those who have received the truth.

13 And I think it right, as long as I am in this tabernacle, to stir you up by putting you in remembrance;—His obligation to stir them up by putting them in remembrance of their duties was a continuing one and would terminate only with his death. The "tabernacle" to which he refers is used figuratively of his

up by putting you in remembrance; 14 knowing that the putting off of my tabernacle cometh swiftly, even as our Lord Jesus Christ signified unto me. 15 Yea, I will give diligence that at every time ye may be able after my

fleshly body. By implication, the word suggests the immortality of the soul, the transient nature of this earthly existence, and the ease with which the spirit throws aside at death its tenement of clay. Paul refers to the body by this term (2 Cor. 5: 1-2), and as Peter does here and in the verse which follows, mixes the figure by referring to the body as a building (tabernacle), and then as a garment which must be put off.

14 Knowing that the putting off of my tabernacle cometh swiftly, even as our Lord Jesus Christ signified unto me.—The familiar King James rendering, "knowing that *shortly* I must put off this my tabernacle," makes the apostle to say that the time of his departure draws near and that death was rapidly approaching. The Revised Version more correctly conveys the meaning of the original text. He did not say that he must soon put aside his tabernacle, but that the putting off, when it did come, would be sudden and swift. The verb "signified" is translated from a Greek aorist and indicates a definite time in the apostle's mind when this information was revealed to him. In John 21: 18, 19, the Lord had said to him: "Verily, verily, I say unto thee, When thou wast young, thou girdest thyself, and walkest whither thou wouldest: but when thou shall be old, thou shalt stretch forth thy hands, and another shall gird thee, and carry thee whither thou wouldest not. Now this he spake, signifying by what manner of death he should glorify God." While this text refers primarily to the swiftness with which death would come, Peter was by now an old man and must have known that in the natural order of events death could not be far distant.

15 Yea, I will give diligence that at every time ye may be able after my decease to call these things to remembrance.—In the word "diligence" of this verse the apostle looks back to verse 10. As he had urged diligence upon them, he would not be forgetful to exercise the same in their behalf by leaving an inspired record of instruction for their continued edification after his death. Two words of great significance occur in this section relating to the genuineness of the epistle of Second Peter. *Skene,* translated

[10]decease to call these things to remembrance. 16 For we did not follow cunningly devised fables, when we made known unto you the power and [11]coming of our Lord Jesus Christ, but we were eyewitnesses of his majesty.

[10]Or, *departure*
[11]Gr. *presence*.

tabernacle, and *exodus*, decease, occur in the narrative of the transfiguration. (Luke 9: 31.) Peter was present and powerfully impressed with the events there occurring, and in the use of these terms he gives an undesigned guarantee of the genuineness of the record and the authenticity of the matters recorded.

16 For we did not follow cunningly devised fables, when we made known unto you the power and coming of our Lord Jesus Christ, but we were eyewitnesses of his majesty.—In the verses immediately preceding this, Peter wrote of the things which he was doing; here, he passes from the singular "I" to the plural "we" as he describes matters which involved not only himself, but the other apostles, James and John. (Matt. 17: 1-8; Mark 9: 2-9; Luke 9: 28-36.) The verb "follow" in the text, from the compound *ex-akoloutheo*, means to take the lead and follow the direction of another; and as here used with the negative, is highly significant in that in it the writer clearly disavows secondhand sources of information regarding that about which he was testifying, affirming instead that he and those with him were eyewitnesses. "Fables" *(muthoi)* are myths, legends, fictitious stories without basis of fact. The words "cunningly devised" are from the verb *sophizo,* to invent artificially, to devise artfully. Thus, in making known the power and coming of the Lord, the apostles were not influenced by men who had deceived them by skillfully told fictitious stories, but were themselves eyewitnesses of the things alleged. The word translated "eyewitnesses" *(epoptes)* was current at the time Peter wrote of those who were initiated into the highest order of mysteries of the heathen religions. Such were styled "beholders" (from the word *epopteuo)* from the fact that they had attained to the highest degree possible. This word the apostle adopted to indicate that he, along with James and John, had been admitted to the highest degree of evidence in being privileged to see with their own eyes the glory and majesty of the transfigured Saviour.

The manner in which the power and coming of the Saviour were

17 For he ¹²received from God the Father honor and glory, when there was borne such a voice to him by the Majestic Glory, This is my beloved Son, in whom I am well pleased: 18 and this voice we *ourselves* heard borne out of heaven, when we were with him in the holy mount. 19 And we have the

¹²Gr. *having received.*

---

revealed was both oral and written. This was a familiar theme both in their writing and in their preaching, and the New Testament is filled with it. (Matt. 24: 3; 1 Cor. 15: 23; 1 Thess. 2: 19, etc.) The apostle had written of the matter in his first epistle. (1: 7, 13; 4: 13.) The "coming" referred to is his second advent *(parousia,* presence) when he shall judge the living and the dead. (Matt. 25: 31-46.)

17 For he received from God the Father honor and glory, when there was borne such a voice to him by the Majestic Glory, This is my beloved Son, in whom I am well pleased:— The "honor" which was conferred upon him was the announcement which came from heaven that he was God's Son; and the "glory" he experienced was the transfiguration he underwent when his face shone above the brightness of the Syrian sun. The "majestic glory" from which the Voice which acknowledged his deity was borne was the Shekinah, the visible presence of God. In the Greek translation of Deut. 33: 26, God is described as "the majestic One of the firmament." The Voice which was heard was God speaking, and it came from his divine presence.

Affirmed in the announcement was (a) the deity of Jesus; (b) his relationship to God; (c) the intimacy which obtained between God and his Son; and (d) God's good pleasure in Jesus. The tense of the verb in the latter clause of this verse emphasizes that this pleasure had existed from all eternity. (Cf. Matt. 3: 17; 12: 18.)

18 And this voice we ourselves heard borne out of heaven, when we were with him in the holy mount.—To emphasize the personal connection which he and James and John sustained to the events which he relates, Peter repeats the pronoun and makes it emphatic: this voice we ourselves—and no other—heard. Further, it was when they *were with him* that the events he records transpired, thus making them personal witness of that recorded. It is styled a "holy mount" because of the significance of the events

word of prophecy *made* more sure; whereunto ye do well that ye take heed,

there occurring. (Cf. "holy hill of Zion," Psalm 15: 1; "holy ground of Horeb," Ex. 3: 5.) The exact location and identity of the mount of transfiguration is unknown. The context places Jesus in the vicinity of Mount Hermon shortly before this time (Matt. 16: 13; 17: 1), though the later tradition is that he was transfigured on Mount Taber. The location, at this date, cannot be definitely determined.

19 And we have the word of prophecy made more sure; whereunto ye do well that ye take heed,—The "word of prophecy," literally, "the prophetic word" *(ton prophetikon logon)*, refers to the revelations received and recorded by the Old Testament prophets. (Verse 21.) The apostle thus affirms, "And we have the prophetic word more sure." More sure than what? Many expositors assume that the comparison which the apostle draws is between the transfiguration scene which he had witnessed during the personal ministry of Christ and the prophetic word which he mentions, thus making him to say that these prophecies were more convincing and constituted better evidence of the deity of Jesus than that which he had just related concerning his experiences in the "holy mount." Such was the view of the King James translators, hence their rendering, "We have also a more sure word of prophecy." Had the apostle been writing exclusively of others, it is barely possible that he might have intended to convey such an idea; it will, however, be seen that he includes himself—in the personal pronoun *we*—among those who have the prophetic word more sure. It is inconceivable that Peter could have regarded any evidence, whatever the source, as more convincing than that which he received on the occasion of the Lord's transfiguration. He saw the light above the brightness of the noonday sun flash about the Saviour. He looked upon the transfigured face of his Lord with his own eyes. He witnessed the appearance of Moses and Elijah, and was so enraptured with the scene that he wanted to build three tabernacles there. He heard the Voice from heaven identify Jesus as deity. Surely no word of Isaiah, Jeremiah, Daniel, or other Old Testament prophet could have supplied more irrefutable and convincing evidence than this. A more reasonable and satisfactory

as unto a lamp shining in a ¹dark place, until the day dawn, and the day-star

---

¹Gr. *squalid*.

---

view—and that which the American Standard translators adopted, as their translation indicates—is that the word of prophecy was made more sure and further confirmed by that which he had witnessed, and which he was, in turn, passing on to his readers. Being additional evidence, it would serve to strengthen, to corroborate, and to make more sure the faith already existing which, in the final analysis, was based on the testimony of the Old Testament prophets. The transfiguration scene confirmed the testimony of these prophets concerning the deity of Jesus, and established more clearly the relationship which obtains between God and his Son. The testimony of these prophets was thus made more sure by that which Peter, James, and John had witnessed in the holy mount, and which Peter was then reciting.

"Whereunto" is dative of the relative and refers to the prophetic word. To this prophetic word Peter's readers would do well to take heed. "To take heed" is, literally, to give attention to, to fix the mind upon. The participle (*prosechontes*) is present, hence suggesting continuous and uninterrupted action, "Whereunto ye do well to keep on taking heed. . . ." The testimony which he had given regarding the transfiguration was not designed to supplant the evidence which the prophets supplied of the deity and identity of the Lord, but to confirm and strengthen it.

As unto a lamp shining in a dark place, until the day dawn, and the day-star arise in your hearts:—The term translated "dark place" is that which denotes a squalid, filthy, and dark dungeon, a fitting description of the condition which characterizes men without the light of truth. Into such a world the lamp of prophecy sheds its light bringing hope and cheer. To such a lamp Peter's readers were to look "until the day" should dawn through the gloom of night and the daystar (Christ) should shed its full brilliance upon them. It is not likely that there is any reference here to the second coming of Christ. The meaning is rather that as darkness flees before the light, so the gloom of a sinful world fades as the daystar is allowed to throw its light upon the heart. As the appearance of the daystar heralds the approach of day, so the re-

arise in your hearts: 20 knowing this first, that no prophecy of scripture is

ception of the prophecies—confirmed by the story of the transfiguration—would light up the gloom of the world and bring happiness to all who allow themselves to be bathed in its refulgent beams.

20 Knowing this first, that no prophecy of scripture is of private interpretation.—The words "knowing this first" would be better rendered "this first understanding. . . ." As a primary requisite to the study of prophecy, it must be recognized that it is not of "private interpretation." "Prophecy of scripture" refers to all prophecy whether in the Old Testament or the New. The verb "is" in this passage is of significance and sheds much light on the meaning of the passage. It is translated from the verb *ginomai*, to become, to spring into being, and not from the simple and ordinary *eimi*, is. The meaning is, No prophecy comes or springs into existence by means of private interpretation. "Private" *(idias)* refers to that which is peculiarly one's own; and "interpretation" is from *epilusis*, explanation, exposition. It follows, then, that no prophecy of the scripture came into existence merely as the result of the prophet's own personal explanation, but originated, as he points out in the verse which follows, by holy men of God who were influenced by the Holy Spirit. Since the prophecy of scripture is not a product of those who delivered it, nor did it originate as expositions of their own intellects, but came by the inspiration of the Spirit of God, Peter's readers would indeed do well to give heed thereto," as unto a lamp shining in a dark place."

Catholics, in an effort to support their doctrine of the right of the pope to interpret all scripture for them, cite this passage for the purpose of showing that it is impossible to understand the Bible without infallible aid. Their effort in this is reduced to an absurdity; for, either (a) one can understand this passage, and their contention is shown to be false; or (b) if it is impossible to understand *any* scripture unaided, then one cannot understand *this* passage, and they stand guilty of admitting as evidence that which they concede is impossible to understand. If one can understand this verse, their theory is false; if one cannot understand it, how do they know that it teaches that one cannot understand the scriptures? The private interpretation refers, not to those who read

of ²private interpretation. 21 For no prophecy ever ³came by the will of man: but men spake from God, being moved by the Holy Spirit.

²Or, *special*
³Gr. *was brought.*

the prophecy, but to those who delivered it—the prophets themselves. The passage teaches nothing about men interpreting or explaining the scriptures, but deals exclusively with the manner in which the prophets received and delivered the messages for which they were instruments in the hands of God. Often they themselves did not understand the significance of the things which they spoke. (1 Pet. 1: 10-12.)

21 **For no prophecy ever came by the will of man: but men spake from God, being moved from the Holy Spirit.**—"For" (*gar*) introduces the reason for the statement of the preceding verse, that no prophecy of scripture had its origin in the prophet's own mind. Instead, it is affirmed that (a) men spake *from God;* and (b) those who thus spake were *moved* by the Holy Spirit. "Moved" is from *pheromenoi,* present passive participle of *phero,* to bear; hence, to be borne along as a sailing vessel before the wind. The prophets are thus declared to be passive instruments in the hand of God, being directed in what they wrote by the Holy Spirit. Since the prophecies are not of human origin; since they did not originate in the will of man; and since they were delivered by men of God who spake as they were moved by the Holy Spirit, they have the weightiest possible claims on our reverence, our most serious consideration and prayerful study.

SECTION TWO

WARNING AGAINST FALSE TEACHERS
2: 1-11

1 But there arose false prophets also among the people, as among you also there shall be false teachers, who shall privily bring in ⁴destructive heresies, denying even the Master that bought them, bringing upon themselves

⁴Or, *sects of perdition*

1 **But there arose false prophets also among the people, as among you also there shall be false teachers,**—The word "but" with which this verse begins puts it in contrast with matters dealt with at the close of the preceding chapter. There, the apostle had emphasized the fact that the prophetic word is a product of inspiration; that it was delivered by men who spake from God; and that those who thus spoke were moved to do so by the Holy Spirit. Lest from this his readers should conclude that all who affected to be prophets were thus influenced, he hastened to add that as in times past false prophets had risen to lead the people of Israel astray (Deut. 14: 1-5; Isa. 9: 15; Jer. 14: 14; Ezek. 13: 3; Zech. 13: 4), so false teachers were to be expected among them. Such teachers constituted a constant menace to the early church, and many warnings against them appear in the New Testament. (Matt. 24: 5, 24; Acts 20: 29, 30; 1 Tim. 4: 1ff.; 2 Tim. 4: 1ff.; 1 John 4: 1.)

Who shall privily bring in destructive heresies, denying even the Master that bought them, bringing upon themselves swift destruction.—"Who" refers to the false teachers mentioned in the second clause of the verse. "Privily" *(Pareisago)* means to slip in by the side of, and indicates that these teachers had artfully and slyly introduced their false doctrines by the side of the truth in such fashion as to deceive those who had accepted them. Such doctrines are described as "destructive heresies." They were heretical, because they were false; and they were destructive from the fact that they brought ruin upon all who accepted them, as well as upon those who propagated them. The doctrine to which Peter particularly alludes here led people to deny "the Master who bought them." (1 Cor. 6: 20; Heb. 10: 29.) There were many heresies afloat near the close of the first century, all tending to this end. The Lord's *deity* was questioned by some

swift destruction. 2 And many shall follow their lascivious doings; by reason of whom the way of the truth shall be evil spoken of. 3 And in covetousness shall they with feigned words make merchandise of you: whose sentence now from of old lingereth not, and their destruction slumbereth not.

(1 John 4: 15), his *humanity* by others (1 John 4: 2). Some teachers then, as now, denied the threefold personality of the godhead, maintaining that there is but one person, with three manifestations. Others held to the doctrine that the body of Christ was not real, but only imaginary; while still others, by their wicked and corrupt lives, denied their Master by using their bodies as their own and not his. Reference to denying the Lord by Peter is significant, in the light of his own previous conduct. To him this involved the greatest possible apostasy. But when Peter denied his Lord, the price of redemption had not been paid. How much graver the offense of those who today treat with contempt that precious purchase price! (Acts 20: 28.)

2 **And many shall follow their lascivious doings; by reason of whom the way of the truth shall be evil spoken of.**—The word "lasciviousness" *(aselgeia)* refers to unbridled lust, abandoned actions of the flesh, extreme wantonness, dissolute habits and all unclean living. These teachers of whom Peter wrote made a religion of lust, and while confounding Christian liberty with license, preached the gospel of libertinism. Errors which allow such liberty have ever been attractive to those who live for the world, and many were led to adopt such and to follow willingly and gladly those who propagated them. In consequence, the "way of truth" was evil spoken of, i.e., reviled, blasphemed. Many unbelievers did not run to such excesses, and failing to distinguish between those professors and those who taught the truth, they regarded such conduct as the usual and ordinary fruits of Christianity, and held the institution of Christianity itself in contempt.

3 **And in covetousness shall they with feigned words make merchandise of you:**—Covetousness—unlawful desire for personal gain—was the motive which influenced these false teachers; and thus motivated, they used feigned words—words artfully and skillfully forged for the occasion—to deceive those whom they could. These teachers "made merchandise" of their dupes by treating them as merchandise, i.e., as objects by which to enhance

4 For if God spared not angels when they sinned, but ⁵cast them down to ⁶hell, and committed them to ⁷pits of darkness, to be reserved unto judgment;

⁵Or, *cast them into dungeons*
⁶Gr. *Tartarus*.
⁷Some ancient authorities read *chains*. Comp. Wisd. 17. 17.

their own wealth. Such proselyted only that they might profit, and promised what they could never deliver from motives of greed and avarice. (See 1 Tim. 6: 5; Tit. 1: 11.)

Whose sentence now from of old lingereth not, and their destruction slumbereth not.—Being evildoers, and therefore under the ban of all who disobey God, their destiny was definite and their damnation sure. (Phil. 3: 19.) Peter solemnly assured his readers that such would not be delayed nor forgotten. "Lingereth not" is from *ouk argei,* is not idle; and "slumbereth not" is from *ou nustazei,* does not nod, thus signifying that these deceivers and all those whom they deceived were hastening toward a judgment and a destiny that did not loiter on the way nor nod off to sleep in forgetfulness!

4 For if God spared not angels when they sinned,—In proof of the proposition that judgment against the wicked is inevitable, Peter cites three well-known instances: (1) angels who sinned; (2) the destruction of the old world in the flood; and (3) the overthrow of the cities of the plain. Angels are created beings, "sent forth to do service for the sake of them that shall inherit salvation." (Heb. 1: 14.) They are moral creatures and answerable to God for their conduct, though apparently outside the redemptive provisions of grace. (Heb. 2: 16.) Thus, when they sin, they are beyond the possibility of salvation. These, despite their rank, the honorable position they occupied, and the holiness they possessed when created, sinned and were not spared. What the *nature* of their sin was *when* they sinned and the *number* of those sinning is not stated. Much speculation has been indulged in regarding the matter. There is a popular view that Gen. 6: 2-4 involves an unholy association between angels and women, and that the sin of the angels was fornication "with the daughters of men." This exposition is based on an erroneous view of Gen. 6: 1-4. There is no reference to angels in that passage. The "sons of God" were human beings. Others, with more reason, have concluded that these angels were the same as those alluded to by Jude when he

5 and spared not the ancient world, but preserved Noah with seven others, ᵃa preacher of righteousness, when he brought a flood upon the world of the

ᵃGr. *a herald.*

said that "they kept not their own principality, but left their proper habitation," and are kept "in everlasting bonds under darkness unto the judgment of the great day." (Jude 6.) Some hold to the view that Satan was a created angel; that he led a revolt in heaven (Rev. 12: 7); that the occasion for the revolt was spiritual pride and a desire for higher position (1 Tim. 3: 6); and that for such arrogance and presumption he was cast out of heaven. Inasmuch as it is inconceivable that God created these angels wicked, the following conclusions seem certain: (a) they were originally holy; (b) they sinned; (c) the occasion of their sin was in abandoning their "proper habitation"; (d) as a result they were thrust down to a place of bondage. What this place was is designated in the clause which follows.

But cast them down to hell, and committed them to pits of darkness, to be reserved unto judgment;—The word translated "hell" here, *tartarosas,* does not occur elsewhere in the Greek New Testament. The word is used in Greek mythology of the place of restraint and punishment for the souls of wicked men after death. It seems likely that Peter, writing in Greek, and to people who would be disposed to understand the words of the language in their ordinary signification, here used the word in its usual import, and that by it he intended to convey the idea that these wicked angels were thrust down to such an abode to await the judgment of the great day. Inasmuch as the nature of the place is the same as that which characterized the rich man in torment in Hades, separated by a great gulf from the righteous there (Luke 16: 23-26), it is reasonable to assume that the places are the same, and that *tartarus* is that compartment in the Hadean realm where wicked spirits are reserved (kept in restraint) until the day of their final condemnation is at hand. The place is described as "pits of darkness," from the fact that darkness is the condition which there prevails. The word "pit," from the Greek *seiros,* denotes an underground opening or den.

5 **And spared not the ancient world, but preserved Noah with seven others, a preacher of righteousness, when he**

ungodly; 6 and turning the cities of Sodom and Gomorrah into ashes condemned them with an overthrow, having made them an example unto those

brought a flood upon the world of the ungodly;—The argument—an *a fortiori* one—continues, and the apostle offers the second illustration of the certainty of judgment upon the wicked. The "ancient world" embraced the people who lived before the flood. Though these people had clear and unmistakable warnings of impending doom, and despite the fact that the time provided them was ample to flee from the destruction which threatened them, they spurned Jehovah's offer of amnesty and died. Only Noah and his family, consisting of his wife, his three sons and their wives, were saved. (Gen. 7: 7; 1 Pet. 3: 20.) The account of the flood is recorded in Gen. 6: 13-8: 19. Noah is called a preacher of righteousness (Psalm 119: 172), from the fact that he both preached and practiced righteousness. "Noah was a righteous man, and perfect in his generations: Noah walked with God." (Gen. 6: 9.) He was a "preacher" (literally, a herald) of righteousness; he denounced the unrighteousness and corruption about him, and exhorted the people to repentance. Josephus, the Jewish historian of the first century, bears this remarkable testimony concerning him: "Noah being grieved at the things which were done by them and being displeased at their counsels, urged them to change for the better their thoughts and actions. But seeing that they did not yield, but were mightily mastered by the pleasure of evil, fearing lest they should kill him, he departed from the land with his wife and his sons and the women whom they had married." (Antiq. I, 3, 1.)

6 **And turning the cities of Sodom and Gomorrah into ashes condemned them with an overthrow, having made them an example unto those that should live ungodly;**—The historical account of this event is recorded in Gen. 19: 23-29. As a third instance of the certainty of God's judgment, the fearful destruction of the cities of the plain—Sodom and Gomorrah—is offered. The prophets cited the destruction which befell these Old Testament cities (Isa. 1: 9, 10; Ezek. 16: 48-56), as also did our Lord (Luke 17: 28-32). Jude, with more detail than Peter, describes the event thus: "Even as Sodom and Gomorrah, and the cities about them, having in like manner with these given themselves over to fornica-

that should live ungodly; 7 and delivered righteous Lot, sore distressed by the lascivious life of the wicked 8 (for that righteous man dwelling among them, in seeing and hearing, ⁸vexed *his* righteous soul from day to day with

⁸Gr. *tormented.*

tion and gone after strange flesh, are set forth as an example, suffering the punishment of eternal fire." (Jude 7.) The "overthrow" which these cities suffered evidenced God's extreme displeasure with their conduct and serves as a warning of the destiny which awaits those who live in similar ungodly fashion today.

7 **And delivered righteous Lot, sore distressed by the lascivious life of the wicked**—See Gen. 19: 16. The case of Lot is introduced to show that God distinguishes between the righteous and the wicked, delivering the former and bringing destruction on the latter. Lot is called "righteous" because he kept himself from the combination of the world about him. The words "sore distressed" are translated from the present passive participle of *kataponeo,* to wear down, to tire out, to harass beyond endurance. The verb thus denotes the distress which Lot felt at the open and shameless ungodliness which was practiced around him. Most of the distress which he felt doubtless came from the ungodly conduct characteristic of his own family. Though he sought to keep them from the corruption of the people of Sodom, "He seemed unto his sons-in-law as one that mocked." (Gen. 19: 14.)

8 **(For that righteous man dwelling among them, in seeing and hearing, vexed his righteous soul from day to day with their lawless deeds)**:—The parentheses in the text explains the nature of the distress which Lot felt in Sodom. He had himself selected the plain of Jordan and the neighborhood of Sodom on the occasion of the dissension between his herdsmen and those of Abraham (Gen. 13: 1-13); and when he made the choice it was said that "the men of Sodom were wicked and sinners against Jehovah exceedingly" (Gen. 13: 13). When the consequences of his choice became apparent to him, it appears that he often desired to leave but was not able. Forced to live daily in the presence of gross and unrestrained licentiousness, and to see and to hear it constantly, he vexed (imperfect active of *basanizo,* kept on tormenting) his righteous soul with the lawlessness about him. It should be observed that it was Lot who tormented his own soul at

their lawless deeds) : 9 the Lord knoweth how to deliver the godly out of temptation, and to keep the unrighteous under punishment unto the day of judgment; 10 but chiefly them that walk after the flesh in the lust of defilement, and despise dominion. Daring, self-willed, they tremble not to rail at

what he witnessed. The words describe the pain that a naturally sensitive and righteous man would experience at the sight of such flagrant lawlessness as that which existed in Sodom. Though in the midst of extreme wickedness, (a) Lot was not corrupted by it; (b) he did not become indifferent to it; (c) he was daily concerned about it. In this he serves as a pattern for us today.

9 The Lord knoweth how to deliver the godly out of temptation, and to keep the unrighteous under punishment unto the day of judgment:—A conclusion drawn from preceding premises. The Lord can deliver his servants, as illustrated by Noah and Lot; and he does keep the unrighteous under punishment, as evidenced in the cases of the angels who sinned, the wicked, antediluvian world, and the cities of the plain. The word tendered "temptation" in this verse is the same as that translated "trial" in 1 Pet. 1: 6, where it refers to the manifold difficulties which Peter's readers then faced. This passage is, therefore, an assurance of deliverance to the righteous whatever the danger which confronts them. The words "under punishment" are from *kolazomenous*, present participle of *kolazo*, to punish, and reveals that the final punishment of the wicked precedes as well as follows the final judgment, a fact also clearly taught in the narrative of the rich man and Lazarus (Luke 16: 19-31), as well as in the reference to the angels who sinned (2 Pet. 2: 4).

10 But chiefly them that walk after the flesh in the lust of defilement, and despise dominion.—"Chiefly" (malista), i.e., especially these above all others God will reserve under punishment. In a parallel passage, Jude said, "Yet in like manner these also in their dreamings defile the flesh and set at nought dominion, and rail at dignities." (Verse 8.) These false teachers of whom Peter writes were not only walking after the flesh; they desired the defilement of the flesh which their lusts produced; they greedily reached forth for the unlawful and polluting use of the flesh to which their sin led them. These were evidently guilty of the unspeakable sins and other darker forms of impurity which Paul

¹⁰dignities: 11 whereas angels, though greater in might and power, bring not a railing judgment against them before the Lord. 12 But these, as creatures

---
¹⁰Gr. *glories.*

---

mentions as prevalent in the Roman empire. (Rom. 1: 24-28.) Moreover, they despised "dominion," i.e., they regarded all authority with contempt. Any effort to restrain them in their wild rebellion they despised.

Daring, self-willed, they tremble not to rail at dignities:—Despite the fact that they knew the penalty for their conduct, they defied the Lord; and arrogant, audacious, and proud, they blasphemed dignities—all authorities—without fear. These words indicate the extreme coarseness, insolence, and hardness of heart characteristic of these false teachers.

11 **Whereas angels, though greater in might and power, bring not a railing judgment against them before the Lord.**—Angels, though greater in every way than these false and designing teachers, do not bring railing judgments, but with becoming modesty and restraint leave such matters in the hands of God. Examples of this attitude may be seen in Zech. 3: 2; Jude 9.

CHARACTERISTICS AND FINAL DESTINY OF FALSE TEACHERS

2: 12-22

without reason, born [11]mere animals [12]to be taken and destroyed, railing in matters whereof they are ignorant, shall in their [13]destroying surely be destroyed, 13 suffering wrong as the hire of wrong-doing; *men* that count it pleasure to revel in the daytime, spots and blemishes, revelling in their [14]deceivings while they feast with you; 14 having eyes full of [15]adultery, and

---

[11]Gr. *natural*.
[12]Or, *to take and to destroy*
[13]Or, *corruption* Comp. 1 Tim. 6. 9.
[14]Some ancient authorities read *love-feasts*. Comp. Jude 12.
[15]Gr. *an adulteress*.

---

12 But these, as creatures without reason, born mere animals to be taken and destroyed, railing in matters whereof they are ignorant, shall in their destroying surely be destroyed,— The fallen angels recognized the moral law of God and felt the wrath which came upon them in their disobedience; whereas, these false teachers, though greatly inferior to the angels (verse 11), were like mere animals in disregarding utterly any laws of a higher world. Like wild beasts of prey which exist solely for the gratification of fleshly appetites, and eventually to be taken and destroyed for the harm they do, these false teachers, as similar creatures without reason or rational conduct, deserved no better fate. In their senseless railing against matters about which they knew nothing, they would eventually suffer the destruction which was wrought out for all whom they deceived. In destroying others, they would, themselves, eventually, be destroyed. Wild beasts are made to be taken and destroyed by man; and these, being of the same nature, also deserved and would receive destruction.

13 Suffering wrong as the hire of wrong-doing;—These words are to be construed with the final clause of the verse which precedes, i.e., these false teachers "shall in their destroying surely be destroyed, suffering wrong as the hire of wrong-doing." The King James rendering, based on a well-supported variation of the Greek text, has here, "and shall receive the reward of unrighteousness." The "reward of unrighteousness" is ruin. Balaam (Num. 31: 8, 19) and Judas (Acts 1: 18) are examples of those who received the reward of unrighteousness in this life, and all the wicked will receive it in the world to come.

that cannot cease from sin; enticing unstedfast souls; having a heart exercised in covetousness; children of cursing; 15 forsaking the right way, they

Men that count it pleasure to revel in the day-time,—Ordinarily, even the wicked confine their excesses to the night; but these, under consideration by Peter, were so abandoned in sin that they extended their revelings into the day, finding pleasure only in ceaseless and unrestrained indulgence. (1 Thess. 5:7.)

Spots and blemishes, revelling in their deceivings while they feast with you;—Hitherto the apostle had dealt with the insubordination and disrespect for authority characteristic of these false teachers; with this verse he begins a description of their abandonment in sin. They were full of spots and blemishes, in contrast with the Lord who is "a lamb without blemish and without spot" (1 Pet. 1:19); and his body, which he desires to be without "spot, or wrinkle, or any such thing" (Eph. 5:27). Further, these teachers had injected themselves into the feasts which the Christians commonly held, and there sported themselves in their deceivings, using such occasions as additional opportunities to deceive the people.

14 Having eyes full of adultery, and that cannot cease from sin;—"Having eyes full of adultery" is, in the Greek, "having eyes full of an adulteress" *(moichalis)*. It is a vivid term, descriptive of a man who is unable to look at a woman without regarding her as an objective for lasciviousness. It is the disposition of heart which violates the injunction of the Lord when he said, "Ye have heard that it was said, Thou shalt not commit adultery; but I say unto you, that every one that looketh on a woman to lust after her hath committed adultery with her already in his heart." (Matt. 5:27, 28.) The hearts of these false teachers were filled with lust, and they ever sought opportunity for the gratification thereof. Thus motivated, they did not, and could not, cease from sin.

Enticing unstedfast souls; having a heart exercised in covetousness; children of cursing;—"Enticing" is derived from *deleazo,* a bait. The word also occurs in verse 18 of this chapter, and is such a term as would be most familiar to Peter, a fisherman. Unsteadfast souls, deceived by their teachers, suffered themselves to be entrapped by the bait which was dangled before them. The

went astray, having followed the way of Balaam the *son* of ¹⁶Beor, who loved the hire of wrong-doing; 16 but he was rebuked for his own transgression: a dumb ass spake with man's voice and stayed the madness of the proph-

---

¹⁶Many ancient authorities read *Boser*.

---

hearts of these men were exercised (practiced) in coveteousness. The word "exercised" is from a term which indicates training in a gymnasium. These teachers were trained in habits of greed. They are styled "children of cursing," a Hebrew idiom expressing character through sonship. Compare "the son of perdition" (John 17: 12); "sons of disobedience" (Eph. 2: 2); "sons of thunder" (Mark 3: 17). These were "children of cursing," because they were a curse to all others, and would themselves suffer the curse of destruction in judgment.

15 **Forsaking the right way, they went astray,**—The "right way" is the "way of truth." (Verse 2.) It is variously designated "the way of the Lord" (Gen. 18: 19); "the way of peace" (Rom. 3: 17); "the way of wisdom" (Prov. 4: 11); "the way of life" (Prov. 10: 17); and "the way of salvation" (Acts 16: 17). The false teachers whom Peter describes in this section of his epistle had "forsaken the right way" and had gone "astray" and were thus apostates to the faith. One cannot forsake a way in which he has never been. These had abandoned the doctrine of Christ, and they no longer conformed in life to the principles which he taught. (Cf. Acts 13: 4-12.)

Having followed the way of Balaam the son of Beor, who loved the hire of wrong-doing;—For the story of Balaam and his effort to curse the children of Israel, see Num. 22: 1-41. Balaam desired the reward which the Moabite messengers brought, here called "the hire of wrong-doing," because he hoped to receive the money for the wicked work he sought to do. These teachers to whom Peter alludes were like Balaam in that they prostituted the doctrine of Christ for personal gain, and taught doctrines contrary to the will of the Lord because they loved the wages of unrighteousness. The word "followed" in the text is translated from a Greek verb which means to follow out to the end. It occurs in 2 Pet. 1: 16 and 2: 2.

16 **But he was rebuked for his own transgression: a dumb ass spake with man's voice and stayed the madness of the**

et. 17 These are springs without water, and mists driven by a storm; for whom the blackness of darkness hath been reserved. 18 For, uttering great

prophet.—Balaam's transgression was in his readiness to go and curse Israel despite the solemn warning he had received from God. The dumb ass was a beast of burden. Actually, it was the angel who hindered Balaam on his way, but the clearer vision of the beast resulted in the first delay, and the miracle which followed —when the ass spake with the voice of a man—brought to his attention the perverseness of his way. It is significant that Peter accepted and adopted the narrative in Num. 22, regarding Balaam and the ass, as authentic. It was, to him, no imaginary incident, no fictitious account. Modernistic scholars, in seeking to eliminate the supernatural from the sacred writings entirely, allege that Balaam merely heard the promptings of an uneasy conscience on this occasion and that the beast did not really speak. Such a view not only impeaches Moses as a historian; it also convicts Peter, an apostle of the Lord, as an unreliable writer. The beast spake; he spake with the voice of a man; he spake audibly, and his words have been recorded and preserved. (Num. 22: 28.) There is no miracle in the Old Testament better authenticated than this.

17 **These are springs without water, and mists driven by a storm; for whom the blackness of darkness hath been reserved.** —The apostle, in the verses which precede this, has described the sins of the false teachers about whom he writes; here, he directs attention to the emptiness and worthlessness of that which they taught. Though they paraded under the guise of teachers of truth, they were as springs without water, toward which tired and thirsty travelers hasten, only to meet with bitter disappointment when they arrive and find there is no water there. Though such teachers make great promises, the promises they make do not materialize. They are like mists driven by a storm containing the promise of rain, but blown quickly by the wind over the land and away. The harassed farmer looks longingly at the skies and hopes that the cloud which he sees will bring moisture to his parched fields, only to observe it fleeing before the tempest. Such was characteristic of these men who, though they offered a blessing, deceived and disappointed those whom they duped. For all such the blackness of darkness has been reserved and awaits. (Jude 13.) The way of

swelling *words* of vanity, they entice in the lusts of the flesh, by lasciviousness, those who are just escaping from them that live in error; 19 promising them liberty, while they themselves are bondservants of corruption; for of [17]whom a man is overcome, of the same is he also brought into bondage. 20

---

[17]Or, *what*

the wicked is often described in the scriptures as a "way of darkness." (Prov. 4: 19; Jer. 23: 9-12.)

18 **For, uttering great swelling words of vanity, they entice in the lusts of the flesh, by lasciviousness, those who are just escaping from them that live in error;**—In the verse which precedes, Peter describes the false teachers of whom he writes in figures; here, we are informed why they are waterless springs and rainless mists: all that they say is vanity. (Eph. 4: 17.) "Vanity" *(mataiotes),* as here used, signifies that which is empty, useless, vain; and the "great swelling words" *(huperogka)* these teachers were accustomed to use, though pompous and high sounding, were nothing more than hollow, vain phrases, sound without substance, mere bombast. Their purpose was to "entice" *in* the lusts of the flesh *by* (dative of the instrument) lasciviousness. The word "lasciviousness" is, in the Greek, plural *(aselgeia);* there was no temptation of that nature which these teachers did not offer. Hence, (a) their motive was to allure and lead astray; (b) their method of enticement was by high sounding words; (c) the sphere in which the enticement was accomplished was in the lust of the flesh; and (d) the bait *(deleazo)* which was dangled before them (verse 14) was gross fleshly indulgence. The victims of these false teachers were those who were just escaping from the dark night of heathenism through obedience to the gospel, only to be thrust back into the shadows of their former manner of life by these deceivers. Those "that live in error" were the heathen who knew not God. These unfortunate victims of deceit who were just escaping from the influence of those who lived in error—through their obedience to the gospel—were seized by these false teachers and thrust back into the benighted state formerly characterizing them.

19 **Promising them liberty, while they themselves are bondservants of corruption; for of whom a man is overcome, of the same is he also brought into bondage.**—The "great

For if, after they have escaped the defilements of the world through the knowledge of [18]the Lord and Saviour Jesus Christ, they are again entangled therein and overcome, the last state is become worse with them than the

---

[18]Many ancient authorities read *our*.

---

swelling words" which these teachers were accustomed to speak included the offer of liberty, a characteristic feature of their teaching. The freedom which the Christian enjoys from the bondage of the law they interpreted to include the privilege of unrestrained indulgence. Disregarding Paul's warning, "For ye, brethren, were called for freedom; only use not your freedom for an occasion to the flesh, but through love be servants one of another" (Gal. 5: 13), their "liberty" became *libertinism,* and they practiced the grossest corruption. While offering liberty to others, they were themselves in the most advanced slavery, the bondage of sin. Overcome by their vices, they were in bondage to them and were the most enslaved of all creatures. They had become the servants of a master who was using them to enslave others, and who would eventually destroy them. (Verse 12.)

20 **For if, after they have escaped the defilements of the world through the knowledge of the Lord and Saviour Jesus Christ, they are again entangled therein and overcome, the last state is become worse with them than the first.**—The antecedent of the pronoun "they" is the false teachers of the preceding verse. These men had obeyed the gospel and had thereby "escaped the defilements of the world through the knowledge of the Lord and Saviour Jesus Christ," only to return to their former state of defilement by a lapse into their earlier manner of living. "Knowledge," here, is not from the ordinary *gnosis,* but the compound *epignosis,* used so often by Paul (Eph. 4: 13; Col. 2: 2; 3: 10; 1 Tim. 2: 4) and Peter (2 Pet. 1: 2, 3, 8) of the highest form of knowledge. These men had thus not always been hypocrites; they had known Christ in the fullest possible sense as their Saviour, only to apostatize from the faith. The "defilements" into which they had fallen were the corruptions of the heathen world from which they had earlier escaped. (2 Pet. 1: 4.) To these corruptions they had returned, and in them they were again entangled. The word "entangled" *(emplakentes)* suggests the figure of fishes entrapped in a net. Though these men boasted of their free-

| 2: 20, 21.] | SECOND PETER | 177 |

first. 21 For it were better for them not to have known the way of righteousness, than, after knowing it, to turn back from the holy commandment delivered unto them. 22 It has happened unto them according to the true

dom, they were, in reality, like fish entangled in a net, the helpless captives of their own enticements, entrapped by the very bait which they dangled before others. (Verses 14, 18.)

The words "the last state is become worse with them than the first" appear to be suggested by a comment of the Lord in the parable of the unclean spirit who was cast out only to return with seven other spirits more wicked than itself. (Matt. 12: 45.) Such is the condition characteristic of those who have been delivered from the corruption of the world only to return to its defilements. The last state for all such is worse than the first: (a) apostates are usually more abandoned in sin than those who have never walked in righteousness; (b) such a state involves more guilt because of the greater knowledge such a one possesses; (c) such individuals are far more difficult to influence for good than those who have never known the way of righteousness.

21 For it were better for them not to have known the way of righteousness, than, after knowing it, to turn back from the holy commandment delivered unto them.—The verb "known" is, like the noun "knowledge" in the preceding verse, from the compound *epignosis*, the fullest possible form of knowledge, and emphasizes the fact that these teachers had enjoyed a clear perception of the principles of Christ which they had now repudiated. Christianity is styled a "way" because it is a course to be followed, and it is a "way of righteousness" because righteousness characterizes those who walk in it. (Isa. 35: 8.) These deceptive teachers had not only "known" this way; they had walked in it and enjoyed its benefits and privileges. Despite this, through yielding to their sensuous desires, they had turned back to the world and had fallen into a state worse than that in which Christianity found them. It would have been better for them never to have known Christ and his teaching than, after having known it, to turn back from "the holy commandment" delivered unto them. The "holy commandment" was the moral law which Jesus taught, and which these teachers disregarded. It would have been better for them never to have known the right way in view of their subsequent apostasy,

proverb, ¹⁹The dog turning to his own vomit again, and the sow that had washed to wallowing in the mire.

¹⁹Prov. xxvi. 11.

for (a) in this event they would not have brought reproach on the cause of Christ; (b) they would not have fallen to such a level of depravity as that which now characterized them; and (c) they would not suffer as great punishment in the last day, since with increased knowledge comes an increase of responsibility and consequently greater condemnation for those who do not avail themselves of the advantages afforded them. (Luke 12: 47, 48.)

22 **It has happened unto them according to the true proverb, The dog turning to his own vomit again, and the sow that had washed to wallowing in the mire.**—Cited in this proverb are two beasts held in greatest contempt in all Oriental lands. The dog is a scavenger, and the swine is regarded as an abomination. Jesus associated these two beasts in an illustration of what is most profane and degrading. (Matt. 7: 6.) Reference to the dog is a variation of a statement made by Solomon in Prov. 26: 11; that of a sow does not occur in the scriptures, though the truth of that which is affirmed is a matter which has come under the observation of all even casually acquainted with the habits of either of these animals. The proverb was one of general currency when Peter wrote. It should be observed that in both instances the animal was *changed*. That each returned to its former offensive habits does not alter the fact that a change had occurred. Advocates of the doctrine of the impossibility of apostasy, in an effort to avoid the obvious force of this passage, insist that the dog remained a dog, the sow a sow. Such is not the point of the proverb. The dog had ejected that which was foul; the sow had been washed. That each returned to its former manner of life reveals that the old nature *returned*. Peter cites the proverb as an illustration of that which had occurred in the lives of these men who, though they had escaped the corruptions of the world through the knowledge of Christ, had become entangled again therein, and overcome, and their last state was thus worse than the first. (Verse 20.)

SECTION THREE

THE SECOND COMING OF THE LORD AND THE END OF THE WORLD

3: 1-13

1 This is now, beloved, the second epistle that I write unto you; and in both of them I stir up your sincere mind by putting you in remembrance; 2 that ye should remember the words which were spoken before by the holy

1 **This is now, beloved, the second epistle that I write unto you;**—Literally rendered, the Greek text here is, "This already *(ede)* a second epistle I am writing to you." In the use of the word "already" *(ede)* rendered "now" in the translation, there is the suggestion that the second epistle came soon after the first. From this it appears that (a) Peter had written an earlier epistle shortly before this; and (b) it had been addressed to the same readers. In pursuing his design to expose the pretensions of the false teachers so minutely dealt with in chapter two, he calls attention here, and in the succeeding verses, to the mockery characteristic of all such in denying the coming of the Lord merely because it was delayed. The vocative "beloved"—a term of endearment—occurs four times in this chapter and indicates the intimate connection which Peter sustained to these addressed.

And in both of them I stir up your sincere mind by putting you in remembrance;—Both of the epistles were, therefore, written for the same purpose: to stir up the minds of his readers by putting them in remembrance of the vital and fundamental matters with which the chapter particularly, and both epistles generally, deal. Repeated here is the thought which occurs in 2 Pet. 1: 13. The word "stir" *(diegeiro)* means thoroughly to arouse; and the adjective "sincere" *(eilikrines)*, occurring also in Phil. 1: 10, denotes that which is clear, open, candid. The minds (understanding) of these to whom Peter wrote were open and reasonable; and he addressed them with the view of arousing them to a recollection of matters that had been taught them but which they might have, for the time, forgotten. What these matters were he reveals in the verse which follows.

2 **That ye should remember the words which were spoken before by the holy prophets, and the commandments of the**

prophets, and the commandment of the Lord and Saviour through your apostles: 3 knowing this first, that ¹in the last days mockers shall come with

¹Gr. *in the last of the days.*

Lord and Saviour through your apostles:—"That ye should remember" is translated from one Greek word *mnesthenai,* aorist passive infinitive of *mimnesko,* to remind; signifying, as in the King James Version, "That ye should be mindful." The things which Peter would have them recall were the principles, the prophecy, the truth, and the doctrine which the apostles and prophets had taught them. The association of "prophets" and "apostles" here makes it likely that the New Testament prophets who had spoken of the coming of the Lord were included, and that the combination is similar to that which occurs in the epistles of Paul. (Eph. 2: 20; 3: 5; 4: 11. Cf. Acts 11: 27; 13: 1; 1 Cor. 14: 29.) Much emphasis is given to prophecy and to prophetic statements in the epistles of Peter. (1 Pet. 1: 10-12; 2 Pet. 1: 19.) It should be recalled that at the time when Peter wrote the New Testament revelation had not been completed; and unable to appeal to it as a final and complete body of truth in the matters under consideration, it was necessary for him to direct his readers to the announcements of the prophets and to the oral deliverances of the apostles. The reference to "your" apostles is significant; they could properly and fittingly be styled the apostles of those to whom they had written or spoken. Peter was included among those thus designated; and also Paul, Peter's readers being acquainted with certain of that apostle's writings. (2 Pet. 3: 15.) The "commandment" was "of the Lord" in that it originated with him, and "through" the apostles in that they were the instruments by which it was borne to the people.

It is equally important that the Lord's people *today* should have their minds stirred to remembrance of the vital teaching issuing from the apostles and prophets of the Lord. Ceaseless vigilance is the price of a pure faith and a faultless practice, and the obligation of all teachers and preachers in this matter is indeed weighty. Remissness in this respect leads to eventual apostasy.

3 Knowing this first, that in the last days mockers shall come with mockery, walking after their own lusts,—"Knowing this first," i.e., recognize this fact in the beginning. See com-

mockery, walking after their own lusts, 4 and saying, Where is the promise of his ²coming? for, from the day that the fathers fell asleep, all things con-

²Gr. *presence*.

---

ments on 2 Pet. 1: 20, where the same phrase occurs. "The last days" embrace the period of the Christian dispensation—the final age of the world. In the words "mockers shall come with mockery" there is a play on the word *empaizo*, to sport, play, jest, or deride *(empaigmonei empaikai)*. The meaning is that these men would ridicule and hold up to contempt the idea that the Lord would return, and that his return would signal the consummation of the age. This, to them, provided an occasion for mocking and jesting; the idea they ridiculed, and the prophecy they held up to scorn. In doing so, they were but "walking after their own lusts," thus revealing that this was the real cause of their cynicism and doubt. "And this is the judgment that light is come into the world, and men loved the darkness rather than the light; for their works were evil." (John 3: 19.)

4 **And saying, Where is the promise of his coming? for, from the day that the fathers fell asleep, all things continue as they were from the beginning of the creation.**—These mockers insinuated that the promise of the Lord's coming was a delusion, and the expectation thereof a vain hope. The Lord had promised it (Matt. 24: 3ff.); Paul frequently alluded to it (1 Cor. 15: 51; 2 Cor. 5: 4); and Peter taught it (2 Pet. 1: 16). Yet, the Lord had not come; and scoffers were pointing to this fact as proof that he never would appear. From the day the "fathers fell asleep" (died) all things continued as they had from the beginning. The "fathers" to whom they referred were evidently the first generation of Christians, many of whom by now had died. These had passed without witnessing the Lord's return, the natural order of the season, seedtime and harvest; the usual continuity of things were as they had been from the beginning. Why, then, should such a radical change be expected as would attend an event of the type predicted? Likely there were many such questions, this being representative of the type propounded. It is possible that some of the Christians of this period inadvertently supplied these scoffers with an occasion for such objections. Some of the saints of the first century entertained erroneous views regarding the time and nature

tinue as they were from the beginning of the creation. 5 For this they willfully forget, that there were heavens from of old, and an earth compacted out

of the Lord's return. To correct the impression that Christ would appear immediately portions of the Thessalonian letters were written. (1 Thess. 4: 13-18; 5: 13; 2 Thess. 2: 1-7.) The question these mockers raised may, in view of these facts, have implied this: The return of Christ has been widely predicted and confidently expected. The fathers with anxious anticipation awaited it. They lived to old age and in the natural order of events died without its realization. Since their departure all things continue as before. Since they were disappointed in his coming, why should we, with no better basis of hope, expect it?

These cavilers were the uniformitarians of the day, the prototype of those who deny any divine superintendency in the universe today. They argued that that which is, is because it has ever been, and must, therefore, ever be.

The reference to the fathers falling asleep as a figure of death is a reminder of the words of the Lord regarding Lazarus: "Our friend Lazarus is fallen asleep; but I go, that I may awake him out of sleep. The disciples therefore said unto him, Lord, if he is fallen asleep, he will recover. Now Jesus had spoken of his death: but they thought that he spake of taking rest in sleep. Then Jesus therefore said unto them plainly, Lazarus is dead." (John 11: 11-13.) The figure is a common one in the scripture. The rest from labor that death involves, the peaceful aspect of those in death, and the position of the body, all symbolize death. In our English word "cemetery" (from *koimeterion,* a sleeping place) the idea is preserved.

5 **For this they wilfully forget,**—Here, Peter begins his reply to those who alleged that the uniformity of nature constituted an argument against such a change as the return of Christ would necessitate. He pointed out that in reaching such a conclusion they had disregarded important facts relevant to the issue. These facts they had not only ignored, they had done so willfully and deliberately. The word "forget" in the text is from *lanthano,* to escape the notice of, to be hidden from. That these facts had escaped them was not due to inadvertency; they had willfully and purposely allowed them to pass. The word "wilfully" is from *thelon-*

of water and ³amidst water, by the word of God; 6 by which means the world that then was, being overflowed with water, perished: 7 but the heav-

³Or, *through*

---

tas, present active participle of *thelo,* to wish or will. Their ignorance of these matters was, therefore, designed and willful; a guilty lack of information of the matters involved. Far from an unvarying constancy in nature from the beginning, as these men had alleged, the most radical changes had occurred, an instance of which the apostle next introduces.

That there were heavens from of old, and an earth compacted out of water and amidst water, by the word of God;— The "heavens were from of old," i.e., they dated from the original creation. (Gen. 1: 1-3.) The earth was "compacted" (formed) out of water, and in the midst of water, being separated from the waters. "And God made the firmament, and divided the waters which were under the firmament from the waters which were above the firmament. . . . And God said, Let the waters under the heavens be gathered together unto one place, and let the dry land appear; and it was so. And God called the dry land Earth; and the gathering together of the waters called he Seas." (Gen. 1: 7-10.) All of this was accomplished by "the word of God." (Cf. "And God said. . . ." Gen. 1: 6ff.)

6 By which means the world that then was, being overflowed with water, perished:—"By which means," i.e., by the waters which were above the firmament and those under it—the waters out of which the earth was formed. The earth was formed by the separation of the waters; it was kept together (compacted) by such a separation; and it was at length destroyed when this separation was no longer maintained. In the deluge "were all the fountains of the great deep broken up" (the waters from below), and "the windows of heaven (from above) were opened." (Gen. 7: 11.) The waters from above and below joined as instruments in the hands of God in the judgment upon the wicked world. It thus "perished" *(apollumi),* i.e., it was destroyed. It was not annihilated, for such the word does not mean. The existing order was changed; the evils of the age were removed, and there emerged a new world cleansed from its former impurities.

7 But the heavens that now are, and the earth, by the same

ens that now are, and the earth, by the same word have been ⁴stored up for fire, being reserved against the day of judgment and destruction of ungodly men.
8 But forget not this one thing, beloved, that one day is with the Lord as a

---

⁴Or, *stored with fire*

---

word have been stored up for fire, being reserved against the day of judgment and destruction of ungodly men.—The "heavens that now are, and the earth" are put in contrast with "the world that then was" in verse 6. As "the world that then was" suffered destruction in the flood, "by the word of God," so the present heavens and earth, *by the same word* (and thus by the same limitless and inexhaustible power which accomplished the destruction of the world in the flood), have been stored up (literally, treasured, preserved, kept) for fire, i.e., for destruction by fire, at the day of judgment and destruction of ungodly men. In this latter clause the word "destruction" is identical in meaning with the verb "perished" in the preceding verse. By this it is not meant that the ungodly will cease to exist, any more than the earth, following the flood, existed no more. What is meant is that there will be a change in their condition attended by penal consequences as great as that which characterized the earth in the flood. Paul reveals that the destruction of wicked men will be accomplished "at the revelation of the Lord Jesus from heaven with the angels of his power in flaming fire rendering vengeance to them that know not God, and to them that obey not the gospel of our Lord Jesus who shall suffer punishment, even eternal destruction from the face of the Lord and from the glory of his might, when he shall come to be glorified in his saints. . . ." (2 Thess. 1: 7-10.)

8 But forget not this one thing, beloved, that one day is with the Lord as a thousand years, and a thousand years as one day.—The apostle's first reply to the scoffers who alleged an unvarying conformity in nature as an argument against the Lord's return (verses 3-7) is that they had willfully and deliberately ignored the lessons of the flood which demonstrate conclusively that all things *have not continued* as they were from the beginning. His second answer to their allegations is that lapse of time between the promise and the realization is not to be interpreted as meaning that God will not fulfill his commitments and discharge his threatenings. "But forget not this one thing" is, lit-

thousand years, and a thousand years as one day. 9 The Lord is not slack concerning his promise, as some count slackness; but is longsuffering to you-ward, not wishing that any should perish, but that all should come to

erally rendered, "let not this one thing escape you," i.e., be primarily impressed with the fact that with the Lord "one day is as a thousand years, and a thousand years as one day." "With the Lord" signifies the manner in which the Lord regards time. With him, a thousand years is as a day; a day is as a thousand years. This does not mean that a day in "God's calendar" is a thousand years long, as materialists allege, or that God will punish the wicked a thousand years for every day they have sinned in this life, as some affirm. The meaning is that the passing of time does not affect the promises and threatenings of God. Whether it be a day or a thousand years between the time of the promise and the reward, the threatening and the retribution, God will perform it. In this he is wholly unlike man, who the greater the interval between the promise and the fulfillment, the less likely that he will accomplish it. There are many reasons why this is so. (1) Man may die; (2) he may forget his promise; (3) he may violate his word and simply refuse to do that which he promised; (4) conditions may arise making it impossible for him to perform it. Since none of these contingencies are ever characteristic of God, it is idle for the wicked to infer that apparent delay in the execution of the penalty is evidence that God has forgotten. (Psalm 90:4.)

9 **The Lord is not slack concerning his promise, as some count slackness; but is longsuffering to you-ward, not wishing that any should perish, but that all should come to repentance.** —A third answer to the scoffers earlier alluded to begins here, an admonition to them to make good use of what they allege is delay by making their own calling and election sure. God does not loiter or delay in the discharge of his purposes; that which unbelief may regard as such is simply the normal development of the will of God which conceived the operation and now works it leisurely out. The words "is not slack concerning his promise" reveal not only that there is no indifference involved, but also that there will be no tardiness in the ultimate accomplishment thereof. The purpose in the apparent delay is to exhibit God's longsuffering, a characteristic they were ironically perverting into an argument against the

repentance. 10 But the day of the Lord will come as a thief; in the which the heavens shall pass away with a great noise, and the ⁵elements shall be dissolved with fervent heat, and the earth and the works that are therein

⁵Or, *heavenly bodies*

truth of his word. The scriptures abound with evidences of God's longsuffering. (Rom. 11: 11-36; 12: 1.) Far from desiring that any should perish, he longs for all to come (move on to, *choresai*) repentance. Any theory which teaches that God does not will the salvation of all men is therefore palpably false.

10 **But the day of the Lord will come as a thief;**—The verb "will come" is in emphatic position in the Greek text; whatever else occurs, *coming surely* is the Lord. The "day of the Lord" is the day when he shall appear in the clouds on the occasion of his second coming for the purpose of raising the dead and instituting the general judgment. (John 5: 28, 29.) The phrase is of frequent occurrence in the Old Testament, where it usually denotes the idea of judgment; and in the New Testament it designates the Lord's coming which will precede the judgment. (1 Thess. 5: 2; 1 Cor. 1: 8; Phil. 1: 6; 2 Thess. 2: 2.) The day will come as a "thief" because it will come with the suddenness and unexpectedness characteristic of a thief. The figure was first used by the Lord (Matt. 24: 43, 44, a passage which must surely have been in Peter's mind when he wrote these words), and Paul and John used it in similar fashion (1 Thess. 5: 2; Rev. 3: 3).

In the which the heavens shall pass away with a great noise, and the elements shall be dissolved with fervent heat,— The "heavens" here include the visible portion of the universe immediately above us in which the birds fly. (Gen. 1: 20.) In the mighty conflagration which shall attend the destruction of the earth great and wonderful changes are destined to occur in the elements immediately surrounding it. Accompanying its dissolution there is to be "a great noise." The word thus translated is *rhoizedon,* an onomatopoeic term, in which the sound denotes the meaning. Its kindred noun, *rhoidsos,* was used in classical Greek of the whizzing of an arrow, the whirring rush of wings, the sound of the wind, and the murmur of waters. Here it describes the crash of dissolving worlds and the tremendous roar of flames as they consume the earth. The "elements" are the rudimental portions of the

shall be ⁶burned up. 11 Seeing that these things are thus all to be dissolved, what manner of persons ought ye to be in *all* holy living and godliness, 12

⁶The most ancient manuscripts read *discovered.*

earth system, the minute parts which comprise the whole. The heavens and the earth are to be dissolved; they are to lose their form and be returned to the original atoms from which they were constructed, all of which sprang into existence in the divine fiat of the omnipotent God.

And the earth and the works that are therein shall be burned up.—The works that are to perish in the fire which shall ultimately destroy the earth are those which belong to the earth and are characteristic of it, whether of God or man. Along with its dissolution there will be the burning of all that man has accomplished of a material nature—houses, cities, monuments, etc. —everything to which he has set his hand here. These, along with all of God's material creation, are to be dissolved, consumed in the heat of the mighty catastrophe. The manner in which the Lord will accomplish this is not stated, and it is idle to speculate. It is sufficient for us to know that it will occur; the manner in which the Lord purposes to do it remains hidden in the counsel of his own will.

11 **Seeing that these things are thus all to be dissolved, what manner of persons ought ye to be in all holy living and godliness,**—An admonition based on preceding premises. The Greek term translated "what manner of persons" is, literally, "of what country," thus emphasizing Paul's reminder that Christians are citizens of the colony of heaven (Phil. 3: 20), and they ought therefore to remember always that they are merely strangers and sojourners here (Heb. 11: 13-16). The verb in the phrase "ought ye to be" denotes continuous being, and might properly be translated, "ought ye to be found," i.e., found constantly engaging in all holy living and godliness. These words—living and godliness— are, in the Greek text, plurals, *livings* and *godlinesses.* They thus sum up all the duties and characteristics of Christians. In view of the transitory nature of the world and all that belongs to it, children of God should cease their concern about it and fix their attention on those matters that are eternal. "While we look not at the things which are seen, but at the things which are not seen, for the

looking for and [7]earnestly desiring the [2]coming of the day of God, by reason of which the heavens being on fire shall be dissolved, and the [6]elements shall melt with fervent heat? 13 But, according to his promise, we look for new heavens and a new earth, wherein dwelleth righteousness.

---

[7]Or, *hastening*

---

things which are seen are temporal; but the things which are not seen are eternal." (2 Cor. 4: 18.)

12 **Looking for and earnestly desiring the coming of the day of God, by reason of which the heavens being on fire shall be dissolved, and the elements shall melt with fervent heat?**— The faithful are to look forward to, and earnestly desire, the coming of the day of God, because it will signal the end of earthly trials here and betoken the ushering in of the eternal and blissful state for which they sigh. "Earnestly desiring" *(spendontas)* is "hasting unto" in the King James Version. There is no ground for the introduction of the preposition "unto." It is, however, possible to render *speudontas,* transitively, i.e., "hastening on," causing the day of God to come more quickly by helping to accomplish the things which must occur before it dawns. Christians are, therefore, not only to desire the Lord's return, but to hurry it on by performing their duties faithfully in his kingdom. It will be by "reason of his" coming that the destruction already described in verse 10 will occur.

13 **But, according to his promise, we look for new heavens and a new earth, wherein dwelleth righteousness.**—The promise of a new heaven and a new earth is in Isa. 65: 17; 66: 22. John had a vision of it which he describes in Rev. 21: 1. The "heavens and earth" to which Peter refers here is described as "new." There are two words translated "new" in the New Testament; one is prospective and indicates that which is young as opposed to old; the other is retrospective and points to that which is fresh in contrast to that which is worn out. It is the second of these *(kainos)* which is used here. The heavens and the earth which the apostle describes in this passage will be fresh and new, and not worn and old, as are the heavens and the earth which now exist. In this new heaven and earth righteousness will dwell. Righteousness dwells wherever righteous people live. The heavens and the earth here contemplated will, therefore, be the abode of righteous and obedient people.

More than this we cannot, with our present store of information, know. Numerous questions men are disposed to raise regarding the matter it was not Peter's intention (or, for that matter, any inspired man's) to answer. Where will the new heaven and earth be located? What will be the nature and characteristics of it? are questions beyond our ken. It is sufficient for us to note that: (a) The new heaven and earth will follow the destruction of the present heavens and earth. (b) The earth that will *then* be *is not* this one. (c) It is this earth which embodies the hopes and expectations of future kingdom advocates. (d) There is no hint of a reign of Christ on the earth which Peter describes. (e) Christ will have terminated his reign and delivered the kingdom to the Father before the events are accomplished which the apostle here details. (1 Cor. 15: 23ff.) (f) There is, therefore, no support whatsoever in this passage for the premillennial theory.

From a careful consideration of the matters set forth in the foregoing passage, these facts seem to appear: (a) The present heavens and earth serve as a figure of the heavens and earth to follow. (b) The words "heavens and earth" are not intended to embrace all of God's material universe, but only that portion where his people dwell. (c) In the antetype, this limitation must be understood, and the words "new heaven and earth" must then be regarded as a designation of where his people dwell, and not a detailed description of the future abode. (d) Heaven is the final abode of the people of God. (e) Therefore, the phrase "new heavens and earth" must be understood as a designation for *heaven!*

CONCLUDING EXHORTATIONS AND DOXOLOGY
3: 14-18

14 Wherefore, beloved, seeing that ye look for these things, give diligence that ye may be found in peace, without spot and blameless in his sight. 15

---

14 Wherefore, beloved, seeing that ye look for these things, give diligence that ye may be found in peace, without spot and blameless in his sight.—The "things" toward which they looked were the matters which the apostle had just presented: the second coming of Christ, the destruction of the world, and the new heavens and earth. Because such stupendous events were certain to occur, it was virtually important that all who desired to escape

And account that the longsuffering of our Lord is salvation; even as our beloved brother Paul also, according to the wisdom given to him, wrote unto you; 16 as also in all *his* epistles, speaking in them of these things; wherein

---

the destruction certain to come upon the wicked should "give diligence" (strive earnestly, 2 Pet. 1: 10) to be found "in peace" (with both God and man), "without spot" (undefiled), and "blameless" (not condemned).

15 **And account that the longsuffering of our Lord is salvation;**—Instead of regarding an apparent delay in judgment upon the world as an indication of slackness on God's part, it should be gratefully received as a token of his longsuffering and patience to enable man to have every possible opportunity to come to repentance.

Even as our beloved brother Paul also, according to the wisdom given to him, wrote unto you;—This second epistle of Peter, like the first, was written to Christians living in Pontus, Galatia, Cappadocia, Asia, and Bithynia. Paul wrote letters likewise bearing testimony to God's patience and longsuffering to brethren dwelling in some of the same provinces, e.g., to the Ephesians, Colossians, and Galatians. From this significant allusion to Paul, we learn that Peter was acquainted with the writings of that apostle; that those to whom he wrote them were familiar with them; that he was on intimate terms with Paul, having addressed him as his beloved brother; and that he considered Paul's writings as inspired and equally authoritative with his own.

16 **As also in all his epistles, speaking in them of these things;**—It is probable that the epistles of Paul were at this time being read in the churches generally and were thus enjoying a much wider circulation than among the congregations to which they were primarily addressed. The brethren would obviously desire to exchange the letters that had been received from the apostle; and from such exchange they must have come to be well known to all the saints. The churches in Asia Minor would thus be acquainted, not only with the letters to the Galatians, the Ephesians, and the Colossians, but also the epistles to the Thessalonians, the Corinthians, the Romans, etc. In each of these there were numerous references to the theme Peter had just been discussing. The judgment is taught in 1 Thess. 3: 13; Rom. 14: 10; the res-

are some things hard to be understood, which the ignorant and unstedfast wrest, as *they* do also the other scriptures, unto their own destruction. 17

urrection of the dead in 1 Cor. 15; heaven, the future abode of the righteous, in 2 Cor. 5: 1-10; the end of the world and the destruction of the wicked in 2 Thess. 1: 7-10; 2: 1-12.

Wherein are some things hard to be understood,—In these epistles were many matters, in the very nature of the case, hard to be understood. Subjects of such profound import would obviously involve difficulties of interpretation, and the preconceived notions which the people had—particularly the Jews—added to the difficulties. It is significant that Peter said that in these epistles were "some things" hard to be understood. It was not his intention to assert that all of Paul's writings were of this nature, but only such as dealt with the themes particularly under consideration. If such were hard to be understood even by Peter, an inspired man, we need not despair if we find them difficult today. And if Peter, an inspired man, regarded them as difficult, it is utter folly to assume that any so-called successor of his could do any better with them. He who seeks earnestly to find his duty in the sacred writings will not be disappointed; the scriptures are able to make one wise unto salvation. (2 Tim. 3: 15.) *"If any man willeth to do his will, he shall know of the teaching . . . "* (John 7: 17.) The difficulties to which the apostle refers are not such as involve the plan of salvation or the duties of the Christian life. On these matters the teaching is clear and explicit, simple and plain.

Which the ignorant and unstedfast wrest, as they do also the other scriptures, unto their own destruction.—The "ignorant" are the "uninstructed," the "unstedfast" those without definite convictions. Such are unable, from lack of accepted principles, to arrive at a conclusion regarding the meaning of a passage because they are unstable in all matters. It will be seen that those who wrest the scriptures to their own destruction are men who are uninstructed in the way of truth and who lack the stability of character necessary to espouse a position and hold it. Such *wrest* the scriptures. "Wrest" *(strebloo)* means to twist, to turn from the proper position, to torture, to pervert. It is used here of those who twist the scriptures from their intended purpose in order to make them teach matters never intended by the sacred writers.

Ye therefore, beloved, knowing *these things* beforehand, beware lest, being carried away with the error of the wicked, ye fall from your own stedfastness. 18 But grow in the grace and knowledge of our Lord and Saviour

Those guilty of doing this did not limit their perversion to the subjects primarily referred to, but to other scriptures, even to those dealing with simple and elementary matters of the Christian life. Such a course leads inevitably to destruction because it produces a manner of life that must eventually result in destruction.

Important considerations which follow from this are: (1) The destruction which results is due, not to the scripture or its writers, but to its improper handling by men. (2) The passage does not teach that all scripture is difficult of understanding and should not be read. (3) It does not lend support to the view that man needs an infallible interpreter of the scriptures. (4) What is taught is that some scripture is hard to understand and that evil men utilize such for ungodly purposes. (5) The lesson, by implication, is that we should be on guard against any interpretation contrary to the general teaching of the Bible. It is clear that Paul's writings were then generally accepted as scripture, and that Peter, another inspired man, so regarded them.

17 **Ye therefore, beloved, knowing these things beforehand, beware lest, being carried away with the error of the wicked, ye fall from your own stedfastness.**—To be "forewarned" is to be "forearmed," and such was the purpose of the apostle's admonition here. The pronoun "ye" is in emphatic position; others had been led astray by false teachers; "ye . . . beware." "Beware" signifies to keep watch, to be on one's guard. The saints to whom Peter wrote were therefore to maintain unceasing vigilance lest they, too, should be "carried away" (led off) by the error of the wicked, and so fall from their own stedfastness. This warning is significant only on the supposition that it is possible to fall. If, as some allege, it is impossible for a child of God to fall from grace, this warning is without force. The conclusion is irresistible that Peter's readers would escape the *destruction* of the wicked only by being constantly on their guard against the *seductions* of the wicked.

18 **But grow in the grace and knowledge of our Lord and Saviour Jesus Christ. To him be the glory both now and for**

Jesus Christ. To him *be* the glory both now and ⁸for ever. Amen.

⁸Gr. *unto the days of eternity.* Ecclus. 18. 10.

---

ever. Amen.—"Grace" is here used to sum up all the favor of God, which favor increases toward us as we advance in stature as his children. To grow in "knowledge" is to become better informed in the doctrine of Christ, and to enter more fully into sympathy with his cause. He is the divine giver of the grace in which Christians are to grow, and the object of the knowledge which they are to possess. The doxology with which the epistle concludes ascribes glory to Christ forever, literally "to the day of eternity." The Greek phrase thus rendered, *eis hemeran aionos,* occurs only here in the sacred writings. It is proper to refer to eternity as a *day,* because it is indeed an everlasting one, without a yesterday to precede it, or a tomorrow to follow it.

A COMMENTARY ON THE FIRST
EPISTLE OF JOHN

CONTENTS

INTRODUCTION

	Page
Authorship of the Epistle	199
Biographical Sketch of the Apostle John	199
General Characteristics of the Epistle	202
Design of the Epistle	204
Persons Addressed	206
Date and Place of Writing	206

SECTION I (1: 1-4)

INTRODUCTION

Introduction	209
Proof of the Manifestation of the Word (1: 1-3)	209
Purpose of Writing (1: 4)	214

SECTION II (1: 5-2: 28)

GOD IS LIGHT

Conditions of Fellowship with God (1: 5-7)	215
Sin and Its Forgiveness (1: 8-10)	218
Jesus Our Advocate (2: 1, 2)	221
Tests of the Christian (2: 3-6)	224
Commandments New and Old (2: 7-11)	227
Little Children, Fathers and Young Men Addressed (2: 12-14)	232
Love of the World Forbidden (2: 15-17)	237
Warnings Against Antichrist (2: 18-29)	241

SECTION III (3:1-5:12)

GOD IS LOVE

God's Love for Man (3: 1, 2) 256

Origin and Characteristics of Sinful Conduct (3: 3-12) 258

Love and Hate Contrasted (3: 13-24) 276

Spirit of Truth and Spirit of Error Contrasted (4: 1-6) 287

Brotherly Love Commanded (4: 7-21) 293

Tests of Faith and Love (5: 1-12) 307

SECTION IV (5: 13-21)

CONCLUSION

Additional Object in Writing (5: 13-15) 318

The Sin Unto Death (5: 16, 17) 319

Divine Assurances (5: 18-21) 323

Additional Note on 1 John 5: 7 324

INTRODUCTION

AUTHORSHIP OF THE EPISTLE

The evidence which obtains regarding the genuineness, authenticity, and canonicity of the Epistle of First John is abundant, reliable, and entirely satisfactory. No other book of the New Testament comes down to us with stronger claims on our credence than this. It may indeed be traced historically almost to the very hand of the disciple himself. Two of John's pupils, Polycarp and Papias, quote from it, attributing it to their teacher. The Muratorian Fragment refers to it in connection with the authorship of the epistle, and it is included in the Peshito and Itala Versions. Tertullian, Clement of Alexandria, Irenaeus, Origen, Cyprian, and many others of the so-called church fathers used it and thus witness to its traditional authorship. On the assumption that it was composed during the last decade of the first century, the witness of Polycarp and Papias extends to within twenty years of its composition; and when to this the consideration is added that these men were themselves students under the apostle and thus fully able to detect any fabrication of the writings of their teacher, yet accepted it as a product of the pen of the apostle to whom it is attributed, the evidence is such as is sufficient to convince any reasonable and candid mind. Inasmuch as much of the form and content of the Gospel according to John is reproduced in the Epistle, those who regard that work as a production of the apostle have no difficulty in attributing the Epistle to the same author. From the earliest period following the apostolic age there has been the conviction that the Epistle presumed to be, and actually was, the work of John the apostle. Inasmuch as the author never names himself, this conviction of writers both ancient and modern cannot be satisfactorily explained save on the ground that it is true, and that it began with the first readers who received the Epistle from the author who was known to them personally, and who thus became competent witnesses of its apostolic origin.

BIOGRAPHICAL SKETCH OF THE APOSTLE JOHN

The name "John" is from the Greek *Ioannes,* a term derived from the Hebrew *Jehohanan,* "Jehovah is gracious." He was the son of Zebedee, a well-to-do fisherman on the Sea of Galilee (Mark 1: 20; Luke 5: 10), and Salome, one of the women who followed the Lord and were with him at his crucifixion (Matt. 27: 56). He had a younger brother, James (Matt. 4: 21), with whom he is often mentioned, and he lived in Bethsaida (Luke 5: 10; John 1: 44). References, in the sacred writings, to "hired servants," his mother's "substance" (Luke 8: 3), his "own home" (John 19: 27), and his acquaintance with the high priest (John 18: 15), indicate a position of influence and means. From John 1: 35-39 we may infer that he was first a disciple of John the Baptist, and later left him to follow Jesus after the stirring announcement of the harbinger: "Behold, the Lamb of God!" (John 1: 35, 36.)

John, the apostle, was a close associate and friend of Simon Peter, and the two are mentioned together with great frequency, both in the books of the Gospel, and Acts of Apostles. They suffered imprisonment together in Jerusalem, following the healing of the lame man at the Beautiful Gate of the temple, and together went to Samaria to impart the Holy Spirit to the converts of Philip there. (Acts 4: 13; 8: 14-25.) James, brother of John, suffered martyrdom under Herod Agrippa. (Acts 12: 2.) John was one of the "pillars" of the church in Jerusalem on the occasion of Paul's visit there, recorded in Gal. 2: 1ff., and assisted in settling the controversy over circumcision which occasioned the conference mentioned in Acts 15.

From implications which occur in the historical references to the apostle in the New Testament we are led to believe that he went to Ephesus, was exiled to Patmos where the visions of the Revelation occurred; that he outlived all, or nearly all, of those with whom he was associated in his earlier years, including the other apostles; and that his lingering years were spent in combatting the numerous heresies which prevailed particularly in Ephesus. Tradition has it that when his capacity to work and to teach was gone, when he lacked even the strength to stand alone, he directed that he be borne to the meeting of the saints where, rising unsteadily and supporting himself with his cane, he would say with quavering voice, "Little children, love one another!"

Though one of the most prominent of the New Testament characters, and of frequent mention in our day because of the books which he left, there is surprisingly little of a historical nature recorded in the Bible concerning him. Though he wrote five books of the New Testament, viz., the Gospel according to John, the Epistles of First, Second, and Third John, and the Revelation—about one-fifth of the entire volume of the New Testament—his name is mentioned in the books of the Gospel only twenty times, and half of these include no more than the mere mention of his name. These books mention John the Baptist more than four times as often as they mention John the Apostle! And, in the five books which he himself wrote, his name occurs only *five times,* and all of these in the Book of Revelation, revealing little more than the fact that the visions there recorded were vouchsafed to him.

The only time he is mentioned alone in the synoptics is when he bore information to Jesus that he had forbidden a man to cast out demons because he did not belong to their company, a spirit of intolerance which Jesus rebuked. (Mark 9: 38; Luke 9: 49.) The only two times the two brothers are mentioned alone in these books are when they sought to call down fire on the inhospitable Samaritans, and when their mother made the unreasonable request that they be allowed to occupy chief positions in the kingdom. And yet Jesus loved John more than any other man who ever lived. He was charged by the Lord with the care of his mother Mary and served faithfully as a son in this honored capacity. He apparently came nearer to the heart of the Master than any other disciple. He appears to have revealed more of the heart of the Saviour than any of the other New Testament writers. Matthew and Mark and Luke busied themselves in the recital of what Jesus *did*; John was particularly concerned in telling us how Jesus *felt* and what he *thought!*

There was a tradition in the apostolic age, grounded on a misapprehension of the Lord's words to Peter, "If I will that he (John) tarry till I come, what is that to thee? follow thou me" (John 21: 21), that John would live until the Lord returned. His lingering age evidently gave credence to this impression, and though John did not himself share the view, yet as if recalling the actual words of the Lord on that occasion, the intense longing of his soul gathered itself up in the heartfelt cry, as he prepared to lay his pen forevermore aside. "Even so, come Lord Jesus!" (Rev. 22: 20.)

Intervening centuries have supplied their full quota of traditional matter regarding the apostle, most of which is either impossible or absurd; and we are without solid ground for drawing any definite conclusions regarding the place, time, or circumstances of his death. In the absence of such factual evidence, perhaps we would do well to remember the Master's rebuke to Peter, "If I will that he tarry till I come, what is that to thee? follow thou me."

For the reasons set out under "Date and Place of Writing," we are justified in drawing the conclusion that all of John's writings were composed late in the apostolic age, and after the death of the other New Testament writers. It was thus his function to supplement the writings of the others, and to close forevermore the sacred canon. For approximately sixteen hundred years men from Moses to John, about forty in number, had been instruments in the hands of the Spirit to reveal God's will to men, and it remained for this disciple whom Jesus loved best to set the seal on the faith once delivered to the saints. This he did when he penned the final words of the Revelation. And though new light may indeed break out from the deposit of truth which is the New Testament, through more accurate translation and from intenser application and more consecrated study, the word itself will receive no further additions. With John's final production, the words of Paul were fulfilled (1 Cor. 13: 18ff.), prophecies failed, tongues ceased, supernatural knowledge ended.

GENERAL CHARACTERISTICS OF THE EPISTLE

The similarity which exists between the First Epistle of John and the "Gospel" which bears his name is striking and obvious. This likeness extends to style, vocabulary, form, and content, and is of such nature as to convince the most casual reader that both compositions are from the same hand. Peculiarities of expression, turns of thought, and a fondness for key words and phrases occurring in the "Gospel" are repeatedly noted in the Epistle. "Life," "light," "love," "darkness," "death," "the world," "fellowship," "truth," are among the words which occur with amazing regularity in both books. Of the approximately two hundred and ninety-five different words in the vocabulary of the Epistle, only sixty-nine of them do not appear in the "Gospel."

There is here the same recurrence of ideas so characteristic of the Gospel according to John. Note, for example, the repetition of *love* in the following passage: "*Beloved,* let us *love* one another: for *love* is of God; and every one that *loveth* is begotten of God, and knoweth God. He that *loveth* not knoweth not God; for God is *love.* Herein was the *love* of God manifested in us, that God hath sent his only begotten Son into the world that we might live through him. Herein is *love,* not that we *loved* God, but that he *loved* us, and sent his Son to be the propitiation for our sins. *Beloved,* if God so *loved* us, we also ought to *love* one another. No man hath beheld God at any time; if we *love* one another, God abideth in us, and his *love* is perfected in us." (1 John 4: 7-12. Cf. John 5: 31-39. See 1 John 5: 7-11 for the recurrence of the word *witness* in the same manner.)

The same vivid and pointed contrasts are noticeable in both books. As in the Gospel, so here in the Epistles, life and death, light and darkness, children of God and children of the devil, love of God and love of the world, righteousness and unrighteousness, Christ and anti-christ, are again and again set over against each other in sharp contrast.

The teaching is identical and is presented in much the same fashion. (1) Christ is announced as the Word *(logos),* the complete expression of deity (John 1: 1; 1 John 1: 1-3), a concept peculiar to the apostle whom Jesus loved. (2) Only in the writings of John is Jesus styled the "only begotten Son." (John 3: 16; 1 John 4: 9.) (3) The books begin with the same idea, they close with the same thought. (Cf. John 21: 25; 1 John 5: 13.) (4) In at least thirty-five passages in the two productions, the thought is parallel, and in many of these instances, the same words and phrases are used. It is therefore not a matter of surprise that almost all scholars who believe that John wrote one of these books ascribes the other to him also. It has been said that it would be more feasible to assign any two of Shakespeare's plays to different authors than the "Gospel" and the First Epistle of John. They are, by all candid and reasonable standards, of the same family, and hence belong together.

The Epistle places great emphasis on love and has been called "The Epistle of Love." The word "love" and its derivatives occur fifty-one times. Various forms of the verb "know" occur in its vocabulary. It was a favorite term with the apostle, possibly in refutation of the peculiar theories of the Sophists and Gnostics who boasted of their superior knowledge. There are many assurances in the Epistle. "We know that we have passed out of death into life. . ." (1 John 3: 14.) "We know that we are of the truth." (3: 19.) "We know that he abideth in us." (3: 24). It is an Epistle of fellowship, the two conditions being righteousness and love. (1 John 1: 7-10.) The book is an Epistle of victory: "Ye are of God, my little children, and have overcome them: because greater is he that is in you than he that is in the world." (4: 4.) In the first chapter, the way to victory over sin is pointed out. The second chapter declares victory over the evil one. The victory of righteousness is proclaimed in the third chapter. In the fourth chapter we are shown the victory of love. The fifth chapter is a glorious demonstration of the victory of faith.

DESIGN OF THE EPISTLE

An indication of the general purpose and design of the Epistle may be gathered from the following affirmations of the apostle himself: "And these things we write, that our joy may be made full. . . ." "These things have I written unto you, that ye may know that ye have eternal life, even unto you that believe on the name of the Son of God." (1 John 1: 4; 5: 13.) By the side of this indication of purpose on the part of the apostle may be placed the declared design of the Gospel according to John. "Many other signs therefore did Jesus in the presence of the disciples, which are not written in this book: but these are written, that ye may believe that Jesus is the Christ, the Son of God: and that believing ye may have life in his name." (John 20: 30, 31.) We are thus to gather that in a general sense the purpose of both productions was to supply, in credible fashion, the evidence essential to faith, to quicken the readers to greater activity in the service of the Lord, and to provide assurance of God's approval upon all those who "believe on the name of the Son of God."

In order to the accomplishment of these objectives, it was necessary for the apostle to combat, in vigorous fashion, the various forms of evil then prevailing, and to warn the saints of the deadly nature thereof. Pernicious teaching regarding the person of Christ was afloat, and there were those in the church who had imbibed its poison and apostatized from the faith. (1 John 2: 19.) Some denied the *deity* of the Lord; others, his *humanity*. The former said that Jesus was not Christ; the latter, that Christ was not Jesus. Unbelieving Jews were in the vanguard of those who denied his deity; the Gnostics questioned his humanity. There were two groups of these Gnostics—the Docetic Gnostics, who denied the actual humanity of Christ, and the Cerinthian Gnostics, who attempted to distinguish between the man Jesus and the Christ which they alleged descended upon Jesus at his baptism and left him on the cross. The word "Gnostic" is derived from the Greek *gnosis,* knowledge, and they were so designated because of their claims to superior knowledge.

Gnosticism, whether of the Docetic or Cerinthian brand, was an admixture of paganism and corrupt Christianity. Basically, the theory regarded evil as an ever-present characteristic of matter, and its advocates were, therefore, unable to accept the doctrine of the incarnation—the assumption of flesh on the part of the Lord—on the ground that they believed it impossible for sinless deity to occupy a material body. They hence argued that the body of Jesus was not real, but an illusion and that the sufferings on the cross were apparent and not actual. The theory, in its practical aspects, was especially pernicious because its devotees were led into a course of conduct essentially wicked and vile in nature. Inasmuch as they regarded their bodies as evil, they concluded that their spirits were independent of them, and thus undefiled by them. They contended that once regenerated, they were pure in spirit, and it mattered not what the body did, since it was inherently evil anyway. They lived lives of unrestrained indulgence, on the ground that a jewel might lie in a dunghill and be just as much of a gem as in the most costly case! They believed that it was inevitable that their bodies should sin, and they argued that a thorough understanding of these matters left them free to indulge in any course of action which they preferred. It was this alleged superior knowledge which prompted them to style themselves the *Gnostics.*

There is a tradition which, if true, indicates the extreme distaste with which John the apostle regarded Cerinthus, advocate of this theory. Irenaeus, a pupil of Polycarp, who was himself a student of John, relates that Polycarp told him that the apostle, "the disciple of the Lord, going to bathe at Ephesus, and perceiving Cerinthus within, rushed out of the bathhouse without bathing, exclaiming, Let us fly, lest even the bathhouse fall down, because Cerinthus, the enemy of the truth, is within." (Against Heresies, Book 3, ch. 3, 4.)

In proof of the reality of the Lord's fleshly body, John offered testimony involving three of his five senses! He had heard, he had seen, and his hands had handled the Word of life, Jesus Christ the Lord. (1 John 1: 1-3.) And, in refutation of the wicked theories of unindulged activity in sin, the apostle repeatedly pointed out in the Epistle that only those who *do* righteousness are righteous, only those who are *pure* have hope, and those who *habitually sin* are of the devil. The Epistle is thus a clarion call to purity, a positive affirmation that those who are children of God have his "seed" in them, and cannot persistently continue in a life of sin because they are begotten of God." (3: 1-9.)

PERSONS ADDRESSED

Inasmuch as the Epistle of First John is without an address or superscription, it may rightly and properly be regarded as a "general" or "universal" Epistle, intended for Christians everywhere and in every age. That it was written primarily for Christians of the first century, and particularly for those of Ephesus where John lived and where the Docetic heresies were current, is a matter admitting of little doubt. The "little children," thus tenderly and familiarly addressed, were known to John and were possibly his own converts. (Cf. 3 John 4.) The fact that the readers were warned of idols (5: 21) indicates that they were of Gentile origin.

DATE AND PLACE OF WRITING

If the testimony of such early writers as Irenaeus (a pupil of Polycarp, who was himself a student under John), who lived in the early decades of the second century, may be regarded as reliable, it seems certain that John spent a number of years near the end of his life at Ephesus in Asia Minor. Inasmuch as the Epistle appears to have been written by an elderly man, we are safe in attributing it to the last years of John, and hence while sojourning in Ephesus, capital of Asia. To this conclusion most conservative scholars have come. There are, moreover, numerous considerations in the book itself which suggest that it was written near the close of the first century. It appeared at a time of external peace. It lacks the admonitions to fortitude under trial characteristic of other and earlier books of the New Testament. It was written to saints of considerable attainment and capable of a profound grasp of theological problems. On the basis of these facts, we assign it to a date just prior to the great outburst of persecution under the Roman Emperor, Domitian, A.D. 94. We think it must have been written about A.D. 90.

A COMMENTARY ON THE FIRST EPISTLE OF JOHN

SECTION ONE

INTRODUCTION
(1: 1-4)

PROOF OF THE MANIFESTATION OF THE WORD
(1: 1-3)

The Epistle opens with an exordium, or introduction (1: 1-4), in which the author sets out the personal experiences which had been his, thus enabling him to offer eyewitness testimony regarding the facts presented and to announce the purpose for which they were offered. This introduction consists of a lengthy and involved sentence, but it may be analyzed as follows: (a) beginning of the sentence in verse 1; (b) its temporary suspension and the insertion of verse 2 as a parenthetical statement to explain verse 1; (c) resumption of the original thought in verse 3 with enough of verse 1 repeated to enable the reader to resume the thought. Omitting the parenthetical statement of verse 2, we may gather up the thought set out in verses 1 and 3 as follows: "That which was from the beginning, which we have heard, which we have seen, which we beheld, and which our hands handled concerning the Word of life, we declare unto you also, that ye also may have fellowship with us."

The striking resemblance between this exordium of the First Epistle of John and the "Gospel" which he wrote is immediately apparent, and will appear clearly in the following parallel:

The Gospel	The Epistle
"In the beginning *(en arche)* was the Word." (1: 1.)	"That which was from the beginning" *(ap' arches)*. (1: 1.)
"And the Word was with God" *(pros ton Theon)*. (1: 1.)	"The Life . . . which was with the Father" *(pros ton patera)*, (Verse 2.)
"In him was life" *(zoe)*.	"The word of life." (1: 1.)
"The light shineth."	"The life was manifested."
"We beheld *(etheasametha)* his glory." (Verse 14.)	"That which we beheld" *(etheasmetha)*. (Verse 1.)

1 That which was from the beginning, that which we have heard, that which we have seen with our eyes, that which we beheld, and our hands

1 **That which was from the beginning,**—Instead of a personal pronoun in the masculine gender which we would ordinarily expect in this instance, the sentence begins with a neuter relative, *that which.* The reference is thus not to Christ contemplated as a person only, but to the attributes and characteristics which he, as the Word, possesses. It was "concerning the Word of life" which John purposed to write, hence the neuter to express a collective or comprehensive whole. The words "from the beginning" are reminiscent of "In the beginning was the Word" (John 1: 1), and "In the beginning God created the heavens and the earth" (Gen. 1: 1.) However, "the beginning" in John's phraseology does not always indicate the same period; in any given instance, the context must be examined to determine its significance. "Beloved, no new commandment write I unto you, but an old commandment which ye had from the beginning" (1 John 2: 7), "the beginning" denoting the time when these to whom John wrote became Christians. "He that doeth sin is of the devil; for the devil sinneth from the beginning." (1 John 3: 8.) Here the beginning points to the time when Satan came into possession of his devilish character— the occasion of his sin and fall. "I have written unto you, little children, because ye know the Father. I have written unto you, fathers, because ye have known him who is from the beginning" (1 John 2: 14), i.e., from all eternity. In our text "from the beginning" points to that period before creation, and therefore into the eternity which precedes it. It is an affirmation of the eternal characteristics of the Lord and the attributes which he possesses.

That which we have heard, that which we have seen with our eyes, that which we beheld, and our hands handled concerning the Word of life.—It will be observed that there is a fourfold repetition of the neuter *that which (ho)* introducing the phrases which follow: (1) that which was from the beginning; (2) that which we have heard; (3) that which we have seen with our eyes; (4) that which we beheld and our hands handled. The first of these, "that which was from the beginning," is an affirmation of the eternal character of that to which reference is made; the

handled, concerning the ¹Word of life 2 (and the life was manifested, and we

¹Or, *word* Comp. Acts 5. 20.

---

three which follow indicate John's relation thereto. That which was from the beginning he (and others) had (a) heard; (b) seen with his eyes; (c) beheld; and (d) handled. Each of the verbs *heard, seen, beheld,* and *handled,* in rising gradation, sharpens the concept and vivifies the thought intended by the writer. The lowest in the scale which he presents is hearing. There is no personal contact in hearing; it may be done from a distance, without design or purpose, indeed, unwillingly. Seeing is likewise involuntary, though the eyes may be averted from that which we do not desire to see. The word "beheld," however, indicates conscious and willful participation; it denotes more than mere seeing *(etheasametha),* from which it is translated, suggests a steady and penetrating gaze designed to hold the object in view until all its characteristics are noted. Also inherent in the meaning of the word is the idea of contemplating with pleasure, looking with delight, finding satisfaction in the object thus contemplated. The verb *handled* suggests the most tangible, intimate, and definite evidence which John offered. In it there was physical contact. Thus three senses—hearing, seeing, and touching—were utilized by the apostle to obtain evidence of the reality of the Word of life about which he testifies here. The reason why the apostle felt it necessary to deal thus minutely with the evidence, and to offer testimony in such detailed fashion is to be seen in the nature of the false doctrines prevalent regarding the person of the Christ. (See under "Design of the Epistle" in the Introduction.) The Lord was not a mere influence, nor yet a shadowy phantom, but a living, vibrant, tangible personality whose voice John had heard, whose body he had seen, and whom he had touched with his own hands.

The testimony which the apostle offered was "concerning the Word of life." This does not mean the gospel, but he who is its source, the *logosa* (John 1: 1), the complete expression of deity. The testimony which John offered was with reference to the Word in the flesh, the second person in the Godhead, the Lord himself. "Of life" is in apposition to "word" *(logosa)* and is descriptive of the Word thus designated. The prepositional phrase "of life" is

have seen, and bear witness, and declare unto you the life, the eternal *life*, which was with the Father, and was manifested unto us; 3 that which we

frequently used by the Lord to describe his various characteristics. He is "the life" (John 11: 25; 14: 6); "the bread of life" (John 6: 35, 48); "the light of life" (John 8: 12). Thus, the neuter relative, "that which," points to the matters concerning, pertaining to, and descriptive of Christ as the Word (the full expression) of life. John was particularly careful to guard his readers against the conclusion that the Word of life was merely some speech or saying delivered by Christ, and hence emphasized that it was the actual, literal, fleshly body of Christ which he had seen, beheld, heard, and his hand had handled. Here, as in the first chapter of the Gospel by the same writer, is refuted the Gnostic heresy that Christ was not really in the flesh but only appeared to be. There, he declared that the "Word became flesh, and dwelt among us" (John 1: 14); here, that he was in possession of tangible, definite evidence of his reality.

2 (**And the life was manifested, and we have seen, and bear witness, and declare unto you the life, the eternal life, which was with the Father, and was manifested unto us**);— This verse is parenthetical and repeats the sense of verse 1, revealing why John and those similarly situated—the other apostles— were able to bear witness of and declare Jesus as the life. To "manifest" is to make visible in the sense of revelation; to make known matters formerly concealed. Because this life was revealed, John had been privileged through investigation—hearing, seeing, gazing upon, and handling—to obtain sensible knowledge of him thus revealed, and hence to be able to bear testimony regarding him. A progression of ideas is to be noted here, each of which, in ascending order, indicates the care which John exercised in leading his readers to the conclusion he desired: (1) the life was manifested (in the incarnation); (2) John had seen it; (3) he was, therefore, competent to testify regarding it; (4) this he was doing in declaring "the life, the eternal life," which, before his advent into the world, had been with the Father.

This life had been with the Father prior to the incarnation and is thus eternal. Here is the first of four stages indicated in the sacred writings regarding the second person of the Godhead and

have seen and heard declare we unto you also, that ye also may have fellowship with us: yea, and our fellowship is with the Father, and with his Son

points irresistibly to his deity: (1) his pre-existence in eternity as the Word prior to creation; (2) his foreshadowing in the Old Testament period as the angel of Jehovah, the anticipated Messiah, etc.; (3) his incarnate life on earth; (4) his present glorified state in heaven at the right hand of God, the Father, on the throne of David. (Acts 2: 25-36.) A complete study of the life of our Lord must proceed from each of these heads.

3 **That which we have seen and heard declare we unto you also, that ye also may have fellowship with us;**—The apostle here resumes the thought begun in verse 1, and asserts the purpose for which the Word of life is declared: "That ye also may have fellowship with us." "Fellowship" *(koinonia)* is partnership, joint sharing. Through the acceptance of the Word of life a unity of faith, practice, and worship is established, and it was for this purpose that the life was being declared. Here, in the most emphatic fashion, the writer points out that only in unity of faith is there communion in religion. It is possible to have fellowship only when there is a common bond established in faith, work, and love.

Yea, and our fellowship is with the Father, and with his Son Jesus Christ:—Where there is communion among the saints, established through the acceptance of the truth, it leads on to fellowship with the Father and his Son, Jesus Christ. (1 Cor. 1: 9.) Here, indeed, is the only way to church unity; a common faith based on unity of teaching and practice. When such obtains, there is unity among the believers, and the bond of fellowship thus established is extended to include both the Father and the Son. We thus learn that the society of the saints is not limited to the earth: it extends into heaven and consists of an intimate bond of sympathy with deity itself. On the other hand, when there is an alienation of fellowship here, there is an inevitable severance of such in heaven. Brethren cannot allow themselves to become alienated from each other here without suffering similar alienation from the Lord himself. That this unity might prevail, Jesus prayed: "Neither for these only do I pray, but for them also that believe on me through their word; that they may all be one; even as thou, Father, art in me, and I in thee, that they also may be in us: that the world may believe that thou didst send me." (John 17: 21.)

PURPOSE OF WRITING
(1: 4)

Jesus Christ: 4 and these things we write, that ²our joy may be made full.

---
²Many ancient authorities read *your*.

---

4 And these things we write, that our joy may be made full.—"These things" were the matters immediately referred to in the early verses of the chapter and, in a secondary sense, in all of the Epistle. The plural pronoun "we" is a common literary device and does not, of course, mean that others were joined with John in the authorship of this Epistle. (Cf. 2 Cor. 1: 1; Col. 1: 1; Phil. 1: 1; Phile. 1: 1; 1 Thess. 1: 1.) The purpose for which "these things" were penned was that the joy of John might abound. Through the announcement of the testimony regarding Christ (verse 1) fellowship would obtain (verse 3), and the effect of this fellowship was joy. The same writer later said, "I rejoiced greatly, when brethren came and bare witness unto thy truth, even as thou walkest in the truth. Greater joy have I none than this, to hear of my children walking in the truth." (3 John 3, 4.)

In the foregoing verses is another of the many parallels which occur between this Epistle and the Gospel by the same writer:

The Epistle	The Gospel
"That ye also may have fellowship with us." (1: 3.)	"That they may all be one." (17: 20.)
"Our fellowship is with the Father and his Son, Jesus Christ." (1: 3.)	"That they also may be one in us." (17: 21.)
"These things we write, that our joy may be made full." (1: 4.)	"And these things I speak in the world, that they may have my joy made full in themselves." (17: 13.)

SECTION TWO

GOD IS LIGHT
(1: 5-2: 28)

CONDITIONS OF FELLOWSHIP WITH GOD
(1: 5-7)

5 And this is the message which we have heard from him and announce unto you, that God is light, and in him is no darkness at all. 6 If we say

5 And this is the message which we have heard from him and announce unto you, that God is light, and in him is no darkness at all.—Again the apostle cites the sensible evidence which he had of the Lord's identity, emphasized so strongly in verse 1, as the ground of his readers' acceptance of the "message" which he was announcing, viz., (1) God is light; (2) in him is no darkness at all. This message John and the other apostles had "heard" from "him," i.e., Christ. The affirmation, "God is light," is not the same as "God is *the* light" or "God is *a* light," but simply God is light, such is his essence; he is of the character of light. The word "light" sums up the divine character on the intellectual side, as "God is love," similarly describes the fullness of his moral nature. He is the "author" of light (James 1: 17), its creator (Gen. 1: 3); he is bathed in perpetual light (1 Tim. 6: 16); and the marvelous light in which Christians are to walk is his (1 Pet. 2: 9). Moreover, "in him is no darkness at all." "Darkness" is a figure of ignorance, superstition, and sin, as "light" represents truth, purity, and goodness. In this manner, God is contrasted with the heathen deities the worship of which promoted immorality, ungodliness, and gross sin. The devil and his agents are styled "the world rulers of this darkness" (Eph. 6: 12), and their domain is called "the power of darkness" (Col. 1: 13). Those formerly enmeshed in the mazes of heathenism were said to have been "once darkness," but now, as the result of their obedience to the gospel, "light in the Lord." (Eph. 5: 8.) Paul gave thanks unto the Father, "who made us meet to be partakers of the inheritance of the saints in light." (Col. 1: 12.)

Though there is much darkness in the world, "darkness *in him* there is none whatsoever." This statement, in the Greek text, is an exceedingly emphatic one, the two negatives, *ouk estin oudemia*,

that we have fellowship with him and walk in the darkness, we lie, and do not the truth: 7 but if we walk in the light, as he is in the light, we have

---

signifying "no, not even one tiny particle!" There is no discoloration, no admixture of darkness in the pure light which streams from the character of God. He is, indeed, "the Father of lights, with whom can be no variation, neither shadow that is cast by turning." (James 1: 17.)

6 **If we say that we have fellowship with him and walk in the darkness, we lie, and do not the truth:**—This verse contains a conclusion drawn from premises in the verse preceding. The situation which he assumes is a hypothetical one: Should one say, "I have fellowship with God," and yet walks in darkness, his words are false, and he does not the truth. "Walk" is a figure of the Christian life, summing up its activities. The Lord said, "I am the light of the world; he that followeth me shall not walk in the darkness, but shall have the light of life." (John 8: 12.) To be in fellowship with God, one must walk in the light; he who claims it, yet does not walk therein, sins both in word and in deed. Here, as often elsewhere in the sacred writings, it is made clear that theory and practice in religion are inseparably connected. Truth, properly held, always exhibits itself in obedience. Those who "walk in darkness" are not only sinful in conduct; their disposition is one of hatred and envy. "He that saith he is in the light, and hateth his brother, is in the darkness even until now. He that loveth his brother abideth in the light, and there is no occasion of stumbling in him. But he that hateth his brother is in the darkness, and walketh in the darkness, and knoweth not whither he goeth, because the darkness hath blinded his eyes." (1 John 2: 9-11.)

7 **But if we walk in the light, as he is in the light, we have fellowship one with another,**—The verb "walk" here *(ean peripatomen)* is present active subjunctive, thus literally, "If we keep on walking in the light. . . ." It must be a continuing walk. Moreover, we are to walk in the light in which the Father is. We are in the light only when fellowship with him obtains; and in this light must we remain. It is conditional whether we are in it, but such is his constant habitation. His dwelling is in "light unapproachable." (1 Tim. 6: 16.) If the element of our daily walk is

fellowship one with another, and the blood of Jesus his Son cleanseth us

the same as God's, "we have fellowship one with another." "Fellowship" *(koinonia)* is partnership, joint participation, communion. Thus only through fellowship with God is fellowship with the brethren possible. Fellowship with the brethren involves mutual assistance in all the difficulties of life; it includes the bearing of one another's burdens (Gal. 6: 2), the sharing of all the sorrows and joys which constitute life. "And whether one member suffereth, all the members suffer with it; or one member is honored, all the members rejoice with it. Now ye are the body of Christ, and severally members thereof." (1 Cor. 12: 26, 27.)

And the blood of Jesus his Son cleanseth us from all sin.—This clause is coordinate with "we have fellowship one with another," and is a statement of the means by which it is possible for us to walk in the light. Thus, by walking in the light two results follow: (1) we have fellowship with each other; (2) the blood of Jesus cleanses us from all sin. Cleansing efficacy is thus attributed to the blood of Christ. Many important considerations follow from this passage: (a) It is not the mere example of Christ's dying that accomplishes our salvation; (b) it is not simply the contemplation of his death which delivers us from the guilt of sin; (c) it is not belief in the moral implications of Calvary which produces the blessing; nor (d) faith in the suffering of Christ on the cross. It is the blood, the shed blood of the Son of God, that cleanses us from sin. Moreover, it cleanses from *sin,* not merely or solely the conscience, but sin *(amartias),* all sin, whether of thought, word, or deed, rash sins, sins of ignorance, of malice, of omission or commission, sins of the flesh, sins of the disposition, sins of pleasure or of pain, sins of every type and kind committed at any time or place.

"Cleanseth" is from the verb *katharizei,* in the present tense, thus revealing that it is a constant process, conditioned on our walking in the light. As we thus walk the blood operates to keep us constantly cleansed from the defilement of sin and the condemnation which attends it. This verse is an exceedingly significant and comprehensive one, in the light of the false doctrines which were in vogue when the Epistle appeared and which it was written to refute. Established beyond reasonable controversy are the following important propositions: (1) the reality of the body and blood of Jesus; (2) the sufferings which he experienced on the tree of the cross; (3) the efficacy of the blood which he shed.

SIN AND ITS FORGIVENESS
(1: 8-10)

from all sin. 8 If we say that we have no sin, we deceive ourselves, and the

---

8 If we say that we have no sin, we deceive ourselves, and the truth is not in us.—Inasmuch as there is no article before the word "sin" in this passage, it is contemplated in essence, abstractly considered. These words were penned to refute the prevailing notion of the heretics—and some to this day advocate the same view—that it is possible for one to live above sin. Those who so affirm (a) deceive themselves, and (b) exhibit the fact that the truth is not in them. Because of the weakness of the flesh and the ever-present problem of temptation, even the best of people inadvertently sin, and hence have need of the cleansing power inherent in the blood of Jesus. Aware of such, John was shortly to write: "My little children, these things write I unto you that ye may not sin. And if any man sin, we have an Advocate with the Father, Jesus Christ the righteous." (1 John 2: 1.) *Those who deny that they have sin, add to the sin they already have, and sin in so affirming!* The ever-present problem of sin is adduced by the apostle as the reason why children of God must have the cleansing power of the blood applied. This clearly refutes the notion that men have lived, or may live in this life, without sin. The truth is not *in* those who so allege. It may be around them or near them, but it is not in them; it does not constitute a part of their character. These to whom John wrote had been forgiven of their past or alien sins; thus reference here is not to any previous state of guilt prior to conversion but to *present sin*, sin at the time he wrote, sins of omission and commission, sins of the flesh and of the disposition, all sin, any sin of which we may be guilty. The recognition and confession of sin is a prerequisite to our approval before God. To refuse such recognition and confession is simply to deceive ourselves and to demonstrate the fact that the truth is not in us.

truth is not in us. 9 If we confess our sins, he is faithful and righteous to

9 If we confess our sins, he is faithful and righteous to forgive us our sins, and to cleanse us from all unrighteousness. —The phrase, "If we say. . . ," a mere formal admission of guilt (verse 8), becomes here "If we confess. . . ," a much more vivid concept. One may indeed "say" *(eipon)* that he has sin without experiencing any deep or abiding sense of guilt or wrong and without being moved to repentance. The confession *(homologe)* here contemplated is a humble acknowledgment of wrong, a penitent attitude essential to forgiveness. The word *homologeo,* from which the word "confess" is translated, means to say the same thing, to speak together, and figuratively implies a dialogue between God and the sinner, in which the Father describes the condition of the sinner, and the sinner finally accedes to the correctness of the description and thus confesses that God is right!

The word "sin" of verse 8, an abstract concept of wrong, becomes "sins," individual and specific acts of wrongdoing in verse 9. It follows, therefore, that the sins we are to confess are the specific and particular manifestations of the sin which all sincere believers of the Word know in their hearts they possess.

The verb "confess" is translated from a present active subjunctive, thus literally, "If we keep on confessing our sins. . . ," indicative of a continuous process. There are two definite and specific types of confession required of the erring in the New Testament: (1) confession before the Father, as here; (2) acknowledgment of sins before others, as in James 5: 16. It is scarcely necessary to add that an additional confession before a priest on the pretext that such a one can absolve sins is wholly unknown to the New Testament, is contrary to the teaching of the scriptures, and inimical to the genius and character of the Christian religion. With Jesus as our Priest, Mediator, and Advocate, we need no other assistance in approaching the Throne of Grace. (Heb. 7: 25; 10: 19, 20; 1 John 2: 1; 1 Tim. 2: 5.)

If we keep on confessing our sins, God "is faithful and righteous to forgive us our sins, and to cleanse us from all unrighteousness." "Faithfulness" and "righteousness" are attributes of the great Jehovah; and when we confess our sins before him, we enter into

forgive us our sins, and to cleanse us from all unrighteousness. 10 If we say that we have not sinned, we make him a liar, and his word is not in us.

and partake of the blessings which result from them. He has promised to forgive us on condition that we confess our sins; and since he is faithful, he will not fail in the performance of his promises. David joined these attributes in Psalm 143: 1: "Hear my prayer, O Jehovah; give ear to my supplications; in thy faithfulness answer me, and in thy righteousness." It is God's *nature* to be faithful and righteous, and it is his *purpose* to cleanse when the conditions—confession and penitence—are met. "Unrighteousness," the opposite of "righteousness," is synonymous with the word sin, of verse 8. Wrongdoing is set forth under various aspects in the scriptures. A collection of terms indicative of its different qualities occurs in Ex. 34: 7.

10 If we say that we have not sinned, we make him a liar, and his word is not in us.—Compare verse 8. Here, again, there is an advance in thought, as in verses 8 and 9. The "if we say we have no sin" (abstractly considered) becomes here, "If we say that we have not sinned . . ." (have not been guilty of specific and concrete acts of sin). Verse 10 designates specific acts of sin; in verse 8 sin is regarded as a state or condition. Those who insist that they have not sinned make God a "liar" and demonstrate the fact that God's word is not in them. Much emphasis is given here to the fact and reality of sin in the lives of us all. Those who deny this *lie* (verse 6) *deceive themselves* (verse 8) make God a liar (verse 10). Taught here, in the most emphatic fashion possible, is the constant and recurring need of pardon on the part of all children of God. Not only is such essential to the alien sinner in order that he may be adopted into the fellowship of God; he must continue to seek it and avail himself of its benefits throughout life. As sin is evermore about us, and, alas, all too often in us, we must continually seek new pardons through the means hereinbefore set forth. This section of the Epistle, far from teaching that the Lord forgave us of all sins, "past, present, and future," as the advocates of the doctrine of the impossibility of apostasy allege, establishes the fact of an ever-present need of the cleansing power of the blood of Jesus Christ our Lord. Happily we have the assurance that "the blood of Jesus his Son keeps on cleansing us from all sin" (verse 7) as we conform to the conditions on which such depends.

Those who deny the fact of sin in their lives make God a liar by contradicting his express statements of man's sinfulness before him, and they demonstrate the fact that the truth is not in them by exhibiting ignorance of the truth in their allegation.

JESUS OUR ADVOCATE
(2: 1, 2)

2 My little children, these things write I unto you that ye may not sin. And if any man sin, we have an ³Advocate with the Father, Jesus Christ the

---

³Or, *Comforter* Jn. 14. 16. Or, *Helper* Gr. *Paraclete*.

---

1 My little children, these things write I unto you that ye may not sin.—The words of this section are to be construed and considered along with the matters set forth in chapter 1. It should be remembered that when John wrote, the chapter and verse divisions now characteristic of the text were not there. This section was designated to show, (1) the *means* by which one is enabled to walk in the light; (2) the *conditions* upon which forgiveness is available, viz., (a) a confession of sins and (b) the forsaking of them.

The chapter begins with a term of endearment: "My little children. . . ." The apostle John, when he wrote these words, was an old man, and the mode of address is such as might be expected from an aged one to those near and dear and *much* younger. There are two Greek words translated by the phrase "little children" in the Epistle. The first of these, *teknia*, plural diminutive of *teknon*, occurs here and at 2: 12, 28; 3: 18; 4: 4; 5: 21, and only elsewhere, in the New Testament, in John 13: 33, where the Lord used it, and which use likely occasioned John's adoption of it here. It is a word which, when figuratively used, designates the spiritual relation of children to a father in the faith. (See 1 Cor. 4: 15, where the idea, but not the word, occurs.) The second word translated by the phrase "little children" is *paidia*, occurring in 2: 13, 18. This word denotes the age and characteristics of childhood, and, as here used, conveys the kind and tender address of age to youth, of authority to subordinates, or wisdom to ignorance.

righteous: 2 and he is the propitiation for our sins; and not for ours only,

"These things" embrace the matters which were written in the closing portion of chapter 1, the purpose of which was to lead the saints to forsake all sin. "That ye may not sin" is a negative purpose clause in the aorist tense, and the apostle thus warned against even isolated acts of sin. Fellowship with the Father and with his Son, Jesus Christ, and with all saints depends on walking in the light, and only those walk in the light who, as far as they are able, abstain from sinful conduct. Thus, those to whom John wrote stood in relation to him as his "little children" in the Lord. He has written to them for the purpose of warning aginst any participation in sinful acts. But what if some, in spite of such counsel, inadvertently fell into sin? Their case was not hopeless.

And if any man sin, we have an Advocate with the Father, Jesus Christ the righteous:—Though the followers of the Lord are ever to strive to avoid any participation in sinful activity, when such occurs, they are not to despair; they have an "advocate," Jesus Christ the righteous. The verb "have" here is, significantly, in the present tense *(echomen),* thus literally, "We keep on having" an ever-present remedy for the isolated acts of sin which, through weakness, ignorance, and inadvertence, we commit. An "Advocate" is a lawyer or an attorney, whose function it is to represent one in court. Jesus thus represents us in the court of heaven, pleading our cause and advocating our case before the bar of God's divine justice. As our Advocate, he is "with" *(pros)* the Father, thus at his side, and ever present to afford us adequate and constant representation. There is no article before the word "righteousness" in the Greek text. The meaning is, Jesus, a righteous one, pleads the cause of unrighteous ones. Only the pleading of such an Advocate could possibly avail. An advocate himself in need of intercession could not hope to influence the great Judge in behalf of others.

2 And he is the propitiation for our sins; and not for ours only, but also for the whole world.—To "propitiate" is to appease and render favorable, to conciliate. The word "propitiation," in the text, occurs only here and in 1 John 40: 10, in the New Testament, though other forms of it are in Luke 18: 13;

but also for the whole world. 3 And hereby we know that we know him, if

Rom. 3: 25; and Heb. 2: 17. Here is announced but one of the many aspects of the death of Christ in our behalf. (1) He propitiates *(Hilasmos)* the Father, thus rendering him favorable toward us. (2) He reconciles *(katallasso)* us to God, enabling us to be at peace with him. (Rom. 5: 11; 2 Cor. 5: 18, 19.) (3) As a ransom *(apolutrosis)* for us, he paid the debt, permitting us to go free from the thralldom and bondage of sin. The blessings of this propitiation extend to the whole world and have been made available to all mankind. Here is positive and undeniable evidence of the falsity of any system of theology which would limit the benefits of the atonement, or deny its blessings to any portion of the human family. Martin Luther well said, "It is a patent fact that thou too art a part of the whole world; so that thine heart cannot deceive itself and think, the Lord died for Peter and Paul, but not for me." No man is outside the mercy of God, except as he deliberately places himself there through the repudiation of the plan which was evolved to save him.

This entire section, 1: 5-2: 2, is a closely-knit and well-ordered argument, designed to reveal the blessings available to us through Christ. (1) There is no darkness in God, for he is light. (1: 5.) (2) If we affirm that we have fellowship with him, yet walk in darkness, we lie, and do not the truth. (1: 6.) (3) If we walk in the light, (a) we enjoy such fellowship, and (b) the blood of Jesus Christ constantly cleanses us from any sin which, through weakness of the flesh, or the infirmities of our nature we commit. (1: 7.) (4) The truth is in us if we acknowledge our sins. (1: 8, 9.) (5) Shall we then disregard all warnings against sin on the ground that the blood of Christ operates to cleanse us? God forbid. (2: 1, 2.) The purpose of the entire section is to warn against this very thing. Avoid sin when possible. But if into it you fall, do not despair. Rely on your Advocate who effectively pleads your case in heaven!

It is significant that John did not say, *"Ye* have an Advocate . . ." nor "Ye have *me* for an Advocate," but *"We* have an Advocate . . ." thus including himself among those in need of the intercession before the throne of grace which Jesus alone can supply. Walking in the light requires: (1) fellowship with the Father and with his Son, Jesus Christ; (2) acceptance of the propitiation provided through the shed blood of the Lord; (3) obedience to the Lord's commandments. This third condition, of walking in the light, John develops in the section to follow.

TESTS OF THE CHRISTIAN
(2: 3-6)

we keep his commandments. 4 He that saith, I know him, and keepeth not

3 **And hereby we know that we know him, if we keep his commandments.**—"Hereby" *(en toutoi)*, literally, "in this," a phrase often used by the apostle, and occurring at 2: 5; 3: 16, 19; 4: 2, 13; 5: 2. It refers to the clause, "If we keep his commandments." "Keep," here, is present subjunctive, thus, "If we keep on keeping his commandments." We are informed here that it is possible for us to "know that we know him." How, or in what way? *If we keep his commandments!* To know him is to have far more than an acquaintance with his nature; it is to enter into the most intimate relationship with him as his child. It is possible to claim a knowledge of God and of Christ and to be deceived. Paul writes of those who "profess that they know God; but by their works they deny him, being abominable, and disobedient, and unto every good work reprobate." (Tit. 1: 16.) One does not know God who does not conform to his will. We may believe intellectually that there is a God; we may affirm the truth of his existence, the facts of his attributes, the reality of his works in nature. But only those who have wholly committed their wills to his know him in his saving power. "And this is life eternal, that they should know thee the only true God, and him whom thou didst send, even Jesus Christ." (John 17: 3.) It if be asked *which* commandments constitute the test here submitted, the answer is, *All* of them! Any commandment we are disposed to break because of our unwillingness to bend our wills to his provides the occasion which demonstrates lack of full knowledge of him. This is the "one thing" which we "lack" and which, like the young ruler's riches, will close the door of heaven in our face.

4 **He that saith, I know him, and keepeth not his commandments, is a liar, and the truth is not in him;**—A conclusion drawn from the foregoing premises, and a further affirmation

his commandments, is a liar, and the truth is not in him; 5 but whoso keep-

of the truth above expressed. The Gnostics boasted of their superior knowledge and spiritual insight and maintained their acquaintance with the Lord despite the fact that they kept not his commandments. With reference to all such the apostle solemnly declares, "He that saith, I know him, and keepeth not his commandments, is a liar, and the truth is not in him." The verbs in the Greek text are in the present tense. He who keeps on saying, I know him, and yet keeps not on keeping his commandments, is a liar, and the truth is not in him. Far from actually and really knowing God, those who refuse to do his will are, in addition to being disobedient characters, liars and without truth. The words "He is a liar" are more emphatic than "we lie," of John 1: 6, and "we deceive ourselves," of 1: 8. His status is not simply that of one who is guilty of a single falsehood, or one who is innocently deceived; his acts of falsehood have become embedded in his character and he is, essentially, a *liar*. Such a one is demonstrating the nature and character of his father, the devil, who is a liar from the beginning. (John 8: 44.) It was evidently no uncommon thing for men, at the time John wrote, who had adopted the pernicious doctrine of the Gnostics to affirm that they, though willfully guilty of sinful acts, were not thereby corrupted. Some of these men maintained that they were no more polluted by sin than gold is by the mire into which it might fall.

As shocking as the foregoing theology is, it has its modern counterparts. Those false teachers, while denying any contamination from sin, did admit the fact of sin in their lives. There are those today who deny *both* the sin and the contamination. A prominent denominational preacher, in a tract entitled, "Do a Christian's Sins Damn His Soul?" wrote: "We take the position that a Christian's sins do not damn his soul. The way a Christian lives, what he says, his character, his conduct, or his attitude toward other people have nothing whatever to do with the salvation of his soul. . . . All the prayers a man may pray, all the Bibles he may read, all the churches he may belong to, all the services he may attend, all the sermons he may practice, all the debts he may pay, all the ordinances he may observe, all the laws he may keep, all the benevolent acts he may perform will not make his soul one whit

eth his word, in him verily hath the love of God been perfected. Hereby we know that we are in him: 6 he that saith he abideth in him ought himself also to walk even as he walked.

---

safer; and all the sins he may commit from idolatry to murder will not make his soul in any more danger. . . . *The way a man lives has nothing whatsoever to do with the salvation of his soul.*" Such theology, whether ancient or modern, is precisely in principle what John condemned when he affirmed that those who say they know him, yet do not keep his commandments, are liars.

5 But whoso keepeth his word, in him verily hath the love of God been perfected.—"Keepeth his word," of verse 5, is synonymous with "keeping his commandments" of verse 4. Here, as in 1: 7, 9, the opposite of that immediately preceding is stated, and the thought advanced one step further. The "love of God" here contemplated is not God's love for us, but our love for God, and the affirmation of the apostle is that he who keeps God's word has his love for God perfected. "Perfected" is perfect passive indicative of *teleioo,* to stand complete. Thus, he who keeps the commandments of God matures his love, for such is the way in which love for God manifests itself. "For this is the love of God, that we keep his commandments: and his commandments are not grievous." (1 John 5: 3.) It is idle for one to claim love for God while neglecting or refusing to do his commandments. Such is the acid test of one's love.

Hereby we know that we are in him:—I.e., by keeping his word. The words "in him" indicate a relationship of the most intimate nature. The phrase is a summary of all the blessings available from God. To know God we must keep his word; those who keep his word love him; but those who love him are *in him.* Fruit bearing produced as the result of love for God is evidence of our union with him. "Abide in me, and I in you. As the branch cannot bear fruit of itself, except it abide in the vine; so neither can ye except ye abide in me. I am the vine, ye are the branches: he that abideth in me, and I in him, the same beareth much fruit; for apart from me ye can do nothing." (John 15: 4, 5.)

6 He that saith he abideth in him ought himself also to walk even as he walked.—There is here, as in verse 4, a boastful attitude hinted at. He who represents himself as abiding in the

Lord has the definite obligation to "walk even as he walked," i.e., in the light, in fellowship with God, in keeping his commandments. In this manner alone does one demonstrate the soundness of his claim and the validity of his profession. "Ought," from *opheilo,* to be in debt, denotes the moral obligation here to exhibit the basis of one's profession. To walk as Christ walked is to follow him as the perfect model and guide that he is. Nothing less than this will meet the demands of the case. The *walk* of the Lord which we are to imitate is, obviously, to be found in the religious, moral, and spiritual activities of his life on earth. There is no reference here to the miraculous powers which Jesus exhibited on earth. As Martin Luther fittingly remarks, it "is not Christ's walking on the sea that we are to imitate, but his ordinary walk." The verb "walk" is figuratively used to denote the activity which must characterize us as children of God. Jesus used it in this sense (John 8: 12; 12: 35), as did Paul (Eph. 2: 10; Col. 3: 7; Rom. 6: 4). But how did Christ walk? The answer is to be found in the whole of the things recorded concerning him in the sacred volume. These words sum up the life of Christ on earth.

COMMANDMENTS NEW AND OLD
(2: 7-11)

7 Beloved, no new commandment write I unto you, but an old commandment which ye had from the beginning: the old commandment is the word

---

7 Beloved, no new commandment write I unto you, but an old commandment which ye had from the beginning: the old commandment is the word which ye heard.—The apostle had just commanded his readers to walk as Christ walked. (Verse 6.) This walk was grounded in, and originated in, love. Hence, the commandment to love God was not a new one, i.e., a novel, unusual thing. These to whom John wrote had been aware of this obligation, yea, had in some measure followed it from the beginning of their Christian life. Far from being a *new* thing, this commandment was essential to their salvation from sin; they were already in possession of it; they had possessed it from the beginning. This commandment was the "word" which they had "heard." The "word" sums up the message they had received; "heard" indicates the manner of reception. They had "heard" it; it therefore came

which ye heard. 8 Again, a new commandment write I unto you, which thing is true in him and in you; because the darkness is passing away, and

to them through preaching. The *time* when they heard it was at the beginning of their Christian experience.

8 Again, a new commandment write I unto you, which thing is true in him and in you; because the darkness is passing away, and the true light already shineth.—Though the commandment to love is as old as the race (1 John 3: 1ff., particularly verses 11, 12), from another aspect it is always new. To walk as the Lord walked and hence to comply with the requirements of the "old commandment" is as old as religion, but each new compliance therewith constitutes a new and fresh approach thereto. Love, as old as man, becomes new with each experience. It was the Lord himself who designated the command to love one another as a *new* one: "A new commandment I give unto you, that ye love one another; even as I have loved you, that ye also love one another." (John 13: 34.) The newness was not merely or solely in the command to love; the law and the prophets required this. (Deut. 10: 19; Mic. 6: 8, etc.) It was the *measure* or *extent* of the love that made it new: "even as I have loved you." Never before the Christian age had such a love been required of man. It was henceforth to be a condition precedent to discipleship; indeed, the badge and token thereof: "A new commandment I give unto you, that ye love one another; even as I have loved you, that ye also love one another. *By this shall all men know that ye are my disciples, if ye have love one to another.*" (John 13: 34, 35.)

The darkness of ignorance, superstition, bitterness, and hate was passing; the "true light," which radiated from the Lord, was shining, thus dispelling the gloom and darkness of unbelief. The text does not affirm that the darkness had already passed. Then, as now, there was much error in the world. But, as the truth was preached, the light was extended, and the darkness receded as man came into the refulgence thereof. Jesus said, "And this is the judgment, that the light is come into the world, and men loved the darkness rather than the light; for their works were evil. For every one that doeth evil hateth the light, and cometh not to the light, lest his works should be reproved. But he that doeth the

the true light already shineth. 9 He that saith he is in the light and hateth

truth, cometh to the light, that his works may be made manifest, that they have been wrought of God." (John 3: 19-21.) "Again therefore Jesus spake unto them saying, I am the light of the world: he that followeth me shall not walk in darkness, but shall have the light of life." (John 8: 12; cf. 1 John 1: 4-10.)

9 He that saith he is in the light and hateth his brother, is in the darkness even until now.—Another hypothetical case, of which there are many in the Epistle (1: 6, 8, 10; 2: 9; 4: 20), is stated, and the inconsistency between the profession and the fact pointed out. He who affects to be in the light, i.e., the light of truth about which the apostle had been writing, yet hates his brother is, notwithstanding his pretension, in darkness. The brother of this passage is a fellow believer. He who hates one of a common origin and with the same loving Father is, despite his claim to being in the light, in darkness, "even unto now," i.e., up to the present. Jesus commanded us to love one another (John 15: 17); he made love the badge of discipleship (John 13: 35); and without it, one remains in darkness—the element which characterizes all away from God. It is significant that the apostle leaves no middle ground either here or elsewhere in the contrasts which he draws between light and darkness, right and wrong, truth and error. With him, on the one side is God, and on the other, the world; here is life, there is death; here love, there hate; there is no common ground. Such is in harmony with the Lord's affirmation: "He that is not against you is for you" (Luke 9: 50, and the converse, "He that is not with me is against me" (Luke 11: 23). One is either for God, in which case the principle of his life is *love*, the sphere in which he moves *light*, and the desire of his heart *obedience*; or, he is against him, in which event, though he may hide his hatred, and craftily conceal his worldliness and evil, the fountain from which his moral life emerges is not God, but the world—he is yet in death, he loves nothing but himself, and his proper element is darkness. The word hate *(miseo)* here does not indicate the *degree,* but merely the *fact* of such a disposition. When it exists in any degree, he who manifests it is yet in the darkness. Let him who holds malice in his heart against a brother in Christ recog-

his brother, is in the darkness even until now. 10 He that loveth his brother abideth in the light, and there is no occasion of stumbling in him. 11 But he

nize his position and see the folly of pretension which his conduct belies. He deceives no one by his allegation.

10 **He that loveth his brother abideth in the light, and there is no occasion of stumbling in him.**—The verb "abideth" means more than merely *being* in the light; to abide is to remain *(Menei)*, and the tense (present indicative active) reveals a continuous action rather than a temporary state. He who loves his brother is evermore remaining in the light; the fact of the love guarantees continuation in the sphere. Moreover, the force of the tense indicates that he has not only entered upon this sphere; he has settled down into it as if it were his home. It is, of course, unnecessary to add that love, with John, indeed with all of the New Testament writers, is much more than affection. Here, it is made to stand for all the graces which adorn the character of the Christian, all the duties owed to those who are our brethren in Christ. This comprehensive aspect of the term is observable throughout the apostle's writings. "My little children, let us not love in word, neither with the tongue, but in deed and in truth." (1 John 3: 18.) "Hereby we know that we love the children of God, when we love God and do his commandments. For this is the love of God, that we keep his commandments: and his commandments are not grievous." (1 John 5: 2, 3.) The principle is the same as that alluded to by our Lord when he declared that to love God supremely and one's neighbor as one's self embraces (in principle) all that is in the law and in the prophets. (Matt. 22: 34-40.) He did not by this mean that love for God or man is accepted in lieu of obedience; there is, indeed, no such thing as love apart from obedience. (1 John 5: 3.) What is meant is that he who truly loves God and his neighbor will be prompted thereby to discharge his full duty to both.

Not only does one who loves his brother abide in the light, in addition there is no occasion of stumbling in him. An occasion for *whose* stumbling? His own, or another's? The verb "stumble" *(skandalon)* is derived from a word which designates a snare or trap. In Matt. 18: 7, it obviously refers to an occasion of stumbling in the way of others. Here, however, the context, and par-

that hateth his brother is in the darkness, and walketh in the darkness, and knoweth not whither he goeth, because the darkness hath blinded his eyes.

ticularly the verse which follows, appears to indicate that John had in mind an occasion of stumbling in one's own self. The apostle thus emphasizes here that those who walk in the light and abide in the truth are protected from the snares and pitfalls into which they would otherwise fall. Certainly, one who loves his brother as himself will never find occasion to give expression to the evil passions of envy, malice, hate, and revenge. Those who walk in darkness stumble, because they are unable to see their way; those who walk in the light can recognize, and therefore avoid, the snares which beset their way. One who truly loves his brother will conduct himself in such fashion as to avoid any semblance of friction or difficulty, and will thus neither stumble nor fall in his relationship with him. "Owe no man anything, save to love one another: for he that loveth his neighbor hath fulfilled the law. For this, Thou shalt not commit adultery, Thou shalt not kill, Thou shalt not steal, That shalt not covet, and if there be any other commandment, it is summed up in this word, namely, Thou shalt love thy neighbor as thyself. Love worketh no ill to his neighbor; love therefore is the fulfillment of the law." (Rom. 13: 8-10.)

11 But he that hateth his brother is in the darkness, and walketh in the darkness, and knoweth not whither he goeth, because the darkness hath blinded his eyes.—Three conditions are here affirmed of him who hates his brother: (1) he is "in the darkness"; (2) he "walketh in the darkness"; and (3) he "knoweth not whither he goeth," the reason being that "the darkness hath blinded his eyes." Such is the fearful status of those who hate their brethren. The inner condition is one of *darkness*; the outward life is a walk in darkness. The element which is his natural sphere has possessed him; he has partaken of the realm in which he habitually moves. Moreover, he has lost his sense of direction; "He knoweth not whither he goeth." His way is dark; he neither knows its direction or its end. He is like the insects of Mammoth Cave in Kentucky, which have no eyes, the faculty of sight being so long disused it is gone. The poet Tennyson, in vivid verse, though with reference to sorrow rather than sin, sets forth the fatal result:

"But the night has crept into my heart and begun to darken my eyes."

The state which the apostle describes is all the more fatal because unrecognized by those in it. "They know not, neither do they understand; they walk to and fro in darkness." (Psalm 82: 5.) "Blinded" here is from the same verb and form occurring in 2 Cor. 4: 4: "In whom the God of this world hath blinded the minds of the unbelieving, that the light of the gospel of the glory of Christ, who is the image of God, should not dawn upon them." Thus the blindness which characterizes the alien is that which possesses him who hates his brother. The grace of love is so basic that he who lacks it is deficient in all the virtues of Christianity. Where it does not exist, no other can.

LITTLE CHILDREN, YOUNG MEN, AND FATHERS ADDRESSED
(2: 12-15)

The verses which immediately follow, 12, 13, 14, involve matters admittedly difficult, and which have long taxed the ingenuity of Bible students, expositors, and commentators. An analysis reveals that there are six clauses, divided into two sets of three each by the different tenses of the verb *grapho*, I write. They may be arranged thus:

1. I am writing unto you *(grapho)*:
   - (a) children *(teknia)* — You are forgiven
   - (b) fathers — *because* — You know the Lord
   - (c) young men — You have overcome
2. I have written unto you *(egrapsa)*:
   - (a) children *(paidia)* — You know the Father
   - (b) fathers — *because* — You know the Lord
   - (c) young men — You are strong, and have overcome

Numerous questions arise, the answers to which are essential to the understanding of this section. (1) Why did John use the present tense, "I write" *(grapho)*, in the first three clauses, and "I have written" *(egrapsa),* epistolary aorist, in the second three? (2) To what writing does he refer in the first instance? In the second? (3) What is the meaning of the word "children" in the first clause of each of the divisions? (4) Why did he use the word *teknia* in the first reference to children, and *paidia* in the second? (5) In what sense is the reference to "fathers" and "young men" to be taken, literal or figurative?

Here, as often elsewhere in the Epistle, the opinions which have been advanced are many, and merely to list them would extend the limits of this commentary far beyond that which the plan justifies. In seeking the answers to these questions, it is not our purpose to burden the reader with views which have accumulated across the years, only to refute them; those interested may examine them at their sources. We shall, instead, set forth the grounds which, after much careful consideration and study, we have adopted as, on the whole, the most reasonable exegesis of the passage.

Why did John use the present, "I write" *(grapho),* in the first three clauses, and "I wrote" *(egrapsa),* epistolary aorist, or as it may be rendered in English, "I have written," in the second? "I write" is from the viewpoint of the writer—as the matter occurred to John as he actually wrote. The "I wrote," or, as it may be translated, "I have written," is the viewpoint of the reader. The first reflects the author's position; the second, his readers. "I write" these matters to you; when you read them, your position will be with reference to that which is written.

To what writing does he refer in the first instance? In the second? In both instances the reference is the same: to the Epistle which he was then writing. Efforts to make one refer to the Epistle, the other to the Gospel which he wrote; or, the first to the whole Epistle, and the second to that which preceded what he was then writing, we reject as unsound. A simpler and more satisfactory conclusion is that both words embrace the same composition, the entire first Epistle.

What is the meaning of the word "children" in the first clause of each of the divisions? All of John's readers, so most expositors think. And, that such is the significance of the word in 1 John 2:1 ("My *little children,* these things I write unto you. . . .") seems certain. But that the word has this significance here, we are disposed to doubt. (a) The designations "children," "fathers," and "young men" appear to be a detailed analysis of all his readers. There was, it seems, evident definite design on the part of the writer to particularize those addressed. (b) On the assumption that "children" embrace the whole of those addressed, who are the "fathers" and the "young men?" (c) Why, if the term is used thus comprehensively, did the writer use two different Greek terms—*teknia, paidia*—to designate the children? Does not this fact lead to the conclusion that it was the author's purpose to assign a specific, and therefore, a limited meaning, to the terms used? On the whole, it seems more in keeping with all the facts to assign to the word "children" a limited significance, and to conclude that those thus addressed were the ones among John's readers who had but lately obeyed the gospel, and whose sins had accordingly but recently been forgiven. This view is supported by the fact that the reason given why John addressed them particularly is "because your sins are forgiven you for his name's sake."

Why were two different Greek words, *teknia, paidia,* used to designate this particular group? The reason is not immediately apparent. It is obvious, from the context, that both terms describe the same individuals; and this consideration leads to the conclusion that the variation was resorted to, not for the purpose of distinguishing between two groups, but to emphasize the different characteristics of the same group. The answer to our question must, therefore, be sought in the difference of meaning in the terms themselves. *Teknia,* plural of *teknion,* designates the fact of childhood; *paidia,* the infancy of those thus designated. The words, in their literal sense, denote those of tender age; and, as here figuratively used, denote those who are babes in Christ. The first reveals that those thus designated were children; the second, that they were infant children. Not literal babies, of course, but those lately born into the family of God. (John 3: 3-5; 1 Pet. 2: 1, 2.)

In what sense are the words "fathers" and "young men" to be taken, as a literal designation, or a figurative one? If literal, then no elderly men, not fathers, were addressed in this connection by John. In such an instance, no women whatsoever were included. It must, therefore, be obvious that the words "children," "fathers,"

12 I write unto you, *my* little children, because your sins are forgiven you for his name's sake. 13 I write unto you, fathers, because ye know him who is from the beginning. I write unto you, young men, because ye have overcome the evil one. ¹I have written unto you, little children, because ye know

¹Or, *I wrote*

---

and "young men" were used to describe three different classes of people among John's readers. The *children* were the recent converts; the *young men*, those who had reached maturity and were possessed of great spiritual strength in the Lord; and the *fathers* were those who had been in Christ the longest, and had therefore attained to the greatest spiritual growth.

12 I write unto you, my little children, because your sins are forgiven you for his name's sake.—Those thus addressed were familiarly styled "little children"; the occasion for the address was that their sins had been forgiven them; and the reason assigned for their forgiveness was "for his name's sake." "For his name's sake" means on the basis of his name, i.e., God, the Father, forgives on account of Christ's name and because of his advocacy of our cause. (1 John 2: 1.) It is through the name of Christ that we are privileged to approach the Father. "Jesus said unto him, I am the way, and the truth, and the life; no one cometh unto the Father, but by me." (John 14: 6.) "And in none other is there salvation: for neither is there any other name under heaven, that is given among men, wherein we must be saved." (Acts 4: 12.) The words "are forgiven" are translated from a Greek perfect *(apheontai)*, a tense pointing to past action with existing results. "You have been, and consequently stand forgiven of your past, or alien, sins."

13 I write unto you, fathers, because ye know him who is from the beginning.—As there was a special reason for addressing those who had but lately obeyed the gospel, so John also felt it needful to include instruction for those of more maturity in the Christian life, and who had long been faithful disciples of the Lord. The fathers were, therefore, addressed because "ye know him. . . ." The word "know," as here used, means far more than casual acquaintance. The verb is in the perfect tense *(egnokate)*, "You came to know, and now know," and describes the rich and full experience which these fathers had with the Lord. He who is

the Father. 14 ⁴I have written unto you, fathers, because ye know him who is from the beginning. ¹I have written unto you, young men, because ye are strong, and the word of God abideth in you, and ye have overcome the evil

¹Or, *I wrote*

"from the beginning" was the word, the second person of the Godhead: "In the beginning was the Word, and the Word was with God, and the Word was God." (John 1:1.)

I write unto you, young men, because ye have overcome the evil one.—Here, and often elsewhere in the Epistle, as also through the New Testament, the personality of Satan is clearly indicated. Far from being merely or solely an influence, he is revealed as a definite and distinct agent who must be resisted, repelled, and overcome by the saints. (See comments on 1 John 3: 8, 10.) Those thus addressed by the apostle had "overcome the evil one." This they had done by remaining stedfast in the faith and not succumbing to the seductions of the devil. "And this is the victory that hath overcome the world, even our faith." (1 John 5:4.)

I have written unto you, little children, because ye know the Father.—For a full discussion of the various terms used, an analysis of the passage, and reasons assigned for the change in tense here, see above at the beginning of the section. The word "know" here is of the same tense, and has the same significance as in verses 3 and 4, literally, "you have come to know, and now retain this knowedge of the Father." Such knew him as their Father, because they were his children; they had been adopted into his family, and were by him regarded as such. In verse 12, those alluded to as children are declared to have been forgiven, to know the father. The ideas are correlative and dependent; only those who are forgiven know the Father; only those who know the Father have been forgiven.

14 **I have written unto you, fathers, because ye know him who is from the beginning.**—He who is from the beginning is the Word (John 1: 1, 2; 1 John 1: 1-3); the reference is thus to the pre-existent Christ who occupies eternity. The nature, attributes, and characteristics of the Eternal One constitute a profound study; but these mature saints, from long and careful consideration

of the facts available to them, had come to possess a knowledge of him who thus bridges the brief span of time before and after which is the eternity without end. It is a subject especially intriguing to those advanced in years and mature of mind.

I have written unto you, young men, because ye are strong, and the word of God abideth in you, and ye have overcome the evil one.—Three characteristics of these young men are mentioned: (1) They were strong; (2) the word of God abode in them; and (3) they had overcome the evil one. The occasion of their strength was in the fact that the word of God was in them and the consequence of this indwelling was their triumph over the evil one. In no other fashion may one achieve victory over Satan. Only as the word dwells in us richly (Col. 3: 16), do we become strong in the Lord and in the power of his might (Eph. 6: 10), and are we protected from sinning against God (Psalm 119: 11).

LOVE OF THE WORLD FORBIDDEN
(2: 15-17)

one. 15 Love not the world, neither the things that are in the world. If any man love the world, the love of the Father is not in him. 16 For all that is

---

15 **Love not the world, neither the things that are in the world.**—Those addressed in the verses immediately preceding—The children, fathers, and young men—though each is commended for having triumphed in his respective sphere, were nevertheless yet in the world, yet subject to its allurements and temptations, yet within the reach of the Evil One. There was, therefore, need that such an exhortation be given.

What is the "world" here contemplated? How do the "things of the world" differ from the world itself? What is the significance of the word "love" in this passage? In view of the fact that "God so loved the world" (John 3: 16), does the world which he loved differ from that which we are not to love, or is the difference in the "love" which is to be exercised, or both? Obviously, the answers to these questions are essential to any proper exposition of this passage.

The "world" which John's readers were forbidden to love was not the material universe, God's original creation (Rom. 1: 20), the people who inhabit it (John 3: 16); the earth (John 1:

in the world, the lust of the flesh and the lust of the eyes and the vainglory

9), or the visible and tangible elements of our surroundings which are in themselves neither good nor bad. By the *world* John did not mean the sunshine and the rain, the mountains and the seas, the sunset and the stars, the loveliness of the night, the sparkling freshness of the morning, the sweet song of the birds, or the fragrance of the flowers. He did not mean the dust from which our bodies are composed, the earth which supplies us with our food, and in whose gentle embrace we must at last eventually rest. Nor does the word "love" denote the tenderness of affection and the warmth of heart which characterize God and man toward those whose attributes encourage and stimulate such feeling. The "world" of this passage is a sphere or cosmos *(kosmos)* of evil, an order which is opposed to God, and to whose pursuit those who abandon the Lord have dedicated themselves. The "love" which men entertain for this world is evil desire. The love contemplated in John 3: 16 is that of divine compassion and redeeming mercy; here, it is the emotion of selfish desire, of avarice and worldly pride. The love of the Father is an affection grounded in utter selflessness; that which man cherishes for the world is a greedy reaching for its affairs. The "world" which God loves is mankind; that which man is forbidden to love is an evil order or sphere.

But not only did the apostle's exhortation embrace the "world," it is extended to include the *"things* of the world." The prohibition is exceedingly emphatic: "Love not the world, neither *(mede) no not either the things of the world."* The meaning is, Do not love the world, no, nor anything that may be in it. There is, therefore, a distinction drawn between the world and the things in it: a distinction between the general and the specific, the whole and the particular. We are forbidden to love even a specific or particular part of the world—an exhortation needful then and now. There are those who have repudiated the world, but for one particular, as for example the rich young ruler, who but for his love of riches would have surrendered his life wholly to the Lord. The "one thing" which we "lack"—be it the love of pleasure, of riches, of ease; the attraction of a home, a farm, or a business; the desire

of life, is not of the Father, but is of the world. 17 And the world passeth

for fame, prominence, and worldly honor, is the particular or specific thing, though we may have repudiated the world as such, which will eventually close the door of heaven in our faces.

If any man love the world, the love of the Father is not in him.—Love for the world and love for the Father are wholly incompatible; they cannot exist in any heart at the same time. "No man can serve two masters; for either he will hate the one, and love the other; or else he will hold to one, and despise the other. *Ye cannot serve God and mammon.*" (Matt. 6: 24.) The antithesis drawn is the same as that in Rom. 8: 5: "For they that are after the flesh mind the things of the flesh; but they that are after the Spirit the things of the Spirit." The warning is similar to one from James: "Ye adulteresses, know ye not that friendship of the world is enmity with God? Whosoever therefore would be a friend of the world maketh himself an enemy of God." (James 4: 4.) On the principle here enunciated is the exhortation of Paul: "Wherefore come ye out from among them, and be ye separate, saith the Lord, and touch no unclean thing; and I will receive you, and will be to you a Father, and ye shall be to me sons and daughters." (2 Cor. 6: 17, 18.)

16 **For all that is in the world, the lust of the flesh and the lust of the eyes and the vainglory of life, is not of the Father, but is of the world.**—The things of the world have their origin, not in the Father, but in the world of which they are a part; and they are designated as (1) the lust of the flesh; (2) the lust of the eyes; and (3) the vainglory of life. The "lust of the flesh" is evil desire which finds its origin in the flesh and through the flesh finds expression. It is a lust *after* the flesh; but it is more; the genitive is subjective, the flesh is thus designated as the seat in which the evil desire dwells. The word "flesh" as here used does not denote skin and muscle and tissue; it is used in that darker sense so often seen in Paul's writings of the animal nature, the source of evil appetites. (See Gal. 5: 16-24; Eph. 2: 3; 2 Pet. 2: 18; Col. 2: 18.) The lusts of the flesh exhibit themselves in the *works* of the flesh, a catalog of which is listed in Gal. 5: 19ff.

away, and the lust thereof: but he that doeth the will of God abideth for ever.

It is significant that John sums up, in this section, the three avenues of approach which Satan, in his efforts to seduce, follows. The appeal which he ever makes is based on (1) carnal desires; (2) desires awakened through the appeal of objects of sight; and (3) vanity, pride, worldly honor. Such was, precisely, the course followed in the seduction of Eve and in the unsuccessful attempt on the Saviour. "And when the woman saw that the tree *was good for food* (the lust of the flesh), and that it was *a delight to the eye* (the lust of the eyes), and that the tree was to be *desired to make one wise* (the vainglory of life), she took of the fruit thereof, and did eat; and she gave also unto her husband with her, and he did eat." (Gen. 3: 6.) In similar fashion, and by following the same procedure, Satan suggested that Jesus, after forty days of fasting, should command the stones to become bread, thus appealing to the lust of the flesh; he showed the Lord all the kingdoms of the world and promised them to him on condition that he do him homage, an appeal to the lust of the eyes; and in bidding the Lord to exercise his powers of divine protection by flinging himself down from the pinnacle of the temple there was an evident appeal to a sense of pride and vainglory which such an achievement, in the breasts of some, would have been certain to create.

17 And the world passeth away, and the lust thereof: but he that doeth the will of God abideth for ever.—The world will pass, and with it every lustful pleasure; but he who does the will of God abides through the ages. The transitoriness of the one—the world—is contrasted with the permanence of the other, the one doing the will of God. God himself is eternal; and those who abide in his will share in his eternal nature. In view of the temporal nature of the world, it is supreme folly for one to cling tenaciously to it, when it will inevitably be dissolved and cease to be. The tense of the word "passeth" is present middle indicative, "is passing away," the process is even now in operation, and will continue until the present evil age is no more. But, notwithstanding its passing, he who does (literally, *keeps on doing*) the will of the Father, abides unto the ages.

WARNINGS CONCERNING ANTICHRISTS
(2: 18-29)

18 Little children, it is the last hour: and as ye heard that anti-christ

18 Little children, it is the last hour:—Again we meet with the designation, "little children" *(paidia),* as in 2: 1, 12, 13; and the meaning here, as in 2: 1, is obviously, the entire body of disciples addressed by the apostles. For the reasons why a more limited significance is to be assigned to the expression in 2: 12, 13, see the notes there.

The words "It is the last hour" are to be closely construed with the verses which immediately precede them. The apostle had described the transient nature of the worldly sphere and had pointed out that only those who do the will of the Father shall abide unto the ages. Here, he continues his exhortation by solemnly directing attention to the fact that his readers were even then in the period of "the last hour," and that events known to foretoken it were already appearing.

What is the last hour here referred to? The termination of the Jewish state, so many think; the last hour of the world before the consummation of all things, so others. Both views are erroneous. The Jewish state had already ended when the Epistle was written, and thus could not have been the "hour" to which the apostle alluded. And, to understand John as affirming that the last hour of the world was imminent in his day is to ascribe to him a position which the passing of the centuries has proved to be untrue. The first view is thus historically incorrect; the second impeaches the inspiration of the writer; and we hence reject both.

Three Greek words are variously used in the New Testament to indicate *time,* as such. *Chronos* is time with reference to duration or succession; *kairos* is time contemplated with reference to events; and *hora* is time with reference to a fixed date or period. It is the last of these words—*hora*—which occurs in the text, and the meaning is, therefore, a fixed date or period. The word is of obvious figurative significance, and thus describes a determinate period fixed in the divine mind and the last of the events thus predetermined by the Father. The word designates time, time conceived of as a definite period, this period being the *last* in the succession of periods similarly determined by deity. It therefore des-

cometh, even now have there arisen many anti-christs; whereby we know

---

ignates the Christian dispensation, the last of the great periods or ages arranged by the Father. (Isa. 2: 2-4; Acts 2: 17; Heb. 1: 2.)

And as ye heard that anti-christ cometh,—The apostle's readers were already in possession of information regarding "antichrist"; they had heard it through the preaching of the writer and others. Those who had been their teachers, among them John himself, had earlier warned of the appearance of this antichrist.

Who, or *What,* is "anti-christ?" The word itself suggests two possible meanings, accordingly as the preposition *"anti"* used in composition, here, is understood to signify (a) *over against,* or (b) *opposed to.* If the former, the word denotes one who puts himself in the place of Christ; if the latter, one who stands in opposition to Christ. The word appears only in the writings of John; here, and in 2: 22; 4: 3; and 2 John 7. His characteristics, as indicated in those verses, are, (1) he is a liar; (2) a deceiver; (3) a denier that Jesus is the Christ; and (4) he refuses to acknowledge that Jesus Christ has come in the flesh.

References to a similar individual, in the language of the Lord, and the writings of Paul, enable us to fix his identity more definitely, and indicate that the word combines the two meanings suggested above, viz., one who not only opposes Christ, but who usurps the place of Christ. "For many shall come in my name, saying, I am the Christ; and shall lead many astray." "For there shall arise false Christs, and false prophets, and shall show great signs and wonders; so as to lead astray, if possible, even the elect." (Matt. 24: 5, 24.) "Let no man beguile you in any wise; for it will not be, except the falling away come first and the man of sin be revealed, the son of perdition, he that opposeth and exalteth himself against all that is called God or that is worshipped; so that he sitteth in the temple of God setting himself forth as God." (2 Thess. 2: 3, 4.) The individual here described is designated as "the man of sin" and the "son of perdition." (a) He opposes his will to that of God; (b) he exalts himself against God; (c) he sits in the temple of God; and (d) he sets himself forth as God. He is, moreover, (1) the personification of sin; (2) the son of

that it is the last hour. 19 They went out from us, but they were not of us;

perdition; (3) a participant in signs and lying wonders, the purpose of which is (4) to deceive. Like the antichrist described by John, and the false Christs predicted by the Lord, he seeks to identify himself with deity; he, like them, seeks to deceive, and has arrayed himself against the Lord and his Christ, and opposes them. To the candid mind the conclusion is irresistible that the "man of sin," whom Paul describes, as identical with the "anti-christ," to which John refers. And, in the centuries which have passed since these words were penned, no character in history so nearly conforms in minute detail to the representation here given as *the pope of Rome!*

To deny that these prophecies find fulfillment in him is to close one's eyes to the facts in the case, utterly to ignore the evidence which obtains, and to reduce Biblical exegesis to mere caprice.

Even now have there arisen many anti-christs; whereby we know that it is the last hour.—If it be asked why John added that already there had arisen many antichrists (long before the development of the apostasy and the appearance of the first pope), the answer is obvious: while the great antichrist predicted by John and described by Paul had not come, many were evidencing and exhibiting the same spirit as would be characteristic of him, and were, therefore, properly styled antichrists. We, today, refer to men as papists who evince the spirit of and support the papacy; and with equal propriety those of John's day who preceded the popes but possessed his spirit were similarly designated. False and heretical teachers were then active, some of whom denied the deity of Jesus, and others his humanity, men who were clothed in the attributes of and possessed the spirit of the antichrist to come. If it be insisted that the pope does not today deny the Christ or oppose him, but, on the contrary, supports his cause and defends his name, we deny it. As the so-called *vicar* of Christ, he affects to be the Lord's personal representative on earth; he blasphemously claims the prerogative of Christ in forgiving sins; and he alleges that he sits in the seat of Christ on earth. He is, therefore, a parody of the Christ, a counterfeit Christ; and though he imitates some of the characteristics of Christ, this is precisely what is expected of one who seeks to deceive.

for if they had been of us, they would have continued with us: but *they went out,* that they might be made manifest ²that they all are not of us. 20 And ye

²Or, *that not all are of us*

The appearance of these antichrists was evidence that the "last hour" had been ushered in, such being tokens predicted by Christ to appear before the consummation of the age. (Matt. 24: 5, 24-27.)

19 **They went out from us, but they were not of us; for if they had been of us, they would have continued with us: but they went out, that they might be made manifest that they are not of us.**—The antecedent of "they" is the word "anti-christ," of the preceding verse. The preposition *ek*, rendered "out from," indicates origin from the center; and these were, therefore, formerly among the disciples, and members of the church. They became apostates from the fold by going out. They were not "of" the disciples, i.e., they did not possess the same spirit of obedience characteristic of the disciples, for if they had "they would have continued with" the disciples. In going out, i.e., in apostatizing from the faith, they were "made manifest" (shown to be), not of the disciples, and for the reason assigned above.

This passage, often cited by advocates of the doctrine of the impossibility of apostasy for the purpose of showing that those who abandon the cause are mere professors or pretenders, and were never sincere, falls far short of the effort; for (a) they were once with the disciples; (b) they went out from them; (c) one does not go out from a place where he has never been; (d) had they possessed the same love for the Lord and equal desire to serve him as those from whom they went out, they would have continued with them; (e) they did, in fact, continue for a time, and then ceased to be faithful. (f) It follows, therefore, that they simply apostatized from the right way. We learn from this that (1) there was no necessity from without which made it impossible for these people to forsake the right way; (2) they were under no compulsion such as would have been true if the doctrine of decrees and predestination, as taught by Calvinists, is true. (3) Some obey the gospel and, like him of whom the Saviour spoke in the parable of the soils, "heareth the word, and straightway with joy receiveth it; yet hath he not root in himself, but endureth for a while; when tribula-

have an anointing from the Holy One, ³and ye know all things. 21 I have

³Some very ancient authorities read *and ye all know.*

---

tion or persecution ariseth because of the word, straightway he stumbleth." (Matt. 13: 20, 21.) Others, like those of this text, adopt false and heretical doctrines, forsake the church, and make shipwreck concerning the faith. (1 Tim. 1: 19.)

20 **And ye have an anointing from the Holy One, and ye know all things.**—This passage asserts that these to whom John wrote: (1) had an anointing; (2) this anointing they received from "the Holy One," Christ; (3) as a result of this anointing they knew all things.

The word "anointing" is translated from the Greek *chrisma*, a term originally signifying an oil or ointment rubbed on the skin, and later, the anointing itself. There is a play on words in the Greek Testament here, not observable in the translation. If the false teachers were *anti-christoi*, these to whom John wrote were *christoi*, anointed ones. The reference here is to a custom characteristic of the law of Moses of anointing with perfumed oils those elevated to positions of trust or power. In compliance with the will of Jehovah, kings (1 Sam. 10: 10), priests (Ex. 29: 7), and prophets (Isa. 61: 1) were anointed; and ointment is both figuratively, and in the act itself, a symbol of the Holy Spirit. Jesus was the anointed one (Acts 4: 27), and that with which he was anointed was the Holy Spirit (Acts 10: 38).

Some hold to the view that the anointing alluded to by John was for "ordinary measure" of the Spirit, believed by them to be vouchsafed to all believers. References cited in support of this view are Gal. 4: 6; Eph. 3: 16; Phil. 1: 19; and 2 Cor. 3: 17ff. This conclusion is based on an unwarrantable assumption. It should be noted that the test makes no mention whatsoever of the time when, nor the manner in which the anointing was received. It merely affirms the fact of its occurrence, and not the manner or mode thereof. To affirm that this is the "ordinary measure of the Spirit which all Christians receive in conversion" is to inject a meaning into the passage, rather than to draw out the meaning that is there.

This was not an "ordinary measure" of the Spirit, and for the

not written unto you because ye know not the truth, but because ye know it,

following reasons: (1) The context is against this view. Antichrists, formerly among the disciples, and now apostates, were advocating false and heretical doctrines designed to lead the disciples astray. These teachers were readily recognizable because the faithful had received an anointing from the Lord. In this anointing these saints had been supplied with an endowment enabling them to discern false spirits, and their teaching—to detect those who falsely asserted their inspiration: "Beloved, believe not every spirit, but prove the spirits, whether they are of God; because many false prophets are gone out into the world." (1 John 4: 1.) This test they were able to make by comparing the teaching of the Spirit within them with the pretensions of those teachers who affected to be similarly led. (2) This anointing which they had received enabled them to know "all things." This phrase, "all things," is, of course, to be interpreted in the light of the context, and with reference to matters there considered. It was not the apostle's purpose to imply that such anointing made those who received it omniscient; otherwise, why was he, an inspired apostle, writing to them at all? If, through the inspiration of the Holy Spirit, they had come into possession of all knowledge, why this Epistle to them? The "all things" must, therefore, be limited to include the things pertaining to the antichrists. (3) The anointing supplied them with such information as they needed to recognize and refute the false teachers who had gone out from among them. So, the apostle later affirmed: "These things have I written unto you concerning them that would lead you astray. As for you, the anointing which ye received of him abideth in you, and ye need not that any one teach you; but as his anointing teaches you concerning all things, and is true, and is no lie, and even as it taught you, ye abide in him." (1 John 4: 26, 27.)

We conclude, therefore, that the "anointing" which these to whom John particularly wrote had received a miraculous measure of the Spirit; that this measure enabled them to recognize and refute the false teachers which plagued the church at that time; and that the anointing is not to be confused with any so-called "ordinary measure" of the Spirit available to Christians today. In the absence of a written revelation, it was needful that an infallible test

and ¹because no lie is of the truth. 22 Who is the liar but he that denieth that Jesus is the Christ? This is the anti-christ *even* he that denieth the

¹Or, *that*

be supplied the early saints by means of which they were able to discern and to expose the pretensions of those who sought to lead them astray. Such was the purpose of the "anointing" here contemplated. See further on this in the comments on 1 John 2: 27.

21 I have not written unto you because ye know not the truth, but because ye know it, and because no lie is of the truth.—Here, again, the reference is to the immediate context, and to the matters which had claimed the apostle's attention above. Certainly he is not to be understood as affirming that the reason he wrote the truth to them was because they already possessed all the truth which he wrote. If they already had it, why did he write? The "truth" which they possessed was with reference to the false teachers about them; the manner in which they received this truth was through inspiration, styled in the verse preceding, "an anointing," a miraculous gift enabling them to discern false and lying spirits. The "lie" which is opposed to the truth was that which the antichrists taught. (Verse 18.)

22 Who is the liar but he that denieth that Jesus is the Christ—The "lie" had claimed the apostle's attention in verse 21; here, the one who originated it. Passing from the abstract to the concrete, John identified the liar as "he that denieth that Jesus is the Christ." Many false theories regarding the nature and the attributes of the Saviour were afloat when John wrote this Epistle. The Gnostics alleged that Jesus and Christ were two different persons; that Christ merely appeared to have flesh, but in reality did not; and that the one designated as Jesus was without divine origin. The effect of this heresy was, in the case of Christ, to deny his humanity; and in the case of Jesus, to deny his deity. (See under "Design of the Epistle," in the Introduction.)

This is the anti-christ, even he that denieth the Father and the Son.—Here, the word "anti-christ" is used in the same sense as in its second occurrence in verse 18, to identify those who possessed the character and attributes of the great antichrist to come. He who taught the things attributed to him here was of the same purpose and spirit as antichrist, and thus might properly bear

Father and the Son. 23 Whosoever denieth the Son, the same hath not the Father: he that confesseth the Son hath the Father also. 24 As for you, let

his designation. To deny the humanity and deity of Jesus was to repudiate his Messiahship; and to reject the Messiahship was, in effect, to reject the Father himself. "He that honoreth not the Son honoreth not the Father that sent him." (John 5: 23.) The Son reveals the Father (John 1: 18; 14: 9), and our approach to the Father is through the Son (John 12: 6). Thus to reject the Son is to repudiate the only method by which it is possible to reach the Father. This is the reason why an acknowledgment of the Son before men is a prerequisite to acknowledgment by the Father: "And I say unto you, Every one who shall confess me before men, him shall the Son of man also confess before the angels of God: but he that denieth me in the presence of men shall be denied in the presence of the angels of God." (Luke 12: 8. Cf. Matt. 10: 32.)

23 **Whosoever denieth the Son, the same hath not the Father: he that confesseth the Son hath the Father also.**—A conclusion drawn from preceding premises. He who disowns the Son, in the same act rejects the one who is his Father. Inasmuch as it is not possible to know the Father but by the Son, such rejection must inevitably extend to the Father also. This truth is stated both negatively and positively in this verse. It emphasizes what is often taught in the sacred writings that no man can have a clear knowledge of God the Father who does not learn of and familiarize himself with the attributes and characteristics of the Son. "No man hath seen God at any time; the only begotten Son, who is in the bosom of the Father, he hath declared him," i.e., revealed him, made him known. (John 1: 18.) Since the appearance of the Son no one can truthfully object to the acceptance of deity on the ground that such is unknowable. The Father has revealed himself to man through his Son.

While these words were primarily written to refute the ancient Gnostics who plagued the church with these heresies at the time John wrote, they are not without a very definite and pertinent relevancy in our time. The seeds of the ancient Cerenthian heresy are to be seen in the modern rationalism which affects to believe in God but which rejects Christ as his Son and the Scriptures as a

that abide in you which ye heard from the beginning. If that which ye heard from the beginning abide in you, ye also shall abide in the Son, and in

---

revelation from him. God, without Christ, is simply not! Such a being is utterly without existence. The attempt to visualize God, without Christ, is to reduce him to a metaphysical abstraction, eventuating in pantheism, or atheism. Voltaire, the famous French infidel, entranced by the unspeakable beauty in the Swiss Alps, shouted, "God the Father! I adore thee," and then, as if ashamed of his outburst, immediately added that he did not worship the Son, an illustration of the conclusion which the apostle draws that it is impossible to acknowledge the Father without confessing the Son also.

It will of course be unnecessary to add, to the thoughtful reader, that to confess the Son is much more than merely saying that one believes that Jesus is the Christ, the Son of God. The Lord himself said, "Not every one that saith unto me, Lord, Lord, shall enter into the kingdom of heaven; but he that doeth the will of my Father who is in heaven. Many will say to me in that day, Lord, Lord, did we not prophesy by thy name, and by thy name cast out demons, and by thy name do many mighty works? And then will I profess unto them, I never knew you: depart from me, ye that work iniquity." (Matt. 7: 21-23.) Here, as in 1 John 4: 2, to confess the Son is to acknowledge him for what he is, and to render to him the obedience such an acknowledgment implies. The apostle had earlier shown that the Gnostics, in denying that Jesus is the Christ, had, in so doing, repudiated the Father. Conversely, those who confess the Son, by implication, also acknowledge the Father.

24 As for you, let that abide in you which ye heard from the beginning.—That which they had heard from the beginning was the truth; the beginning was their earliest acquaintance with the gospel; and the manner in which it was brought to them was by means of preaching. This which they had thus heard they were to allow to abide in them, literally, to let it settle down and find, as it were, its permanent home in them. The exhortation is, therefore, one to steadfastness, and admonition to hold fast to that which had been taught them.

the Father. 25 And this is the promise which he promised [5]us, *even* the life

[5]Some ancient authorities read *you*.

If that which ye heard from the beginning abide in you, ye also shall abide in the Son, and in the Father.—Here, as in the clause immediately preceding, the word "abide" *(meno)* means to settle down and dwell, as in one's permanent home; if the truth is thus permitted to settle down in us, we shall, in turn, be privileged to settle down, and have our home in the Son and in the Father. The conditional particle "if" governs the sentence and determines the conclusion. *If,* i.e., on condition "that which ye heard from the beginning abide in you, ye also shall abide in the Son and in the Father." Here is another of the many passages in the scripture clearly establishing the conditionality of salvation and emphasizing the necessity of continued faithfulness. See this same truth taught in John 6: 56; 15: 1ff.; 17: 23; Eph. 3: 17; 1 Cor. 3: 16; 6: 17.

25 **And this is the promise which he promised us, even the life eternal.**—From this verse we learn, (1) eternal life is a promise; (2) this promise is conditioned on our holding fast to that which we heard from the beginning. It follows, therefore, that eternal life is not a present possession, but a promise, a promise conditional and dependent on our remaining faithful. Passages, such as John 5: 24, apparently asserting that the believer is in possession of eternal life already must be understood as declaring that it is had in *prospect only.* "In hope of eternal life, which God, who cannot lie, promised before times eternal." (Tit. 1: 2.) One does not *hope* for that which he already has. (Rom. 8: 24, 25.) "Jesus said, Verily I say unto you, There is no man that hath left house, or brethren, or sister, or mother, or father, or children, or lands, for my sake, and for the gospel's sake, but he shall receive a hundredfold now in this time, houses, and brethren, and sisters, and mothers, and children, and lands, with persecutions; *and in the world to come eternal life.*" (Mark 10: 29, 30.) The Lord often promised eternal life to those who abide faithful: "Father, the hour is come; glorify thy Son, that the Son may glorify thee: even as thou gavest him authority over all flesh, that to all whom thou hast given him, he should give eternal life. And this is life eternal that they should know thee the only true God, and him whom thou didst send, even Jesus Christ." (John 17: 1-3.)

eternal. 26 These things have I written unto you concerning them that would lead you astray. 27 And as for you, the anointing which ye received

26 These things have I written unto you concerning them that would lead you astray.—Those seeking to lead John's readers astray were the "anti-christs" (verse 18), false and heretical teachers of that period who were exceedingly active in their efforts to lead the faithful away from the true faith. In view of this constant and persistent threat to the security and well-being of the saints, it was especially needful that John should pen these words of warning. False teachers early appeared in the apostolic church, and many warnings regarding them were given. To the elders of the church in Ephesus, Paul said: "I know that after my departing grievous wolves shall enter in among you, not sparing the flock; and from among your own selves shall men arise, speaking perverse things, to draw away disciples after them." (Acts 20: 29.) And to Timothy, the same apostle wrote, "But the Spirit saith expressly, that in later times some shall fall away from the faith, giving heed to seducing spirits and doctrines of demons, through the hyprocrisy of men that speak lies, branded in their own conscience as with a hot iron; forbidding to marry, and commanding to abstain from meats, which God created to be received with thanksgiving by them that believe and know the truth." (1 Tim. 4: 1-3.) And John, himself, to put his readers constantly on guard against false teachers affecting to be led by the Spirit, wrote, "Beloved, believe not every spirit, but prove the spirits, whether they are of God; because many false prophets are gone out into the world." (1 John 4: 1.)

27 And as for you, the anointing which ye received of him abideth in you, and ye need not that any one teach you; but as his anointing teacheth you concerning all things, and is true, and is no lie, and even as it taught you, ye abide in him.—The meaning of this verse is identical with that of verse 24, except that what is set forth there as a command is stated here as a fact. Two things essential to the proper understanding of this must be noted: (1) When the apostle said, "Ye need not that any one teach you," he is to be understood as having reference to the matters of the context, and including the things but recently under considera-

of him abideth in you, and ye need not that any one teach you; but as his

tion, viz., the ability to discern between false and true teaching. (2) The ones who had no need of teaching were those who had been anointed, i.e., had received a miraculous measure of the Spirit, thus enabling them to exercise discernment essential in such instances. This gift, the discernment of spirits, as in the case of all the spiritual endowments of the apostolic age, was not a universal gift; and those who exercised it did so because they were specially endowed by the Holy Spirit for such a purpose. The ones exercising this gift were those referred to in verse 24, and not the entire body of believers. (Cf. 1 Cor. 12: 10.)

It is an unwarranted extension of the apostle's remarks here, to apply them to all believers; to urge that one does not need to be taught the truth of the gospel today because he is already in possession of it; or to conclude that the "anointing" here contemplated is the "ordinary measure" of the Holy Spirit, which all children of God, by virtue of their sonship, receive. (Gal. 4: 6, 7.) See the comments on verse 24, above.

The meaning is that those thus endowed were able to weigh the claims of the teachers about them; they were in possession of the means with which to apply an infallible test thereto; and they could, therefore, know whether such men spoke for God or not. There is no support here whatsoever for the theory that all Christians have the anointing of the Holy Spirit or that the inspiration of the Holy Spirit extends to all believers today; or that men are justified in setting aside the revealed and written word of God to follow the leading of the so-called revelations with which they affect to be endowed. Such a theory is a hurtful and dangerous one, and is responsible for the extreme and ridiculous fanaticism prevalent among those who profess to be thus anointed.

This gift of discernment respecting the false doctrines then being propagated remained with those selected to exercise such at the time John wrote; the ability to judge of the claims of the teachers of such doctrines was not a passing thing, being necessary until the complete deposit of truth had been permanently embedded in a written record; and the anointing thus received rendered further apostolic teaching, with reference to this particular matter, unneces-

anointing teacheth you concerning all things, ^aand is true, and is no lie, and

^aOr, *so it is true and is no lie; and even as &c.*

sary. Here, again, is evidence of the correctness of our exposition that this information thus vouchsafed was limited to the matters embraced "in all things" pertaining to the false teachers under consideration. If all the disciples were embraced in these remarks; if all received the anointing of the Holy Spirit; if all possessed a knowledge of "all things"; and if none of them needed that any one should teach them, *why the Epistle itself?* On the assumption that the gift of the Spirit here contemplated extended to include all believers, the Epistle itself is rendered superfluous, John's effort unnecessary, and indeed, the Bible itself a useless book! The conclusion is, therefore, irresistible, that the "anointing" was a miraculous gift; it was of limited duration; and it was, along with all the gifts of a miraculous nature, removed when the church reached maturity. "Love never faileth: but whether there be prophecies, they shall be done away; whether there be tongues, they shall cease; whether there be knowledge, it shall be done away. For we know in part, and we prophesy in part; but when that which is perfect is come, that which is in part shall be done away. When I was a child, I spake as a child, I felt as a child, I thought as a child; now that I am become a man, I have put away childish things." (1 Cor. 13: 8-11; cf. Eph. 4: 11-13.)

The leading of the Spirit, received in the miraculous gift referred to as the "anointing," was true, it was no lie; and it might, therefore, be safely depended on to guide in the right way. So long as those endowed therewith followed the direction of the gift which they possessed, they were able to "abide" in him—Christ. The mere possession of spiritual gifts did not guarantee to the possessor thereof the impossibility of apostasy.

It is well to remember that the direction of the Spirit in miraculous fashion was never designed to supplant the written word; it was, on the contrary, merely a temporary device, to supply the early church with the means of discerning false teaching until such time as the record was completed. The New Testament is the complete and final deposit of truth in this age, and an allegation of

even as it taught you, [7]ye abide in him. 28 And now, *my* little children, abide in him; that, if he shall be manifested, we may have boldness, and not be ashamed [8]before him at his [9]coming. 29 If ye know that he is righteous,

---

[7]Or, *abide ye*
[8]Gr. *from him.*
[9]Gr. *presence.*

---

additional information from the Lord must be, regardless of its source, repudiated. (See comments of verse 20, above.)

28 **And now, my little children, abide in him; that, if he shall be manifested, we may have boldness, and not be ashamed before him at his coming.**—Here is the tender address of 2: 1, and the admonition and exhortation of 2: 24, 27, repeated. It is an address of age to youth, an admonition essential to their continued well-being. The manifestation of Christ, and his coming is, of course, the same event. The conditional phrase, "if he shall be manifested," indicates John's uncertainty as to the time of the event, thus confirming the teaching of Christ with reference to the matter. (Mark 13: 32.) The exhortation which this verse contains is grounded in the desire of the apostle that when such an event does occur both he and his readers might (a) have boldness, and (b) not be ashamed before the Lord.

The word "boldness" *(parresia),* as here used, signifies "freedom of speech," the right to speak out as one thinks, and was used by the ancient Greeks of their privilege as free citizens. It was the apostle's hope that all those to whom he wrote as well as himself might live in such fashion as to be able to stand unafraid in the presence of the Lord, and to be free to express their confidence in their position. "Ashamed," from *aischunomai,* "to grow pale, to change color from shame," is used to indicate the effect which the coming of Christ will produce on those who are unprepared to meet him. Those who are ashamed will, in that day, shrink from the Lord in guilty fashion, fully aware of the fact that they are unprepared to meet him. Cf. 2 Thess. 1 : 7-9.

29 **If ye know that he is righteous, ye know that every one also that doeth righteousness is begotten of him.**—At first glance it would appear that the antecedent of the pronoun "he" of the first clause refers to Christ; but, in view of the fact that "of him" in the last clause must be referred to the Father, the reference must be to the Father here. It is, therefore, God who is

[2: 29.] FIRST JOHN 255

²⁹ye know that every one also that doeth righteousness is begotten of him.

²⁹Or, *knew ye*

"righteous"; it is "of God" that every one that "doeth righteousness" is begotten. One is never, in the scriptures, said to be born or begotten of Christ, but always of God. (1 John 3: 9, 18; 4: 7.)

The word "know" of the first clause is from the Greek *oida*, to know theoretically; the second is from *ginosko*, to know experimentally. The meaning is, if you know (i.e., recognize theoretically) that God is righteous, you have practical knowledge that he who does righteousness is begotten of God. If one intuitively recognizes God as possessed of such principles, reason suggests that whoever habitually does righteousness *(ho poion,* present linear action) as a mode of life is begotten of God. This inference the members of the apostle's proposition make clear: (1) God is righteous. (2) As such, he is the source of righteousness. (3) When, therefore, one exhibits righteousness as a manner or mode of life, it follows that God is the source thereof. (4) Those who exhibit God's nature must receive it through regeneration. Hence, (5) "Every one also that doeth righteousness is begotten of him."

Righteousness is right-doing, moral rectitude in all of the relationships of man, and obedience to the commandments of God. (Psalm 119: 172.)

Though the doctrine is clearly and positively taught elsewhere (e.g., Matt. 7: 21; Mark 16: 15, 16; Rev. 22: 13, 14), this passage cannot be properly cited in support of the view that doing righteousness, i.e., keeping the commandments, is a condition precedent to salvation from past, or alien, sins. (1) The righteousness here contemplated is that which one does *as a child of God,* and not in order to become one. (2) The logical order of the premises leading to the conclusion of the apostle shows that it was his design to exhibit the fact that "doing righteousness" is *evidence* that one *is* a child of God, and is not offered as a condition on which one *becomes* a child. Nor is there any significance in the fact that *gennao* is rendered "begotten," rather than "born." Here the word is descriptive of the new birth, but is properly rendered "begotten," (a) because it is incongruous and awkward to predicate birth of a masculine personality; and (b) the scriptures, properly translated, never refer to *a birth of God!*

SECTION THREE

GOD IS LOVE
(3: 1-5: 12)

GOD'S LOVE FOR MAN
(3: 1, 2)

3 Behold what manner of love the Father hath bestowed upon us, that we should be called children of God; and *such* we are. For this cause the world

1 Behold what manner of love the Father hath bestowed upon us, that we should be called children of God; and such we are.—The first verses of 1 John 3 continue and advance the thought set out in the final verse of the second chapter of the Epistle. Having declared that those who exhibit righteousness in their lives evidence the fact that they are the begotten sons of God, the apostle proceeds to dwell upon the marvelous blessings which such a relationship suggests.

"Behold" *(eidete)* means to see, to take notice of, to be impressed with. Its design, as in John 1:29; 19: 5; Mark 13: 1, and often elsewhere in the New Testament, was to fix the attention of John's readers on the measure of the love which had been revealed in their behalf. "Manner of love" is a phrase descriptive of the quality of the love which the Father has vouchsafed to his children. In it is revealed not only the size, but the blessedness of it. "What glorious, sublime, immeasurable love the Father hath bestowed upon us. . . ." Included in the manner of it is the freeness, the greatness, the preciousness, the scope, the duration—in a word, all that is summed up in the word, "For God so loved the world, that he gave his only begotten Son. . . ." (John 3: 16.) This love God "bestowed" (literally, *gave),* eventuating in our being "called children of God." Inasmuch as the Lord makes us what we are, to be called his children by him is to be such, and to sustain this relation to him in all the affairs of life. "And such we are" is a positive affirmation of that which had just been said.

For this cause the world knoweth us not, because it knew him not.—The first clause of this sentence is a conclusion drawn from the premise which the second clause contains. The world knows us not. Why does the world know *us* not? Because

knoweth us not, because it knew him not. 2 Beloved, now are we children of God, and it is not yet made manifest what we shall be. We know that, if ¹¹he shall be manifested, we shall be like him; for we shall see him even as

¹¹Or, *it*

---

it knew *him* not. Since the world does not know the Father, of course it does not recognize the Father's children! The word "know" here, as in many other instances in John's writings, is used to mean much more than merely superficial knowledge. The world knows, of course, that Christians are in it; they are aware of the fact that Christians worship God; but they do not approve of the lives of Christians, nor do they acknowledge the Christian's God as their Sovereign and King. Of similar import are the words of the Lord: "If the world hateth you, ye know it hath hated me before it hated you. If ye were of the world, the world would love its own; but because ye are not of the world but I chose you out of the world, therefore the world hateth you." (John 15: 18, 19.)

2 Beloved, now are we children of God, and it is not yet made manifest what we shall be.—We are children of God *now*, in spite of the nonrecognition of the world. Though the world about us refuses to recognize us for what we are, God does, and this is enough. And, the fact that "it is not yet made manifest what we shall be," does not raise a question regarding our *present* status. Grant that we do not possess a full knowledge of matters pertaining to the next life; let it be admitted that here is much with reference to the future which we do not know. Does this, in any fashion, raise a presumption of doubt regarding our present relation to the Father? Certainly not. We are children of God; we are children of God now; and as such, all the blessings of sonship are ours.

We know that, if he shall be manifested, we shall be like him; for we shall see him even as he is.—To "be manifested," is to be made to appear, to be brought to the light, to be known. The phrase, "if he shall be manifested," refers to the Lord's second coming. When this event occurs, our imperfect conceptions will vanish in the perfect knowledge of him which will then be ours. Then it is that we shall see him even as he is, and shall be like him. The meaning is: we are children of God now, as much so as we shall be when the Lord comes; but at the present we are waiting for an inheritance which we do not fully comprehend; when he comes we shall still be children and, in addition, in possession of that for which we now wait. Moreover, we shall then have perfect understanding of matters with reference to our future state which now we do not fully understand.

The glorious anticipation of being "like him" should prompt us to utilize every faculty we possess in his service, and thrill us with the prospect of awakening in his likeness. To be like him is to be as he is, in both spirit and body. It is to partake of his glorious characteristics of mind and heart, of soul and spirit; to come into possession of the spiritual graces which are his. It is to be like him in purity, in holiness, in kindness and in love; it is to share with him the complete approval of our Father and God. It is, further, to be like him in body; to possess the immortal nature which he possesses, and to be no longer, as he is no longer, subject to death. "For our citizenship is in heaven; whence also we wait for a Saviour, the Lord Jesus Christ: who shall fashion anew the body of our humiliation, that it may be conformed to the body of his glory, according to the working whereby he is able even to subject all things unto himself." (Phile. 3: 20, 21.)

The wondrous blessing which this promise includes—of being like him—should not be lightly regarded or passed over hurriedly. It is a summary of all the good things which the Father has in reserve for his own. There is a story often told of a group of heathen converts who, when they came to this verse in translating into their language, unable to believe that such could possibly be in store for sinful man, stopped and said, "No! It is too much. Let us write that we shall be permitted to kiss his feet."

ORIGIN AND CHARACTERISTICS OF SINFUL CONDUCT
(3: 3-12)

he is. 3 And every one that hath this hope *set* on him purifieth himself, even

3 And every one that hath this hope set on him purifieth himself, even as he is pure.—The "hope" which we have is in being like him when he shall appear; and he who is in possession of this hope keeps himself pure, even as Christ, whom we shall be like when he appears, is pure. The meaning is, we have a hope;

3: 3, 4.] FIRST JOHN 259

as he is pure. 4 Every one that doeth sin doeth also lawlessness; and sin is

this hope is to awake in the likeness of the Saviour; the possession of this hope leads one to keep himself pure, this being a condition precedent to its realization; the pattern for this purity is Christ himself. The verb "purifieth" *(hagnizei,* present active indicative), is a continuous act, *keeps on purifying,* an essential prerequisite to the maintenance of the hope which we have in him. Taught here, in the most emphatic fashion is, (1) the conditionality of our salvation; (2) the necessity of abstaining from every form of impurity; (3) the encouragement to faithfulness which hope affords; and (4) the example of purity which Christ himself supplies.

This passage may not be legitimately cited to sustain the view that it is possible for a child of God to live above sin here. (1) Such a view is opposed to other statements by the same writer. (John 1: 8; 2: 1.) (2) Such is a misapprehension of what is here taught. If this passage teaches that one can purify himself to the extent he is above sin, it teaches that every one who has hope in Christ can do so, in which case all who have hope in the Lord are above sin. We are purified by complying with the conditions on the basis of which the Lord forgives us: "If we walk in the light as he is in the light we have fellowship one with another, and the blood of Jesus his Son cleanseth us from all sin. If we say that we have no sin, we deceive ourselves, and the truth is not in us. If we confess our sins, he is faithful and righteous to forgive us our sins, and to cleanse us from all unrighteousness." (1 John 1: 7-9.) This passage, instead of teaching us that it is possible to live above sin, actually teaches the opposite of this, by indicating the means by which we overcome the effect of sin in our lives. By striving for the purity which the Lord possesses we reach for the goal which will be finally realized when he appears.

4 Every one that doeth sin doeth also lawlessness; and sin is lawlessness.—Here, again, the connection with what has gone before, in the Epistle, is immediately apparent, and should not be overlooked. The theme of this section is set forth in 2: 29: "If ye know that he is righteous, ye know that every one also that doeth righteousness is begotten of him." Verses 1-3, of this chapter, in the development of this theme, emphasize the fact that the doing of righteousness is proof of the new birth; and when such evidence does not exist, there is no sonship. Verses 4-10 establish the utter impossibility of reconciling sin with the work of redemption, with fellowship with Christ, and with the new birth. These connecting links are not to be ignored in the study of the Epistle; they are, indeed, essential to the understanding of the design of the author. Having shown, in the foregoing verses, what the fatherhood of God (and the consequent sonship which relates) *includes*, he then proceeds to show what it *excludes*.

In the statement which constitutes a definition of sin, the apostle wrote, "Every one that doeth sin doeth also lawlessness; and sin is lawlessness." It is easily possible that it was the purpose of the apostle to encourage his readers to refrain from sin by showing its essential and inherent nature, more than to set out a formal definition thereof, but it still remains that his statement is a definition of sin, simply and plainly put. *Sin* is translated from the Greek *hamartia*, the literal meaning of which is "to miss the mark," and as here used, to veer away from that which is right. It is a general term embracing every form of wrongdoing, all divergence from that which is right. The verbs "Doeth" in the first clause are both in the present tense, the force of which, in Greek, is to indicate continuous action. It is the *habitual practice* of sin which is here contemplated. "Lawlessness" *(anomia)* is that state or manner of life wherein one fails to conform to law, whether in positive disobedience thereto, or in failing to come up to its demands. It is action contrary to law, whatever the form in which the action takes place. It embraces sin both positively and negatively; it includes sins of omission as well as sins of commission.

The meaning is that whoever practices sin is a lawless person; by his sinful life he has become a violator of the law for "sin is the transgression of the law." (1 John 3: 4AV.) This John wrote in order to impress his readers with the fact that all sin is a violation of the law of God; and since the violation of his law leads to condemnation, no sin, however small or insignificant it may appear to us to be, should be regarded lightly. In view of conditions which then prevailed this was a sorely needed lesson. Certain heretical sects of the time held that their superior knowledge (the Gnostics) made them immune from the demands of the law, and

3: 4, 5.] FIRST JOHN

lawlessness. 5 And ye know that he was manifested to ¹²take away sins; and

---
¹²Or, *bear sins*

---

that God did not, in their case, impute to them wrongdoing even though their conduct was in conflict with God's law. The apostle here shows that the wickedness of sin is in the fact that it is disregard for, and disobedience to, the law of God, for sin, all sin, any sin, is lawlessness. It follows, therefore, that any sin is serious, because it puts one under condemnation of the law.

In the Greek text, both *sin* and *lawlessness* have the article before them; each term is the equivalent of the other and they are, therefore, interchangeable. Sin is lawlessness; and lawlessness is also sin. One who veers away from the right is a lawless person; a lawless person is one who veers from the right. To "miss the mark," whether it be going beyond that which is right, or in failing to measure up to it, puts one in the position of being a law violator, and one who violates the law of God is, of course, a sinner. The connection with the context thus becomes apparent: if we would sustain and preserve the hope which we possess, we must continue to purify ourselves. A failure to do so is to lapse into a life of sin; and a life of sin is lawlessness.

5 And ye know that he was manifested to take away sins; and in him is no sin.—Two additional reasons are thus advanced why Christians are not to engage in the practice of sin: (1) Christ was manifested to take away sins; (2) in him, who is our example, there is no sin. The manifestation of Christ here referred to was his entrance into the world, in the flesh, the purpose of which was to "take away sins." (Matt. 1: 21.) The article (the) appears before the word "sins" in the Greek text, and the meaning is, Jesus came into the world to take away the sins of the world, all sin, not merely one sin here and another there.

The design of the Lord's appearance was, therefore, in part, to take away sins. The verb *take away* is translated from *arei*, first aorist subjunctive of *airo*, occurring also in John 1: 29. It conveys the idea of a burden or load which is lifted in order that it may not crush him upon whom it rests; and, as here figuratively used, it signifies the lifting and carrying away of sins that they may be upon us no more. Being in the aorist tense, the act is a

in him is no sin. 6 Whosoever abideth in him sinneth not: whosoever sin-

once-for-all process, in which by one offering the Lord accomplished his purpose henceforth and forever. Implied in the word is the idea of atonement, reconciliation, expiation and sanctification, all of which the Lord accomplished in his death, though the primary meaning here is the bearing away of sin. The lesson the apostle desired to teach is that all sin must be shunned and avoided for Christ came into the world for the purpose of removing sin from us, and to continue to participate therein would frustrate his purpose and thwart his plan for those for whom he suffered. Forms of the word thus translated occur in the Septuagint translation in Isaiah 53: 11, and in Hebrews 10: 4, 11, in each of which the primary meaning "to take away" is retained. In taking away sin, the Lord abolishes the guilt, the power, and the punishment thereof, thus making it possible for his children to entertain an assured hope of salvation. Such Paul must have had in mind when he wrote, "Christ . . . gave himself for us, that he might redeem us from all iniquity, and purify unto himself a people for his own possession, zealous of good works." (Titus 2: 14.)

In view of the fact that the Lord became incarnate in order that he might take away our sins, the proper regard for this should serve as a mighty incentive to all Christians to refrain from all wilful participation therein. (1) To engage in sin, in view of the design which led to his death, is to thwart the purpose and plan of the Lord and to render his sacrifice in vain. (2) As disciples of his, it is proper that we should follow such a course as would result in the furtherance of his purposes and plans for men. (3) To indulge in sin is to practice that which was the occasion for the ignominy and shame which were heaped upon the Lord at his crucifixion. (4) To persist in such practices in view of what sin did to him reveals a perverseness and depravity of heart wholly inconsistent with that which characterizes those who love and serve him.

The second clause, "and in him is no sin," is, if literally rendered, *"and sin in him is not."* It is an emphatic and positive affirmation of the Lord's freedom from sin. Being himself absolutely free from sin, and without any admixture of wrong in him whatsoever, it is only as we "purify" ourselves, (verse 3), and abstain from all sinful practices, that we are able to approach the perfect

neth hath not seen him, neither ¹³knoweth him. 7 *My* little children, let no

---

¹³Or, *hath known*

---

standard his life constitutes. That our Lord was wholly free from sin every moment of his life is a fact clearly taught in the sacred writings. Jesus declared it himself (John 7:18; 8:46); and it was often affirmed of him (2 Cor. 5: 21; Heb. 4: 15; 7: 26; 9: 13). It follows, therefore, that those who would imitate him in manner of life today must strive for the same inherent purity. "For hereunto were we called because Christ also suffered for you, leaving you an example, that ye should follow his steps: who did no sin, neither was guile found in his mouth: who, when he was reviled, reviled not again, when he suffered, threatened not; but committed himself to him that judgeth righteously." (1 Pet. 2: 21-23.)

6 **Whosoever abideth in him sinneth not; whosoever sinneth hath not seen him, neither knoweth him.**—The ideas which this verse contains were favorite ones with the apostle, and are repeated, in one form or another, throughout his writings. The word "abideth," for example, occurs (in one of its various forms) in John 5: 38; 6: 56; 14: 10; 15: 4, 5, 6, 7, 9; 1 John 2: 6, 10, 14, 17, 27; 3: 6, 25; 4: 12, 13, 15, 16. It was likely suggested to him by the Lord in the familiar and impressive statement of John 15: 4-6: "Abide in me, and I in you. As the branch cannot bear fruit of itself, except it abide in the vine; so neither can ye, except ye abide in me. I am the vine, ye are the branches: he that abideth in me, and I in him, the same beareth much fruit: for apart from me ye can do nothing. If a man abide not in me, he is cast forth as a branch, and is withered; and they gather them and cast them into the fire, and they are burned." The word "abide" is translated from a word *(Meno)* which means to settle down and remain, as in one's permanent home. Here, in addition to its literal meaning, it denotes the intimate relationship which exists between the Lord and his disciples, the close and continuing connection which obtains between him and those who derive their life from him. Not only does the word itself suggest an abode in Christ; the tense necessitates this conclusion also, *"whosoever keeps on abiding. . . . "*

"Whosoever keeps on abiding in him *sinneth not.*" Here, too, the apostle gives utterance to an idea which is often expressed in one way or another in his Epistles. (1 John 2: 24; 3: 9; 5: 18; 3 John 11.) (1) Whosoever abides in him sins not; (2) whosoever is begotten of God does not sin; (3) he that does evil has not seen God. These propositions are developed in much detail throughout the first Epistle; and the ideas which they contain were favorite ones with John. The apostle did not intend to affirm that one who abides in Christ is not capable of committing a single act of sin; such a concept would be in conflict with his affirmation of the universal prevalence of sin, even among the saints (1 John 1: 8); moreover, the designation of the means by which to overcome sin through the intercession of Christ (1 John 2: 1) implies its possibility. Thus to teach it is possible or even probable that one will attain to a life of sinlessness here is in conflict with his own teaching in the instances cited, and must not be attributed to him here.

The meaning of this verse, and indeed, all of those of similar import in the writings of the apostle John (e.g., 3: 9; 5: 18; 3 John 11), is to be sought and found in the significance which attaches to the *tense* of the verbs which set forth the action involved. The word "tense" as applied to the Greek verb is misleading, if it be accorded its literal signification, for it is derived from the French *temps,* time, and originally the Greek tense had no reference to time, as such. This characteristic, so prominent in the English verb, is only incidental in the Greek, the tense of the Greek verb having to do with the state of action, and not necessarily with the time when it occurred. Its function is to indicate the state of the action, accordingly as it is conceived of as an indefinite event (aorist tense), an action in progress (present tense), or a completed action with existing results, (perfect tense). Other tenses, such as the imperfect, etc., are variations of one or the other of these types of action. In the English language the time element is the prominent feature of the verb, and we think of an act as either past, present, or future.

The present tense, in Greek, indicates action in progress at the present time. It is thus distinguished from the aorist tense which is a single act indefinitely conceived of, without regard to time.

The distinction between the present and the aorist tenses may be seen in the following manner:

The present tense: (_____) an act continuing.
The aorist tense: (•   ) a single act.

In the passage under consideration, the verb *sinneth not* is the translation of *ouch hamartanei,* third person singular, of the present indicative active, of *hamartano*. Inasmuch as the chief characteristic of the Greek present tense is to indicate action in progress contemporary with the time of speaking, whereas the English verb does not distinguish between such action in progress, and a single act occurring, the significance of the verb *sinneth,* as used by the apostle, does not fully appear in the translation. It can be brought to the attention of the English reader only by an expanded translation thus: "Whosoever continues to abide in him, does not keep on sinning" (i.e., habitually as he did before his conversion). Had the apostle intended to convey the idea that one who abides in Christ is incapable of committing a single act of sin, he would have utilized the aorist tense. In such a case, however, he would have been in conflict with his own previous statements which assert the fact of sin in the lives of Christians, and the means provided for their removal. The meaning of the verse is, He who has taken up his abode in Christ, and settled down to a permanent existence in him, has terminated his former manner of life and has ceased the practices then characteristic of him. He no longer engages in habitual and persistent sin. That he has broken the hold of sin in his life, and no longer regularly yields to evil impulses as a manner of life, however, is far from asserting that there are never occasional lapses into sin through weakness or ignorance. (Cf. 1 Cor. 9: 27; Phil. 3: 12.) For these inadvertent lapses, a plan has been provided. (1 John 2: 1.)

"Whosoever sinneth hath not seen him, neither knoweth him." The verb "sinneth" here, as in the first clause of the verse, is in the present tense. Whosoever sins following his conversion demonstrates the fact that he has neither seen nor known the Lord. This passage, as translated, appears to teach that sinful conduct on the part of one who affects to be a child of God is evidence of the fact that such a one is not only not saved at the time, but *never has been!* This conclusion is obviously erroneous, because it is in

man lead you astray: he that doeth righteousness is righteous, even as he is

conflict with other statements in the same Epistle, and by the same author. He had earlier said that Jesus is our Advocate when we sin, and that "if we confess our sins, he is faithful and just to forgive us our sins, and to cleanse us from all unrighteousness." (1 John 1: 7-9; 2: 1.) How is it possible to confess sins never committed? Why do Christians need an Advocate for them when they sin, *if they never sin?* The verb *sinneth*, as in the first clause, indicates a continuous practice. "Whosoever *keeps on sinning* . . ." has neither seen nor known him. The verbs "seen" (*heoraken*) and "knoweth" (*egnoken*) are Greek perfects. The Greek perfect tense denotes action absolutely past, which lasts on in its effects. It is the function of the Greek perfect to indicate the result which follows the action, the action, meanwhile, dropping out of view. In this respect it differs greatly from the English perfect which keeps the action in view and in which the past idea predominates. When, for example, we say, "I have known," the mind instinctively attributes the time of knowing to the past; in this, the true function of the English perfect is seen. In the Greek perfect, however, the time element is lost sight of, and the force of the tense is to point to an existing state produced by the action which has already terminated. Thus, the significance of "I have known," regarded from the viewpoint of the Greek perfect, is, "I know" *(now)*.

Thus, in the study of this verse if we keep in mind that the verbs *seen* and *knoweth*, as here used, express *result*, the meaning becomes clear. "Whosoever continues to abide in him does not keep on living a life of sin; whosoever does keep on living such a life, does not see him or know him." Obviously, one who has lapsed into a life of habitual sin, such as characterized him before his conversion, no longer sees (enjoys) God, nor knows (recognizes) God in his life.

In the implication that one who abides in Christ *sees* the Father, we do not, of course, infer from this that it is possible for one to look upon, with physical eyes, the likeness of the great Jehovah. "No man hath seen God at any time." (1 John 4: 12.) The seeing which is thus possible is to exercise the knowledge and insight which such a relationship allows—the perception possible to

righteous: 8 he that doeth sin is of the devil; for the devil sinneth from the

the faithful. To *see* in the New Testament is a figure often used of such spiritual insight. (John 1: 18; 6: 46; Heb. 2: 8.)

7 My little children, let no man lead you astray: he that doeth righteousness is righteous, even as he is righteous:—The address here is the same, and the same ones are addressed as in 2: 1 and 2: 18. The warning, "Let no man lead you astray," appears, in one form or another, often in the Epistles. (1: 8; 2: 18, 26; 3: 1-3.) These words have particular reference to men who sought to deceive the saints of that day by alleging that it is possible to live a life of habitual sin, and yet have the approval and approbation of God. Such views were propagated by false and heretical sects of the time, and many were deluded and led into a life of sin by them. (See under "Design of the Epistle," in the Introduction.) These false teachers advocated the view that they pleased God without living a life of righteousness, and that whatever might be the case with others who were without their alleged superior knowledge (*gnosis*), there was no need for *them* to work righteousness, because they were eternally saved by the grace of God, regardless of what their works might be. The effect of this teaching was to lead those who accepted it into a life of gross and unrestrained indulgence, and that in the name of religion!

To counteract such teaching the apostle laid down the maxim that "He who doeth righteousness *is righteous,* even as he (Christ) is righteous," i.e., the man who does righteousness is righteous, and no other is. It is a positive affirmation that character and conduct cannot be separated. It matters not how much one may assert his righteousness; it is of little consequence to what extent one may declare his love for the Lord; the acid test is, *does he do righteousness?* If yes, he is a righteous man; if no, his claims are false.

Here, as in 2: 29, the doing of righteousness is not a condition precedent to righteousness, but evidence that such salvation exists. However tempted we may be to cite these passages in support of the scriptural doctrine that obedience is essential to salvation from past, or alien, sins, such is an unwarranted use of them. It is never allowable to take passages from their context and use them in support of a proposition even though the proposition we seek to

beginning. To this end was the Son of God manifested, that he might de-

prove is taught elsewhere in the scriptures. A passage should never be used in any sense other than that for which it was originally written by the sacred writer. The use of texts out of their contexts, so common to denominational preachers, has led people to the conclusion that it is possible to *prove anything* by the Bible. It is well to remember that "a text, taken from its context, becomes a mere pretext." It was John's design to show here that the doing (practice) of righteousness is the only test of a righteous (approved) person, whatever his claims may be. Long ago Luther truthfully said, "Good works of piety do not make a good pious man, but a good pious man does good pious works . . . fruits grow from the tree and not the tree from the fruits."

The verb "doeth" in this verse, as often elsewhere in the Epistles of John (e.g., 2: 29; 3: 4; 3: 7; 3: 9, etc.), is a present active participle in the Greek text *(poion)*, and signifies *to keep on doing*. As occasional lapses into sin through weakness, inadvertence, or ignorance do not demonstrate that one has never been saved, so isolated and infrequent acts of righteousness (outward conformity to some of God's laws) do not justify the conclusion that such a one is a righteous man. To be righteous, one must practice righteousness as a settled habit in life. Such a one, the apostle affirms, is a righteous man; no other is.

"Even as he is righteous" is a reference to Christ. "Even as" does not signify that one attains to the same righteousness as that Christ possesses; it means that Christ constitutes the model or pattern of righteousness toward which all of his followers are ever to strive. As he is righteous, so are we to seek to be; and such righteousness is attained through right-doing. (Psalm 119: 172; Acts 10: 34; Matt. 3: 14.) The right-doing essential to such righteousness includes the duties and responsibilities of the Christian life.

8 **He that doeth sin is of the devil; for the devil sinneth from the beginning.**—He who lives a life of habitual sin is of the devil; he demonstrates his relation to Satan by his conformity to the character which the devil possesses. The devil has sinned (has been sinning, *ap' arches hamartanei,* present active indicative) from the beginning, i.e., from the first sin which resulted in his becoming the devil. Being the first sinner, the devil is the

3: 8.]   FIRST JOHN   269

stroy the works of the devil. 9 Whosoever is begotten of God doeth no sin,

source of sin, the fountain from which it springs, the father of all those who practice it. "Ye are of your father the devil, and the lusts of your father it is your will to do. He was a murderer from the beginning, and standeth not in the truth, because there is no truth in him. When he speaketh a lie, he speaketh of his own; for he is a liar, and the father thereof." (John 8: 44.) Inasmuch as the devil is the original sinner, and since he has persisted in sin without interruption from the occasion of the first sin, it follows that whoever sins thus persistently partakes of the character of him who is their spiritual father. Such being the pattern of his existence, those who conform thereto must be regarded as his offspring and imitators.

But here, again, we must not confuse mere occasional lapses into sin with a life of persistent and willful transgression. (1) To affirm that this passage teaches that it is possible to live a sinless life here is to (a) ignore the significance of the terms employed and (b) to put the writer in conflict with himself in other passages in the same Epistle. (1 John 1: 7-9; 2: 1.) (2) Such a claim is refuted by the sober consciousness of all thoughtful persons who, though it may have been years since they have engaged in willful sin, are aware of defects of character, and the like, which occasionally lead them inadvertently into sin. (3) The wisest, greatest, and best characters of whom we read in the scriptures never laid claim to sinlessness in this life, but, on the contrary, exhibited the weaknesses common to humanity, and often confessed them with penitence and shame. (Cf. the lives of Abraham, David, Peter, and Paul.) (4) It must not be overlooked in the consideration of this passage that the evil contemplated is that which flows uninterruptedly from an evil heart, and is deliberate, willful, and persistent. The steady stream of pollution unmistakably reveals that the source is equally corrupt. It follows, therefore, that the type of sin under contemplation here is that which is habitual. Those who live as the devil lives must be regarded as belonging to the devil; in exhibiting the traits and characteristics of the devil, they evidence the fact that they are his children.

Here, incidentally, is additional proof of the personality of the devil—a fact often taught in the scriptures. (a) He exists; (b)

because his seed abideth in him: and he cannot sin, because he is begotten of

he has existed from the beginning; (c) he is the spiritual progenitor of all who sin as he does; and (d) false teachers are his agents in seeking to seduce and lead astray the saints.

To this end was the Son of God manifested, that he might destroy the works of the devil.—"To this end" indicates the purpose for which the Son of God was manifested (appeared in the world), that he might "destroy" (bring to naught) the "works of the devil." The "works of the devil" include his plans, purposes, designs, schemes, aims, and ends which he hopes to accomplish. These Jesus came to "destroy" *(luso),* literally, to weaken, deprive of power, abolish in principle. Included among the works of the devil are not only sins, but the consequences of sin—pain, sorrow, misery, and death. Christ has abolished death "and brought life and immortality to light through the gospel." (2 Tim. 1: 10.) The eventual triumph over death will be realized in the resurrection: "But when this corruptible shall have put on incorruption, and this mortal shall have put on immortality, then shall come to pass the saying that is written, Death is swallowed up in victory. O death, where is thy victory? O death, where is thy sting?" (1 Cor. 15: 54, 55.) There, too, will all sorrow, pain, and misery be forevermore terminated: "And I heard a great voice out of the throne saying, Behold, the tabernacle of God is with men, and he shall dwell with them, and they shall be his people, and God himself shall be with them, and be their God: and he shall wipe away every tear from their eyes; and death shall be no more; neither shall there be mourning, nor crying, nor pain any more: the first things are passed away." (Rev. 21: 3, 4.)

9 **Whosoever is begotten of God doeth no sin, because his seed abideth in him; and he cannot sin, because he is begotten of God.**—The familiar rendering, "Whosoever is born of God doth not commit sin," of the King James Version, has given place to the American Standard rendering, "Whosoever is begotten of God doeth no sin," and here, as often elsewhere, the Standard rendering is the preferable one, though it, too, as we shall later see, does not fully and adequately convey the meaning of the text. (1) The phrase "begotten of God" is a decided improvement over "born of God" *(gegennemenos ek tou theou),* for *gegennemenos,*

God. 10 In this the children of God are manifest, and the children of the

from *gennao*, means to beget. (2) Correctly translated, the scriptures never refer to a "birth of God." (3) It is absurd to predicate the act of birth of a masculine personality exclusively. We are not, however, from this to infer that the reference here, or in the numerous other instances where the phrase occurs, signifies an embryonic or prenatal state. Obviously, here and in 2: 29 and 5: 18, the reference is to children of God. While the context establishes the fact that children of God are contemplated, accuracy of translation necessitates the rendering "begotten of God" rather than "born of God."

Whosoever is begotten of God "doeth no sin." "Doeth no sin" is translated from the phrase, *hamartian ou poiei*, present active indicative of *poio*, does not keep on doing sin (as a life habit.) The reference here is to persistent, continuous, willful sin, such as that contemplated in 3: 6, and the remarks there (which see) apply with equal force here.

But why does the one begotten of God refrain from habitual and persistent indulgence in sin? Because his seed remains in him and he cannot sin. Whose seed? God's. What is God's seed? The word of God: "The seed is the word of God." (Luke 8: 11.) In whom does this seed abide or remain? In the child of God. What does the word "abide" signify? That the word of God has made its home, as it were, in the heart of the one begotten. Is this a scriptural concept? "Let the word of Christ dwell in you richly in all wisdom" (Col. 3: 16), which we translate more vividly, "May the word which Christ speaks to you have in your hearts in all its fullness its home." What is the result of such? The child of God cannot sin.

Does this mean that it is impossible for a child of God, under any circumstances, to commit a single act of sin? No. The phrase "Doeth no sin" does not adequately convey the meaning of the original text. Here, as in 3: 6, in order to discover the full significance of the verb *doeth*, it is essential to take into consideration the tense thereof, a better rendering of which would be, "worketh no sin." (See comments on 1 John 3: 6.) What reasons have we for concluding that it was not the intention of the apostle to teach that it is impossible for a child of God to commit a single

devil: whosoever doeth not righteousness is not of God, neither he that lov-

act of sin? (1) Such a conclusion is in conflict with 1 John 1: 7-9; 2: 1, and many other passages in the scriptures. (2) The words "he cannot sin" cannot be correctly construed to mean that one cannot commit a single act of sin after being begotten of God. Why is it alleged that such a conclusion is in conflict with what the apostle taught elsewhere? Because he affirmed, in the references cited, that children *do* sin, and he moreover revealed the conditions on which they may be forgiven.

Why is it thought that the phrase "he cannot sin" may not be correctly interpreted to mean that it is impossible for a child of God to commit a single act of sin? "And he cannot sin" is translated from the phrase *"kai ou dunatai hamartanein." Hamartarein* is a present active infinitive, the force of which is, "he cannot continue to live a life of sin" (as before). But why cannot he continue to live such a life? The seed, which is the word of God, and which is in him, forbids it. How did David recognize and apply the principle taught here? "Thy word have I laid up in my heart, that I might not sin against thee." (Psalm 119: 11.) How did Jesus resist the seductions of Satan? By relying on the same power. Suppose one is tempted to steal. Such a one remembers that the Word says, "Thou shalt not steal." So long as this injunction remains in the heart and governs the life, one *cannot* steal. "It is written" is as effective in resisting the blandishments of Satan today as it was when the Lord utilized it on the mount of temptation. Why, then, cannot one thus begotten persist in sin? (1) The seed (the word of God), which forbids it, is in him, controls his life, and directs his energies. (2) A life of sin is inconsistent with the spiritual parentage of the one thus begotten. But does this mean that it is never possible for one possessed of this nature to sin? No. All, through weakness, error, ignorance, and inadvertence, occasionally sin; but children of God do not work sin as a life principle, for its author—Satan—they have repudiated and his nature abandoned. When, in such instances, sin occurs, it is a momentary lapse; it is due to an imperfect holding of the word in the heart; it is recognized as contrary to the higher impulses of the person thus sinning, and it is confessed and put aside with shame.

Paul and John are in strict harmony in their teaching on the dif-

eth not his brother. 11 For this is the message which ye heard from the

ference between such occasional lapses into sin and a life wholly devoted to it. The former wrote, "What shall we say then? Shall we continue in sin, that grace may abound? God forbid. We who died to sin, how shall we any longer live therein? Or are ye ignorant that all we who were baptized into Christ Jesus were baptized into his death? We were buried therefore with him through baptism into death: that like as Christ was raised from the dead through the glory of the Father, so we also might walk in newness of life. For if we have become united with him in the likeness of his death, we shall be also in the likeness of his resurrection; knowing this, that our old man was crucified with him, that the body of sin might be done away, that we should no longer be in bondage to sin." (Rom. 6: 1-6.) We are thus no longer to continue in sin, for (a) we have died (separated ourselves) from the practice thereof; (b) we have risen from the baptismal grave to walk a new life; (c) the body of sin has been done away; (d) we have been delivered from the bondage of sin. The careful distinction which the inspired writers make between a life of continuous and habitual sin and the infrequent deviations of children of God who, while they ever reach upward toward a nobler life, now and then falter through weakness or error, may be seen by a comparison between Rom. 6: 1, "Shall we continue in sin" *(epimenomen tei hamartiai,* present active subjunctive) and 6: 15, "Shall we sin" *(hamartesomen,* first aorist active subjunctive), "Shall we commit a single act of sin?" (because we are not under law, but under grace). Carefully and pointedly the apostle to the Gentiles makes it clear that even isolated acts of sin were not to be indulged in on the assumption that the grace under which we live, instead of the law, would make provision for such.

Properly interpreted, neither 1 John 3: 9 nor any other scripture countenances the view that it is impossible for a child of God to live above sin in this life; and theories to this end, whether drawn from this passage or some other, are clearly erroneous.

10 In this the children of God are manifest, and the children of the devil:—That is, in the matters immediately preceding. We indicate by our manner of life our parentage. The word "manifest" means to make known, to reveal. Children of

beginning, that we should love one another: 12 not as Cain was of the evil one, and slew his brother. And wherefore slew he him? Because his works

God and children of the devil are readily distinguished from each other by the fact that the former abstain from a life of unrelieved sin, whereas such a life is ever characteristic of the latter. The nature exhibits itself in the individual and reveals who is his father. As a life of constant and continuous sin justifies the conclusion that such a one is a child of the devil, so a life of righteousness is evidence of the fact that such a one is a child of God. "Ye know that every one also that doeth righteousness is begotten of him." (1 John 2: 29.) "Every one that doeth sin doeth also lawlessness; and sin is lawlessness." (1 John 3: 4.)

Whosoever doeth not righteousness is not of God, neither he that loveth not his brother.—The first clause of this verse relates to what had just been said; the second expands it and makes it applicable not only to the spiritual, but also to the social side of life. The love under consideration here is that which one brother in Christ should have for another and where it does not exist, there is an absence of divine parenthood. We are taught here that he who does not love his brother actually *has no brother to love,* for in his failure to comply with this normal and natural principle, he demonstrates that God is not his Father. In refusing to love one of God's family, he simply excludes himself from the family itself!

11 **For this is the message which ye heard from the beginning, that we should love one another:**—"For," i.e., with refrence to what had just been written, "Whosoever doeth not righteousness is not of God, neither he that loveth not his brother." John's readers had heard this "message" from the beginning of their acquaintance with Christianity, since this was a cardinal principle of the movement itself. (John 13: 34, 35.) It is called a message from a word which, in the New Testament, signifies things announced in order that they may be done. It is referred to here as a message, instead of a commandment, though such it was, and is, because it was announced in words, and conveyed by messengers. See further on this in the comments on 1 John 2: 9.

12 **Not as Cain was of the evil one, and slew his brother.**— This statement is put in contrast with that of verse 11, and Cain is

were evil, and his brother's righteous.

offered as an example of what children of God are not to do. The meaning is, We should love one another, and not be as Cain was, who was of the evil one, and slew his brother. (Gen. 4: 1-17.) Those who do righteousness are "of God"; Cain, who did not obey the commandment to love, was "of the evil one," i.e., the devil. He demonstrated the fact that he was of the devil by killing his brother Abel. The word translated "slew" here *(sphazo)* means, literally, to butcher, to slit the throat with a knife; and from this it may be inferred that this was the manner in which Cain took the life of Abel. If the word is to be taken in its literal import, this conclusion follows, though it is, of course, possible that it is used figuratively to kill, and thus without any indication of the method by which the murder took place.

And wherefore slew he him? Because his works were evil, and his brother's righteous.—The question, "Wherefore slew he him?" is immediately answered, "Because his (Cain's) works were evil, and his brother's (Abel's) were righteous. The reason for God's rejection of Cain's offering and his acceptance of Abel's, though not detailed in the Genesis record, is made clear in the reference thereto by the writer of Hebrews: "By faith Abel offered unto God a more excellent sacrifice than Cain, through which he had witness borne to him that he was righteous, God bearing witness in respect of his gifts; and through it he being dead yet speaketh." (Heb. 11: 4.) Cain's offering was "of the fruit of the ground," Abel's "of the firstlings of his flock and of the fat thereof." (Gen. 4: 3, 4.) "And Jehovah had respect unto Abel and his offering; but unto Cain and to his offering he had not respect." Inasmuch as Abel made his offering "by faith," it follows that the Lord had specified the nature and the type of offering to be made, since faith comes by hearing God's word. (Rom. 10: 17.) Cain's offering was rejected because it was in violation of express instructions from Jehovah. Though not stated in the Mosaic account, it is implied in the following statement: "And Cain was very wroth, and his countenance fell. And Jehovah said unto Cain, why art thou wroth? and why is thy countenance fallen? If thou doest well, shall it not be lifted up? and if thou doest not well, sin coucheth at the door; and unto thee shall be its desire; but do thou rule over it." (Gen. 4:5-7.)

Resentful because his brother's offering was accepted and his own rejected, and filled with envy at Abel because his brother enjoyed the approbation of Jehovah while he smarted under the rebuke which he had received, "it came to pass that when they were in the field, that Cain rose up against Abel his brother and slew him." (Gen. 4:8.) In this terrible deed, Cain acted from envy, he was influenced by the evil that was in him, and he was directed by Satan whose servant he was. In citing this well-known Old Testament instance of the first murder, it was evidently the apostle's design to show the extent to which one is led when under the influence of envy, bitterness, and hate. His reasoning appears to have followed this pattern: Cain murdered his brother; therefore Cain hated his brother; hate is a characteristic of those who are children of the devil; therefore, Cain was of the devil. (Verse 12.) One who hates his brother identifies himself as of the same spirit as Cain, and likewise demonstrates that his works are evil. Basic in every difficulty and dispute between brethren today is the absence of brotherly love. Whatever may be the immediate occasion which prompts such, each difficulty and dispute may, in principle, be traced to the resentment which the evil feel toward the good. Why did Cain murder Abel? Because his works were evil, and Abel's works were righteous.

LOVE AND HATE CONTRASTED
(3: 13-24)

13 Marvel not, brethren, if the world hateth you. 14 We know that we

13 Marvel not, brethren, if the world hateth you.—"Marvel not," i.e., do not be surprised or astonished that the world hates you. The hatred of the good by the bad is nearly as old as the race; hence, it is not a thing to be surprised at, however much it may be regretted. This disposition was exhibited by Cain in the early morning of the race; and man's subsequent history has been filled with similar examples. Jesus, in teaching the disciples the obligation of love, referred to this attitude: "These things I command you, that ye may love one another. If the world hateth you, ye know that it hath hated me before it hated you. If ye were of

have passed out of death into life, because we love the brethren. He that the world, the world would love its own; but because ye are not of the world, but I chose you out of the world, therefore the world hateth you." (John 15: 17-19.)

It is significant that only here, in the Epistle, does John refer to his readers as "brethren," the address being elsewhere, "little children," "beloved," etc. The designation "brethren," literally, *brothers,* was especially appropriate here, in view of his discussion of brotherly love.

14 **We know that we have passed out of death into life, because we love the brethren.**—The connection which this verse sustains to the context in which it appears is very close, and must not be disregarded if the meaning of the text is to be determined. Love of the brethren is that which distinguishes between the children of God and the children of the devil. (Verse 10.) The obligation of Christians to love one another is definite and positive, and has been taught them from their earliest acquaintance with Christianity. (Verse 11.) The feeling of hate which the world evidences toward the good is ever present, and is, therefore, to be expected, however much it may be regretted. (Verses 12, 13.) But, in spite of this, children of God have the blessed assurance of knowing that they have passed "out of death into life" *because* "they love the brethren." They thus have more about which to rejoice than to regret in this fact, since they are in life while the world remains in death. "Death" is the status of the unregenerate; "life," of the good. These terms, opposites in their reference to the condition of the good and the bad, are often used in this fashion in the scriptures. (Eph. 2: 1, 5; Col. 2: 13.) Children of God "have passed" (migrated) from the spiritual death which formerly characterized them (and that which yet characterizes the world into the life which is obtained through union with Christ. "He that hath the Son hath the life; he that hath not the Son of God hath not the life." (1 John 5: 12.) The pronoun "we" with which the verse begins is in the emphatic position in the sentence: whatever the world may do, or feel, toward us, *we* (in contrast with those of it) *know* (have certain, definite knowledge) that we have passed from a state of death into life because we love the brethren.

loveth not abideth in death. 15 Whosoever hateth his brother is a murderer:

Just here care should be exercised in avoiding an obvious and common misinterpretation of this text. It was not the apostle's purpose to affirm, nor did he affirm, that love of the brethren is *the* (or even *a*) condition of salvation from past, or alien, sins. Brotherly love is here declared to be the condition, *not of our salvation*, but of the certainty of *our* knowledge of it. It affords the evidence by which we may know that we have passed out of death into life. The test is human, not divine; it is one we are to apply to ourselves for the purpose designated. It is such a test by which the individual and (as John 13: 34, 35 shows) the world about him may determine the reality of his profession. "We know that we have passed out of death into life *because* . . . we have been baptized? *Because* . . . we meet on the first day of the week? *Because* . . . we give liberally of our means? However important these matters are, in their respective spheres, it remains that such do not constitute the test here set out. "We know that we have passed out of death into life, *because we love the brethren*." "By this shall all men know that ye are my disciples. . . ." (John 13: 35.) Why? Because you say you are? Because there is outward conformity to the ceremonials of Christianity? Because you believe that you are? These are not the tests which the Lord ordained. "By this shall all men know that ye are my disciples, *if ye have love one for another*."

This does not mean that love alone is the basis of our acceptance before God. What it does mean is that love is the base on which all other virtues rest; where it exists, the others may be implied; yea, they must exist. He who loves his brother will not only discharge his whole duty to him; he will be led, by the same considerations which prompt such love, to love God, and so to comply with all the requirements which such a relationship involves.

He that loveth not abideth in death.—In the absence of love, the state in which one dwells is death. As the presence of love signifies life, so its opposite, hate, indicates death. The reference is not to future death; it already exists and will reach its consummation in the next life. "He that believeth on him is not judged: he that believeth not hath been judged already, because he hath not believed on the name of the only begotten Son of God." (John 3:

and ye know that no murderer hath eternal life abiding in him. 16 Hereby

18.) The absence of love is not the *cause* of his death, but the *sign* of it by which it is evidenced to others. "He that loveth not" is, literally, *the not loving* man; and "abideth" suggests a state into which one has settled down permanently. The death is spiritual death—separation from God and all that is good.

15 **Whosoever hateth his brother is a murderer:**—The phrase "he that loveth not" *(ho me agapon)* is followed by "whosoever hateth" *(pas ho mison)*, thus indicating that the two are of identical meaning: it was the design of the writer to show us that in the absence of love there is hate; there can be no middle ground. Not loving is hating; it is impossible to avoid one or the other of these opposites. In the teaching of the apostle, love and hate, as life and death, light and darkness, mutually exclude each other. He who has not the one must be regarded as possessing the other. It follows, therefore, that the only protection against hate in the heart is love.

The affirmation of the text is that he who hates his brother is a murderer. This does not mean that he has committed the act of murder; or, that he is as guilty as if he had committed the act of murder; or, that God will hold him responsible for the act of murder. What is meant is, he has exhibited the disposition and spirit of a murderer; he has allowed passions to arise in his heart which, when carried to their ultimate ends, result in murder. The reason such a one does not commit murder is not that he lacks the disposition or desire; the restraint which prevents it is not inward, but outward. Either the opportunity is lacking, or the courage or the means with which to accomplish it wanting. He refrains from the overt act, not from restraint which he himself has imposed, but a restraint from others. Murder is simply hate expressed in an overt act; and when it does not issue in this fashion, it is due to other causes than those which reside in the heart of the hater. If hate does not result in murder, the reason is to be sought, not in the hate, but in the lack of opportunity or means, or courage, of the hater.

It was this which prompted the Lord to forbid that which leads to hate. In his explanation of the commandment, "Thou shalt not kill," he said, "Ye have heard that it was said to them of old time,

know we love, because he laid down his life for us: and we ought to lay

Thou shalt not kill; and whosoever shall kill shall be in danger of the judgment: but I say unto you, that every one who is angry with his brother shall be in danger of the judgment; and whosoever shall say to his brother, Raca, shall be in danger of the council; and whosoever shall say, Thou fool, shall be in danger of the hell of fire." (Matt. 5: 21, 22.) Unnecessary anger and words of provocation are thus shown to violate, in spirit, the command to do no murder, since such often leads to it. Cain, who slew his brother Abel (1 John 3: 12), affords an example of the fruits of hate; and the devil, who was a murderer from the beginning (John 8: 44), became such by sowing the seeds of hate in those whom he seduced.

And ye know that no murderer hath eternal life abiding in him.—Obviously, spiritual life and spiritual death cannot abide in the same soul. Where hate is, there is death; where there is death, there can be no life. He who entertains hatred for another, whether it follows its normal course and results in murder, or from outward restraints imposed, stops short of the overt act, it still remains that such a one is utterly incapable of possessing life. Several phrases of similar import are discernible in the context. He is not of God who loveth not his brother. (Verse 10.) He that loveth not abideth in death. (Verse 14.) He who hates his brother has no life abiding in him. (Verse 15.) Thus, to be not of God, to abide in death, and to be without eternal life in the sense here intended, is the same. (1) In view of this, how important it is that we search our hearts diligently and purge from them every semblance of bitterness, hate, and envy. (2) How we should guard with ceaseless vigilance our own hearts lest such evil dispositions possess us. (3) How grateful we should be that we have fallen under the influence of the glorious gospel of Christ, which enables us to subdue the feelings of hate and bitterness and envy, and to triumph over the dispositions of the flesh and carnal mind.

16 Hereby know we love, because he laid down his life for us:—Every word in this verse is of the utmost importance and justifies the most minute and careful study. "Hereby" is, literally, "in this," *(en touto)*, i.e., in that which is about to be stated. "Know we" *(egnokamen*, perfect active indicative of *ginosko*, from

down our lives for the brethren. 17 But whoso hath the world's goods, and

an investigation of the facts we have come to possess certain knowledge of) "love," what it is, its nature, its sacrifices, its extent, and its design. This knowledge we have come to apprehend, for the reason that Christ *laid down* his life *for* us *(huper hemon)*, in our behalf, for our protection. The verb "laid down," is, significantly, the same mode of expression as that which the Lord utilized in his narrative of the shepherd and the sheep: "I am the good shepherd: the good shepherd layeth down his life for the sheep." . . . "Therefore doth the Father love me, because I lay down my life, that I may take it again. No one taketh it away from me, but I lay it down of myself. I have power to lay it down, and I have power to take it again." (John 10: 11, 17, 18.) The meaning is, we have become acquainted with love; we know what it is from having seen it displayed in Christ in his death *for* us. The preposition "for" here *(huper)* indicates the purpose of the death of Christ, and sheds much light on the nature and effects thereof. The picture in the preposition is of one who sees, for example, another who has fallen, wounded, in grave danger, and about to perish, and who rushes to him, stands over him, fights in his behalf, and enters the fray in his stead. This, and more, Jesus did for us in his death on the cross. He took our place; he suffered the penalty of law to be executed in his own person; "him who knew no sin he made to be sin in our behalf; that we might become the righteousness of God in him." (2 Cor. 5: 21.) We thus have, in both the Father and the Son, a clear demonstration of love, in all that it is and does. (John 3: 16; 5: 13; Rom. 5: 18.)

And we ought to lay down our lives for the brethren.—In view of what Christ and God have done for us, we (the children of God) ought (are morally obligated) to lay down our lives (die) for the brethren (our brothers and sisters in Christ). The meaning is, Christ's death was the greatest possible proof of love; if, therefore, we imitate him as we ought, the same evidence of love which prompted him to die for others will be seen in us. "This is my commandment, that ye love one another, even as I have loved you. Greater love hath no man than this, that a man lay down his life for his friends." (John 15: 12, 13.) This, of course, does not mean that there is the same efficacy in the death of one Chris-

beholdeth his brother in need, and shutteth up his compassion from him, how

tian for another as there was in the death of Christ for the world; nor was it the writer's design to compare the effects which follow such sacrifices. The subject is love; the comparison which is drawn is designed to demonstrate what love is; and the example of Christ's sacrifice is offered for our emulation. Under what circumstances it is the duty of one child of God to die for another is not stated; but in any instance, we may assume, when more good would be accomplished for him by dying than by living. In any case, where a brother's welfare depends on such a sacrifice, love prompts it, without regard to the cost that might result. The contextual force of the apostle's teaching is clear: Cain is an example of hate; Christ, of love. Cain killed his brother Abel because of selfishness; Christ died for all men because of his unselfishness. If we are to avoid the hate which motivated Cain, we must adopt the love which influenced Christ. The willingness to give what one has, even his life, for the sake of others, is of the essence of true love.

17 But whoso hath the world's goods, and beholdeth his brother in need, and shutteth up his compassion from him, how doth the love of God abide in him?—In an argument from the greater to the less, the apostle shows, in the application of the principle taught in the verse preceding, that if a brother's welfare should require that we give up our life for him, we surely ought to make those smaller sacrifices involving only material things. A refusal to make such comparatively minor sacrifices is to demonstrate that the love of God does not abide in us. The "world's goods" here is, literally, "the life of the world" *(ton bion tou kosmou);* and the "world" contemplated is not the order of evil often set forth by this term (1 John 2: 15), but the material sphere in which we live. The "life" of the world is not the higher spiritual life *(zoe),* but the organic life *(bios),* which is sustained by the things of the world. The meaning is, He who has in his possession the necessary means to sustain life and who sees his brother in need yet refuses to be touched by a feeling of sympathy for his unfortunate condition or be moved to supply the things needed, how does the love of God abide in him? The question is rhetorical for emphasis; its significance is, the love of God *does not* abide in him.

doth the love of God abide in him? 18 *My* little children, let us not love in word, neither with the tongue; but in deed and truth. 19 Hereby shall we know that we are of the truth, and shall ¹assure our heart ²before him: 20

¹Gr. *persuade.* Comp. Mt. 28. 14.
²Or, *before him, whereinsoever our heart condemn us; because God &c.*

The "love of God" here is not God's love for us, but our love for him. Here, as often elsewhere in the Epistle, and, indeed, throughout the sacred writings, we are taught the important lesson that it is impossible to separate theory and practice. Theology and religion are inseparable handmaids; theology without religion is an empty shell; religion without theology simply does not exist. Our obligation to our less fortunate brethren is clear and unmistakable; we have the example of Christ (Matt. 20: 28); we have the admonition of the inspired apostle (Gal. 6: 10); only through compliance therewith do we exhibit the religion which is both pure and undefiled (James 1: 27).

18 **My little children, let us not love in word, neither with the tongue; but in deed and truth.**—These words contain a summary of the ideas developed by the apostle in the verses immediately preceding. It was not his purpose to condemn affectionate speeches, nor did he forbid us to express our love for others in word. The meaning is, "Let us not love in word *only,* neither with the tongue *alone,* but let us *also* love in deed and truth." It is an admonition to exhibit our love in such fashion as to demonstrate its reality. As the Lord forbade words of hypocrisy in the sermon on the mount (Matt. 6: 5), so, here, John forbids the mere babble of brotherly love, when neither the word nor the tongue is attended by the fruits of brother love.

19 **Hereby shall we know that we are of the truth, and shall assure our heart before him:**—Hereby, i.e., by what has just been said, we are enabled to know that we are of the truth, and have the means by which to assure our hearts before him. If our love is not merely in word or in tongue, but truly in deed and truth, in this *(en touto)* we shall know (come to possess the knowledge) that we are of the truth. "Of the truth" is, in significance, the equivalent of the phrase, "of God," so often occurring in the Epistle. These words of the apostle were likely an echo of the Lord's affirmation before Pilate: "Every one that is of the truth heareth my voice." (John 17: 38.) Possessed of this informa-

because if our heart condemn us, God is greater than our heart, and knoweth all things. 21 Beloved, if our heart condemn us not, we have boldness toward God; 22 and whatsoever we ask we receive of him, because we keep his commandments and do the things that are pleasing in his sight. 23 And this

---

tion, we "shall assure our heart before him." The word "assure," from the verb *peitho,* means to still, persuade, placate; and the meaning here is, the knowledge of the reality of the love which we possess for others enables us to quiet the fears which arise in our own hearts and restrain the questionings which confront us from imagined deficiencies of life and conduct.

20 Because if our heart condemn us, God is greater than our heart, and knoweth all things.—If, in spite of the assurances provided, we yet suffer the uneasiness which springs from the realization of our own weaknesses and the consciousness of our own imperfections, let us remember that God is greater than our heart; he knows all things; and he will deal with us, not according to our conscience, but in harmony with the eternal and unchangeable principles of right. Knowing all things, he knows us better than we know ourselves, and he will deal with us accordingly. Let us then not be disturbed by the promptings of conscience, but conform, as far as possible, to the standard of right, with the assurance that he will approve our course at the last day.

21 Beloved, if our heart condemn us not, we have boldness toward God;—If in addition to the assurance we have from God that we are approved of him, we also have the approval of our own heart, we thus experience even greater confidence of the fellowship that is ours. It will be, of course, unnecessary to add, to the thoughtful reader, that John has under consideration here individuals whose hearts were fully attuned to the gospel and whose consciences were awakened to the relation which all sustain to God. Obviously the apostle does not here refer to men of wicked and depraved conscience whose hearts have been hardened to the influences of the truth and the restraints of right. The reference is to a time of judgment; the court is that of the conscience; and the judgment rendered is one of approval. The approval is that which the individual recognizes as bestowed upon him from the Father.

22 And whatsoever we ask we receive of him, because we keep his commandments and do the things that are pleasing in

is his commandment, that we should ᵃbelieve in the name of his Son Jesus Christ, and love one another, even as he gave us commandment. 24 And he

ᵃGr. *believe the name.*

his sight.—In proof of the fact that the assurance alluded to above is well grounded, the Father is attentive to the prayers of his children and bestows upon them whatever they ask. Two reasons are assigned: (1) they keep his commandments; (2) they do the things that are pleasing in his sight. The promise of the passage is, of course, to be understood within the limitations of his promises regarding prayer elsewhere set forth: viz., that the prayer must be in faith, in confidence, according to his will, and in keeping with his instructions regarding prayer. The truly faithful child of God seeks ever to learn what the will of the Father is, even in matters pertaining to prayer, and does not ask for those things which he discovers to be contrary to the Father's will. The verbs are all in the present tense here and emphasize continuous action; whatever we keep on asking, we keep on receiving, because we keep on keeping his commandments and habitually practice the things that are pleasing in his sight.

23 And this is his commandment, that we should believe in the name of his Son Jesus Christ, and love one another, even as he gave us commandment.—It is significant that the word "commandment" here is singular; it sums up the duties involved in the injunctions which follow it: (1) to believe in the name of God's Son, Jesus Christ; and (2) to love one another. This emphasizes a principle needing constant attention, and one often taught in the Bible; it is impossible to separate faith and practice, duty and dogma. Belief, in order to bless, must eventuate in love; love, without belief, is an impossibility. Faith is the ground not only of love, but of all obedience; it is that which leads to and produces it. And obedience is that which perfects and validates faith. "But wilt thou know, O vain man, that faith apart from works is barren." (James 2: 20.) The name of Christ here is put for him and for all for which he stands; to believe in his name is to accept him for what he is and all that he does. The commandment, involving the duties herein set forth, was frequently on the lips of the Lord. (John 13: 34; 15: 12, 17.)

24 And he that keepeth his commandments abideth in him,

that keepeth his commandments abideth in him, and he in him. And hereby we know that he abideth in us, by the Spirit which he gave us.

and he in him.—Here is a reference to the Lord's own words, "If a man love me, he will keep my word: and my Father will love him, and we will come unto him, and make our abode with him." (John 14: 23.) To "abide" in him is to have fellowship with him, to live and move in that realm of conduct which he approves, and thus to have the abiding presence of deity in the heart. While the context seems to require that the words "in him" refer to the Father (see verse 23), the affirmation is also true of the Son, and is so taught elsewhere. (Eph. 1: 7; Col. 1: 13, 14, etc.) The apostle had earlier referred to this same fellowship. (1: 3.)

And hereby we know that he abideth in us, by the Spirit which he gave us.—This verse declares, (1) God abides in us; (2) we have knowledge of his abiding presence; (3) we possess this knowledge by the Spirit which he has given. It should be observed that it is not the *manner of entrance* nor the *mode* of the Spirit's dwelling which is here referred to, but the *fact* of it. The Spirit assures of approval by motivating its possessor to do those things which enable the Father and the Son to abide in us. If it be asked *how* the Spirit does this, the answer is, Through the word of God, the only motivating force in immediate contact with the individual. Neither here nor elsewhere do the scriptures teach a direct operation of the Holy Spirit, either before or after conversion. It is as erroneous to assume an immediate impact of the Spirit on the Christian's heart as it is to argue similarly with reference to such impact on the sinner's heart. The fact of the Spirit's indwelling is often affirmed in the sacred writings. The manner or mode of such is an entirely different question. The two are not always distinguished; and the result is, a prepossession for some theory thereon creeps easily into our exegesis and colors our explanation, if we are not careful. The fact that the scriptures assert that the Spirit dwells in the Christian does not justify the conclusion that this indwelling is personal, immediate, and apart from the Word of God. Christ is in us (Col. 1: 25); from this we do not infer that in some mysterious, incomprehensible way he has, in his own person, taken up an abode in us. Why should we fall into similar error with reference to the third *person* of the Godhead—the Holy Spirit?

SPIRIT OF TRUTH AND SPIRIT OF ERROR CONTRASTED
(4: 1-6)

4 Beloved, believe not every spirit, but prove the spirits, whether they are of God; because many false prophets are gone out into the world. 2 Hereby

1 Beloved, believe not every spirit, but prove the spirits, whether they are of God;—The fervent address of love with which this verse begins, "beloved," occurs three times in this chapter, verses 1, 7, and 11, and indicates the tender warmth of affection characteristic of the writer for those addressed. To it a warning is appended with reference to false teachers which then abounded. Such were the "spirits" referred to, and often elsewhere alluded to in the Epistle. (E.g., 2: 18, 22, 26; 4: 5, etc.) The sense of the admonition is, therefore, "Refrain from believing every teacher who claims to be from God, but prove (test) them and see whether or not they really are of God." This warning was especially needful at the time because Asia Minor generally, and Ephesus particularly, was rampant with magic and mysticism, heresy and error, and the advocates of each cult claimed supernatural direction and aid. Affecting to be led by the power of God, they sought to support their theories in the same fashion, and by means of the same claims as false teachers today.

The readers of the Epistle were thus admonished to "prove" the spirits *(dokimazete ta pneumata)*, run an assay on them as a metallurgist does his metals, and determine whether they were of God. This, they were able to do, either by exercising miraculous power in the discernment of spirits (1 Cor. 12: 4-11), or by comparing the claims of these men with the known teaching of the Holy Spirit through properly accredited representatives. (See the comments on 1 John 2: 27ff.) There was undoubtedly a wide diffusion of spiritual gifts during the miraculous age of the church in order to supply the deficiency obtaining in the absence of an infallible, documented report of the Spirit's teaching such as we have in the New Testament today. It is significant that it was John's *readers* who were to make the test and not some ecclesiastical dignity or official head. Here, by implication, is positive proof of the falsity of the claim to infallibility by the pope of Rome and the consequent denial of the right of private judgment in matters religious as is done in the Catholic Church today.

know ye the Spirit of God: every spirit that confesseth that Jesus Christ is

Because many false prophets are gone out into the world. —The reason for the injunction delivered in the earlier clauses of this verse. These false prophets are referred to by John in 2:18 as "antichrist," and the Lord, during his public ministry, warned that such would appear: "And many false prophets shall arise, and shall lead many astray." (Matt. 24: 11.) It was, therefore, a time of crisis; and the welfare of the cause of Christ and the salvation of their own souls were dependent on the immediate repudiation of these deceivers and antichrists. Such still abound, and the injunction is equally applicable to us today. Men still affect to be led by the Spirit of God; still claim to be representatives of the Most High; yet attempt to propagate their doctrines on the basis of supernatural aid. These we are to prove (try, test) by the infallible standard we possess—the New Testament. It matters not how pious or religious a teacher may affect to be, he is worthy of belief *only* when his teaching is in complete harmony with the word of God. If it is not in harmony therewith, he ought to be, he must be, speedily repudiated. To do otherwise is to imbibe the poison of unbelief; it is to espouse false doctrine; it is to become a party to the propagation of error. "If any one cometh unto you, and bringeth not this teaching, receive him not into your house, and give him no greeting: for he that giveth him greeting partaketh in his evil works." (2 John 10, 11.) Because Satan ever attempts to counterfeit the work of the Lord, false prophets have ever abounded. (Luke 6: 26; Acts 13: 6; Rev. 16: 13.) We must be constantly watchful, we must exercise ceaseless vigilance lest we, too, succumb to their allurements and surrender to their seductions.

2 Hereby know ye the Spirit of God: every spirit that confesseth that Jesus Christ is come in the flesh is of God:—The test by which certain false teachers then prevalent might be discerned and identified is here indicated: "Every spirit that confesseth that Jesus Christ is come in the flesh is of God." Conversely, any man who denied that Jesus had come in the flesh was not of God. Numerous false doctrines regarding the nature of Christ were then being propagated. Some of these questioned his *deity;* others, his *humanity.* (See under Introduction, "The Design of

come in the flesh is of God: 3 and every spirit that [4]confesseth not Jesus is not of God: and this is the *spirit* of the anti-christ, whereof ye have heard that it cometh; and now it is in the world already. 4 Ye are of God, *my*

[4]Some ancient authorities read *annuleth Jesus.*

the Epistle.") The apostle thus provided a test by which false and true teachers might be distinguished in the matters *then* confronting the church: those who confessed that Jesus had come in the flesh were of God. (a) Those who acknowledged such, confessed the deity of Jesus by admitting that he was the Christ, and thus the Messiah of the Old Testament prophets; (b) in confessing that he had come in the flesh they repudiated the doctrine of the Docetic Gnostics who denied this. These men denied the humanity of Jesus by alleging that he only appeared to have a body of flesh but, in reality, did not. Thus, in acknowledging both the humanity and the deity of Jesus one vindicated his claim to the Spirit's direction. Paul similarly said, "Wherefore I make known unto you, that no man speaking in the Spirit of God saith, Jesus is anathema; and no man can say, Jesus is Lord, but in the Holy Spirit." (1 Cor. 12: 3.)

The verb "is come" in this verse is translated from a Greek perfect, thus indicating past action with existing results. The incarnation was past as to its occurrence, but its effects—benefits and blessing—yet remain, and will continue to do so throughout time and eternity, involving the sum of all that Christianity has vouchsafed to man. This confession embraces the basic truth on which Christianity rests, the foundation stone on which the church is built. (Matt. 16: 13-20.) To deny it is the mark of the false teacher; to acknowledge it, with all that this involves, is to vindicate one's claim to the truth. It thus supplies an infallible test: and by it the true may be separated from the false.

3 And every spirit that confesseth not Jesus is not of God: and this is the spirit of the anti-christ, whereof ye have heard that it cometh; and now it is in the world already.—This is a negative statement, embodying the same truth as that which is positively put in verse 2, with the additional information that to refuse to confess both the deity and the humanity of Jesus is to manifest the spirit of the antichrist. (See comments on 1 John 2: 22, for the identity of the antichrist.) Warnings had been given that such would appear; and now they were there. Though these false teachers were not *the antichrist* primarily designated in this fashion, they exhibited the spirit of the antichrist, in their opposition to Christ and his teaching. In this sense, all false teachers, including those in the world today, are of the antichrist. They are of the antichrist in that they are opposed to the teaching of Christ, his church, and his people; and though they pretend to be of him, they have, in reality, arrayed themselves against him. The fact that they teach much that is true does not justify their claim of being of the Lord; the error which they teach and the opposition which they exhibit establish their true spirit—the spirit of the antichrist. The Catholic Church teaches many things that are true; but this monstrous ecclesiasticism is so formidably arrayed against the truth and the cause of the Lord that it is on the side of Satan, and so of all the denominational and sectarian world.

It is the spirit of the antichrist to do as they do, and all who manifest this spirit derive it from the same source. It originates from the love of error and from an unwillingness to abide in the truth. It is indeed possible for one to have the spirit of truth, i.e., a love for truth while in error; and, conversely, to have a spirit of error while holding much truth. The former repudiate, without hesitation, error as they learn the truth; the latter, though holding much truth, are often motivated by the same spirit as that which characterizes the world. Those of this class are sometimes met with in the church. Prejudice is not a peculiarity of the denominational world alone.

4 Ye are of God, my little children, and have overcome them: because greater is he that is in you than he that is in the world.—"Ye" is in emphatic position in the Greek text which, literally rendered, is: "Ye out of God are, little children. . . ." a clause indicative of John's love for them *("my* little children"), his relation of a counselor and father ("my *little children"),* and their relation to God ("Ye are *of God").* Emphasis is given to the pronoun for the purpose of setting his readers over against the false teachers under consideration in the context. They were thus sharply distinguished from each other, the saints were on one side the false teachers on another; and thus the test provided might be easily applied.

than he that is in the world. 5 They are of the world: therefore speak they *as* of the world, and the world heareth them. 6 We are of God: he that

"Overcome" is translated from a perfect verb, thus indicating that John's readers had earlier reached a decision regarding the nature of these teachers and had rejected them; and an abiding conviction of the matter yet remained with them. They had overcome the false teachers by refusing to listen to their false doctrines, and by repudiating that which these teachers sought to impose upon them. The reason assigned why they were able to do this was that "He who was in them is greater than he that is in the world." God was in them and thus the power which motivated them was greater than that of Satan who is in the world. "We know that we are of God, and the whole world lieth in the evil one." (1 John 5: 19.) Satan is the prince of this world. Hence, Christians are taught to "Love not the world, neither the things that are in the world. If any man love the world, the love of the Father is not in him." (1 John 2: 15.) Satan is the guiding spirit of all those who are of the world, and hence "Whosoever therefore would be a friend of the world maketh himself an enemy of God." (James 4: 4.)

5 **They are of the world: therefore speak they as of the world, and the world heareth them.**—These men who were teaching false doctrines were of the world; the world, therefore, was the origin and source of that which they were and taught. In a similar statement, and to Jews who were advocates of false doctrines, though not that here particularly contemplated, but possessed of the same spirit of error, Jesus said, "Ye are of your father the devil, and the lusts of your father it is your will to do. He was a murderer from the beginning, and standeth not in the truth, because there is no truth in him. When he speaketh a lie, he speaketh of his own: for he is a liar, and the father thereof." (John 8: 44.) In this verse John may have been echoing words he had heard from the Lord: "If ye were of the world, the world would love its own: but because ye are not of the world, but I chose you out of the world, therefore, the world hateth you." (John 15: 19.) The word "world" in these passages is a term used to denote unregenerate human nature and all that is in harmony with it—that sphere which is dominated by the devil and which willingly submits to his domination.

knoweth God heareth us; he who is not of God heareth us not. By this we know the spirit of truth, and the spirit of error.

To guard the saints against any disappointment they might experience in observing that the preaching of these men was attended with success, more success, perhaps, than that which followed the preaching of the true gospel, John pointed out that the popularity of their preaching was due to the fact that it was suited to the desires and inclinations of the world. Such is equally true today. It is a sad commentary on human nature that the masses of people prefer to listen to pleasing falsehoods, rather than unpleasant truth. This disposition has not always been exclusively of the world. Frequently, in the past, and occasionally in the present, members of the church have exhibited the same attitude. Having charged Timothy to preach the word, Paul assigned as the reason why he should "reprove, rebuke, and exhort," that "the time will come when they will not endure the sound doctrine; but having itching ears, will heap to themselves teachers after their own lusts; and will turn away their ears from the truth, and turn aside unto fables." (2 Tim. 4: 1-4.)

6 **We are of God: he that knoweth God heareth us; he who is not of God heareth us not.**—"We" is emphatic, and those included in it are put in contrast with the false teachers earlier considered. It does not embrace all of the saints (if so, who were those who heard them?), but the apostles primarily, and in a secondary sense, those who taught the same truth. Those who are "in tune" with God are "in tune" with each other; hence, "He that knoweth God (recognizes him for what he is) heareth us"; and, conversely, "He who is not of God heareth us not." Jesus said, "He that is of God heareth the words of God: for this cause ye hear them not, because ye are not of God." (John 8: 47.) "Knoweth," in this verse, is translated from a present active participle, and designates "one who keeps on knowing God," i.e., an individual ever increasing in the knowledge of the one and only true God. Such a one, in knowing God, recognizes God's truth when it is preached, and hears it gladly; whereas, one who is not of God hears it not. This, indeed, is one reason why some consider some sermons as uninteresting and dull, as others regard the same efforts as highly interesting and inspirational. The gospel was, to

the Jews, a stumbling block, and to the Greeks, foolishness (literally, *silliness*); and to all who are not of God today, the gospel is a boresome, tiring thing. The reflection in all such instances is not on the message, or on him who presents it, but on the person exhibiting such a disposition. Of such, Jesus said, "Ye hear them not because ye are not of God." One may determine his spiritual level by measuring the degree of interest which he feels in the preaching of the gospel of God. How could such a one find the prospect of heaven inviting, when he experiences so little interest in the work of the Lord here? John knew what it was to be chilled and discouraged by the indifference and disdain of worldly hearers, even as every gospel preacher does today.

By this we know the spirit of truth, and the spirit of error. —"By this," i.e., by the attitude people manifest toward the preaching of the truth it is possible to distinguish between those who hold to the spirit of truth and those who are influenced by the spirit of error. The Holy Spirit is styled "the Spirit of truth" in John 14: 17, and but for the fact that it is put here in contrast with "the spirit of error," the assumption would be that the Holy Spirit is directly referred to here. It appears, however here, that the "spirit of truth" is a disposition favorable toward the truth, as the "spirit of error" is a disposition friendly to error. In view of the fact that the word "spirit" in the text of the American Standard Version is spelled with a small letter "s," it follows that this was the view of that eminent body of translators. Inasmuch as John had just been discussing the difference between those who hold to the truth and those who advocate error, the context supports this view. See the comments on verse 3.

BROTHERLY LOVE COMMANDED
(4: 7-21)

7 Beloved, let us love one another: for love is of God; and every one that

---

7 Beloved, let us love one another; for love is of God;— Again, the writer exhibits tenderness and genuine love in addressing his readers as "Beloved." He was the "apostle of love," and the frequency with which he enjoins love reveals the importance he attached to this characteristic of true saints. The regularity with

loveth is begotten of God, and knoweth God. 8 He that loveth not knoweth

which he taught it is not surprising; he often heard it from the lips of the Lord during the public ministry. (Cf. John 13: 34, 35; 15: 9-23.) Inasmuch as love is the foundation stone of all the commandments (Mark 12: 29, 30), it was imperative that each saint should be impressed with its essentiality. John was later to write, "If a man say, I love God, and hateth his brother, he is a liar: for he that loveth not his brother whom he hath seen, cannot love God whom he hath not seen." (4: 20.) It is very possible that there were those in the early church, as among us today, who, despite the fact that they claimed to be Christians, yet exhibited hatred for their brethren, and thus the great emphasis which John gives to the theme in all his Epistles.

"Love is of God," i.e., it finds its origin in him and proceeds from him; and one who loves God must, as a necessary consequence, love his brother. "He that saith he is in the light and hateth his brother, is in the darkness even until now." (1 John 2: 9.)

Every one that loveth is begotten of God, and knoweth God. —Love for others is so peculiarly Christian in its origin that where it exists there is evidence of the new birth. Only one who has received the spiritual life which comes through the birth from above exhibits such a disposition. Love, in this passage, is a sign and proof of the new birth, and not a condition precedent to it. The writer is here showing how the claim to the new birth may be tested. Does genuine love fill the heart of the one affirming it, and does such a one really know God? If the answer is *Yes,* the birth from above may be assumed; if *No,* whatever the claim, it is weighed in the balance and found wanting. *Love is the one characteristic of the Christian religion which it is impossible to counterfeit!* While deploring the phraseology, the following quotation from the theologian Augustine, made many hundreds of years ago, is a marvelous statement of truth: "A wicked man may have baptism. He may have prophecy. He may receive the Sacrament of the Body and Blood of Christ. (1 Cor. 11: 29.) All of these things a wicked man may have. But no wicked man can have love." How wonderfully true this conclusion is! How important

not God; for God is love. 9 Herein was the love of God manifested ⁵in us, that God hath sent his only begotten Son into the world that we might live

⁵Or, *in our case*

---

it is that every child of God strive to exhibit this characteristic of the genuinely converted one!

8 He that loveth not knoweth not God; for God is love.—The verb here—loveth—is translated from the present active participle of *agapao*, "He who does not continue to love does not know (is without an acquaintance) God. "Knoweth now" is aorist active indicative *(ouk egno ton theon),* has not *once* known, hence, has *never* known, God. The meaning is that one who claims to be a child of God, but does not, and has not, felt the love which exists between true children of God, demonstrates the fact that he not only does not know God, he has never known him—was thus never genuinely converted. (See the comments on 1 John 3: 6.) Love is an indispensable requisite of Christian character. Where it does not exist, there is no Christian love. God is love, and love thus becomes the infallible test of the birth from above. God is love because love originates with him; he is the very essence of love; and only those who truly love are born of him. (Verse 7.) This definition was not designed to be exhaustive; from John we learn that God is also *light* (1 John 1: 5) and *spirit* (John 4: 24). He is also a great many other things, such as power, and wisdom, and goodness; it is impossible for man to apprehend the divine nature. Inasmuch as love is a characteristic of his nature, it follows that all who partake of his nature acquire the characteristic of love; in its absence, sonship itself is wanting.

9 Herein was the love of God manifested in us, that God hath sent his only begotten Son into the world that we might live through him.—From this we learn, (1) God's love for man exists; (2) it has been manifested, i.e., revealed, made known; (3) it was revealed in the gift of God's Son; (4) the purpose of this gift was that we might live through him. Here is, (a) evidence of the falsity of the theory of the creeds that God was angry with man and that Jesus came to appease the wrath of a vengeful God; (b) proof that we did not first receive God's love in consequence of the death of Christ, but that the sending of the Son resulted from love already existing: "But God commendeth his own love toward us,

through him. 10 Herein is love, not that we loved God, but that he loved us, and sent his Son *to be* the propitiation for our sins. 11 Beloved, if God

---

in that, while we were yet sinners, Christ died for us" (Rom. 5: 8); (c) it is absurd to assume that the love of God was evoked by the prior love of man for him. God loved us; loved us before we loved him; loved us while we were yet sinners, and gave his Son for us. The passage is reminiscent of that affirmed in John 3: 16: "For God so loved the world, that he gave his only begotten Son, that whosoever believeth on him should not perish, but have eternal life."

Of vital significance here is the phrase (also occurring in John 3: 16), "his only begotten Son" *(ton huion autou ton monogene)*, literally, "His Son, the only-begotten." *Monogene,* the word translated "only begotten," signifies the-only-one-of-its-kind, and was so used to distinguish Jesus from all other sons of God. All who are members of God's family are sons of God, and often so styled in the sacred writings; Jesus, alone, is the only begotten Son. He is a Son in a sense characteristic of no other being in the universe; and to assign to him a position inferior to this, as modernists do, is infidelity. Attention is directed to the unique position of Christ to sharpen and enhance our concept of the vastness of God's love—it being so great that he was willing to send such a Son into the world that we might "live through him." The life thus provided is spiritual life; and it is through him, because in him only is life. "He that hath the Son hath the life; he that hath not the Son hath not the life." (1 John 5: 12.)

10 Herein is love, not that we loved God, but that he loved us, and sent his Son to be the propitiation for our sins.— "Herein," i.e., in the gift of the Son is love—a demonstration of its vastness, its comprehensiveness, its quality. And, as already indicated in the verse preceding, it was manifested, not because we loved God and thus provoked God to love us, but because prior love existed on his part toward us. "For we also once were foolish, disobedient, deceived, serving divers lusts and pleasures, living in malice and envy, hateful, hating one another. But when the kindness of God our Saviour, and his love toward man, appeared, . . . he saved us." (Titus 3: 4, 5.) The gift of God's Son was the

so loved us, we also ought to love one another. 12 No man hath beheld God at any time: if we love one another, God abideth in us, and his love is per-

highest possible manifestation of love, and in the nature of things could have issued only from a benevolent Father.

The contextual force of the apostle's reasoning should not be ignored. God is love. (Verse 8.) The love which God possesses has been revealed to us in the gift of his Son, the only-begotten (Verse 9.) This love was the result of no act on our part, but was antecedent to the love we now have for him. (Verse 10.) A consequence of the love was that Christ came as "propitiation for our sins." The word translated "propitiation" *(hilasmos)* occurs only here, and in 1 John 2: 2, in the Greek New Testament, though often in the Septuagint Version (Greek translation of the Old Testament), where it signifies a sacrifice of atonement. (Lev. 6: 6, 7; Num. 5: 8, 9; Ezek. 44: 27.) In referring to the death of Christ as a propitiation, John had reference to the sacrifice for sins which the Lord made in suffering himself to die upon the cross for our sins. (1 Pet. 2: 24; Matt. 26: 28.) The essentials of a sacrifice are two: (1) a priest to offer, and (2) a victim to be offered. Christ was *both*, in that he offered up *himself* for our sins. (Heb. 9: 14.) The propitiation makes it possible for all men to be saved (Heb. 2: 8, 9); and salvation becomes a reality to all who allow themselves to be reconciled to God (2 Cor. 5: 19-21). See the comments on 1 John 2: 2.

11 Beloved, if God so loved us, we also ought to love one another.—The particle "if" here raises no doubt, but directs attention to the inference based on that which had just been written. Inasmuch as, i.e., in view of the fact that, God loved us to the extent of giving his Son to die in our behalf, *we also ought* to love one another. The passage affirms not only God loved us, but that he *so* loved us, i.e., in such measure as to give the priceless treasure of heaven as a sacrifice to die in our stead. The adverb not only indicates the immeasurable extent of the love, it also designates the quality of it. (Cf. Rom. 8: 32.) The word "also" establishes a basis of comparison: since God loved us to such an extent, and with such a selfless quality of love we, *on our side,* ought to love *(agapain, keep on* loving) one another.

12 No man hath beheld God at any time:—(John 1: 18.)

fected in us: 13 hereby we know that we abide in him and he in us, because

The noun God *(theos)* is without the article here, and thus reference is made to the divine nature, and not to the first person of the Godhead, exclusively. The word God is properly applied to each of the divine persons of the Godhead, since it is the name of the *nature* which each possesses in common. By an ordinary figure of speech in which the whole is put for a part, each of the divine persons is so designated in the scriptures. E.g., 1 John 4: 9, where the reference is to the first person; John 1: 1-3, to the second; Acts 5: 3, 4, to the Holy Spirit, the third. The meaning is, no man has seen the divine nature, the real essence of the Godhead, inasmuch as it is invisible to the physical eye. Deity (God) can be seen only through its manifestations, and the revelation which it has made of itself in the incarnation. "No man hath seen God at any time; the only begotten Son, who is in the bosom of the Father, he hath declared him," i.e., revealed him. (John 1: 18.) Since the advent of the Son into the world, it can be no longer pleaded that God is unknowable; Jesus has revealed him, made him known. Though God, deity, the divine nature, is not seen with the eye, this does not mean that he is not near us; on the contrary, he is so near he abides in us, providing we love one another and his love is perfected in us.

Since there is but one divine nature, there is *but one God*. Each of the persons of the Godhead possesses the divine nature, and thus each is properly referred to as God. It is, hence, entirely in order to say, "God, the Father," "God, the Son," and "God, the Holy Spirit," since each is possessed of the one divine nature, and is styled God in the sacred writings. The Father, the Son, and the Holy Spirit do not constitute three separate Gods; there is but one God. (Deut. 6: 4.) These three divine personalities are of but *one* essence, *one* nature; and this one nature is God *(theos)*. There are, therefore, *three* persons in *one* God.

If we love one another, God abideth in us, and his love is perfected in us:—On condition that we love one another, two things result: (1) God abides in us; (2) his love is perfected in us. How does God abide in us? Not literally, physically, or bodily, but through that inward relationship which establishes fellowship with him. "That which we have seen and heard declare we

he hath given us of his Spirit. 14 And we have beheld and bear witness that

unto you, that ye also may have fellowship with us: yea, and our fellowship is with the Father, and with his Son Jesus Christ. . . . . If we say that we have fellowship with him and walk in the darkness, we lie, and do not the truth." (1 John 1: 3, 5.) God thus abides in us as we conform to his will and walk in harmony with his precepts. And thus, though God, in his essence and divine nature is invisible to our eye, we may enjoy the blessed privilege of his abiding presence *if we love one another!*

When we love one another, not only does God abide in us, his love is perfected in us. That which is perfected has been brought to maturity. We thus develop and make mature our love for God as we love one another more and more. Love for others is a token of the love which we have for God. "If a man say, I love God, and hateth his brother, he is a liar: for he that loveth not his brother whom he hath seen, cannot love God whom he hath not seen. And this commandment have we from him, that he who loveth God love his brother also." (1 John 4: 20, 21.)

13 Hereby we know that we abide in him and he in us, because he hath given us of his Spirit.—As a token by which we may know that we abide in him and he in us, he has given us "his Spirit"—the Holy Spirit. But how does the presence of the Spirit in us supply evidence of such an abiding presence? The *first* fruit of the Spirit is love: "But the fruit of the Spirit is *love,* joy, peace, longsuffering, kindness, goodness, faithfulness, meekness, self-control. . . ." (Gal. 5: 22, 23.) How may we know that the Spirit dwells in *our* heart? Because we love God *and* one another! Why does this love dwell in us? "And hope putteth not to shame; because the love of God hath been shed abroad in our hearts through the Holy Spirit which was given unto us." (Rom. 5: 5.) For the manner in which the Spirit dwells in the Christian, see the comments on verse 14.

14 And we have beheld and bear witness that the Father hath sent the Son to be the Saviour of the world.—Though no one had seen the divine nature, John and the other apostles had beheld *(tetheametha,* perfect middle or *theaomai,* to behold with adoring wonder), the Lord in the flesh (1 John 1: 1-3), and were thus qualified to bear testimony to the fact that the Father had in-

the Father hath sent the Son *to be* the Saviour of the world. 15 Whosoever

deed sent the Son into the world. The perfect tense designates an act that is past the results of which continue to exist; John had, during the public ministry of the Lord, minutely scrutinized him, obtained clear and distinct impressions regarding him and these remained to convince him forevermore of the identity of Jesus as Lord. Such was, in part, the mission of the apostles; and to equip them for this, the Holy Spirit was given them. "But when the Comforter is come, whom I will send unto you from the Father, even the Spirit of truth, which proceedeth from the Father, he shall bear witness of me: and ye also bear witness, because ye have been with me from the beginning." (John 15: 26, 27).

Indicated also in this verse is the mission which prompted the Lord's advent into the world. He was sent; he was sent from the Father; he was sent to be the Saviour; he was sent by the Father to be the Saviour of the world. The world, which he came to save, embraces all accountable and responsible beings. And so here, again, is emphasized what is often taught in the scriptures: the blessings of the atonement are available to all who will appropriate them to themselves on the conditions on which they are offered. The sacrifice of Christ was neither partial nor limited in its scope. "And he is the propitiation of our sins, and not for ours only, but also for the whole world." (1 John 2: 2.)

We thus learn that the Spirit has been given; that through this divine person love has been shed abroad in our hearts. But how is the Spirit given to us? Paul inquired of the Galatians: "This only would I learn from you, Received ye the Spirit by the works of the law, or by the hearing of faith?" (Gal. 3: 2.) This is a rhetorical question, put in this manner for emphasis. The meaning is, "You did not receive the Spirit by the work of the law. You received the Spirit by the hearing (marginal reading, *message*) of faith. How does faith come? "So then belief (faith) cometh of hearing, and hearing by the word of Christ." (Rom. 10: 17.) Paul's affirmation is, therefore, that the Galatians received the Spirit through hearing the word or message of faith—that is, the gospel. The word of truth—the gospel—is the instrument by which the Spirit exercises his influence on both saint and sinner. Thus, as one receives the truth into his heart *and allows it to motivate his*

shall confess that Jesus is the Son of God, God abideth in him, and he in life he is, to this extent, motivated and influenced by the Spirit, and enjoys his abiding presence. This is, of course, not to be interpreted as meaning that the Holy Spirit *is* the word of truth; the Holy Spirit *uses* the word of truth as the medium by which he influences; and his influence is limited to this medium. The Spirit prompts love for others through the instruction which he has given in the scriptures.

The Epistles of John are filled with instruction touching the duty of the children of God to love one another, as indeed, much of the New Testament. If it is the Spirit, independent of the word of truth, which produces such love, why was such instruction given? Why, indeed, is there teaching on *any* theme if all faithful children of God, then and now, possess a measure of the Spirit from which they derive (independently) such instruction? The question is not, Do children of God possess the Spirit? this, the verse before us and numerous others (e.g., Rom. 8: 9; Gal. 4: 16), affirm. Neither is it, Are children of God influenced by the Spirit today? This, too, the scriptures abundantly assert. The question is the *manner* or *mode* of such indwelling, and not the *fact* of it, which we raise. This Paul settles in the rhetorical question alluded to above. The only impact of the Spirit on the heart of either alien or Christian is by means of the Word of truth. Unfortunately, some brethren, while denying the direct operation of the Holy Spirit on the alien sinner, contend for just such an immediate and direct operation on the Christian following his baptism. The only difference between the positions is the *time when* the operation occurs. The denominational world contends for a direct operation on the sinner in order to his conversion. Those who hold to the view of a personal and immediate indwelling of the Spirit in the Christian, maintain that the operation of the Spirit is immediately following conversion. The one is as untenable as the other, and both wrong. The Spirit dwells in the heart of the Christian; the Father and the Son, likewise; with reference to the latter, it would be absurd to contend that this indwelling is literal, actual, in their own persons. But, because the denominational idea of a mysterious, incomprehensible, intangible being as the Holy Spirit is alleged to be has been adopted in some circles, brethren have allowed themselves to fall into such an error respecting the Holy Spirit.

God. 16 And we know and have believed the love which God hath ⁵in us.

15 Whosoever shall confess that Jesus is the Son of God, God abideth in him, and he in God.—Obviously, the apostle is not to be understood here as affirming that deity, actually, literally, and bodily takes up his abode in a human being. One who confesses that Jesus is the Son of God confesses the truth. The truth thus abides in him. Since God is of the essence of truth, God abides in such a one. In similar manner does the Spirit abide. This verse, with many other similar ones in the first Epistle (e.g., 2: 23; 3: 10; 4: 7; 5: 18), must be interpreted in the light of conditions then prevailing. Certainly it was not the apostle's intention to teach that one who merely gives lip service to the deity of Jesus abides in God, and God in him. Supercilious believers and indifferent professors concede this without hesitation; and even the demons acknowledged Jesus as the Son of God. (Mark 1: 24.) Moreover, the Lord said, "Not every one that saith unto me, Lord, Lord, shall enter into the kingdom of heaven; but he that doeth the will of my Father who is in heaven. Many will say to me in that day, Lord, Lord, did we not prophesy by thy name, and by thy name cast out demons, and by thy name do many mighty works? And then will I profess unto them, I never knew you: depart from me, ye that work iniquity." (Matt. 7: 21-23.)

The Ebonites declared that Jesus was a mere man; the Cerenthians maintained that his body was, for a time, occupied by an *aeon* (or demon) called Christ; the Docetae argued that he only appeared to possess a body, but was, in reality, only a shadowy phantom. The confession, "Jesus *is* the Son of God," was a repudiation of each of these heretical positions, and those who thus acknowledged him confessed (a) his humanity, (b) his deity, (c) his reality. Such a confession, therefore, established the fact that the one making it had not imbibed the poison of these positions, but did indeed accept him for what he is: the divine Son of God.

Implied in the confession is, of course, the complete surrender of the will to the Lord, such surrender expressing itself in willing obedience to his commands. This confession evidences the disposition of mind and heart which prompts to obedience. Jesus said, "If a man love me, he will keep my word: and my Father will love him, and we will come unto him, and make our abode with him." (John 14: 23.)

Moreover, the aorist tense *(homologesei,* confesseth), the exact force of which is difficult to render into English, reveals that the confession is a once-for-all act by which the one making it is committed to this concept of Christ with all the faculties of mind and body. God abides in us as we allow his teaching to fill us and motivate our lives; we abide in him as we practice the precepts of the gospel and find fellowship with him and his children in life.

16 And we know and have believed the love which God hath in us.—"We know" *(egnokamen,* perfect, active), "We have arrived at this knowledge, and continue to possess it, and have believed (and continue to do so) the love which God has in us." How was this knowledge arrived at? Jesus had taught it during his ministry: "O righteous Father, the world knew thee not, but I knew thee; and these knew that thou didst send me; and I made known unto them thy name, and will make it known; that the love wherewith thou lovedst me may be in them, and I in them." (John 17: 25, 26.) Note the three steps indicated: (1) God's name was made known; (2) the purpose for which the name was made known was to reveal that the love which the Father had for the Son was available to the saints; and (3) the indwelling of the life of the Son in them by which they were brought to the Father.

God is love; and he that abideth in love abideth in God, and God abideth in him.—The clause, "God is love," is a repetition of that which occurs in verse 8. See the comments there. The second clause, "And he that abideth in love abideth in God, and God abideth in him," is similar to the latter portion of verse 15. This verse thus combines the ideas advanced in verses 8 and 15. The meaning is, One who abides in love abides in God, and God in him, because God is love.

17 Herein is love made perfect with us, that we may have boldness in the day of judgment; because as he is, even so are we in this world.—Herein is love made perfect in us, i.e., in

the day of judgment; because as he is, even so are we in this world. 18 There is no fear in love: but perfect love casteth out fear, because fear hath

the fact that he who abides in love, abides in God, and God abides in him. (Verse 16.) All of whom such may be affirmed may indeed have boldness (confidence, assurance), because in loving God and their brethren they may be sure that they will not be condemned by the judge of all at the last day. The more we increase in love and perfect it, the less we have to fear that in that day we shall be found wanting. Love expresses itself in service to others (James 2: 1-6); and by this standard men are to be judged in the great day of accounts. "Then shall the King say unto them on his right hand, Come, ye blessed of my Father, inherit the kingdom prepared for you from the foundation of the world: for I was hungry, and ye gave me to eat; I was thirsty and ye gave me drink; I was a stranger, and ye took me in; naked, and ye clothed me; I was sick, and ye visited me; I was in prison, and ye came unto me. Then shall the righteous answer him, saying, Lord, when saw we thee hungry, and fed thee? or athirst, and gave thee drink? And when saw we thee a stranger, and took thee in? or naked, and clothed thee? And when saw we thee sick, and in prison, and came unto thee? And the King shall answer and say unto them, Verily I say unto you, Inasmuch as ye did it unto one of these my brethren, even these least, ye did it unto me." (Matt. 25: 34-40.)

The occasion or ground of the confidence those who love feel is that they resemble Christ in this respect. In loving all men they imitate Christ; and in following his example they do that which will obtain his approbation, and not his condemnation, in the day of judgment. Certainly, he will not condemn those who strive to make themselves like him. He is the embodiment of perfect love; those who follow him as their pattern and guide may be sure of his approval and acceptance in the day when all shall stand before him as their judge.

18 **There is no fear in love: but perfect love casteth out fear, because fear hath punishment; and he that feareth is not made perfect in love.**—Confidence excludes fear; and since those who love have confidence, they have no fear. "Fear," as here contemplated, is not that which the Psalmist declares is "the beginning of wisdom" (Psalm 111:10), a reverential, godly fear,

punishment; and he that feareth is not made perfect in love. 19 We love, because he first loved us. 20 If a man say, I love God, and hateth his

which shrinks from any action which would displease God, the fear which an obedient child has for a loving father, *en phoboi* (1 Pet. 1: 17); but *terror, dread, slavish fear,* such as is characteristic of a slave in the presence of a cruel and heartless master. We are taught to perfect holiness "in the fear of God" (2 Cor. 7: 1); to submit ourselves to one another "in the fear of God" (Eph. 5: 21); and to work out our salvation with "fear and trembling" (Phil. 2: 12). This is the true fear of God; an attitude of respect, or reverence, of holy awe. The fear that is absent from genuine love is the fear of the whip in the hands of the master; the dread of the chastisement which comes to the disobedient. Perfect (mature) love casts out such fear, because it cannot exist where genuine love is. "Fear hath punishment," because in the anticipation of the punishment expected in the future there is torment in the present. In the realization that it is impending, there is a foretaste of it before it actually begins. The child, aware that punishment is deserved and is pending, suffers before the lash is felt.

When, therefore, one entertains fear of the judgment, such evidences imperfect love; it indicates that there is not the development of Christian character which would have purged itself of such slavish fear, and eliminated all anxiety regarding the possibility of punishment. There are at least two kinds of fear referred to in the sacred writings: that which possesses men as a result of their evil deeds and from the dread of God's anger; and that of which the Psalmist wrote, "The fear of Jehovah is clean, enduring for ever." (Psalm 19: 9.) Perfect (mature) love casts out (literally, throws out, *exo ballei*) fear, a strong figure indicating the vigor with which it is excluded.

19 We love, because he first loved us.—Love obtains in the regenerate heart. This love finds its object in both God and man. But why do we love? In order that we may induce God to love us? On the contrary, he loved us before we loved him. Our love for him is thus evoked by a prior love on his part for us. "First" is in emphatic position in the original text, and is a thorough refutation of the creedal statement that Jesus came into the world to appease the wrath of an angry God. John 3: 16 and Rom.

brother, he is a liar: for he that loveth not his brother whom he hath seen, ⁰cannot love God whom he hath not seen. 21 And this commandment have we from him, that he who loveth God love his brother also.

⁰Many ancient authorities read *how can he love God whom he hath not seen?*

5: 8 constitute effective proof, along with this statement, that such a position is at variance with the teaching of the scriptures, and is a base slander on the character of God himself! As Christians we love. In this, we do not obligate God. He loved us before we loved him, and expressed his love by giving his Son to die in our behalf. Only an ingrate would refuse to love him in return.

20 **If a man say, I love God, and hateth his brother, he is a liar: for he that loveth not his brother whom he hath seen, cannot love God whom he hath not seen.**—Taught here is a principle often emphasized in the sacred writings that it is impossible to separate love for God and man. He who affirms that he loves God, and at the same time hates his brother, *is a liar!* Though John was the "Apostle of Love," the very thought of one claiming to love God who, at the same time, hated his brother, led the apostle indignantly to reject his claim, and to style such a one a liar. It is a characteristic of love to fix its attention on that which is visible and near; if, therefore, one does not love his brother whom he has seen, it is impossible to love God whom one has not seen. Ordinarily it is easier to love that which is seen and near; if, therefore, one fails in the easier task of loving that which is seen —his brother—he will obviously fail in the more difficult task of loving God. The love which we feel for our brethren is produced by the qualities in them which they have acquired from God. It follows, therefore, that if one is repelled by the qualities of goodness in his brother which are derived from God, he will feel the same aversion toward these same qualities in God himself! It is thus literally true that one who does not love his brother cannot love God. The one may be verified by the other. If genuine love for man exists, there is a corresponding love for God. Conversely, where one does not love his brother, it is proof that he does not love God. If he says he does, he is a liar.

21 **And this commandment have we from him, that he who loveth God love his brother also.**—In support of the argument of the verse which precedes this, an argument supported by anal-

ogy, by common sense, by the inspiration of the writer himself, there is added here the testimony of Christ. He has given commandment that he who loves God is to love his brother also. When and where was this commandment given? In principle, Jesus stated it often, viz., John 13: 34, 35; 15: 13; and in essence it is set out in the great summary of the law in the Lord's reply to the lawyer who said to him, "Teacher, which is the great commandment in the law? And he said unto him, Thou shalt love the Lord thy God with all thy heart, and with all thy soul, and with all thy mind. This is the great and first commandment. And a second like unto it is this, Thou shalt love thy neighbor as thyself. On these two commandments the whole law hangeth, and the prophets." (Matt. 22: 35-40.) Though it may be difficult to love men *as men,* we are to love them because they are in the image of God, and to love this image as it is reflected in them, though often obscured by sin and impaired by depravity. And, we are to love them, not only because of our kinship to them, but also because of our relationship to God who is our common Father and federal head.

TESTS OF FAITH AND LOVE
(5: 1-12)

It is fatal to correct exegesis to ignore, as is so often done, the context here, and the theme under consideration by the apostle in this section of the Epistle. Unfortunately, many in total disregard of the context, lift the first clause of 1 John 5: 1 from its setting, and cite it in support of views which were never in the writer's mind. It should be remembered that the chapter and verse divisions were no part of the original composition of the Apostle and are, therefore, to be disregarded in the study of the Epistle.

At the close of chapter 4, John was enjoining the duty of brotherly love. One who loves God must, as a necessary consequence, love his brother. *Who is one's brother?* Answer: "Whosoever believeth that Jesus is the Christ is begotten of God: and whosoever loveth him that begat loveth him also that is begotten of him. Hereby we know that we love the children of God, when we love God and keep his commandments." (1 John 5: 1, 2.) The thought, developed here, is this: He who believes that Jesus is the

5 Whosoever believeth that Jesus is the Christ is begotten of God: and whosoever loveth him that begat loveth him also that is begotten of him. 2

Christ is begotten of God; one begotten of God is a son of God; those who love him who begets—God—must necessarily love him who is begotten—one's brother. How do we know that we love those who have been thus begotten? Answer: (1) because we love God; and (2) because we do God's commandments.

1 **Whosoever believeth that Jesus is the Christ is begotten of God:**—"Whosoever believeth," is, literally, "Whosoever continues to believe" *(pas ho pisteuon)*, i.e., whose faith is firmly fixed and abiding in the proposition that Jesus is the Christ. It is, obviously, not a speculative belief; it is not simply or solely intellectual assent to the truthfulness of the proposition; it is such persuasion of the truth of the matter that the one exercising it is influenced to, and actually does act upon, the principle involved, and becomes obedient to him who is the object of the faith exercised. It is faith which includes obedience, since such is the only kind of faith that avails: "But wilt thou know, O vain man, that faith apart from works is barren? Was not Abraham our father justified by works, in that he offered up Isaac his son upon the altar? Thou seest that faith wrought with his works, and by works was faith made perfect: and the scripture was fulfilled which saith, And Abraham believed God, and it was reckoned unto him for righteousness; and he was called the friend of God. Ye see that by works a man is justified, and not only by faith . . . For as the body apart from the spirit is dead, even so faith apart from works is dead." (James 2: 20-26.) Inasmuch as faith, apart from works, is barren; and since the faith under contemplation here is such that results in sonship, it must follow that it includes obedience to the commandments on the basis of which one becomes a child of God. (Gal. 3: 26, 27.) No other faith avails.

It was not the design of the apostle here to announce a condition of salvation, nor were the words of this verse addressed to alien sinners. It was his purpose instead to supply the test by which one might determine whether one is a child of God. One claims to be a son of God. Is he, really? The test is: Does he believe (with all such belief involves) that Jesus is the Christ? Only those who thus do measure to the divine standard of what is re-

Hereby we know that we love the children of God, when we love God and

quired to be a child of God. The proposition, "Jesus is the Christ," was such as effectively sifted out the heretics with reference to whom John was writing. See the comments on 1 John 4: 15. Some denied that Jesus *was Christ,* thus repudiating his deity; others said that Christ was *not Jesus,* hence denying his humanity. Still others maintained that his fleshly body was merely an apparition, thus denying his reality. To confess that Jesus is the Christ is to acknowledge his deity, his humanity and his reality. It was therefore just such a test as would reveal the true believers and expose the heretics which then plagued the church with their false teaching. Those who truly believed this proposition were begotten of God. (For an explanation of the phrase, "begotten of God," see the comments on 1 John 3: 9.)

And whosoever loveth him that begat loveth him also that is begotten of him.—"Whosoever loveth" of this clause is exactly parallel with the "Whosoever believeth," of the first clause of the verse, and embraces the same individuals. It is the same idea as that already advanced by the apostle in 1 John 4: 20, where see the comments. The reasoning of the apostle here is in the logical form of a *sorites,* an abridged series of syllogisms in a group of propositions arranged in such fashion that the predicate of the first becomes the subject of the second, the conclusion uniting the subject of the first proposition with the predicate of the last. The order follows:

1. To believe that Jesus is the Christ is evidence that one is begotten of God.
2. To be begotten of God necessitates loving God.
3. To love God requires one to love God's children.
4. Those who love God's children have been begotten of God.
5. Therefore, to believe that Jesus is the Christ requires one to love God's children, and evidences the fact that one is begotten of God.

But how are we to know that we truly love God's children?

2 Hereby we know that we love the children of God, when we love God and do his commandments.—"Hereby," i.e., *in this,* the test to be supplied, we are able to know that we love

do his commandments. 3 For this is the love of God, that we keep his com-

the children of God. What is the test? When, (1) we love God; and (2) keep his commandments! Here is additional and corroborative evidence out of the correctness of the interpretation above. There, it was pointed out that the faith by which one accepts the proposition that Jesus is the Christ, the evidence of sonship, must include obedience. There, *faith* is declared to be the test of sonship; here, *love of God* and *obedience*. It follows, therefore, that the love and obedience of this verse are embraced in the faith of that. So intimately associated is love for God and man that as 1 John 4: 20 teaches that love for brethren is a token and necessary condition of our love for God, so here the relationship is reversed and this passage teaches that our love for God, exhibited in the keeping of his commandments, is proof of our love for his children. We thus learn that love of God and love of the brethren are inseparable duties, and each becomes the test of the other. But why is such a test effected or needed? Is not one capable of knowing whether he loves his brother or not? In what way does the fact that one loves God and keeps his commandments supply evidence that one loves his brother? One may entertain affection for others from many considerations not related to religion, such as kinship, friendship, business relations, etc.; but such do not afford the motives for the love under contemplation here. This love is such an emotion which springs from a heart filled with good wishes for others, genuine regard based on a common parentage, common interests, common responsibilities and a common reward. How may we know that we possess such? When (1) we love God, and (2) do his commandments, one of which is *to love one another!* A new commandment I give unto you, that ye love one another; even as I have loved you." (John 13: 34.)

3 **For this is the love of God, that we keep his commandments: and his commandments are not grievous.**—In what way is it possible for us to exhibit and demonstrate our love for God? By keeping his commandments. The verb "keep" in the text is present active subjunctive; it is the love of God that we *keep on* keeping his commandments! Here is the acid test of love for him. Do we persist in keeping his commandments and in

mandments: and his commandments are not grievous. 4 For whatsoever is begotten of God overcometh the world: and this is the victory that hath

doing his will to the extent of our ability? If such be characteristic of us, we have the evidence of our love for him. If such be lacking, whatever may be our pretensions thereto, they are weighed in the balance and found wanting.

These commandments from a kind and benevolent Father are not grievous *(bareiai),* heavy, burdensome, distressing. Love lightens them, makes them easily borne. A nine year old lad, struggling to carry his crippled five year old brother, smiled and said, "He's not heavy; he's *my brother!"* Love truly lightens the load, makes us anxious to assist those of our brethren who struggle under heavy burdens. "Bear ye one another's burdens and so fulfil the law of Christ." (Gal. 6: 2.)

4 For whatsoever is begotten of God overcometh the world: and this is the victory that hath overcome the world, even our faith.—To indicate to us why the commandments of God are not grievous (weighty, galling, burdensome), these words were penned. The argument of the apostle follows this pattern: The commandments of God are not burdensome for, despite the difficulties, the hardships, the privations necessarily suffered as Christians, all such will eventually result in victory; those who triumph over all such conquer the world; and hence, none need fear failure or contemplate defeat. For the meaning of the phrase, "begotten of God," see the comments under 1 John 3: 9. For an explanation of the word "world," as here used, see under 1 John 2: 15.

We have here, as often elsewhere in the scriptures, evidence of the conquering power of faith. It is faith which enables men to resist temptation, to avoid the entanglements of the world, to reject false teachers and the doctrines of men. It was faith which guarded the ancient worthies, enabled them to triumph over the seductions of Satan, and filled them with determination to serve the great Jehovah whatever the difficulties, obstacles, impediments in their way. Chapter 11, of the Book of Hebrews, is Inspiration's Hall of Fame. Enshrined in that memorial are the records of grand old men out of an ancient past, worthy patriarchs, prophets, priests and kings who, through faithfulness and courage, earned

overcome the world, *even* our faith. 5 And who is he that overcometh the world, but he that believeth that Jesus is the Son of God? 6 This is he that came by water and blood, *even* Jesus Christ; not ¹with the water only, but

---

¹Gr. *in.*

---

for themselves imperishable honor, and serve for all succeeding ages as examples of undying faith and tremendous courage. They overcame the world. They overcame the world by their faith. They thus serve as worthy examples for our emulation.

The verb "overcometh" is in the present tense *(nikai ton kosmon)* and thus denotes a continuous struggle. There is constant victory only because there is continuous struggle. The faithful one continues to overcome because "his seed" (the Word of God, Luke 8: 11) continues to abide in him. (1 John 3: 9.)

5 **And who is he that overcometh the world, but he that believeth that Jesus is the Son of God?**—It may be asked, What is involved in the proposition which one must believe in order to overcome the world? The answer is: *"Jesus is the Son of God."* Here, again, attention is fixed on both the humanity (Jesus) and the deity (the Son of God) of the Lord. The two natures, the human and the divine, were united in one personality. Those who accept this proposition (with all that it implies) overcome the world, by escaping its guilt, its pollution, its power, and in large measure, its presence.

6 **This is he that came by water and blood, even Jesus Christ; not with the water only, but with the water and with the blood.**—This verse and the ones immediately following have been rightly regarded as the most difficult of the Epistle; and they have given rise to a vast number of interpretations through the years since the apostle John penned these words. Their importance deserves and demands the most careful consideration. An analysis reveals that (a) one came; (b) the one who came was Jesus Christ; (c) Jesus Christ came by water and blood; (d) he did not come by water only, but *with* the water and *with* the blood. Essential to the understanding of this passage are the answers to the following questions: (1) What coming of the Lord is referred to here? (2) What is meant by his coming "with the water," and "with the blood"? There appears to be little doubt that the "coming" under consideration here was his advent

¹with the water and ¹with the blood. 7 And it is the Spirit that beareth

into the world. In coming into the world, he came with the water and with the blood. Why did the writer cite his coming in this fashion? From verse 8, we learn that it was for the purpose of establishing witnesses to the fact of his coming, the witnesses being *water* and *blood*.

It seems clear, therefore, that the reference to the water is an allusion to his baptism; and that of the blood to his death. He came with water at his baptism (Matt. 3: 15); with blood, in his death on the cross (John 19: 34). To these facts, the Spirit bears witness. (Verses 7, 8.) The Spirit was manifested at the Lord's baptism; the Spirit recorded and thus bore witness to both his baptism and his death. Some have seen in the "water" and the "blood," of this passage, a reference to the blood and water which flowed from the "riven side" of the Saviour on the cross. (John 19: 34.) There, however, the order is (1) blood; (2) water; but here, (1) water; (2) blood. Moreover, it was the design of the writer to point out historical facts in the life of the Lord established by the testimony of the Spirit and designed to serve as evidence of his coming. It seems unaccountable that as proof of his coming the evidence would be limited to events occurring almost at the moment of death. We conclude, therefore, that the water here refers to his baptism; the blood to that shed in his death—the first witness being at the *beginning* of his public ministry, the other as its *close*. These two instances in the life of our Lord were doubtless cited, because in the first, his baptism, he publicly received acknowledgment from heaven as the Son of God; and there entered formally upon his public ministry; and on the cross his work was terminated, and the announcement made, "It is finished." (John 19: 30.) If it be asked, Why the repetition, "not by water only, but with the water and with the blood," the answer must be found in the desire of the writer to emphasize both witnesses, and perhaps to distinguish him clearly from John the Baptist, who baptized in water only. (John 1: 26.)

7 And it is the Spirit that beareth witness, because the Spirit is the truth.—The Spirit here referred to is the Holy Spirit; the function which he is said to perform is that he bears

witness, because the Spirit is the truth. 8 For there are three who bear witness, the Spirit, and the water, and the blood: and the three agree in one.

---

witness; that to which he witnesses is the deity of Jesus; his testimony is reliable because the Spirit is the truth (i.e., of the essence of truth); and that to which he bears testimony were the matters primarily under consideration in the verse preceding this—the water and the blood. As indicated both here and in the verses which follow, the Spirit becomes the *third* witness to the identity of the Lord, the first and second being the water and the blood. The Spirit bore witness to Jesus at his baptism by descending in the form of a dove and lighting upon him. (Matt. 3: 15.) John the Baptist accepted this as a token of the Spirit's witness to Christ, when he said, "I have beheld the Spirit descending as a dove out of heaven; and it abode upon him. And I knew him not: but he that sent me to baptize in water, he said unto me, Upon whomsoever thou shalt see the Spirit descending, and abiding upon him, the same is he that baptizeth in the Holy Spirit. And I have seen and have borne witness that this is the Son of God." (John 1: 32-34.) See additional note at the end of the chapter.

8 For there are three who bear witness, the Spirit, and the water and the blood: and the three agree in one.—The Spirit (the Holy Spirit, the third person in the Godhead), the water (of baptism) and the blood (which flowed from the Lord's side on the cross), are here declared to bear witness, i.e., to testify. That to which they bear witness is the deity of Jesus, the lordship of him who was baptized in Jordan and from whose side the blood flowed. These three—the Spirit, the water and the blood—agree in one, i.e., their testimony harmonizes, and point to the same end. The Spirit is mentioned first, because he is the only living witness, and the testimony of the water and the blood depend on the revelation of the Spirit. As there are three divine persons in one God, so there are three witnesses on earth testifying. The testimony which these witnesses give is constant; the Spirit's revelation in the scriptures speaks to all generations; the act of baptism, for nearly twenty centuries, has been picturing the central fact of redemption—the burial and resurrection of Christ—and the blood is that which makes redemption possible. (Heb. 10: 1-4.) Compare 1 John 5: 10; Rom. 6: 1-6; 1 Cor. 11: 23-29. Wherever

9 If we receive the witness of men, the witness of God is greater: for the witness of God is this, that he hath borne witness concerning his Son. 10 He that believeth on the Son of God hath the witness in him: he that believeth not God hath made him a liar; because he hath not believed in the witness

the people of God assemble on the Lord's day, there is, in the Lord's supper which they observe, a memorial of the blood which was shed. (For additional notes and an explanation of the variation in the text here and that which is characteristic of the King James Version, see the "Additional Note" at the end of the chapter.)

9 If we receive the witness of men, the witness of God is greater: for the witness of God is this, that he hath borne witness concerning his Son.—This is an argument *a fortiori,* styled in logic *a minori ad majus,* reasoning from the less to the greater, a conclusion which, when compared with some other, is even more necessary. We *do* accept the testimony of men; thus we should the more readily accept the testimony of God which is greater. That to which particular reference is made is the witness which God has borne concerning his Son. The meaning is, We ordinarily believe the testimony of men; inasmuch as God is infinitely greater and better than the best of men, we are logically bound to accept his testimony; and since he has testified that Jesus is the Son of God, this we ought to believe.

10 He that believeth on the Son of God hath the witness in him:—Literally, "He that keeps on believing in the Son," *(ho pisteuon eis ton huion),* "continues to have *(echei)* the witness in him, i.e., in himself. We have earlier seen that one of the witnesses to the reality of the Christian religion is the Holy Spirit. (Verse 8.) This Spirit, whose abiding presence is in all believers (Acts 5: 32; Rom. 8: 9; Gal. 4: 6), is thus an ever-present witness to the facts on which faith rests. The word, the instrument of the Spirit, is the basis of our faith; this faith supplies us with confidence that the witness is true; and this confidence is ever with us. We thus have a continual witness to the reality of that to which we have committed our lives.

He that believeth not God hath made him a liar; because he hath not believed in the witness that God hath borne concerning his Son.—To reject the deity of Jesus—the Sonship

that God hath borne concerning his Son. 11 And the witness is this, that God gave unto us eternal life, and this life is in his Son. 12 He that hath the Son hath the life; he that hath not the Son of God hath not the life.

---

of the Lord—is to make God a liar; for, to this fact he has testified in his word. He who does not believe this testimony implies, in the rejection of it, that all God has said of his Son is false. Thus, to deny the deity of Jesus is not only unbelief; it is a studied insult to the veracity of God! Inasmuch as the Christian religion is founded on the truth of the proposition that Jesus is the Christ, to reject this is to repudiate all that God has said. Such a one has rejected prophecy, miracle, the character and life of the Lord, the resurrection, the marvelous spread of Christianity, and every other proof that may be adduced in support of the cause for which Jesus died.

11 **And the witness is this, that God gave unto us eternal life, and this life is in his Son.**—God gave us testimony; the testimony which he gave is with reference to eternal life; this eternal life to which he testified is in his Son. This testimony is abundant: John 10: 10; 14: 6; 17: 3. To this end Paul also testified: "For ye died, and your life is hid with Christ in God. When Christ, who is our life, shall be manifested, then shall ye also with him be manifested in glory." (Col. 3: 3, 4.) The manner in which this life is possessed is indicated in the verse which follows:

12 **He that hath the Son hath the life; he that hath not the Son of God hath not the life.**—Only those who have the Son have the life; and since having the Son is conditioned on faithfulness and devotion to him, it follows that the life here contemplated is conditional. It is in this sense only that one has eternal life here. Eternal life is not a present possession of the Christian: it is a promise: "There is no man that hath left house, or brethren or sisters, or mother, or father, or children, or lands, for my sake, and for the gospel's sake, but he shall receive a hundredfold now in this time, houses, and brethren, and sisters, and mothers, and children, and lands, with persecutions: *and in the world to come eternal life.*" (Mark 10: 29, 30.) "In hope of eternal life, which God, who cannot lie, promised before times eternal." (Titus 1: 2.) One does not hope for that which he already has. (Rom. 8: 24.) "And this is the promise which he promised us, even the life eter-

nal." (1 John 2: 25.) Those passages which apparently assert the possession of eternal life here, e.g., John 5: 24; 6: 47; 17: 3, etc., are to be understood as referring to it *in prospect,* and not in reality. The believer has eternal life in prospect and promise, but not in realization. He possesses life, as he possesses the Christ, who is the life, i.e., the source, the origin, the preserver of life. The believer, however, may cease to believe; he may forsake him who has the life. "Having damnation because they have cast off their first faith." (1 Tim. 5: 12 AV.) "But shun profane babblings: for they will proceed further in ungodliness. And their word will eat as doth a gangrene: of whom is Hymenaeus and Philetus; men who concerning the truth have erred, saying that the resurrection is past already, *and overthrow the faith of some.*" (2 Tim. 2: 16, 17.)

"He that hath not the Son hath not the life." He may have money, fame and fortune; intelligence, education and talent; influence, reputation and honor; but, if he has not the Son, he has not the life! He who would have life, must have the Son; there is no substitute.

SECTION FOUR

CONCLUSION
(5: 13-21)

ADDITIONAL OBJECT IN WRITING
(5: 13-15)

13 These things have I written unto you, that ye may know that ye have eternal life, *even* unto you that believe on the name of the Son of God. 14 And this is the boldness which we have toward him, that, if we ask anything

---

13 These things have I written unto you, that ye may know that ye have eternal life, even unto you that believe on the name of the Son of God.—In a general sense, the entire Epistle was written with the design here indicated, though it appears probable that the reference is, particularly, to that of the immediate context, e.g., 5: 1-12. These words are very similar to those occurring in John 20: 31. For the manner in which one possesses eternal life here, see the comments on verse 12. The meaning here is, John wrote; he wrote that men may know that they have eternal life; those who have eternal life in prospect and promise (2: 25), or those who believe (literally, keeping on believing *(tois pisteuousin eis)* in the name of the Son of God. The "name," as here used, sums up the characteristics which make up the personality of Christ.

14 And this is the boldness which we have toward him, that, if we ask anything according to his will, he heareth us: See 1 John 3: 21, and the comments there. The conjunction, *and,* with which this verse begins, associates the ideas which it contains with the verse preceding, and the meaning is: We have the promise of eternal life; the realization of this assures and gives us confidence; this confidence expresses itself, for example, in the assurance we have that if we ask anything according to his will, he hears us. His will is set out in the sacred writings; to ask according to his will, is to ask in harmony with what he has taught regarding prayer. Jesus recognized this condition, and hence prayed: "My Father, if it be possible, let this cup pass away from me: nevertheless, not as I will, but as thou wilt." (Matt. 26: 39.) The Father wills for us only that which is for our good. If we, through ignorance, greed, avarice or some other evil motive, ask

according to his will, he heareth us: 15 and if we know that he heareth us whatsoever we ask, we know that we have the petitions which we have asked

for that which we should not have, the Father, in kindness, withholds it. "Ask, and it shall be given you; seek, and ye shall find; knock, and it shall be opened unto you: for every one that asketh receiveth; and he that seeketh findeth; and to him that knocketh it shall be opened. Or what man is there of you, who, if his son shall ask him for a loaf, will give him a stone; or if he shall ask for a fish, will give him a serpent? If ye then, being evil, know how to give good gifts unto your children, how much more shall your Father who is in heaven give good things to them that ask him?" (Matt. 7:7-11.)

15 **And if we know that he heareth us whatsoever we ask, we know that we have the petitions which we have asked of him.**—The assurance which we have that God does indeed answer the prayers of his faithful children encourages us to ask, and enables us to know that we receive the things for which we ask. If we know that God *hears* our prayers we know that the petitions which we make are granted, though we may not be able to see them supplied in the particular way we had expected. The Father sometimes says, *Yes!*, by saying No! That is, he answers a prayer for our good by denying the petition made but by supplying, in his wisdom, our need otherwise. Three times Paul besought the Lord to remove the thorn from his flesh; and though this was denied him, the prayer was answered in a fashion which Paul was himself later to approve. (2 Cor. 12:7-10.)

THE SIN UNTO DEATH
(5: 16, 17)

of him. 16 If any man see his brother sinning a sin not unto death, ²he shall

²Or, *he shall ask and shall give him life*, even to *them &c.*

16 **If any man see his brother sinning a sin not unto death, he shall ask, and God will give him life for them that sin not unto death. There is a sin unto death: not concerning this do I say that he should make request.**—The connection between this statement and the verse which precedes it is close, and should be carefully considered in determining the significance of

ask, and *God* will give him life for them that sin not unto death. There is this passage. We have boldness (confidence) toward the Father. (Verse 14.) This boldness prompts us to make our petitions with the assurance that if we ask according to his will, he hears us. Though we are unable to "see" the answer to our prayers, in some instances, the confidence which we have in him enables us to know that "we have the petitions which we have asked of him." (Verse 15.) As an instance of this, if we see a "brother sin a sin not unto death," we are encouraged to ask in his behalf, assured that God will give us life for "them that sin not unto death." We are not, however, from thence to infer that God will give us life for "them that sin unto death." There is such a sin; and though we are not forbidden to pray in behalf of one thus sinning, we are not commanded to do so, and there is no assurance that God will hear and answer our petition if we do.

This passage is not to be confused, as is often done, with Matt. 12: 31, 32—"the sin against the Holy Spirit." Here, reference is to a *brother* who sins; there, the Pharisees were primarily in the mind of the Saviour, these being the ones particularly addressed. (Matt. 12: 14-24.) "Any man," of the first clause, is to be understood only of those who are members of the body of Christ and approved of God; it follows, therefore, that the "brother" contemplated as sinning is an erring child of God.

The rendering of the King James or so-called Authorized Version of the New Testament reads, "If any man see his brother *sin a sin* which is not unto death he shall ask. . . ," The American Standard Version, however, has it thus: "If any man see his brother *sinning a sin* not unto death, he shall ask. . . ." This appears, at first glance, to mean that if one sees a brother in the actual commission of sin, he may ask and God will forgive such a one *while* sinning. Such a conclusion is alike repugnant to reason and revelation; opposed both to scripture and to our own sense of the fitness of things, and is obviously false. Jesus said, "Except ye repent, ye shall . . . perish." (Luke 13: 3.) There is no offer of amnesty to the rebellious and impenitent. We may be sure that John did not intend that such a conclusion should be drawn from his words here. Why then, the present active participle *hamartanonta* (sinning) here? The participle agrees grammatically with

ᵃa sin unto death: not concerning this do I say that he should make request.

ᵃOr, *sin*

---

adelphon (brother), and with the cognate accusative *hamartian* (sin); it is a sinning brother who stands, as it were, before our very eyes. This is, therefore, not to be construed to mean that the brother is engaged in sin at the moment prayer is made in his behalf.

An analysis of the passage reveals, (1) a child of God can sin; (2) there is a sin not "unto death"; (3) we are instructed to pray for those thus sinning, with the assurance that our prayers will be heard and answered; (4) there is a sin "unto death"; (5) for those guilty of such it is useless and futile to pray. What is the sin thus contemplated?

(a) It is obvious that no single sin, contemplated as an overt act, was in the apostle's mind. Correctly rendered, the passage does not designate *the* sin, or even *a* sin, but mere sin, sin in essence, sin abstractly considered. (b) The sin was such that a brother could discern it, i.e., identify it: "If any man *see* . . ." (c) The death referred to was not bodily death, the loss of physical life; but spiritual death, separation from God and all that is good. (d) It was such a sin as only children of God could be guilty of. Any interpretation that is correct must take account of each of these considerations, and embrace them. (1) The sin contemplated here is not such as is usually classified as capital, i.e., such sins as idolatry, murder, adultery, blasphemy, etc. (2) The effects of it were visible and obvious—such as could be seen. (3) It was possible for one who prays to distinguish between the sin unto death, and the sin not unto death. To what type of sin then, did John refer?

There is much about sin and its forgiveness in the first Epistle of John. Its fact, in the lives of all Christians, is affirmed (1 John 1: 8-10), its origin indicated (3: 8), the means by which it may be avoided revealed (3: 9). In the event of sin in one's life, there is "an Advocate, with the Father, Jesus Christ, the righteous" (2: 1), and the promise that "if we confess our sins, he is faithful and righteous to forgive us our sins, and to cleanse us from all unrighteousness" (1: 8). The apostle's teaching on the theme is thus

17 All unrighteousness is sin: and there is ᵃa sin not unto death.

abundant, and the significance thereof clear. It is susceptible of being reduced to logical form:

1. The Lord will forgive every sin, of whatever nature, that a brother confesses. (1 John 1: 8.)

2. There is, however, a sin which the Lord will not forgive. (1 John 5: 16.)

3. Therefore, the sin which the Lord will not forgive, is simply *a sin, any sin, all sin that a brother will not confess!*

If this conclusion does not follow, it is because either the major or minor premise of the syllogism is defective. The major premise is that the Lord will forgive every sin a brother confesses. This is stated in 1 John 1: 8. The minor premise is obviously implied in 5: 16. It follows, therefore, that since the Lord will forgive every sin, of whatever nature, that a brother confesses and turns away from; and as there is a sin which the Lord will not forgive, the conclusion is irresistible that the sin which the Lord will not forgive is a sin which a brother will not confess. The context corroborates this view. If my brother sins, and manifests penitence, I not only may, it is my duty to, pray in his behalf: "Confess therefore your sins one to another, and pray one for another, that ye may be healed." (James 5: 16.) If, however, my brother exhibits stubborn impenitence and persistent rebellion, following the commission of his sin, it is useless to petition the Father in his behalf. The sin unto death is thus a disposition of heart, a perverseness of attitude and an unwillingness of mind to acknowledge one's sin and from it turn away. Such a disposition effectively closes the door of heaven in one's face.

17 **All unrighteousness is sin: and there is a sin not unto death.**—Here, sin is negatively defined. Sin is unrighteousness. God's commandments are righteousness. (Psalm 119: 172.) A failure, therefore, to keep God's commandments, is to be guilty of sin in his sight. A positive definition of sin is set out by the apostle in 3: 4: "Sin is lawlessness." Sin thus consists of doing (a) that which is wrong; and of (b) neglecting to do that which is right. The former we classify as the sin of commission; the latter, the sin of omission. "Unrighteousness" is that state or

condition which is opposed to righteousness. It is a general term indicative of the absence of righteousness for whatever cause.

DIVINE ASSURANCES
(5: 18-21)

18 We know that whosoever is begotten of God sinneth not; but he that was begotten of God keepeth ⁴himself, and the evil one toucheth him not. 19 We know that we are of God, and the whole world lieth in the evil one. 20 And we know that the Son of God is come, and hath given us an understanding, that we know him that is true, and we are in him that is true, *even*

⁴Some ancient authorities read *him*.

---

18 **We know that whosoever is begotten of God sinneth not; but he that was begotten of God keepeth himself, and the evil one toucheth him not.**—Verses 18, 19 and 20 each begins with the verb "we know" *(oidamen)*. Compare also, 3: 2, 14; 5: 15. It is a term which indicates full persuasion and complete confidence. For the meaning of the phrase, "begotten of God," see the comments on 1 John 3: 9. For the meaning of the verb "sinneth not," see the notes on 3: 6. For the manner in which one who is begotten of God keeps himself from sin, see on the phrase, "and his seed remaineth in him, and he cannot sin." (3: 9.) The "evil one" of this passage is the devil. See notes on 3: 8.

19 **We know that we are of God, and the whole world lieth in the evil one.**—"Of God," is, literally, "from God"; being begotten of him, we are his offspring. (1 John 3: 10; 4: 6.) The word "world" here is not the material universe in which we live, but the race of wicked men about us. These, because they have abandoned themselves to a life of sin, are in the "evil one." The evil one—the devil—is the prince of this world, the ruler of its citizens. (Eph. 2: 2; 1 Pet. 5: 8; Eph. 6: 11; Col. 1: 13.)

20 **And we know that the Son of God is come, and hath given us an understanding, that we know him that is true, and we are in him that is true, even in his Son Jesus Christ.**—"Is come" of the first clause is in the present tense, but it has the force of the perfect, *has come,* and such is its significance here. By supplying us with credible testimony, the Father has enabled us

in his Son Jesus Christ. This is the true God, and eternal life. 21 *My* little children, guard yourselves from idols.

---

to know him, to accept him as true, and thus also to accept his Son Jesus Christ, and to be in him. (Rom. 6: 3; Gal. 3: 27.)

This is the true God, and eternal life.—To know—to have an understanding of the true God, and to be in his Son, Jesus Christ, is to have the assurance of eternal life. (1 John 2: 25.) These words are an echo of those in his prayer in the shadows of Gethsemane. "And this is life eternal, that they should know thee the only true God, and him whom thou didst send, even Jesus Christ." (John 17: 3.) And thus, at the close of the Epistle, the apostle re-emphasizes that with which it began: the eternal life which has been manifested: "That which was from the beginning, that which we have heard, that which we have seen with our eyes, that which we beheld, and our hands handled, concerning the word of life (and the life was manifested, and we have seen, and bear witness, and declare unto you the life, the eternal life, which was with the Father, and was manifested unto us)." (1 John 1: 1-3.) This is the paramount theme of both the Gospel and the Epistle of John.

21 **My little children, guard yourselves from idols.**— Idolatry was rampant in the land and age when John wrote, and the danger exceedingly great that some of the saints would succumb to the seductions and allurements of the worship which attended it. They were thus admonished to be evermore vigilant against any effort which would involve them in this awful evil. Though the apostle must have had primarily in mind graven images, those fabricated by men, we must not overlook the fact that anything is an idol which supplants the place of deity in our hearts whether persons, property or pleasure.

ADDITIONAL NOTE ON 1 JOHN 5: 7

Those familiar with the King James or "Authorized" Version of the scriptures will have noticed a variation in the text in the Version on which these notes are based at 1 John 5: 7. The King James Version has the words, "And it is the Spirit that beareth witness, because the Spirit is truth," in verse 6, and in the verse which follows, this statement, "For there are three that bear record in heaven, the Father, the Word, and the Holy Ghost: and these three are one." The American Standard Version—the translation followed in this Commentary—omits entirely the words, "for there are three that bear record in heaven, the Father, the Word, and the Holy Ghost: and these three are one," and advances from the sixth verse to the seventh, the words, "and it is the Spirit that beareth witness, because the Spirit is the truth."

While obviously not within the scope of such a work as this to enter into a detailed examination of the critical questions involved, it is believed that the reader of this commentary would appreciate a brief review of the facts in order that he might be in position to form some opinion in the matter, and to this end the details are set out in abridged form for those who may be interested.

The Greek text, from which present-day translations are made, is determined by ancient manuscripts, versions and early writings of the so-called "Church Fathers," some of which extend almost to the apostolic age. With reference to the major portion of the sacred writings—perhaps ninety-nine per cent or more—there never has been the slightest doubt as to their apostolic origin; the readings thereof are supported by overwhelming evidence from all of the original and reliable sources. In a few instances, however, spurious readings have crept in, readings which lack such universal support as that regarded essential to eliminate all doubt as to their genuineness and reliability. In proportion as such a reading is found to be missing from ancient documents on which the text is founded, doubt arises as to its authenticity; and when it is discovered to be wanting from a respectable number of such sources it is regarded as spurious—that is, an inserted passage, without inspiration or divine authority.

With reference to that portion omitted from the American Standard Version, the most conservative scholars have, on weighing the evidence which obtains regarding it, unhesitatingly rejected it. The grounds on which this conclusion is reached are as follows:

1. The verse does not appear in *any* of the Uncial Greek Manuscript, these being the one most important source in determining the text.

2. It appears, for the *first* time, in a Cursive Manuscript, translated in the fifteenth or sixteenth century.

3. It is omitted in *all* of the ancient Versions, including the Vulgate by Jerome, though interpolated in modern editions of this work.

4. The so-called Greek Fathers do not have it, even when producing texts in support of the doctrine of the "Trinity," unaccountable on the supposition that it was then a part of the sacred text.

5. Many of the "Latin Fathers" omit it.

6. It first appears in the Latin writers at the end of the fifth century.

7. Historically, the words appear to have been originally included in an exegesis by Cyprian, and to have made their way, via a copyist, into the margin of the text, and then, later into the text itself.

In view, therefore, of the overwhelming manuscript evidence against the insertion of the verse, it is properly omitted from the American Standard Version, and all New Testament Greek texts today. It would never have found its way into the "Received Text" (basis for the older translations), had not Erasmus promised to insert it if it could be found in *any* Greek manuscript; and discovering that it was in the late Codex Britannicus, in keeping with his commitment, put it in the Complutensian edition of 1514. The most conservative scholars have referred to this act of Erasmus as "stupidity," and the effort itself, "mere caprice." There is, therefore, not the slightest ground for assuming that these words were a part of the original composition of the apostle John, or entitled to a place in the sacred text; nor is there any loss whatsoever in yielding them up as spurious, since nothing is taught in them not abundantly taught elsewhere in the New Testament.

A COMMENTARY ON THE SECOND EPISTLE OF JOHN

CONTENTS

INTRODUCTION TO THE SECOND AND THIRD EPISTLES OF JOHN

Page

General Characteristics 331

The Author of the Epistles 332

Purpose and Design of Second and Third John 333

Time and Place of Writing 334

An Analysis of Second John 334

An Analysis of Third John 335

THE SECOND EPISTLE OF JOHN

Address and Salutation (Verses 1-4) 337

Admonitions (Verses 5, 6) 343

Warnings (Verses 4-11) 344

Conclusion (Verses 12, 13) 350

AN INTRODUCTION TO THE SECOND AND THIRD EPISTLES OF JOHN

GENERAL CHARACTERISTICS

The Second and Third Epistles of the Apostle John are so closely associated, so similar in structure and form, so much alike in purpose and design, that they may be best considered together. That they were written by the same hand is admitted by even the most radical of the destructive critics. In both letters the same general outline is followed, much of the same phraseology occurs, they agree in the use of similar grammatical construction, in the adoption of the same ideas, in the definition given to leading terms, and in the purpose for which written, viz., the strengthening of faith, encouragement under trial, and warnings against, and with reference to, false teachers. They have been called "twin sisters," and it is obvious that they belong together, having issued from the hand of their author near the same time and with the same general design in mind.

Second John contains (1) An Address and Greeting (verses 1-3); (2) The Main Portion of the Epistle, in which the writer expresses great satisfaction in the loyalty to the truth known to exist on the part of some of the members of the family of the woman addressed, and enjoins love, which he identifies as walking "after the commandments," and warns against false teachers and their doctrines (verses 4-11); (3) a conclusion, in which the author reveals an intention of visiting the person addressed.

Certain expressions and dominant terms occur repeatedly in the Epistle, and may, therefore, be regarded as keynotes. "Truth," for example, occurs five times; "love," four times; "commandment," four times. The word "walking" is also of frequent mention in the short missive. Those addressed are commanded to walk in harmony with the Lord's commandment which is declared to be evidence of one's love. (Verses 4, 6.) Walking in truth, keeping the commandments, and continuing in love were favorite themes of the author and were sentiments often alluded to by him, both here and elsewhere in his writings.

Third John has (1) an address and greeting (Verse 1); (2) the main body of the Epistle, in which John wished Gaius financial and spiritual prosperity, expressed joy at his faithfulness and fidelity to truth, complimented him for his hospitality, and denounced Diotrephes for his assumption of dictatorial powers in the congregation to which he belonged (verses 2-12); (3) a conclusion, in which the author expressed the expectation of seeing Gaius soon, and closing salutations (verses 13, 14). The word "truth" occurs six times in the Third Epistle of John, a dominant note in all of that apostle's writings, whether in the biography of Christ (the Gospel According to John), the First, Second, and Third Epistles, or the Revelation. The name "God" appears twice in Third John; "Jesus" or "Christ," not at all, though of course, it is implied in the phrase, "For the sake of the Name." (Verse 7.)

These Epistles, though brief, are of much value to us today in that they afford us intimate glimpses into the affairs of the early church in a manner not characteristic of the lengthier and more profound Epistles. They also reveal that all was not always harmonious, even in the apostolic age, and that human nature, in its darker forms, carried over into the church, and influenced the actions of men even as now. They contain warnings sorely needed in our time, and which should not be ignored or disregarded. We see in them the danger of denying Christ; of failing in genuine love of the brethren; of not keeping the commandments. And, they supply us with a demonstration of the Christian spirit which should ever pervade and permeate our missives and thus constitute a pattern of Christian correspondence of the highest possible type. They are (a) brief; (b) to the point; (c) stripped of unnecessary verbiage; (d) courteous, sympathetic, and *true*. We would do well to bring our letter writing into conformity with the standard here given.

THE AUTHOR OF SECOND AND THIRD JOHN

The author of both of the Epistles is identified simply as "The elder" *(ho presbuteros,* literally, the presbyter) but believed by all conservative scholars to have been the apostle John. The evidence on the basis of which this conclusion is reached is abundant, and both internal and external in nature. The Epistles are anciently ascribed to that apostle by numerous writers of the early centuries; and they bear on their face unmistakable tokens of such authorship. Clement of Alexandria cited them; Dionysius noted that John did not name himself in his Epistles, "not even in the Second and Third Epistles, although they are short Epistles, but simply calls himself a presbyter." (Eusebius, H.E. VII, xxv.) Cyprian introduced a quotation from 2 John 10, as written by "John the Apostle." The internal evidence is even more convincing, and such as to be wholly sufficient for the candid and reasonable mind. The three Epistles of John embody the same language, the same ideas, the same ideals. There is little that is peculiar to them, as distinct from the First Epistle, or the Gospel according to John; and of the Second Epistle, seven or eight of the thirteen verses are found in the First Epistle. In the Third, the writer describes himself in the same fashion, writes largely in the same style, and utilizes many of the same phrases. It is, therefore, not surprising that from the earliest ages of Christianity these books have been regarded as productions of "the disciple whom Jesus loved"—John the Apostle.

PURPOSE AND DESIGN OF SECOND AND THIRD JOHN

The Second Epistle of John was written as a result of information which had come to the apostle regarding the children of the faithful sister addressed in it. He had heard that certain of her children were "walking in truth," and he wrote to rejoice with her in this; to admonish her to persist in the same manner of life; and to avoid the seductions of the false teachers regularly coming her way.

Third John was addressed to Gaius, a name of frequent mention in the New Testament, and one, therefore, not possible to identify with certainty. (Acts 19: 29; 20: 4; Rom. 16: 23; 1 Cor. 1: 14.) Whether one of these men named "Gaius," or a man by this name not elsewhere mentioned or referred to in the New Testament, we have no means of knowing. He appears to have been neither an elder nor a deacon in the congregation where he worshipped, but a man of benevolence, of some financial standing, and greatly devoted to the truth. Third John was written, (a) for the purpose of commending Gaius for his faithfulness, fidelity, and hospitality shown to missionaries which had come his way, to encourage him to continue in this grace and not be deterred by the opposition which had risen; (b) to rebuke Diotrephes for his arrogance, love of pre-eminence, and perverseness; (c) to commend Demetrius, a faithful disciple, whom Gaius is admonished to imitate. Three persons are thus dealt with in this brief missive: *Gaius,* the dependable disciple, liberal, hospitable, devoted; *Diotrephes,* a church boss, dominating, boastful, proud; *Demetrius,* commended by all, humble, kindly, worthy. These are representative types of men often observed in the church today.

TIME AND PLACE OF WRITING

With reference to neither time nor place is it possible to speak with definiteness and certainty. From the many similarities of style obtaining in both Second and Third John we infer that they were written about the same time and, we may presume, from the same place; but, inasmuch as neither of these matters is indicated in these Epistles, it is not possible to know either when or where they were written. The author appears to have been an aged man (cf. "The elder," verse 1); he often referred to his readers as his "little children"; the apostle John died near the end of the first century; and it is, therefore, likely that the Epistles were written near the end of his life. The scholarly Lardner says that John "was somewhat advanced in age, and that he had resided a good while in Asia, before he wrote any of these Epistles; consequently I am disposed to think that these two were not written sooner than the first. And as it was before argued that the First Epistle was written about the year 80, these two may be reckoned to have been written between the years 80 and 90." We are disposed to feel, in view of the known facts, that the date would be nearer A.D. 90 than A.D. 80, or earlier.

AN ANALYSIS OF SECOND JOHN

I. Signature and Salutation. (Verses 1-4.)
  1. John's love for those who walk in the truth.
  2. Appreciation for their loyalty and faithfulness.

II. Admonitions. (Verses 5, 6.)
  1. To walk in love and keep the commandments.

III. Warnings. (Verses 7-11.)
   1. Deceivers were abroad.
   2. The deceivers identified.
   3. Those who go beyond what Jesus taught do not have God.
   4. Such are not to be received into one's house, nor be greeted.
   5. To shelter false teachers is to partake of their evil works.
IV. Conclusion. (Verses 12, 13.)
   1. Things to say better expressed by word than by paper and ink.
   2. An expectation of an early visit.
   3. Salutation from an elect sister's children.

AN ANALYSIS OF THIRD JOHN

I. Signature and Salutation. (Verses 1-4.)
   1. Author's prayer for Gaius' health and prosperity.
   2. Satisfaction on hearing that he walked in truth.
II. The New Testament Law of Missions. (Verses 5-8.)
   1. They go forth for the sake of the Name.
   2. They take no support from unbelievers.
   3. The church's duty to support them.
   4. Those who thus do share in the blessings of the work.
   5. Mutual cooperation thus implied.
III. Endorsement of the Work by the Apostle John.
   1. A letter written admonishing the church to receive the missionaries.
IV. The Church Under the Domination of Diotrephes. (Verses 9, 10.)
   1. Diotrephes used ugly words against the apostle and helpers.
   2. Forced the church to reject the letter which the apostle wrote.
   3. Forbade the congregation to receive the missionaries.
   4. Excluded from fellowship those who did receive them.
   5. Gaius one of those thus excluded.
V. Faithfulness of Demetrius. (Verses 11, 12.)
VI. Letter Written to Encourage Gaius. (Verse 13.)
VII. Closing Salutations. (Verse 14.)

A COMMENTARY ON THE SECOND EPISTLE OF JOHN

ADDRESS AND SALUTATION
(1-4)

1 The elder unto the elect ¹lady and her children, whom I love in truth;

¹Gr. *in*.

1 The elder—The apostle John. For the grounds which prompt to the view that the author of this Epistle was the apostle John, see the Introduction. Numerous reasons may be assigned why the writer styled himself "the elder" *(ho presbuteros)*. He was, in point of years, an exceedingly old man when he wrote this missive, and the relationship which he sustained to his readers was that of a father counseling his children. Inasmuch as the article appears before "elder," emphasis is given to the writer as a person, rather than to an official position. He is here called an elder because he was an old man.

Unto the elect lady and her children, whom I love in truth; and not I only, but also all they that know the truth.—Second John is thus addressed to "the elect lady and her children," identified as individuals whom John loved "in truth," as well as all others who knew the truth. Much diversity of opinion exists regarding the person or persons thus addressed. The words, "elect lady," are translated from the Greek phrase, *eklekte* (elect) *kuria* (lady), and this circumstance has led some to the conclusion that one or the other of these terms should be regarded as a proper name, some assuming that the phrase should be translated "the lady Eclecte," and others, "the elect Cyria." Thus translated, the woman's name is designated by the apostle, being either *Eclecte,* or else, *Cyria,* depending on which of the terms is regarded as the proper name.

Cyria is the English spelling of the Greek *kuria,* and, etymologically, means *lady*. This, however, alone considered, is not significant, since all Bible names mean something, viz., Jacob, "supplanter"; Israel, "one who prevails with God"; Jesus, "Saviour." On the assumption that either *eklekte* or *kuria* is to be regarded as a proper name, the presumption is that it is the latter, rather than

and not I only, but also all they that know the truth; 2 for the truth's sake

the former, inasmuch as the choice must be between "the lady Eclecte" or "the elect Cyria," and women are never called *ladies* in the New Testament. The word *"kuria"* (lady) occurs nowhere else in the New Testament (other than in this Epistle) though the word *woman,* often. Moreover, in 1 Pet. 5: 13, there is a similar reference to an elect sister where, obviously, an individual, though not named, is designated. The marginal reading in the American Standard Version supports the view that the sister addressed by the apostle was named *Cyria*.

Others have thought that a *church* is thus figuratively designated by the apostle, using the allegory of a woman in keeping with the mystical use of Rev. 12. This, however, is highly improbable. To reach this conclusion, one must translate the Greek word *Kuria* as "lady," interpret the word "lady" as a church, and then construe the Greek word *tekna*, children, as members of the church! Only in the highly figurative portions of the scriptures is the church ever referred to as a woman; and it seems very unlikely that the apostle, in this brief treatise, should have used the word thus figuratively. Moreover, other serious difficulties in the way of such a rendering are immediately apparent. If the "lady" was the church, who were the children of the lady addressed? The church has no existence apart from those who constitute its membership. The elect lady had a sister who also had children. (Verse 13.) On the assumption that the elect lady was the church, and her children the members of the church, who then was the sister, and what did she and her children represent? From all the facts in the case, the preponderance of evidence seems logical to lead to the conclusion that the terms under consideration are to be literally interpreted; that the elect lady was some faithful sister known to John; and that she may have borne the name Cyria. More than this it is not possible to know.

Little biographical information is available regarding this woman, and only that which the Epistle contains. From it we learn that she was a faithful disciple of the Lord; that John felt much affection for her and her children; that she was the mother of several children, some of whom were equally faithful; and that she was given to hospitality. The apostle expected soon to visit

which abideth in us, and it shall be with us for ever: 3 Grace, mercy, peace

her, though whether he later did does not appear. Inasmuch as no mention is made of her husband, it would seem to be a reasonable hypothesis that he was either dead, or else an unbeliever.

John loved this sister and her children "in truth," i.e., sincerely, genuinely, truly. (Cf. 1 John 3: 18.) He loved them for their inherent worth, for their devotion to the cause of Christ, because they were Christians. So well known was this sister's faithfulness and loyalty, others were drawn to her, and likewise loved her. From verse 10 we learn that she was accustomed to receiving teachers of the word into her home, and this thus provided occasion for a wider acquaintance among the saints than otherwise would have existed.

Here, again, emphasis is given to a matter which often recurs in the apostle's writings, viz., that the fellowship of love is as wide as the fellowship of faith. All who know *(hoi egnokotes,* perfect active participle, who learned and have come to know the truth), love those equally possessed. It is the communion of love, and is as extensive as the communion of faith. Inasmuch as Jesus is the embodiment of "the truth," one does no injustice to the text to substitute for the word "truth," *Christ*. He is, indeed, the way, the truth, and the light.

2 For the truth's sake which abideth in us, and it shall be with us for ever:—Here the reason is assigned why all who know the truth, love those in truth: it is for "the truth's sake which abideth in us." John loved this faithful sister and the children embraced in the address, not because of an unusual attractiveness which they may have possessed, nor for any personal charm they may have exhibited, but because of the truth which dwelt both in him and in them. It is a vivid and impressive description of the reason for the love each faithful disciple feels for all other disciples. It was the truth which abode in them all which supplied the occasion for the love thus expressed. Only those who have love *for* the truth love *in* truth. This truth which had settled down and made its home in them *(meno)* would, the apostle confidently believed, abide thus with them forever. Despite the opposition which the truth engendered, the difficulties which beset their way, and the

shall be with us, from God the Father, and from Jesus Christ, the Son of the Father, in truth and love.

antagonism of ungodly men, John assured them that the truth would find its true home in them forever.

3 **Grace, mercy, peace shall be with us,**—Grace is the principle on which God extends mercy and peace, and hence must ever precede them. Grace has reference to the transgressions of man, mercy to the misery which such transgressions produce, and peace to the contentment and serenity which obtain as the result of the operation of grace and mercy and their appropriation through obedience to the Lord's commandments. God's free grace is extended to men in their sins, and his mercy rids them of the misery which a consciousness of sin produces. Peace is the resultant state where grace and mercy have operated. The words together constitute a common greeting which, with variations, often occurs in the New Testament. (Rom. 1: 7; 1 Tim. 1: 2; 2 Tim. 1: 2.) For the significance of the terms used as a greeting, see the notes on 1 Pet. 1: 2. Grace *(charis)* evidences the state of God's mind toward the sinner; mercy *(eleos),* the act of love; and peace *(eirene),* the gift of love—the effect resulting from grace and mercy. These terms marvelously reveal the wondrous scope of God's goodness to man from the beginning to the end. Grace suggests the first approach, the loving disposition on the part of the great Jehovah to supply the means of salvation to a rebellious and recreant race. Mercy is grace expressing itself in action, and peace is the blessed condition of heart redeemed by blood and restored by grace to the status of reconciliation.

From God the Father, and from Jesus Christ, the Son of the Father,—Repetition of the word *from* here is indicative of the twofold relation which man sustains to the Father *and* to the Son of the Father. It was the function of the Son to reveal the Father (John 1: 18); i.e., to make him known. Since the advent of the Son into the world, it is not possible for man to plead that God is unknowable. The blessings of grace, mercy, and peace spring from God, the Father, and Jesus Christ, the Son of the Father. They may be obtained from no other source.

In truth and love.—Grace, mercy, and peace flow out to man in truth and love, keynote words of the Epistle, and embody-

4 I rejoice greatly that I have found *certain* of thy children walking in

ing the two things nearest the heart of the "apostle of love." John would have his readers ever to remain faithful to the truth which they had received, and to display always the love which issues from that truth. The word "truth" occurs *five* times in the second Epistle, *six* times in the third.

4 I rejoice greatly that I have found certain of thy children walking in truth,—Literally rendered, the words with which this verse begins would be rendered, "I rejoiced greatly" *(echaren lian,* second aorist passive of *chairo)*, but the translators rightly regarded the verb as an "epistolary aorist," and thus translated by the English present. This idiom of the Greek verb represents the action as taking place from the viewpoint of the receiver of the letter and is thus properly rendered in this fashion.

It was an occasion of much rejoicing to the apostle that he had found "certain" of this woman's children "walking in truth." "I have found *(heureko,* perfect active indicative of *heurisko,* cf. our English word, eureka), suggests that John had chanced to see these children of the sister to whom he wrote, and from personal knowledge was able to say that they were walking in truth. Does the implication follow that certain others of her children *were not* walking in truth? Some expositors think so. This conclusion, however, does not necessarily follow, and appears to be opposed to the great joy which the apostle expressed. Had he been aware that other children of this faithful sister were ungodly, this would have tempered the joy which he felt at the faithfulness of others. We are justified in assuming no more than what appears on the surface of the text: with some of this woman's children John had come in contact. They were walking in truth. In this he found great satisfaction; and with joy he communicated this fact to their mother, assured that she would be glad to know that her children, away from home, and in the midst of ungodly influences, were faithful to her teaching. With reference to other children which she had, no mention is made, and for the probable reason that the apostle was not in possession of any information regarding their present manner of life.

These children were "walking" *(peripatountas)* in truth, a term

truth, even as we received commandment from the Father. 5 And now I

which, in the scriptures, is often used to indicate manner of life or behaviour. It denotes not only action, but habitual action, and progress toward a goal. It was just such everyday conduct on the part of these children that brought joy and satisfaction to the heart of the great apostle.

This interesting circumstance, of an apostle writing a note to a faithful sister, and rejoicing with her over the faithfulness of her children, is wonderfully revealing, in that it indicates a tender, personal touch characteristic of the relationship which obtained between the early saints. It is just such a circumstance as has been duplicated again and again, through the years, by gospel preachers and Christian families. Countless letters have been written through the centuries by the faithful to each other in which joys, sorrows, and the circumstances of life have been shared in Christian love and sympathy. Other than the fact that this woman to whom John wrote was a faithful member of the church, she was not otherwise distinguished. The family was, by the world's standard, only ordinary people, not unlike millions of others about them; and yet, they were Christians, and being Christians, were worthy of the notice and commendation of an apostle of Christ.

Even as we received commandment from the Father.—I.e., to walk in truth. The children of this sister in "walking in truth" were carrying out the commandment which they had received from the Father to walk in this manner. "And this is the message which we have heard from him and announce unto you, that God is light, and in him is no darkness at all. If we say that we have fellowship with him, and walk in the darkness, we lie, and do not the truth: but if we walk in the light, as he is in the light, we have fellowship one with another, and the blood of Jesus Christ his Son cleanseth us from all sin." (1 John 1: 5-7.) "And hereby we know that we know him, if we keep his commandments. He that saith, I know him, and keepeth not his commandments, is a liar, and the truth is not in him." (1 John 2: 2.) "Beloved, no new commandment write I unto you, but an old commandment which ye had from the beginning: the old commandment is the word which ye heard." (1 John 2: 7.)

ADMONITIONS
(5, 6)

beseech thee, ¹lady, not as though I wrote to thee a new commandment, but that which we had from the beginning, that we love one another. 6 And this is love, that we should walk after his commandments. This is the commandment, even as ye heard from the beginning, that ye should walk in it. 7 For

---
¹Or, *Cyria*

---

5 And now I beseech thee, lady,—"And now," i.e., on the basis of what has just been written by the apostle, "I beseech thee. . . ." "Beseech" is translated from *eroto,* a stronger word than our English word *beseech.* It is a petition, but such a petition as one has a right to make, a right in this instance based on the law of love. "Lady" *(kuria,* vocative case) raises again the question of verse 1: Is the noun *kuria* a proper name, or not? If it is, then this is an instance of direct address: "I beseech thee, Cyria. . . ." If it is not, again reference is made to a "lady" not otherwise identified. For additional details in the matter, see the comments on verse 1 of this Epistle.

Not as though I wrote to thee a new commandment, but that which we had from the beginning, that we love one another.—The design of all of God's commandments is that we should love one another, since love is the fulfilling of the law. The love which the commandment requires is not a new commandment, but one which had been repeatedly emphasized from the beginning, i.e., from the beginning of the gospel of Christ. It will be observed that the plural pronoun "we" indicates John's awareness of equal responsibility in the obligation. This duty, the apostle often heard from the lips of the Lord: "A new commandment I give unto you, that ye love one another; even as I have loved you, that ye also love one another. By this shall all men know that ye are my disciples, if ye have love one to another." (John 13: 34, 35.) For the reasons why reference is made to commandments both new and old, regarding the obligation of love, see the comments on 1 John 2: 7, 8.

6 And this is love, that we should walk after his commandments.—Again, the two great keynotes of John's writings become manifest: *love* and *duty.* The one issues in the other; love prompts to the keeping of the commandments. "For this is the love of God that we should keep his commandments." (1 John 5: 3.) Emotion, unrelated to obedience, is worse than useless. Love, in the absence of obedience, degenerates into fanaticism; duty without love is cold formalism. Where love does not exist, the keeping of God's commandments is irksome and hard. To the faithful, the keeping of his commandments is not grievous, because love makes them light.

This is the commandment, even as ye heard from the beginning, that ye should walk in it.—(See 1 John 2: 7-11; 3: 23, 24.) Brotherly love and obedience to God are inseparable; the one fails in the absence of the other. "We love, because he first loved us. If a man say, I love God, and hateth his brother, he is a liar; for he that loveth not his brother whom he hath seen cannot love God whom he hath not seen. And this commandment have we from him that he who loveth God love his brother also." (1 John 4: 19-21.) The phrase, "this is the commandment," designates the obligation we have to love one another, and is singled out because it serves as the basis for all the other commandments. Jesus said, "If ye love me, ye will keep my commandments. . . . He that hath my commandments and keepeth them, he it is that loveth me: and he that loveth me shall be loved of my Father, and I will love him, and will manifest myself unto him." (John 14: 15, 21.)

WARNINGS
(7-11)

many deceivers are gone forth into the world, *even* they that confess not that

7 For many deceivers are gone forth into the world, even they that confess not that Jesus Christ cometh in the flesh.—The preposition "for," with which this verse begins, obviously links the thought which it contains with that which immediately precedes. The meaning, expanded, runs, It is imperative that you be joined together in love and allow this love to issue in Christian conduct, always keeping the commandments which have been given. To do so is to erect the strongest possible barriers against error. That there is an ever-present threat of it is obvious from the fact that many deceivers are gone forth into the world. The word "deceivers" *(planoi)* suggests the idea of wanderers, rovers,

Jesus Christ cometh in the flesh. This is the deceiver and the anti-christ. 8

moving about for the purpose of seducing and leading astray those whom they induce to accept their teaching. (Cf. 1 Tim. 4: 1ff.) These deceivers had gone forth as roving bands, their motive being to deceive, delude, lead the saints away from the faith. The fact that some were said to have gone forth from the disciples (1 John 2: 18) establishes the presumption that these here referred to may have been the apostates there described, though the verb "gone forth" may mean no more than that they regarded the world as the field in which to propagate their doctrine, and were thus industriously extending their efforts.

These deceivers were those who "confess not that Jesus Christ cometh in the flesh." To "confess not" is the equivalent of denying that Jesus had come in the flesh, and this they were doing. "Cometh" is translated from a present participle in the original text, and reveals that the apostle regarded the incarnation as a continuing fact, the denial of which made one a deceiver and false teacher. John did not mean by this that Jesus was yet in the flesh; though in his glorified state when these words were penned, the truth of the incarnation yet remained, and shall ever do so, and to deny it is to repudiate the truth. Judaism denied that Jesus *had come* in the flesh; Gnosticism, the current heresy of the time when John wrote, denied that he *could come* in the flesh. Either doctrine was heretical, and the propagators thereof deceivers.

This is the deceiver and the anti-Christ.—For the characteristics and identity of the anti-christ, see the comments on 1 John 2: 18, 22; 4: 3. In the text here, as in the passages in which the term anti-christ occurs, it will be seen that the apostle sometimes refers to many anti-christs, and again to but one. The great anti-christ was the symbol, the representative of the class whose spirit, disposition, design the others adopted. The anti-christ is the head of the apostate church—the church of Rome—and all who teach false doctrine, however much they may differ in detail in their teaching, or oppose one another in their actions, are one in their opposition to the Lord and the cause for which he died. Of what consequence is it that men array themselves against each other in minor details when together they form a solid phalanx against the truth of the gospel of Jesus Christ our Lord? How quickly do

Look to yourselves, that ye ²lose not the things which ³we have wrought, but that ye receive a full reward. 9 Whosoever ⁴goeth onward and abideth not

²Or, *destroy*
³Many ancient authorities read *ye*.
⁴Or, *taketh the lead* Comp. 3 Jn. 9.

---

men resolve their differences of a denominational nature when they are confronted with a genuine representative of the truth! The denominational world has ever recognized the church of the Lord as a common enemy; and where it is active, they have disregarded their own distinctive interests to form a common front against the truth. The spirit of the anti-christ is the motivating factor in every false teacher.

8 **Look to yourselves, that ye lose not the things which we have wrought, but that ye receive a full reward.**—"Look to yourselves," i.e., take an introspective view into your own hearts and test the defences which you have against such in order that you may be sure you will not succumb to the allurements of these teachers and so lose the things wrought out by the apostles. That which was wrought out by the apostles was the gospel delivered through them by means of the Holy Spirit to the people to whom they preached. Taught here in emphatic fashion is, (1) the possibility of apostasy; (2) the importance of constant and careful self-examination; (3) the vital necessity of ceaseless vigilance against the blandishments of the evil one. That which this faithful sister stood in danger of losing was the most priceless possession she had: the salvation of her soul. The admonition is equally applicable to us today. Our first and paramount concern should be our own standing before God, and this is to be maintained only by an unswerving adherence to his will and way as taught in the scriptures. Any threat thereto, such as these false teachers posed, should be rejected speedily and permanently.

9 **Whosoever goeth onward and abideth not in the teaching of Christ, hath not God:**—Verse 8, immediately preceding this, warns of the loss to be sustained in listening to the false teachers and "deceivers" mentioned in verse 7. Here, the loss is identified and explained: it is the loss of God himself! Whosoever goes onward and abides not in the teaching of Christ *"hath not God!"* The verbs "goeth onward" and "abideth not" are descriptive of the same act: the first presents it positively, the second, negatively.

in the teaching of Christ, hath not God: he that abideth in the teaching, the

The "teaching of Christ" here is not teaching about Christ, or teaching which is Christian in substance or nature; it is the teaching which Christ did personally and through those whom he inspired. It is the teaching of Christ, because he is, in the final analysis, its author, and from him it issued. It is thus an infallible standard, and no deviation from it is possible without apostasy.

To go onward and not abide in this teaching is to lose God. The verb "goeth onward" is from the Greek *proago*, to progress. The meaning thus is: Whosoever becomes *progressive* and abides not in the teaching of Christ hath not God. Men often boast that they are progressive, and movements religious have arisen both in and out of the church through the years whose watchword and slogan was *progressiveness*. Progress is good only when it is in the direction of Christ, and not away from him; and in some matters it is far preferable to be non-progressive, particularly in not going beyond what the Lord has said. Any movement which is away from the teaching of Christ is progress in the wrong direction, and results eventually in the loss of God himself. The price of a sound church is a pure faith and a faultless practice; and this may be had only by faithful adherence to the truth as it is in Christ Jesus. We must ever be on our guard against any semblance of departure from that which is written, whether in teaching or practice; and we should remember always that the teaching of Christ and his apostles constitutes the only safe and all-sufficient rule of faith and practice for the saints of God.

He that abideth in the teaching, the same hath both the Father and the Son.—This is the same thought as that of the clause preceding, but stated positively, and with the addition of the phrase, "and the Son." (Cf. 1 John 2: 23.) "He that abideth" *(ho menon,* keeps on abiding) in the teaching (of Christ) is the individual who recognizes the inviolate character of the teaching and veers neither to the right nor left of it. He regards the teaching of Christ (and that continued through his apostles) as the complete deposit of truth for this dispensation to which nothing more will be added, and from which nothing may be taken, and which is, therefore, the infallible standard of Christianity. He who

same hath both the Father and the Son. 10 If any one cometh unto you, and bringeth not this teaching, receive him not into *your* house, and give him no

recognizes this, and abides in it faithfully, has both the Father and the Son. There is such an intimate relationship subsisting between the Father and the Son that to have one is to have the other. Conversely, he who has not the one cannot have the other. And, one has neither when he fails to adhere steadfastly to the teaching of Christ.

Modernism, under the guise of progressiveness, is shrewd and adroit in its method of approach. It begins by reminding us that we live in the twentieth century, not the first; that conditions have changed and in our day necessitate a different and modernized approach; that the New Testament was never intended to be a stereotyped arrangement for all succeeding ages; and that "sanctified common sense" must be utilized in adapting its message to our time.

We should regard with grave suspicion anyone who would disparage the value of the New Testament or lessen its influence in any way for our time. All such should be solemnly reminded of Paul's warning to the fickle Galatians: "I marvel that ye are so quickly removing from him that called you in the grace of Christ unto a different gospel; which is not another gospel: only there are some that trouble you, and would pervert the gospel of Christ. But though we, or an angel from heaven, should preach unto you any gospel other than that which we preached unto you, let him be anathema." (Gal. 1:6-8.)

10 **If any one cometh unto you, and bringeth not this teaching, receive him not into your house, and give him no greeting:**—The Greek construction here (indicative with *ei*), presents an actual case, and not a hypothetical one, as would have been indicated by *ean* with the subjunctive. The meaning is, "When one comes to you bringing not this teaching, receive him not into your house, and give him no greeting." "This teaching" is the teaching of Christ, the teaching in which we must abide, and beyond which we must not progress, if we are to possess God. (Verse 9.)

In the first century, accommodations were few, and the means to

greeting: 11 for he that giveth him greeting partaketh in his evil works.

obtain them often non-existent on the part of the teachers and preachers of the word. Moreover, there was the obligation to extend Christian hospitality (Rom. 12: 13), as well as the natural desire to share their fellowship. The faithful sister to whom John wrote, of a benevolent disposition, possessed of a home, and evidently with sufficient means to entertain visitors, would occasionally be faced with the problem of deciding whether the teachers who came her way and who would claim her hospitality were worthy or not. The test which the apostle supplied her to use in such instances was this: Do they advocate the teaching of Christ? (verse 9), and particularly, Do they confess that Jesus Christ has come in the flesh? If not, she was not to receive them into her house; she was to show no hospitality to them; she was not so much as to give them greeting. The greeting was *"Chairo!"* literally, *goodspeed* or *Godspeed.* This greeting was more than mere formality; it was an approval of the course being pursued by the one thus greeting, and included a desire for success in the effort attempted.

11 For he that giveth him greeting partaketh in his evil works.—And thus the reason why no such greeting should be extended to the advocates of false doctrine of whom John warned. To do so was to become a party to, and thus to be guilty of, the evil works characteristic of such. The severity of the injunction here given, and the apparent inhospitality which it contains, has led some to question the spirit which prompted it, and to attribute it to the fiery disposition of him who once sought to call down fire from heaven upon a village which treated the Lord with contempt. (Luke 9: 51-55.) Such is, of course, to misunderstand what the apostle said, and to misapprehend the circumstances under which he said it.

(1) John does not here forbid hospitality to strangers, or, for that matter, to false teachers when, in so doing, false teaching is neither encouraged nor done. Were we to find a teacher known to be an advocate of false doctrine suffering, it would be our duty to minister to his need, provided that in so doing we did not abet or encourage him in the propagation of false doctrine. (2) What is

12 Having many things to write unto you, I would not *write them* with paper and ink: but I hope to come unto you, and to speak face to face, that

forbidden is the reception of such teachers in such fashion as to supply them with an opportunity to teach their tenets, to maintain an association with them when such would involve us in the danger of accepting their doctrines. The passage teaches that we must do nothing that would in any way support or encourage the teaching of that which is not true. To do so is to share in the guilt of the teachers themselves. The principle here taught may not be legitimately extended to include association or hospitality extended to unbelieving relatives, strangers, or even false teachers when in so doing we do not (a) aid them in their work; (b) lend encouragement to their efforts; (c) subject ourselves to the danger of corruption from them. The test is, Does one become a partaker by the action contemplated? If yes, our duty is clear; we must neither receive them nor give them greeting; if No, the principle here taught is not applicable.

12 **Having many things to write unto you, I would not write them with paper and ink: but I hope to come unto you, and to speak face to face, that your joy may be made full.**— There were other matters the apostle desired to write, but for the time being did not deem it expedient, either from the nature of the things in mind, or from the fact that it was his purpose soon to visit with the sister, and thus to communicate them to her face to face. The apostle's heart was full, and the missive was a hurried one, and he would simply wait until he could see and speak face to face with her of all the matters he had stored up for her.

The "paper" *(chartes)* was prepared by taking the pith of the papyrus plant, pressing it into sheets and pasting them together. Paper, such as we use, was not invented until comparatively recent times, and long after the apostolic period. The "ink" *(melan)* was a substance made from mixing soot and water and thickened with gum. While the apostolic epistles were frequently dictated (cf. Rom. 16: 22), it appears that John must have written this brief communication with his hand. "Face to face" is literally "mouth to mouth" *(stoma pros stoma),* a phrase also occurring in 3 John 14, and indicating personal presence and conversation. This meeting John desired that (1) he might communicate to her the other

your joy may be made full. 13 The children of thine elect sister salute thee.

matters he had in mind, the result of which would be (2) her joy would be full.

13 The children of thine elect sister salute thee.—The salutation was from the children of the sister of the woman to whom John wrote. The mother was not included, either from the fact that she was dead, or else lived elsewhere. These children, being in the vicinity of where John was, joined in the salutation (greeting) to their aunt. This godly woman, a sister of the one particularly addressed by the apostle, was a Christian, because she is described as "elect," i.e., *called* or *chosen*. (See the comments on 1 Pet. 2: 4.) No further information regarding her is available, yet from what is said, certain deductions follow: (1) She had reared her children to be Christians, and though apparently dead, her influence lived on in them. (2) She was *a mother*, not a *nun,* and thus performed her true function in life. (1 Tim. 2: 15.) And though unknown to us by name, she is enrolled in that innumerable army of the faithful who have lived and served and passed on to the joys of their Lord. Blessed and fortunate indeed will we be if as much may be said of us.

A COMMENTARY ON THE THIRD
EPISTLE OF JOHN

CONTENTS

THE THIRD EPISTLE OF JOHN

Address and Salutation (Verses 1-4) 357

New Testament Law of Missions (Verses 5-8) 360

John's Apostolic Approval (Verse 9) 363

Domination of Diotrephes (Verses 9, 10) 363

Faithfulness of Demetrius (Verses 11, 12) 364

Conclusion (Verses 13, 14) 366

A COMMENTARY ON THE THIRD EPISTLE OF JOHN

ADDRESS AND SALUTATION
(1-4)

1 The elder unto Gaius the beloved, whom I love in truth.
2 Beloved, I pray that in all things thou mayest prosper and be in health,

1 The elder unto Gaius the beloved, whom I love in truth.—The author is thus the same as the writer of the second epistle, "the elder," i.e., the apostle John. (See the Introduction to the Second and Third Epistles of John.) The missive was addressed to Gaius. The name occurs in Acts 19: 29; 20: 4; Rom. 16: 23; and 1 Cor. 1: 14, but inasmuch as it was a common name in the Roman Empire of the time, we are not justified in inferring that it was one of those thus referred to. The description, "the beloved," reveals the esteem in which Gaius was held by those who knew him. "Whom I love in the truth" was John's specific affirmation of regard, in addition to that in which the disciple Gaius was generally held. For the significance of the phrase "in truth," see the comments on Second John 1.

2 Beloved, I pray that in all things thou mayest prosper and be in health, even as thy soul prospereth.—Four times, in this brief letter, the word "beloved" occurs, viz., verse 1, here, and in verse 5 and 11. This verse thus contains an address of affection; it reveals that John was praying for his beloved friend and brother in the Lord; it informs us that that for which he prayed was that Gaius might (a) prosper (financially); and (b) be in health; that such should be to the extent that his soul prospered. Here, incidentally, is the standard by which to determine how rich one may safely become: *just so long as the soul prospers!* So long as one enjoys soul prosperity, his riches bless and benefit not only himself, but others; when they impair spiritual health, the interests of the soul demand, as in the case of the rich young ruler (Mark 10: 17, 31), that a surgical operation be performed and they be severed from us!

It would appear from the apostle's petition that Gaius' health was not good and that he was also not a prosperous man. It is

even as thy soul prospereth. 3 For I ¹rejoiced greatly, when brethren came

¹Or, *rejoice greatly, when brethren come and bear witness*

possible his soul health was better than either his physical or financial health, hence the prayer that these might equal that. On the other hand, it may be that the prayer was a simple petition for the welfare of Gaius without any implication that either his financial condition or physical health was good or bad, but that they might be as good as his soul already was. In either view, the principle is the same: a recognition of the superior importance of the interests of the soul. The apostle was speaking in the spirit of his Master's admonition when he said: "But seek ye first his kingdom, and his righteousness; and all these things shall be added unto you." (Matt. 6: 33.) Having put first things first, it was entirely in order that Gaius should have health and prosperity. It is a lesson so sorely needed among us today. We should ever remember to subordinate the material to the spiritual, and never allow the world to gain precedence in our thoughts and lives.

3 For I rejoiced greatly, when brethren came and bare witness unto thy truth, even as thou walkest in truth.—The apostle rejoiced; the occasion of his joy was the witness which the brethren brought of the faithfulness of Gaius that he walked in truth. The verbs, "came," and "bear witness," are present participles *(erchomenon, marturounton),* and thus suggest repetitive action, i.e., "brethren are constantly coming, and continually bearing witness to me of thy truth." The clause, "even as thou walkest in truth," is not an independent one by which the apostle added the testimony of his own to that of the brethren; but is epexegetical of the former, and gives the substances of the testimony which they brought.

The brethren who bore this testimony regarding Gaius to John are not certainly known, though they may well have been those to whom the apostle refers in verse 5. These brethren had carried a letter of recommendation to the church, which John had written, and though entertained by Gaius and given hospitality by him had been rejected by the church through the influence of Diotrephes. (Verse 5-11.) These would, therefore, be able to testify of the kindness and faithfulness of Gaius, in contrast with the unbrother-

and bare witness unto thy truth, even as thou walkest in truth. 4 Greater joy have I none than ²this, to hear of my children walking in the truth.

²Or, *these* things, *that I may hear*

---

liness of Diotrephes. It seems reasonable to assume that these bearing witness particularly referred to here were indeed the brethren whom the apostle had sent. The final clause of verse three, rendered, "Even as thou walkest in truth," has, in the original text, the pronoun "thou" in emphatic position: *"Thou* (in contrast with Diotrephes), walkest in truth."

From verses 5 and 6, it appears that Gaius' faithfulness consisted not only of devotion to the cause of the Lord, but in liberality, hospitality and good works. In these matters that disciple continued; and this, John described as *walking in truth!* Again, there is emphasized here, that which is repeatedly taught throughout the Bible: it is not possible to separate theory and practice in genuine Christianity. "What doth it profit, my brethren, if a man say he hath faith, but have not works? can that faith save him? If a brother or sister be naked and in lack of daily food, and one of you say unto them, Go in peace, be ye warmed and filled; and yet we give them not the things needful to the body; what doth it profit? Even so faith, it if have not works, is dead in itself. Yea, a man will say, Thou hast faith, and I have works: show me thy faith apart from thy works, and I by my works will show thee my faith. Thou believest that God is one; thou doest well: the demons also believe, and shudder. But wilt thou know, O vain man, that faith apart from works is barren? Ye see that by works a man is justified, and not only by faith." (James 2: 14-20, 24.) There is thus no genuine faith without works, nor are works of value without faith, or such as are produced by faith. It is only when the two are united that the practice of genuine Christianity results.

4 Greater joy have I none than this, to hear of my children walking in the truth.—"Greater, here *(meizoteran)*, is a double comparative, and thus a term of great emphasis. Compare the "more better" of Paul in Phil. 1: 23. These forms are of frequent occurrence in both biblical and classical Greek. In Eph. 3: 8, there is a comparative on a superlative: "Unto me, who am *less than the least* of all saints. . . ." In this manner did the apostle indicate the tremendous satisfaction he derived from the knowledge that his children (those whom he converted to the truth, or with whom he had been closely associated in the work of the Lord) walked in truth. That which brought joy to the apostle's heart is likewise a source of much satisfaction to all faithful gospel preachers today. To know that those we have been instrumental in leading to the truth are continuing stedfastly in faith and good works warms the heart and stirs the emotion of all true teachers of the word.

NEW TESTAMENT LAW OF MISSIONS
(5-8)

5 Beloved, thou doest a faithful work in whatsoever thou doest toward them that are brethren and strangers withal; 6 who bare witness to thy love before the church: whom thou wilt do well to set forward on their journey

5 **Beloved, thou doest a faithful work in whatsoever thou doest toward them that are brethren and strangers withal;—** In verse 4, John had commended Gaius for the fact that he walked in truth. Here, he makes particular mention of the acts in which Gaius had exhibited faithfulness: he had supplied hospitality for the "brethren," and "withal" (and that also) to "strangers." This faithful disciple had not limited his bounty to those known to him; he had extended it to the strangers who came, i.e., to brethren personally unknown to him. Missionaries, properly accredited, were certain to find a welcome at his house, whether he had previously known them or not. From what follows in the Epistle, we may infer that Gaius had been sharply criticised by Diotrephes (a domineering church boss) for what he had done; and John carefully put the stamp of apostolic approval on his work in emphatic fashion. To provide for those who were bearers of the message of salvation was a faithful work; and the apostle urged Gaius to continue in it.

6 **Who bare witness to thy love before the church:**—The antecedent of "who" is both the brethren and the "strangers" of verse 5. Though strangers, they were brethren, but brethren formerly unknown to Gaius. These testified to the church of Gaius' faithfulness and acts of love. The congregation before which they appeared and bore this witness is not stated, though we may infer

worthily of God: 7 because that for the sake of the Name they went forth,

that it was the church in Ephesus, since here, according to reliable tradition, John lived when, it is believed, his Epistles were written. That it was before the public meeting of the church when Gaius was commended, follows from the fact that the article does not appear before the word "church" in the text. (Cf. 1 Cor. 14: 35, *en ekklesiai,* "*in church.*") The commendation was uttered, so we believe, in the midst of a report being made to the church of their evangelistic activities.

Whom thou wilt do well to set forward on their journey worthily of God:—From this it would appear that this same group of missionaries were contemplating another visit to that region, and would need the aid of Gaius; and the apostle, therefore, admonished him that he would "do well" to continue to evidence his faithfulness by setting them forward on their journey in a manner worthy of a follower of God. The custom then prevailed to start a guest on his journey by accompanying him for some distance, by providing money and food for the trip, and by bidding him Godspeed on the way. To this gracious custom Paul refers in Rom. 15: 24, and Titus 3: 13. The phrase, "to set forward on their journey," means thus not only to accompany one a portion of the way, but also to supply the ordinary means for such a journey. (Cf. Acts 21: 5.)

7 Because that for the sake of the Name they went forth. —The *name* for which these missionaries went forth was the name of Jesus Christ. (Cf. Acts 5: 4; James 2: 7; 1 Pet. 4: 16.) Thus early in the history of Christianity, the *name* represented all that Christ was and taught and did. When the shadow of Dark Ages descended upon the world, the word became a passport in dangerous places, serving as an introduction and protection to those who accepted the Lord's standard. When the agents of persecution came to ferret out the martyr, and when civil and papal edicts shut the door of sympathy, occasionally help could be obtained by knocking at the door of others, and whispering, "*In the Name!*" As the *name* in the Old Testament stands for Jehovah so in the New Testament, it is the synonym for *Christ.*

These words explain why the hospitality which Gaius accorded

taking nothing of the Gentiles. 8 We therefore ought to welcome such, that we may be fellow-workers ³for the truth.

³Or, *with marg.*

the missionaries which came his way was so essential and important. They "went forth," not in their own name, or by their own authority, but "in the name of" (by the authority of) Christ, to bear his message to the lost. They were thus entirely worthy of the bounty bestowed upon them, the shelter and food which they received.

Taking nothing of the Gentiles.—It would have been unseemly for these who carried the message of salvation to depend for support on those to whom they preached. Such would have exposed them to the charge that they sought material advantage for themselves, and that their preaching was merely a pretext to obtain that. There is nothing which so quickly wins men to a sympathetic hearing as the realization of complete unselfishness on the part of those who bear the message to them: and it is absolutely requisite that in all missionary efforts the missionaries be wholly independent financially and materially of those to whom they preach. (Cf. 2 Cor. 11:3.)

8 We therefore ought to welcome such, that we may be fellow-workers for the truth.—That missionaries are not to receive support from the heathen or unbelievers to whom they go does not mean that they are not worthy of support, or that the church is released from the obligation to provide for them. On the contrary, "we" (who are children of God) "ought" (are morally obligated) to "welcome such," *(hupolambanein,* present active infinitive), keep on welcoming such, as a regular practice in life, in order that we may be fellow-workers for the truth. As those who welcome and support those who preach false doctrines become partakers with them (2 John 9), so those who receive and maintain those who preach the truth become fellow-workers for the truth. The word "welcome" is translated from a word which, in the first century, signified the reception of people into one's house, the association which attends such receptions; the fellowship which obtains; and the readiness with which, under such circumstances, provisions are supplied them.

JOHN'S APOSTOLIC APPROVAL
(9)

9 I wrote somewhat unto the church: but Diotrephes, who loveth to have

9 I wrote somewhat unto the church: but Diotrephes, who loveth to have the preeminence among them, receiveth us not. —Apparently, John had written a brief letter to the church in which Gaius held membership; perhaps it had been sent along by the missionaries which had come their way; but it had been suppressed and destroyed by Diotrephes, a man of prominence and leadership in the congregation, perhaps an elder or preacher. Because he loved to have the "preëminence," he refused to acknowledge John's apostleship, or the missionaries in the fellowship of the apostle, and, hence, received them not. This personal letter to Gaius was a warning with reference to this designing man. The word "preëminence," *(philoproteuon,* present active participle), is derived from *philoprotos,* a fondness for being first; and is, alas, a disposition too often observable in our ranks today. The spirit manifested by this man Diotrephes is wholly foreign to the New Testament and opposed to the teaching of the Lord himself. All self-serving and personal aggrandizement must be eschewed and avoided if we would measure to the standard of primitive Christianity.

DOMINATION OF DIOTREPHES
(10)

the preëminence among them, receiveth us not. 10 Therefore, if I come, I will bring to remembrance his works which he doeth, prating against us with wicked words: and not content therewith, neither doth he himself receive the brethren, and them that would he forbiddeth and casteth *them* out of the

10 Therefore, if I come, I will bring to remembrance his works which he doeth, prating against us with wicked words: and not content therewith, neither doth he himself receive the brethren, and them that would he forbiddeth and casteth them out of the church.—The apostle entertained the hope that he would soon be able to visit Gaius and the congregation where he worshipped, and where Diotrephes was exercising such dominance, and he assured the faithful Gaius that when he came he would not ignore what this church-troubler was doing. The great apostle was not intimidated by Diotrephes, and he promised that he would deal with him adequately when the opportunity presented itself. The verb "doeth," in the phrase, "works which he doeth," *(poiei)*, is present active indicative, "which he keeps on doing," thus revealing a persistent course on the part of Diotrephes.

The extent of Diotrephes' lordship over the congregation is seen in the fact (1) he prated *(phluaron,* to babble, to accuse idly and falsely) against John and his associates with wicked words, (not merely idle, but actually *evil* words); (2) he refused to receive the brethren which came from John; (3) he forbade others in the congregation to do so; (4) those who refused to bow to his will he expelled from membership in the congregation. This does not mean that Diotrephes was able actually to sever faithful members from the body of Christ; the Lord added them to the church (Acts 2: 47), and it was obviously beyond the power of this ungodly man to turn them out of the body of Christ; but, exercising domination over the congregation, and having imposed his will and way over the saints here, he could and did expel them from membership in it. He was an ambitious, unscrupulous, church boss, opposed alike to apostolic authority and missionary work, a servant of Satan and an agent of the devil. Diotrephes' conduct was insubordination of the most advanced type and the apostle promised to deal in summary fashion with him when he arrived. Just what course John would follow, he does not indicate; we may be sure that he would expose the rebellious disposition characteristic of the man, exhibit the ungodliness he was manifesting, and warn the saints against him. He would, of course, be divested of any further authority in the congregation; and if he did not repent, would be speedily excluded from the fellowship of the church.

FAITHFULNESS OF DEMETRIUS
(11, 12)

church. 11 Beloved, imitate not that which is evil, but that which is good. He that doeth good is of God: he that doeth evil hath not seen God. 12

---

11 Beloved, imitate not that which is evil, but that which is good.—Having shown the true nature of Diotrephes, and having warned Gaius of such conduct as he had seen in him, he then exhorted him to follow and to copy *(mimou,* mimic) that which is good. (Cf. 1 Cor. 11: 1.) The verb is a present active imperative, "keep on imitating that which is good." Diotrephes afforded an example of conduct not to be imitated; Demetrius, one which Gaius might safely follow.

He that doeth good is of God: he that doeth evil hath not seen God.—Inasmuch as God is the source of all good, he who does good is of God. This does not refer to isolated acts of goodness which may appear in the lives of evil men, but to that of a life habitually good, good from proper motives, good because influenced from the proper source. Here, again, the verb "doeth" is a present participle *(poion)*, and thus denotes a settled mode of life. Conversely, he who practices evil continually evidences that he has not seen God, i.e., has never become acquainted with him. See the comments on 1 John 3: 6.

12 **Demetrius hath the witness of all men, and of the truth itself: yea, we also bear witness; and thou knowest that our witness is true.**—Demetrius (in contrast with Diotrephes), was universally regarded; those who knew him did not hesitate to ascribe to him the highest possible attainment in Christian living. Moreover, the apostle and those with him also bore witness to the faithfulness of this disciple, and Gaius knew that this testimony was true. The phrase, "and of the truth itself," an additional testimony to Demetrius' character is obscure, and its meaning not readily apparent. On the whole, the best explanation is that conformity to the truth, which was characteristic of Demetrius, was itself a public witness of the type of man he was, and thus the truth to which he adhered approved his course. As one who breaks the law is condemned by the law, so one who keeps it is approved by it. The truth itself thus becomes an independent witness to the faithfulness of those who walk in harmony with it.

CONCLUSION
(13, 14)

13 I had many things to write unto thee, but I am unwilling to write *them* to thee with ink and pen: 14 but I hope shortly to see thee, and we shall

---

13 I had many things to write unto thee, but I am unwilling to write them to thee with ink and pen:—There were many matters which John desired to communicate to his beloved brother and friend Gaius, but he was not disposed to do so with ink and pen. (Cf. 2 John 12.) The "pen" *(kalamos)* was a reed used for the purpose of a stylus; the "ink" *(melas)*, a black substance prepared from soot and oil. Ink is mentioned three times in the New Testament; here, in 2 John 12 and 2 Cor. 3:3.

14 But I hope shortly to see thee, and we shall speak face to face.—The reason why John did not desire to communicate the matters he had in mind. He hoped soon to see Gaius, and to be privileged to talk with him face to face, a much more effective and satisfactory method than that of the laborious and tedious medium of writing with pen and ink.

Peace be unto thee.—A usual greeting *(eirene soi)*. Cf. the Lord's greeting following the resurrection. (John 20:19, 26.) This greeting was especially appropriate, because *peace* is the sum of the divine blessings through Christ. The salutation is one which all genuine disciples extend to others. Those who are good and happy wish joy and peace to be the portion of all those about them. Peace, genuine peace, lasting peace comes only through willing service and complete obedience to the will of Christ. In disobedience there is rebellion; and where rebellion obtains between God and man, the result is a state of war and not peace. (Cf. Rom. 5:1.)

The friends salute thee.—The apostle is joined, in the salutation, by friends of Gaius who were associated with him, perhaps in the congregation and city of Ephesus. Who these friends were does not appear; we may, however, be certain that they were faithful members of the body of Christ themselves.

Salute the friends by name.—In saluting "by name" the heart-warming experience to have people remember us, and to call us by name. The statement is reminiscent of the only other in-

speak face to face. Peace *be* unto thee. The friends salute thee. Salute the friends by name.

---

stance where the phrase "by name" occurs in the New Testament: "To him the porter openeth; and the sheep hear his voice: *and he calleth his own sheep by name.*" (John 10: 3.) The apostle thus wanted to follow the example of his Master by his own recognition of each lamb of Christ by name! And so this brief and tender missive ends; an exceedingly short letter, compared with other New Testament Epistles, but one of great importance to us today, in its revelation of the inner feelings of the beloved apostle, and the glimpse which it affords us of the personal life of John and those whom he knew and loved so well. From it we learn that the apostles were not always involved in written or oral discussions of profound theological themes; they did not spend all of their time in intricate and involved dissertations or subtile and learned essays such as Romans and Hebrews; they had their tender and personal sides, and the world is greatly blessed by this short letter to Gaius by the apostle whom Jesus loved.

A COMMENTARY ON THE EPISTLE OF JUDE

CONTENTS

INTRODUCTION TO THE EPISTLE OF JUDE

Page

General Characteristics 373
Author of the Epistle 374
Authenticity 375
The Persons Addressed 376
Date and Place of Writing 376
Resemblance of Jude to Second Peter 377
An Analysis of the Epistle 378

SECTION ONE

Introduction (1-4) 381
Salutation (1, 2) 381
Occasion for Writing the Epistle (3, 4) 383

SECTION TWO

Examples of Condemnation (5-7) 388
Wicked and Good Contrasted (8-10) 392
Condemnation of Evil-Doers (11-13) 394
The Prophecy of Enoch (14-16) 397

SECTION THREE

Exhortations to Faithfulness (17-23) 402

SECTION FOUR

Benediction (24, 25) 407

INTRODUCTION

GENERAL CHARACTERISTICS

The Epistle of Jude was written to meet the need of the hour in which it was produced, and this circumstance determined its form and content. It appears to have been originally the intention of the author to write a treatise on the common salvation (see the comments on Jude 3), but an emergency suddenly arose which prompted him to revise his plan and to substitute this brief Epistle. False teachers, deceitful workers appeared on the scene the aim of whom being to seduce the saints and to corrupt the people of God; and the exigency of the situation led the writer to abandon his original plan and to write hurriedly this solemn warning.

These facts account for the vigorous style in which the book is written; this explains the rich and varied vocabulary which it contains. It is denunciatory in nature, severe in tone, and full of warning against those whose evil and ungodly activity was threatening the peace and security of the church. It is an impassioned effort in which example after example of destruction upon the wicked is produced; charge after charge hurled, and the sternest of warnings issued. The author hurried from one warning to another as if his words were not sufficient to contain the torrent of invectives which he felt the occasion demanded. The aroused writer referred to these false teachers as ungodly, lascivious, infidels, murmurers, faultfinders, hypocrites, liars, deceivers and sensualists. He compared them to Cain and Baalam and Korah, to the cities of the plain and to the fallen angels. Its descriptions of false teachers are sharp, incisive, convincing; its exhortations touching, tender, full of warmth; its conclusion sublime, beautiful and vivid. The doxology with which it concludes is one of the most beautiful in the New Testament.

The author of the Epistle evidently had a fondness for triple arrangements, and the book is filled with ideas set out in groups of threes. Those whom he addressed are, "called, beloved in God the Father, and kept for Jesus Christ." (Verse 1.) He wishes for them mercy, peace and love. (Verse 2.) Instances of judgment upon the ungodly are the Israelites in the wilderness, the angels who sinned, and the cities of the plain. (Verses 5-7.) The filthy dreamers he mentions are corrupt, rebellious, and railing. (Verses 8-10.) They had walked in the way of Cain, Baalam and Korah. (Verse 11.) They were murmurers, discontented, self-willed; they were church dividers, sensual, without the Spirit. (Verses 16-19.) Those in error were to be regarded in three classes, the first to be dealt with in mercy, the second snatched as it were from the fire, the third pitied. (Verses 22-23.) Saints are to keep themselves in the love of God, pray in the Spirit, and await the mercy of Christ at the last day. (Verse 21.) Glory to God is ascribed before all time, in the present, and throughout eternity. (Verse 24.) Eleven times in twenty-five verses this arrangement of triple effect may be discerned, a circumstance unparalleled in so short a space in any other portion of the sacred writings.

AUTHOR OF THE EPISTLE

The author is by the Epistle itself designated as "Jude, a servant of Jesus Christ, and brother of James." The "James" to whom reference is made here was the "James" prominently mentioned in connection with the church in Jerusalem (Acts 15: 13; Gal. 1: 18; 2: 9), one of the sons of Joseph and Mary, and hence a brother of Jesus in the flesh. (Matt. 13: 55; Mark 6: 3.) Inasmuch as "Jude" was a brother of this "James," he, too, was a fleshly brother of the Lord.

Very little information of a biographical nature is available concerning him. He was not an apostle; he appears to have designedly excluded himself from the ranks of the apostles (verse 17); and from motives of modesty and humility refrained from any mention of his relation to the Lord in the flesh. From the fact that he is mentioned last in Matthew's list of the sons of Mary and Joseph, and third in Mark's list, we are led to infer that he was either the youngest, or the next to the youngest of the children—at least of the sons. Along with the rest of his brothers, he was an unbeliever in the deity of Jesus during the Lord's personal ministry. (John 7: 3-8.) That they were with Mary in the upper room in Jerusalem after the ascension indicates that they were convinced of the Lord's claims by the resurrection. (Acts 1: 14.) Jude was married; he appears to have traveled considerably, and to have been accompanied by his wife on his journeys. (1 Cor. 9: 5.)

Eusebius preserves a story which he derived from Hegesippus that in the time of the Roman Emperor Domitian, two grandsons of Jude, Zocer and James, were summoned before the king for examination on the ground that they belonged to the royal line of David and might seek to regain the throne. When he saw that they were poor peasants, that their hands were horny with toil, and that they owned only thirty-nine acres of land he dismissed them with contempt. From the same source, we learn that these men became elders, and lived until the time of Trajan; and that they were greatly honored because of their faithful testimony before the king.

AUTHENTICITY

Along with other New Testament books (e.g., James and 2 Peter), Jude was slow in gaining acceptance by the religionists of the second and third centuries and doubts were expressed by them regarding its right to a place in the sacred canon. But it should be remembered that these men were not inspired; they were without any supernatural direction in determining what should be regarded as canonical and what should not; and they were influenced by theological considerations as are their counterparts today. That it was seldom quoted in the early centuries is due to the fact that it is short; the themes with which it deals are limited; and it would obviously lack the prominence which would characterize a production of Paul or John or Peter.

That it is not without ecclesiastical sanction follows from the fact that Tertullian believed it to be genuine and apostolic; Clement of Alexandria quoted it as scripture and commented on it; Origen accepted it and Didymus of Alexandria wrote a commentary on it. The councils of Laodicea, A.D. 360, of Hyppo, A.D. 393, and Carthage, A.D. 397 put it in the canon where it has remained ever since. Questions which have since arisen regarding the right of certain books to appear in the canon of scripture have resulted from prepossessions of theologians whose theories were in conflict with the teaching of these books (Luther and the book of James, for example), or rationalists and modernists who seek to destroy what they cannot explain.

The question of apocryphal quotations which it is alleged the book contains is outside our province and purpose here and the reader is referred to more exhaustive works for a consideration of this matter. If it were granted that the writer did indeed quote from them, it does not follow that he endorsed other portions which *he did not quote!* Paul quoted from three heathen poets, and to one of the quotations added, "This testimony is true," but this does not mean that the whole poem is true. (Acts 17: 28; Tit. 1: 12, 13.)

THE PERSONS ADDRESSED

The address, occurring in the outset of the Epistle, is "to them that are called, beloved in God the Father, and kept for Jesus Christ." (Jude 1.) Being thus without geographical detail, it is not possible to know certaintly to whom it was originally sent. In a secondary sense we may be sure that it was the design of the writer to prepare a treatise which would have universal appeal, and be utilized by Christians in all ages and places, though it obviously was written to meet a local need. The churches generally, both in Palestine and in Asia Minor, were constantly beset with false teachers during the apostolic age, and much of the New Testament was written to refute the various heresies which arose from time to time. It may be inferred that the readers for whom it was primarily written were of Jewish background from the fact that so many references and examples are cited from the Old Testament; but this is not conclusive evidence, since even Gentile Christians would be interested in, and accept as evidence these writings.

DATE AND PLACE OF WRITING

With reference to neither date nor place is it possible to speak with any degree of assurance, inasmuch as no data exist either in the Epistle, or out of it, from which such information may be derived. From the Jewish undertones of the Epistle, traditions regarding the residence of Jude and his descendants, and the fact that other members of Joseph's and Mary's family resided in Palestine, the supposition is that such was the residence of Jude, and that the Epistle was written from there and perhaps the city of Jerusalem itself. All of which we may be sure is that it was written during the latter half of the first century of the Christian era; and that it has been preserved for us as a product of inspiration. Neither the date nor the place of writing involves matters of importance to us today.

RESEMBLANCE OF JUDE TO SECOND PETER

There is a close and obvious relation between the Epistles of Jude and Second Peter; and the effort to determine which preceded the other—whether Jude borrowed from Peter or Peter from Jude, or whether both borrowed from a common source—has long occasioned the ingenuity of commentators, Bible expositors and students generally. To those of us who accept both Epistles as inspired productions, the matter is of little consequence. Inasmuch as Peter was an apostle and Jude was not, it seems more likely that Jude would expand the teaching of an apostle than that an apostle would depend on Jude for what he wrote; and an examination of the internal evidence leads plausibly to the conclusion that Jude followed the apostle. In verses 17 and 18, Jude appears to quote 2 Peter 3: 3. Testimony to the apostolic office in the phraseology of this verse indicates Jude's knowledge of 2 Peter, and his use of it, a procedure entirely proper in his case, but difficult to believe if reversed. Jude confessed dependence on what the apostles had taught as ground for the acceptance of matters; whereas, Peter never acknowledged, even in the most indirect fashion, dependence on another.

As evidence of the close connection between the two Epistles, it may be noted that both warn of heretics who deny the Lord that bought them (2 Pet. 2: 1; Jude 4); these false teachers, in both instances, were turning the grace of God into lasciviousness (Jude 4; 2 Pet. 2: 2); they had crept into the congregations privily and were doing their work deceptively (2 Pet. 2: 1; Jude 4); their motive was covetousness (Jude 11; 2 Pet. 2: 3, 15); in both references the heretics despised authority, and railed at dignitaries (2 Pet. 2: 10; Jude 8); both writers call attention to the fact that they employed swelling words of vanity (2 Pet. 2: 18; Jude 16); they are described in both Epistles as ignorant, being influenced by neither reason nor the gospel, but acting like brutes (2 Pet. 2: 12; Jude 10); they are likened to Baalam (2 Pet. 2: 5; Jude 11); and to "springs without water," and "clouds carried along by winds" (2 Pet. 2: 17; Jude 12).

378　　　　　　　　　INTRODUCTION

From the foregoing instances, and numerous others which might be offered, it seems certain that either Jude or Peter was familiar with, and followed, in some detail, the work of the other, though which it is not possible to pronounce with certainty. Again we would emphasize that it is of little consequence; both are divine productions, both dealt with similar conditions; and it was, therefore, entirely legitimate to follow the same pattern and plan and utilize the same arguments. If the apostles Peter, John and Paul could cite Old Testament prophecy in support of their inspired utterances, what objection could be raised to a New Testament writer citing a prior production for the same reason?

AN ANALYSIS OF THE EPISTLE

1. Introduction. (Verses 1-4.)
   1. Salutation. (Verses 1, 2.)
   2. Purpose of the Epistle. (Verse 3.)
   3. Immediate occasion of the Epistle. (Verse 4.)
2. WARNINGS. (Verses 5-15.)
   1. Three examples of punishment from the Old Testament, as evidence of the fact that the heretics of which he warned would not escape the vengeance of God.
      (a) The unfaithful Israelites in the wilderness. (5, 8.)
      (b) The angels which sinned. (6, 9.)
      (c) The cities of the plain. (Verses 7, 10.)
   2. Three instances of individual wickedness. (Verse 11.)
      (a) Cain, an example of disobedience.
      (b) Baalam, an example of greed.
      (c) Korah, an example of railing.
   3. An analysis of the wicked men against whom he warned, with three tokens by which their condemnation would be manifested. (Verses 12-19.)
      (a) An illustration from nature. (Verses 12, 13.)
      (b) Recognized from identity of conduct with those about whom Enoch wrote. (Verses 14, 15.)
      (c) By their ungodly language, and their evil thoughts. (Verse 16.)

(d) By fulfilling the prophecy of the Apostles. (Verses 17, 18.)
(e) By their unfaithful conduct. (Verse 19.)

3. EXHORTATIONS. (Verses 20-25.)
  1. As to themselves. (Verses 20, 21.) They were to be
    (a) Firm in faith. (Verse 20.)
    (b) Stedfast in love. (Verse 21a.)
    (c) Confident in hope. (Verse 21b.)
  2. With reference to the wicked among them. (Verses 22, 23), they were to treat some of them
    (a) With gentle measures. (Verse 22.)
    (b) Others with sternness and vigor. (Verse 23a.)
    (c) But all with abhorrence of their sins. (Verse 23b.)
  3. With reference to God, all were to thank him for
    (a) His assistance in preserving them. (Verse 24a.)
    (b) His grace in saving them. (Verse 24b.)
    (c) His wisdom in keeping them. (Verse 25.)

A COMMENTARY ON THE EPISTLE OF JUDE

SECTION ONE

INTRODUCTION
(1-4)

SALUTATION
(1, 2)

1 ¹Jude, a ²servant of Jesus Christ, and brother of ³James, ⁴to them that

---
¹Gr. *Judas.*
²Gr. *bondservant.*
³Or, *Jacob*
⁴Or, *to them that are beloved in God the Father, and kept for Jesus Christ,* being called

---

1 Jude, a servant of Jesus Christ, and brother of James.— The author of the Epistle affirms three things of himself in the first sentence of the opening paragraph of the Epistle, (1) his name was "Jude"; (2) he was a servant of Jesus Christ, and (3) a brother of "James." For a detailed discussion of the reasons which prompt to the view that this individual so designated was a son of Mary and Joseph, and therefore, a brother in the flesh of our Lord, see under "Author of the Epistle," in the introduction.

The name *Jude,* the literal meaning of which is *renowned,* was a common one among the Jews of the first century. There are at least nine persons so designated in the New Testament. (Luke 3: 33; 3: 26; 3: 30; Matt. 10: 3; 13: 55; 10: 4; Acts 15: 22; 9: 11; 5: 37.) Two of the apostles bore the name Jude or Judas (the English Revised Version has the spelling Judas in this verse), these being the apostle designated in John 14: 22; and Iscariot who betrayed the Lord.

Notwithstanding the fact that this writer was a brother of the Lord, he makes no mention thereof in the Epistle, being content merely to style himself "a servant" of "Jesus Christ." Numerous reasons may be assigned why he chose to do this. (1) That which he wrote was *true* and should be accepted on its own merits, and not because of the relationship which the author sustained to the

are called, beloved in God the Father, and kept for Jesus Christ: 2 Mercy unto you and peace and love be multiplied.

Lord. (2) Considerations of humility prompted him to omit any reference to such relationship. (3) Such a reference might have supplied an occasion for envy or jealousy on the part of others. (3) The Lord had taught that those who did his will were possessed of greater distinction than any fleshly relationship might have afforded. (Matt. 12: 46-50.)

The word "servant" is translated from a word *(doulos),* which literally signifies a slave (cf. the margin of the ASV), though with this difference: *doulos* designates one who gladly surrenders his will to another, a disposition not always characteristic of literal slaves, but eminently true of all who resign their wills to that of the Lord. The service is absolute and unrestrained, but willing, and rendered from motives of love, and gratitude and joy. The word appears in the introductions to the Epistles of Romans, Philippians, Titus, James and 2 Peter.

James, identified as "a brother" of the author, was himself author of the New Testament book which bears his name, and who, too, omitted any reference to the relation which he likewise bore to the Lord. Neither of these faithful disciples suffered the inclinations of the flesh to lead them to a boastful announcement of their position, and both with becoming humility laid stress on the fact that they were simply servants. (Cf. James 1: 1.) To be a *bond-servant* of the Lord is truly to occupy the most enviable position possible to man today. See, at length on the identity of Jude and James, the introduction to the Epistle.

To them that are called, beloved in God the Father, and kept for Jesus Christ:—The address is to them that are *called,* and the "called" are identified as (a) beloved in God the Father; and (b) kept for Jesus Christ. All saints are called in to the work which is theirs to do (2 Thess. 2: 14); the *call* is extended through the gospel, and is world-wide and all-inclusive in its nature (Mark 16: 15, 16). Many are called, but few chosen, because all who are called do not heed and hearken and obey.

The "called" are "beloved of God the Father," this indeed being the occasion of their calling. "But God commendeth his own love toward us, in that, while we are yet sinners, Christ died for us." (Rom. 5: 8, see, also, John 3: 16.) Those thus called (through the gospel) are "kept" (preserved) for Jesus Christ, i.e., for his honor and glory. That this keeping is not unconditional in its nature, and hence does not suggest the impossibility of falling away from the grace of God and the divine favor, see Jude 21, where the admonition is to "keep yourselves in the love of God, looking for the mercy of our Lord Jesus Christ unto eternal life." Compare also the remarks on 1 Pet. 1: 4. Though the divine guardianship is here marvelously set forth, there is the corresponding thought of faithfulness and fidelity. Though we are "kept" for Jesus Christ, we must "keep" ourselves (the same Greek verb is employed) in his love. It is paradoxical but eminently true that while we must depend wholly on God for our salvation, we cannot be saved without doing our part. Paul embraced both ideas when he said, "Work out your own salvation . . . for it is God who worketh in you. . . ." (Phil. 2: 12)

2 Mercy unto you and peace and love be multiplied.—With the substitution of "mercy" for "grace" this salutation corresponds with that which occurs in the outset of both of the Epistles of Peter. Mercy, peace and love are associated here, because these graces sum up the blessings most needful for Jude's readers, and for all of us today. All of these proceeded from God, and these Jude desired to be multiplied (abound) in the lives of those to whom he wrote. Compare the salutations occurring in the Epistles of Peter (1 Pet. 1: 2 and 2 Pet. 1: 2), and see the notes there.

OCCASION FOR WRITING THE EPISTLE
(3, 4)

3 Beloved, while I was giving all diligence to write unto you of our com-

3 Beloved, while I was giving all diligence to write unto you of our common salvation, I was constrained to write unto you exhorting you to contend earnestly for the faith which was once for all delivered unto the saints.—The word "beloved," with which the verse begins, is an indication of the warmth of feeling which characterized the writer toward those primarily addressed. It occurs often in the apostolic writings (Rom. 1: 7; 2 Cor. 7: 1; Phil. 2: 12, etc.), being used by Paul, Peter, John and

mon salvation, I was constrained to write unto you exhorting you to contend

Jude. The author had, for some time, been contemplating a treatise, perhaps had already begun composition thereof. The theme on which he proposed to write was "the common salvation." While meditating thereon, information suddenly came to him that those to whom he proposed to write were being threatened by special dangers occasioning his immediate attention. He accordingly suspended his proposed treatise and wrote without delay to exhort his brethren "to contend earnestly for the faith which was once for all delivered to the saints."

That which prompted a change in the writer's plans was news that false teachers had appeared among the saints, seeking to lead them astray. These teachers are particularly described later in the Epistle, and their doctrines revealed. His object was, therefore, to stir his readers to immediate resistance; to impel them to reject these teachers and repudiate their teaching, and to defend with all their might the faith which had been delivered them. A number of vitally important considerations appear in this passage, and some especially relevant to our time.

(1) Jude was not indifferent to the interests of these who were his beloved brethren. (2) He gave "diligence" (exercised himself) immediately in their behalf. (3) As important as the original theme was—the common salvation—the appearance of false teachers made it obligatory that it should for the time be suspended, and warnings and exhortations issued. (4) The saints were admonished to contend earnestly for the faith which had been delivered. (5) We must never be indifferent to, or unmindful of, those who would lead the faithful away from the truth. False teachers evermore constitute a threat to the peace and security of the saints, and must be resisted and refuted. The scriptures, a complete and infallible deposit of truth, are available and constitute an effective means for such confutation.

The "common salvation" about which the author had intended to write is so styled because it is available to all and denied to none who comply with the conditions thereof. Jew and Gentile, bond and free, male and female are entitled to its blessed provisions, and share in its manifold benefits. In Titus 1:4, reference is made to

earnestly for the faith which was once for all delivered unto the saints. 4
the common faith where, as here, emphasis is given to the fact that all Christians are participants as distinct from the alleged knowledge claimed by false teachers as belonging to only a few.

To "contend earnestly" *(epagonizesthai)*, is literally, to wrestle, and as here figuratively used, denotes the extreme efforts which are to characterize the faithful in their defense of the truth, however formidable and numerous its enemies may be. These efforts are, it is surely unnecessary to add, of a moral and persuasive nature only; all force of a physical nature being expressly forbidden the faithful. When Peter sought to defend the Lord with a sword he was rebuked for his pains; and in bidding him sheathe it, he forevermore made it clear that his followers are not to fight with carnal weapons in his behalf. But, if men are forbidden to fight in *his* defense, *in whose defense may they properly fight?* "Jesus answered, My kingdom is not of this world: if my kingdom were of this world, then would my servants fight, that I should not be delivered to the Jews: but now is my kingdom not from hence." (John 18: 36.)

The "faith" for which Jude's readers were thus earnestly to contend, put objectively here for the gospel, is the sum of all that which Christians are to believe and obey. Cf. Acts 6: 7, where it is said that "a great company of the priests were obedient to the faith," and Gal. 1: 23, where Paul is affirmed to have preached "the faith of which he once made havoc." Faith, a *part* is thus put for the *whole,* because belief is basic to the system of Christianity, the proper exercise of which determines the salvation of those who embrace it.

This faith has *once for all* (hapax) not simply formerly as the King James Version implies, but for all time been delivered to the saints. The meaning is that the truth is delivered for all time; it is a permanent deposit, it will never be superseded, amended or modified. As it now stands it is a perfect, adequate, complete and inviolable deposit of truth, providing the means with which to confute the gainsayer, and resist the advocate of false doctrine. This deposit of truth was infallibly delivered, through the inspiration of the Holy Spirit (Gal. 1: 11; 2 Pet. 1: 21), and no part of it is superfluous or unnecessary. "Every scripture inspired of God is

For there are certain men crept in privily, *even* they who were of old ⁵written of beforehand unto this condemnation, ungodly men, turning the

---
⁵Or, *set forth*

also profitable for teaching, for reproof, for correction, for instruction which is in righteousness: that the man of God may be complete, furnished completely unto every good work." (2 Tim. 3: 16, 17.)

4 **For there are certain men crept in privily, even they who were of old written of beforehand unto this condemnation,—** The occasion for the concern which Jude felt, and the immediate reason why he wrote the Epistle is here revealed: false teachers had appeared among the saints; they had slipped in unawares, and were thus all the more dangerous because they were unrecognized. These teachers are described as "certain men," but not otherwise identified; they had "crept in privily," i.e., they had entered, as it were, by a side door *(pareisedusan)* and without revealing their true motive of seducing the saints. Peter, in describing these same teachers, predicted that they would "bring in destructive heresies, denying even the Master that bought them, bringing upon themselves swift destruction. And many shall follow their lascivious doings, by reason of whom the way of truth shall be evil spoken of." (2 Pet. 2: 1, 2.)

The appearance of these men was not unanticipated; it had been predicted—written beforehand—that they would appear to plague the church, and their condemnation had already been announced. These words, often cited by Calvinists in their efforts to defend the doctrine of reprobation by arbitrary decree, fall far short of the effort because in them there is nothing to justify the conclusion that this condemnation was unconditional, or, that it was announced in eternity, or, that it was determined without regard to the moral character of those thus condemned. The word "ordained," appearing in the King James Version, has properly given way to the more accurate rendering, "written of beforehand," literally, placarded or set forth *(progegrammenoi)*, compare the word *programmed;* and this was from of "old" *(palai)*, a word never used of an eternal decree, but always of something occurring in time. All that may properly be deduced from this statement is that from ancient times condemnation had been declared upon all who did as these men were doing, i.e., leading the saints astray. The divine

grace of our God into lasciviousness, and denying our ⁶only Master and Lord, Jesus Christ.

⁶Or, *the only Master, and our Lord Jesus Christ*

law, existing from the beginning, condemned these men and all others who violated it, and no more than this was intended by the inspired writer. Who the writer, or writers, was who made this prediction is not stated. Obviously, the period must be projected into the Old Testament when this condemnation was placarded; but to what period of Old Testament prophecy, or to what prophetic writer of that period, does not appear. The fact that Enoch is mentioned and his prophecy cited lends support to the view that it was the writer's intention to attribute to him this announcement. (Cf. verse 14.) The kind of men these were the writer next describes.

Ungodly men, turning the grace of our God into lasciviousness, and denying our only Master and Lord, Jesus Christ. —They were, in character, ungodly *(asebeis)*; they were utterly without piety or reverence, boldly blasphemous of anything religious. Possessed of this character, they did not hesitate to turn the grace of God into lasciviousness, and to deny the only Master and Lord, Jesus Christ. The "grace" of God is salvation (Eph. 2: 8, 9), vouchsafed to man through the gospel; this gospel, these men perverted by interpreting it as actually allowing or supporting the practice of lasciviousness, gross fleshly indulgence. The words of the writer here are similar to those in 2 Pet. 2: 18, 19, where the apostle there described these teachers as pretending to magnify the grace of God on the basis of Christian liberty but in reality were living base and licentious lives in positive disobedience to the teaching of all the inspired writers. See the comments there, and cf. 1 Cor. 6: 9-18; 1 John 3: 7-10. Such teaching and practice were a denial of Jesus Christ the Lord, both in doctrine and life. The doctrine, of making Christian liberty an excuse for ungodly living, is a pernicious and persistent one, and has been advocated often since the apostolic age. To all who affect such John solemnly declares, "He that saith, I know him, and keepeth not his commandments, is a liar, and the truth is not in him." (1 John 2: 4.) And Paul inquired, "Shall we continue in sin that grace may abound?" a query which he immediately answered, "God forbid." (Rom. 6: 1.)

SECTION TWO

EXAMPLES OF CONDEMNATION
(5-7)

5 Now I desire to put you in remembrance, though ye know all things once for all, that ⁷the Lord, having saved a people out of the land of Egypt,

⁷Many very ancient authorities read *Jesus*.

5 Now I desire to put you in remembrance, though ye know all things once for all, that the Lord, having saved a people out of the land of Egypt, afterward destroyed them that believed not.—Three examples of the divine vengeance upon evildoers are offered by the sacred writer to support his premise that those who disobey shall receive the just recompense of reward. The first of these involved matters perfectly familiar to those to whom he wrote, events looming large on the historical horizon of the Israelite people. In proof of the fact that punishment of the wicked is certain and sure, Jude directed attention to the condemnation visited on the people of Israel after they had been providently delivered from the hand of Pharaoh in Egypt. The reference here parallels Paul's description of the judgment executed upon those people in 1 Cor. 10: 1-11. Israel was delivered and preserved in the wilderness (1 Cor. 10: 1-4), yet, despite their many evidences of God's goodness and graciousness to them, rebelled, and in their grievous sin against him were severely punished. See the same theme alluded to in more detail in Psalm 68. The sins of the people of Israel during this period were exceedingly numerous and grave. Their constant and determined murmuring; their faithlessness in the promises of Jehovah; their unwillingness to go into the land of Canaan; the idolatry of the golden calf; their gross fleshly corruption, are matters duly recorded in great detail by the sacred historian. All of this is summed up under the basic sin of unbelief. The application intended by Jude is that regardless of how secretly men may work, God will eventually ferret them out and deliver them over to the condemnation they deserve. Israel, a mighty nation, perhaps two millions strong, was saved out of Egypt and then the majority of its people, because of unfaithfulness, were destroyed. Though they engaged in the formalities of religion and complied in outward fashion with the ritualism required, they were unwilling to adopt

⁸afterward destroyed them that believed not. 6 And angels that kept not their own principality, but left their proper habitation, he hath kept in everlasting bonds under darkness unto the judgment of the great day. 7 Even as Sodom

⁸Gr. *the second time.*

the principles of righteousness into their hearts and lives. They were opposed to the idea of God ruling the heart, the life, and the nation and they died under the divine and irresistible judgment of God. The implication is that if half a million men were executed for violation of God's law through their disobedience, then these false teachers who were teaching, in principle, that for which these multitudes suffered death, would not escape!

6 **And angels that kept not their own principality, but left their proper habitation, he hath kept in everlasting bonds under darkness unto the judgment of the great day.**—The second instance which the author offers to prove his thesis that the punishment of the wicked is inevitable, is that of the angels who sinned. See at length on this a similar reference in 2 Pet. 2: 4, and the notes there. Angels are created beings. These to whom Jude alludes "kept not their own principality, but left their proper habitation." "Principality" *(arche)* is a term descriptive of office or position; this, these angels abandoned though for what reason or reasons, the writer does not say. There is much speculation on this theme, and Isa. 14: 12-15 is often cited in this connection, a passage obviously primarily applicable to Babylon, but by many believed to have a secondary application to the fall of Satan. As a result of their abandonment of their proper position, these wicked angels are "kept in everlasting bonds under darkness unto the judgment of the great day." The great day alluded to here is the judgment day described in Matt. 25: 41. These wicked angels will suffer punishment, along with evil men, and in everlasting bonds under darkness they await the judgment day. The writer's meaning is, If the angels which sinned do not escape the vengeance of God, so neither will the false teachers referred to in verse 4.

7 **Even as Sodom and Gomorrah, and the cities about them, having in like manner with these given themselves over to fornication and gone after strange flesh, are set forth as an example, suffering the punishment of eternal fire.**—The third instance of evildoers being summarily punished which Jude cites

and Gomorrah, and the cities about them, having in like manner with these given themselves over to fornication and gone after strange flesh, are set

is that of Sodom and Gomorrah "and the cities about them." The nature of the horrible and unspeakable sin of which these cities were guilty and the terrible punishment visited upon them because of it is set out in detail in Genesis 19. The "cities about them," i.e., about Sodom and Gomorrah, were Admah and Zeboim. Zoar, a fifth city in the same general vicinity, was spared from the judgment visited upon the others through the intercession of Lot in order that he might have a place to which to flee. (Gen. 19: 22.) Sodom and Gomorrah, Admah and Zeboim, and the desolation which came upon them for their sin, is alluded to by Moses in Deut. 29: 23.

A fanciful theory, and with many adherents today, is that the antecedent of "these" in this verse is the "angels" of verse 6, and that Jude here describes the sin of the angels as fornication and the lust for "strange flesh." In support of this view, reference is made to Gen. 6: 4, where the phrase "sons of God" is interpreted to mean "angels of God," and the conclusion is thus drawn that the Nephilim, there described as "mighty men that were of old, men of renown," resulted from co-habitation between angels and earthly women! In *some* manuscripts of the Septuagint Version, a translation of the Old Testament from Hebrew into Greek, begun about the third century before the Christian era, instead of the reading, "sons of God," "angels of God" appears. Moreover, it is alleged that the pronoun *toutois* (these) is masculine gender, whereas Sodom and Gomorrah are neuter, and thus do not agree; and since a pronoun must agree with its antecedent in number, the reference is not to these cities but to the angels.

In refutation of this interpretation, the following considerations should be noted: (1) The word "angels" in the Septuagint manuscripts alluded to is not a translation of the original Hebrew text, but an unwarranted interpretation injected from Alexandrian influences. (2) *Toutois,* dative plural of *toutos,* has the same form in both masculine and neuter gender; hence, the objection based on the gender of the pronoun fails. (3) In determining the antece-

forth as an example, suffering the punishment of eternal fire.

⁹Or, *as an example of eternal fire, suffering punishment*

dent of a pronoun, where two or more are grammatically possible, the nearer one is to be selected. (4) *Toutois* (these) refers to that which is nearer in the context. The translators, had they intended to refer to a more distant antecedent, would have supplied *those* instead. (5) The sin which the angels committed was in leaving their proper habitation and in not keeping their principality. There is nothing said in the reference to their sin of any sexual deviation or co-habitation of women by them. (6) The word "Nephilim" occurs in Num. 13: 33, where the reference is obviously to the offspring of men, and not angels. (7) "The Nephilim" were not angelic beings of monstrous prodigies resulting from a crossing of species, but gigantic human beings, men of great renown physically. (8) It is an immutable and inviolable law of reproduction that everything brings forth *after its own kind.* This law is announced and affirmed repeatedly in the book of Genesis. (Gen. 1: 11, 12, 21, 24, etc.) The Lord himself affirmed that angels are sexless beings and never marry. (Luke 20: 35.) It follows, therefore, that any interpretation of Jude 6, which makes the sin of the angels the same as that which characterized the cities of the plain—fornication and unnatural sexual indulgence—is fanciful, erroneous, and absurd. See 2 Pet. 2: 4, and the comments there.

These cities, in the condemnation which befell them, serve as examples of what happens to those who disobey God. The verb "set forth" *(prokeintai)* means to lie exposed, as a corpse laid out for burial. The word example *(deigma),* from a word occurring only here in the New Testament, means to exhibit or show, and as used here to indicate the demonstration which the cities of the plain afford to the vengeance inevitable to those in disobedience. They suffered the punishment of "eternal fire," not that the fire which consumed them is eternal, but that their punishment was so utter and so permanent that the nearest approach to it will be seen in the destruction which shall be characteristic of those who suffer *the eternal fire.* Their destruction thus stands as a symbol of that which shall eventually be the lot of all ungodly men.

WICKED AND GOOD CONTRASTED
(8-10)

8 Yet in like manner these also in their dreamings defile the flesh, and set at nought dominion, and rail at [10]dignities. But Michael the archangel, when contending with the devil he disputed about the body of Moses, durst not bring against him a railing judgment, but said, The Lord rebuke thee. 10

---

[10]Gr. *glories.*

---

8 Yet in like manner these also in their dreamings defile the flesh, and set at nought dominion, and rail at dignities.— Three striking illustrations of the certainty of divine punishment to be inflicted upon those who indulge in gross sin, including Jews, Gentiles, and angels, were presented in the foregoing section. Here, the writer proceeds to apply these examples to the ungodly of his own day; to demonstrate that the conduct of these men was comparable to that of those alluded to in the illustrations presented; and to call attention to the fact that they were, by their conduct, provoking Jehovah to deal with them in similar fashion.

"Yet in like manner" identifies the conduct of these to whom the writer alludes with those of Sodom and Gomorrah, and the other cities of the plain. "In their dreamings" they (1) defile the flesh, (2) set at naught dominion, and (3) rail at dignities. They lived in a dreamy world of impurity; they defiled the flesh by sins unspeakably vile (cf. Rom. 1: 18-32); they exhibited contempt for all authority, whether civil or divine; and they did not hesitate to speak evil of men though they occupied high places. (See the comments on 2 Pet. 2: 10.)

9 But Michael the archangel, when contending with the devil he disputed about the body of Moses, durst not bring against him a railing judgment, but said, The Lord rebuke thee.—Cf. 2 Pet. 2: 2. Michael is first mentioned, in the scriptures, in Dan. 10: 13, and other references to him are in Dan. 10: 21; 12: 1; and Rev. 12: 7. He appears to have been a prince or guardian angel of the Jewish people. He was an "archangel," a term meaning chief or captain of the angels. In Rev. 12: 7-9, he is described as the leader of unfallen angels who war with and conquer Satan and his angels. It is affirmed of Michael in this passage that (1) he contended with the devil; (2) the occasion of this contention was with reference to the body of Moses; (3) in the disputation which arose between Michael and the devil on this matter, he refrained from a railing judgment against Satan, (4) being content merely to say, "The Lord rebuke thee."

When this occurred, the events prompting it, and the effects which followed do not appear either here or elsewhere in the sacred writings. It is, admittedly, the most difficult statement in the entire Epistle, and has given rise to much speculation. Merely to state the views which have been expressed regarding it would require a treatment of the subject far beyond the limits of this commentary. Jewish tradition and Rabbinic literature abound with allusions to such an advent, but such sources are wholly unreliable in reconstructing the facts in the case.

Jude, an inspired writer, affirmed that the event occurred. It is sufficient for us simply to believe it; it is surely unnecessary for us to vindicate Jude's veracity by proving that the facts related occurred and are testified to by other writers. The lesson which the author desired to be drawn from his remarks is obvious. The ungodly characters, about whom he was warning his readers, spoke of angelic dignities in a fashion which even an archangel did not dare adopt in speaking to the devil. The argument is an *a fortiori* one. The meaning is, If one of the highest beings in the angelic world restrained himself from the use of railing judgment against the devil, how much more unjustified was it for these false teachers to disregard the dignity of those against whom they spoke.

10 But these rail at whatsoever things they know not: and what they understand naturally, like the creatures without reason, in these things are they destroyed.—"But these," i.e., the false teachers under consideration, in contrast with the conduct of Michael, do not hesitate to "rail" (speak evil) of matters about which they know nothing, matters wholly outside their sphere of spiritual vision, their only knowledge being their passions, the instinct and impulses which men share with the animal creation. Paul alluded to a similar type of individual whom he described as "dwelling in the things which he hath seen, vainly puffed up by his fleshly mind." (Col. 2: 18.) Those who scorn the higher things of the Spirit and surrender themselves to the appetites of the flesh descend to the level of beasts and forfeit their spiritual standing and their eternal destiny. "In these things," i.e., in the things of the flesh, "are they destroyed." That in which they find the greatest pleasure will, at length, become the occasion of their destruction. Cf. 2 Pet. 2: 12, and the comments there. Though these men boasted of their superior knowledge, and alleged it as the ground on which they defended their licentious and lascivious practices, they were actually, and in reality, on the level of brute beasts in their conduct. Their desires became the rule of their lives, and the flesh the source of their gratification. They were wicked, ungodly men, and their destiny determined and sure. Like Cain, Balaam, and Korah, examples offered in the next section, their error was coupled with disaster and would not long delay its effects.

CONDEMNATION OF EVILDOERS
(11-13)

[11]destroyed. 11 Woe unto them! for they went in the way of Cain, and [12]ran riotously in the error of Balaam for hire, and perished in the gainsay-

[11]Or, *corrupted* Comp. 2 Pet. 2. 12 marg.
[12]Or, *cast themselves away through*

---

11 Woe unto them! for they went in the way of Cain, and ran riotously in the error of Balaam for hire, and perished in the gainsaying of Korah.—The substantive is wanting in the clause "woe unto them," and it is possible to understand it as either in the indicative or optative mood. If the latter, it is a curse, i.e., "Woe *be* unto them"; if the former, a simple statement of the misery that will inevitably descend. . . . "Woe unto them." It is in this sense that the word "woe" *(ouai)* occurs in Matt. 24: 19, and which sense we assign it here.

Three well-known illustrations from Old Testament history are adduced by the writer to prove his thesis that disobedience leads to disaster, Cain, Balaam, and Korah. Cain is cited because he was regarded as one of the most outstanding examples of Old Testament characters who became wicked, one who defied the simplest and most obvious law of God; and who, in addition, followed his own natural instinct rather than the will of the Lord in determining the nature of his offering; Balaam is included because he de-

ing of Korah. 12 These are they who are [13]hidden rocks in your love-feasts

[13]Or, *spots*

graded the prophetic gift for sordid gain; and Korah, because he rebelled against divine authority. (See Gen. 4: 7; Num. 22: 5-7; Rev. 2: 14; 2 Pet. 2: 15; Num. 16: 1-35.) By identifying these false teachers with these Old Testament characters, Jude demonstrated that they were guilty, in principle at least, of murder, covetousness, rebellion, and pride. See the comments of 2 Pet. 2: 15.

The "way of Cain" was the way of disobedience, hate, murder, and ruin; the "error of Balaam" was in seeking to seduce Israel for personal gain; and the "gainsaying of Korah" was rebellion against divinely constituted authority. The evil inherent in these men exhibited itself in the lives of the false teachers threatening the peace and harmony of the church and exists, alas, in some measure today.

12 **These are they who are hidden rocks in your love-feasts when they feast with you,**—With a wealth of imagery and in vivid detail here and in the verse to follow Jude describes those who threatened the peace and purity of the church and against whom he wrote. They are described as "hidden rocks" in the love feasts in which the saints participated. Like sunken reefs which could not be seen on the surface of the water, but which would inevitably wreck any ship which struck them, so these men gave no warning of the threat which they posed. The "love-feasts" were meals common to the apostolic age at which the saints met from social, charitable, and humanitarian reasons. They appear to have had their origin in the practice of wealthier members of the congregation providing food for the poorer ones, and eating with them, in token of their brotherliness. These feasts are not to be identified in any way with the Lord's supper; indeed, when this supper was corrupted into such a meal, it occasioned a sharp rebuke from Paul. (1 Cor. 11: 17-34.) But that saints were accustomed to meet together for common meals follows from this reference to such by Jude, from a similar reference in 2 Pet. 2: 13, and from numerous statements from ecclesiastical writers in the early centuries of the Christian era. They were suspended by the fourth century because men of the type of whom Jude wrote turned them into ungodly revels.

when they feast with you, shepherds that without fear feed themselves; clouds without water, carried along by winds, autumn trees without fruit,

---

Shepherds that without fear feed themselves;—Instead of submitting themselves to the true shepherds of the flock—the elders—they affected to be shepherds themselves, their true motive being to feed themselves! This statement is similar in content to that occurring in Ezek. 34: 2: "Woe unto the shepherds of Israel that do feed themselves! should not the shepherds feed the sheep?" "Yea, the dogs are greedy, they can never have enough; and these are shepherds that cannot understand: they have all turned to their own way, each one to his gain, from every quarter." (Isa. 56: 11.)

Clouds without water, carried along by winds;—Note a similar statement in 2 Pet. 2: 17, "springs without water, and mists driven by a storm." These false teachers were like clouds which offer promises of refreshing showers, but are carried along (borne past, *parapheromenai*) and leave no rain. In a land of little rainfall such as Palestine, indeed, in much of the East, the appearance of clouds offering refreshing rain is eagerly watched by the farmer, but when the cloud is borne along by the wind leaving no moisture hope yields to despair. These false teachers, like clouds devoid of water, were pretentious, boastful, promising. Yet, in their wake they left only disappointment. To an Oriental, it would not be possible to suggest a more expressive and vivid figure than that which here appears. Cf. Prov. 25: 14: "As clouds and wind without rain, so is he that boasteth himself of his gifts falsely."

Autumn trees without fruit, twice dead, plucked up by the roots;—"Autumn" here is from *phthinoporon,* a word meaning, literally, late autumn, hence, trees on which there is no fruit at the season when it is most expected. Jude may have recalled here the parable of the barren fig tree, which teaches the same lesson of legitimate expectation unfulfilled. The lesson, however, is carried further here. The tree was not only barren; it was twice dead, and in addition, plucked up by the roots. There was, therefore, no possible chance for fruit from such a source! Such was the character of the false teachers about whom Jude wrote.

twice dead, plucked up by the roots; 13 wild waves of the sea, foaming out their own [14]shame; wandering stars, for whom the blackness of darkness

[14]Gr. *shames.*

---

13 Wild waves of the sea, foaming out their own shame; wandering stars, for whom the blackness of darkness hath been reserved for ever.—The first two figures which Jude used, hidden rocks and clouds, referred to the false pretensions of the men about whom he warned and their disaster to which their teaching and conduct led. The third, that of the fruit tree twice dead, described their wretched condition of complete barrenness. The two which this verse contains, foaming waves of the sea, and wandering stars, suggest their lawlessness and shamelessness and their ultimate fate. The figure of the foaming sea waves as illustrative of the wicked is used by the prophet Isaiah: "But the wicked are like the troubled sea; for it cannot rest, and its waters cast up mire and dirt." (Isa. 57: 20.) The reference is obviously to the flotsam and jetsam borne on the crest of the waves and cast up from time to time on the beach. These men with their "great swelling words of vanity" (2 Pet. 2: 18) were like the great waves that break in foam and leave the beach littered with tangled and worthless refuse. Or, like wandering stars without direction or orbit, they shine for a while and then pass into utter darkness. For them the blackness of darkness has been reserved forever and ever. Religious teachers are often likened to stars in the sacred writings. (Rev. 1: 16; 2: 1.)

There is striking resemblance between this entire section and that which occurs in 2 Pet. 2: 1-22. The notes should be consulted there in connection with the comments which are made here.

THE PROPHECY OF ENOCH
(14-16)

hath been reserved for ever. 14 And to these also Enoch, the seventh from Adam, prophesied, saying, Behold, the Lord came with [15]ten thousands of

[15]Gr. *his holy myriads.*

---

14 And to these also Enoch, the seventh from Adam, prophesied, saying,—The patriarch Enoch was one of the most illustrious of the Old Testament saints, a man about which little is

his holy ones, 15 to execute judgment upon all, and to convict all the un-

said in the sacred writings, but that of the most complimentary nature. Of him Moses wrote: "And Enoch lived sixty and five years, and begat Methuselah: and Enoch walked with God after he begat Methuselah three hundred years, and begat sons and daughters: and all the days of Enoch were three hundred and sixty and five years: and Enoch walked with God: and he was not; for God took him." The implication here is that Enoch began to walk with God on the occasion of the birth of his son, Methuselah, an indication of the fact that he recognized especially his responsibility to Jehovah after that a son was given him. In recounting the exploits of the faithful, the Hebrew writer wrote: "By faith Enoch was translated that he should not see death; and he was not found, because God translated him: for he hath had witness borne to him that before his translation he had been well pleasing to God." (Gen. 5: 21-24; Heb. 11: 5.)

Though Moses does not mention the fact that Enoch was a prophet, his faithfulness and fidelity, his devotion to truth, and his sense of responsibility to Jehovah to which the lawgiver testifies suggest that he was such a character as would be used by the Lord for such purposes. He was the "seventh from Adam," being seventh in the line of descent from the first man, the details of which appear in Gen. 5: 3-32. The line, as there given, runs: Adam, Seth, Enos, Cainan, Mahaleel, Jared, Enoch, Methuselah, Lamech, and Noah.

To such men as these false teachers against whom Jude was writing, Enoch uttered the prophecy embraced in Jude 14, 15. It was not Jude's intention to convey the idea that Enoch wrote specially or primarily to these; the meaning is that the prophecy which that patriarch delivered was such as might properly be applied to such characters as these about whom Jude was writing.

From what source did Jude obtain the prophecy of Enoch to which he refers? It is sufficient for our purpose merely to answer, *from inspiration,* whether directly or from traditional sources, is of little consequence. Authenticated by the approval of the Holy Spirit under whose inspiration Jude wrote, it matters little what the method was by which it was brought to his attention. It is al-

godly of all their works of ungodliness which they have ungodly wrought, and of all the hard things which ungodly sinners have spoken against him.

leged by many scholars that this prophecy which Jude cites was taken from an apocryphal book entitled "Book of Enoch," copies of which are in existence to this day, and containing the following prophecy: "Behold he comes with ten thousands of his saints, to execute judgment upon them, and to destroy the wicked, and to strive (at law) with all the carnal for everything which the sinful and ungodly have done and committed against him." This "book of Enoch" was discovered shortly before the Revolutionary War —about 1773—in a copy of the Ethiopic Bible, and translated into English in 1821. The book cannot be certainly traced back of the third century, and there is no reliable evidence when it was written. An examination of it reveals that it was written by a Jew; that its author subscribed to the idea of a judgment such as that taught in the New Testament; and that it was influenced by New Testament conceptions. Numerous matters in it suggest a post-apostolic origin. There are sharp variations between the statement allegedly cited by Jude and the actual statement as it appears in Jude. There is more reason for supposing that the book of Jude is older than this so-called "Book of Enoch," and that the author quoted from Jude rather than Jude from him! In the same fashion that Peter knew that Noah was a preacher, that Lot was vexed in Sodom, and that Paul knew the names of the Egyptian magicians; Jude learned of Enoch's prophecy—by inspiration.

Behold, the Lord came with ten thousands of his holy ones, —The prophecy of Enoch was one about judgment, a judgment in which the Lord would come with "ten thousands" (literally, *his holy myriads*, marginal reading) of his holy ones. The reference here is to the angels who are to accompany the Lord on his mission of judgment, and who are mentioned in connection with that event in Matt. 25: "But when the Son of man shall come in his glory, *and all the angels with him*, then shall he sit on the throne of his glory. . . ." (Verse 31.) Compare Deut. 33: 2, 3; Zech. 14: 5.

15 **To execute judgment upon all, and to convict all the ungodly of all their works of ungodliness which they have ungodly wrought, and of all the hard things which ungodly**

16 These are murmurers, complainers, walking after their lusts (and their mouth speaketh great swelling *words*), showing respect of persons for the sake of advantage.

---

sinners have spoken against him.—In the judgment to come Enoch prophesied that the ungodly would be convicted of their evil works and of the hard things which they had spoken. In the Greek text, the words "ungodly sinners" appear at the end of the text and give emphasis to that which the writer sought to convey. The Lord is coming to execute judgment upon all, to convict the ungodly of their evil works, to expose them for the harsh and ugly things which they have spoken against him—*these ungodly sinners!*

From this prophecy of Enoch we learn that the doctrine of a judgment day, with its corresponding rewards and punishments, was known near the beginning of the race. The disposition to feel that those ancient worthies groped blindly in the mists of superstition and ignorance and were without a knowledge of the true God and his way with man, is thus shown to be wrong. The patriarchs were doubtless possessed of a much more profound grasp of truth than is customary to assign them in our day. That the world was later engulfed in ignorance and superstition and lost the knowledge of Jehovah does not argue that they were never in possession of such. The blindness which later characterized them was due to apostasy and to a repudiation of the truth which they once possessed.

16 **These are murmurers, complainers, walking after their lusts (and their mouth speaketh great swelling words), showing respect of persons for the sake of advantage.**—To Enoch's prophecy and description of the ungodly, Jude supplied additional details of the characteristics of these men of the disposition of which that patriarch wrote. They were murmurers *(goggustai)*, individuals who rebelled at their lot in life, and argued that providence was unkind. Being complainers, they were evermore expressing dissatisfaction with all that which was about them, and perhaps, with even God himself. In "walking after their own lusts," they had given themselves over to a life of dissoluteness, licentiousness, and lasciviousness. They had deliberately chosen the lower life for the higher; they live only for fleshly gratification. In

their efforts to deceive, they resorted to "great swelling words," words bombastic and empty, the design of which was to delude those who were influenced by sound and not sense. See the notes on 2 Pet. 2: 18, 19. Moreover, they "showed respect of persons" and this "for the sake of advantage," the rich, the influential, the prominent, they courted; and this, for their own welfare.

It is not unusual to find those similarly influenced today. Many complain at their lot, murmur against providence, and maintain that God is not good because they fall heir to the ills and difficulties of humanity. Others, through specious reasoning and by means of empty phrases, seek to justify their conduct though it is opposed to the simplest and plainest teaching of the New Testament. Such, God will eventually judge, a judgment impending at least as long ago as Enoch, seventh from Adam.

SECTION THREE

EXHORTATIONS TO FAITHFULNESS
(17-23)

17 But ye, beloved, remember ye the words which have been spoken before by the apostles of our Lord Jesus Christ; 18 that they said to you, In the last time there shall be mockers, walking after ¹their own ungodly lusts.

¹Gr. *their own lusts of ungodlinesses.*

---

17 **But ye, beloved, remember ye the words which have been spoken before by the apostles of our Lord Jesus Christ;**—Here, as also in verse 20, the writer directs an appeal to the saints themselves, in which he recalls for them words which they had heard the apostles speak regarding trials certain to come upon them. See Acts 20: 29; 1 Tim. 4: 1ff.; 2 Tim. 4: 1ff.; 1 John 4: 1ff. By his reference to the apostles in the third person we have corroborative evidence of the view advanced in the Introduction that the writer was not himself an apostle. Had Jude been an apostle, as some affirm, it is reasonable to suppose that he would have adduced his apostolic authority; he would have said here, "Remember ye the words which have been spoken before *by* the apostles of our Lord Jesus Christ." The statement is such as would have been made by one not an apostle. The teaching of the apostles, on the theme referred to, is not introduced as something new; Jude's readers were, in fact, familiar with it; and are here reminded of what they already knew. They were, therefore, acquainted with some of the apostles; they had heard them speak and read their writings, and thus would recognize this warning as one originally delivered by them. The phrase, *hoti elegon humin,* "that they said to you," with which the next verse begins, suggests that the warning to which Jude refers was a spoken one, rather than written.

18 **That they said to you, In the last time there shall be mockers, walking after their own ungodly lusts.**—Cf. 2 Pet. 3: 2, 3, where the words are very much the same. Those who are disposed to hold that Second Peter was written earlier than Jude, and that the writer of our Epistle was dependent on that production for many of its sentences, cite this reference as evidence of the claim. It should be noted, however, that Peter, in the words

19 These are they who make separations, ²sensual, having not the Spirit. 20

²Or, *natural* Or, *animal*

---

which immediately precede the statement, refers the prophecy to an earlier announcement than his own: "This now beloved, the second epistle that I write unto you; and in both of them I stir up your sincere mind by putting you in remembrance; that ye should remember the words which were spoken before by the holy prophets, and the commandment of the Lord and Saviour through your apostles; knowing this first, that in the last days mockers shall come with mockery, walking after their own lusts, and saying, Where is the promise of his coming? for, from the day that the fathers fell asleep, all things continue as they were from the beginning of the creation." (2 Pet. 3: 1-4.) The word translated "mockery" here is the same as that which occurs in 2 Pet. 3: 3, and the reference is much the same, though Jude does not detail, as did Peter, the specific form of mockery referred to—sneers at the delay alleged in the coming of the Lord. For an explanation of the terms used, and the meaning of the writer, see the comments on 2 Pet. 3: 1-4.

19 These are they who make separations, sensual, having not the Spirit.—The word translated "make separations" is a rare one in the sacred writings, and means to cause divisions, parties, factions in the church. It is a compound word, made up of the prepositions *apo,* from; *dia,* through; and the noun *oros,* a section line. As here figuratively used, it designates one who draws a line through the church and sets one part over against another. It is a vivid and impressive picture of the actions of church dividers, factionists, troublers of the people of God. Some ancient versions render the phrase, "they who make separations," as "these are makers of sects"; and Luther translated it, "makers of factions." Such men are described as being "sensual," and as "not having the Spirit." The word "sensual," here, is translated from the same word, as "natural," in 1 Cor. 2: 14: "The natural man receiveth not the things of the Spirit of God; for they are foolishness unto him; and he cannot know them, because they are spiritually discerned." The root for the word sensual is the same as that translated "soul" in the scriptures—*psyche.* These men were, therefore, *soulish* characters. The word soul is a generic term;

But ye, beloved, building up yourselves on your most holy faith, praying in

and it is not possible to assign a simple meaning to it which will apply in each instance where it occurs. Here, in contrast with the higher nature of man, it signifies the individual life, and denotes that which pertains to a man as a man; and is, hence, the basis of a manner of life inferior to that which is described as spiritual. The word sometimes denotes the animal life which man possesses in common with beasts (Psalm 78: 50); occasionally it refers to and is used synonymously with the spirit (Rev. 6: 6-9). The soul stands midway between the body and the spirit of man. He who yields himself to the desires and the demands of the flesh becomes a fleshly person; he who, through communion of his spirit with God's Spirit, allows himself to be employed in the duties which he owes to God is properly styled spiritual. The *natural man* is thus an individual who lives on the plane of the soul—a lower nature than that of the spirit, though higher than that of the body—and who refuses to rise to the higher order of his being and to enjoy the communion which is possible between his spirit and God. Man is thus a triune being—he is composed of body, soul, and spirit. (1 Thess. 5: 23.) He is capable of living on either of these planes; and the manner of life he lives is an index to that which orders his life and controls his being. Those who are sensual possess a wisdom which is from below rather than that which is from above, and they "have not the Spirit." Being without the guidance and direction of the Spirit of God, their lives are sensual, earthly, devilish. (James 3: 15.)

20 But ye, beloved, building up yourselves on your most holy faith, praying in the Holy Spirit,—But ye, in contrast with these wicked and ungodly men, building yourselves up on your most holy faith, and praying in the Holy Spirit, "keep yourselves in the love of God." Such was the design of their building up and praying. The metaphor of building, as a figure to represent growth in Christianity, is a common one in the sacred writings. (Eph. 2: 20ff.) With faith as the foundation, they were to build a sacred edifice—a holy temple unto the Lord. (1 Cor. 3: 16, 17.) For "praying in the Holy Spirit," see 1 Cor. 14: 15. For evidence of the fact that the Spirit aids us in prayer, see Rom. 8: 26.

the Holy Spirit, 21 keep yourselves in the love of God, looking for the mercy of our Lord Jesus Christ unto eternal life. 22 ³And on some have mercy, ⁴who are in doubt; 23 and some save, snatching them out of the fire; and on

³The Gr. text in this passage *(And . . . fire)* is somewhat uncertain. Some ancient authorities read *And some refute while they dispute* with you. Comp. 1 Tim. 5. 20; Tit. 1. 9.
⁴Or, *while they dispute* with you

21 Keep yourselves in the love of God, looking for the mercy of our Lord Jesus Christ unto eternal life.—The phrase "love of God" can be understood as signifying either God's love for us, or our love for God, though it is the former—God's love for us—which appears to be its significance here. We keep ourselves in his love by conforming our lives to his will: "Even as the Father hath loved me, I also have loved you: abide ye in my love. If ye keep my commandments, ye shall abide in my love; even as I have kept my Father's commandments, and abide in his love." (John 14: 9, 10.) In admonishing his readers to *keep* themselves in the love of God, human agency in salvation is thus clearly indicated by the inspired writer. While God provides the sphere of salvation—his love—it is man's function to keep himself, through faithfulness, in that sphere; and a failure to so do is to exclude one from the provisions of salvation. The "mercy of our Lord Jesus Christ" sums up all that redemption provides; and all of this looks "unto eternal life," i.e., to its ultimate possession in the next world.

22 And on some have mercy, who are in doubt;—There are various classes of humanity, and vastly different attitudes toward religion manifested by those of the same class, thus our approach to them must be influenced by the attitude characteristic of them. Some, in error, will be honest doubters, and with these we are to deal with infinite tenderness and patience; those who are perplexed, bewildered, confused, are to be tenderly escorted to the truth.

23 And some save, snatching them out of the fire; and on some have mercy with fear; hating even the garment spotted by the flesh.—These are those more advanced in error than those contemplated in verse 22; men who are far along the way to the fiery destruction which inevitably awaits them; and they are, therefore, to be snatched, as it were, from the fire to which they are so dangerously close. In so doing, we are to be careful that we

some have mercy with fear; hating even the garment spotted by the flesh.

do not partake of their uncleanness, "hating even the garment spotted (defiled) by the flesh" (the ways of the flesh). See Zech. 3: 1-4.

SECTION FOUR

BENEDICTION
(24, 25)

24 Now unto him that is able to guard you from stumbling, and to set you before the presence of his glory without blemish in exceeding joy, 25 to the only God our Saviour, through Jesus Christ our Lord, *be* glory, majesty,

---

24 Now unto him that is able to guard you from stumbling, and to set you before the presence of his glory without blemish in exceeding joy,—The doxology is to Jesus Christ, our Saviour, who the writer affirmed was, (a) able to guard his readers from stumbling; and (b) to set them before the presence of his glory without blemish in exceeding joy. The word "guard" indicates the protection which the Lord extends to his saints who "keep themselves" in his love (verse 21), a protection which extends even to *stumbling,* an act to be distinguished from *falling,* since it is possible for one to stumble, and not necessarily to fall. To stumble is a step short of falling, and a condition precedent to it. It follows, therefore, that if one never stumbles, he will never fall. This passage does not teach the impossibility of apostasy; it is not affirmed that God guards all whether they keep themselves in his love or not; on the contrary, only those who avail themselves of the means of escape provided (1 Cor. 10: 12, 13) are thus protected. The verb "to set" means, literally, "to cause to stand," and this the Lord will do for those who are faithful to him to the end. Such shall stand before him "without blemish" (i.e., blameless, faultless, pure), because they have kept themselves from defilement, and have lived in such fashion as to merit his approval. These shall experience "exceeding joy" because of the marvelous blessings there to be vouchsafed them.

25 To the only God our Saviour, through Jesus Christ our Lord, be glory, majesty, dominion and power, before all time, and now, and for evermore. Amen.—Jesus is called God because he possesses the divine nature, was in the beginning with God, and *is God.* (John 1: 1.) The glory, majesty, dominion and power here ascribed to him is past, present, and future, embracing all time, and the whole of eternity. And thus the Epistle closes on a note of genuine faith and trust in the Lord, having

dominion and power, before all time, and now, and ⁵for evermore. Amen.

⁵Gr. *unto all the ages.*

begun with a prayer and a petition that mercy, peace, and love might abound. Fearlessly Jude had rebuked the deceitful workers threatening the peace and security of the church; with scathing denunciation he had condemned those who corrupted the faith and sought to lead the saints astray; and now, with tenderness and faith he commits his readers to the Source of all good—"to the only God our Saviour"—their Protector, Defender, and Lord. May we, through equal fidelity to his will and way, make him ours as well!

This exceptionally valuable material, from the appendix of "The Living Oracles," last published by the GOSPEL ADVOCATE in 1974 and now out of print, is included here as an aid to the study of the Epistles of Peter, John and Jude. Many of the matters discussed have special relevance to these epistles, and will richly reward those who carefully examine the words and definitions given.

TABLE XIV.

APOSTOLIC WORDS AND PHRASES,

WHICH HAVE BEEN SUBJECTS OF CONTROVERSY; ALPHABETICALLY ARRANGED, AND DE-
FINED FROM THEIR CURRENT ACCEPTATION IN THE CHRISTIAN SCRIPTURES.

ADOPTION, Υιοθεσια, huiothesia, adoption, or the choosing for a son, Rom. viii. 15, 23; ix. 4; Gal. iv. 5; Eph. i. 5. Occurring only in the five preceding sentences, its meaning is easily ascertained. The spirit of adoption, is the spirit of a son; the adoption of the body is its redemption from the grave, and its union with an adopted spirit in a glorious immortality. The adoption which pertained to Israel according to the flesh, was their peculiar relation to God from among all nations, and his paternal government over them. But the adoption of men, through Jesus Christ, into the rank of sons and heirs of God, is the transcendent glory of the embassy of Jesus, and of his religion.

AGE, Αιων, Aion, (derived from aei, always, and ων, being.) Its radical idea is indefinite duration. It is in all versions differently translated. We have the phrase eis aiona, or eis ton aiona, in the singular form, thirty-two times; and in the plural form, twenty-six times, translated in the common version, "always" and "forever." The word aion, in other passages, also alludes to duration. The phrase, "Since," and "before the aion, (world) began," occurs in Luke i. 70; John ix. 32; Acts iii. 21; xv. 18; Eph. iii. 9. The phrase, Sunteleia tou aionos, occurs in Matthew five times, rendered "the end of the world;" by Dr. Campbell, "the conclusion of this state;" and in Hebrews ix. 26, in the plural form, rendered, "once in the end of the world." Also, 1 Cor. x. 11, tele tou aionos, (end of the world.) 2 Peter iii. 18, we have it connected with day—"the day of eternity"—tou aionos. Also, with King—"King of Eternity," or "King of ages"—"eternal King." 1 Tim. i. 17. It is also found, Eph. ii. 7; iii. 21; Col. i. 26, rendered ages, Com. Ver., and Eph. iii. 11, rendered eternal. Besides the above, we have the present world, or, "this world," Matt. xii. 32; Mark x. 30; Luke xviii. 30; Gal. i. 4; 2 Tim. iv. 10; Titus ii. 12; Eph. i. 21; Rom. xii. 2—and " the world to come," Matt. xii. 32; Hebrews vi. 5.

To these may be added, "cares of this world," Matt. xiii. 22; Mark iv. 19. "Children of this world," Luke xvi. 8; xx. 34. "Disputers of this world," 1 Cor. i. 20. "Wisdom of this world," 1 Cor. ii. 6. "Rulers of this world," 1 Cor. ii. 6, 8. "Wise in this world," 1 Cor. iii. 18. "God of this world," 2 Cor. iv. 4. "Darkness of this world," Eph. vi. 12. "He made the worlds," and "The worlds were made," Hebrews i. 2; xi. 3. Once only is it rendered course, in connection with κοσμος, kosmos, world; Eph. ii. 2, "The course of this kosmos."

More than sixty times in the common version, aion is rendered by such words as express the longest duration. It also indicates a state of things, or course of arrangements, which we sometimes call a dispensation, state, or age. It is found about one hundred times in the Christian Scriptures.

The word kosmos, translated almost uniformly world, which is found one hundred and eighty-four times in the New Testament, is in some respects very different from aion. Concerning the word kosmos, we would have it noticed, that it is never found in the plural form in the Christian Scriptures. There is but one kosmos, though different aions, found in this volume. Kosmos denotes the material globe with all its elements—sometimes, the universe; and, by a figure called metonomy, which substitutes the thing containing for the thing contained, the human family is often called the world. God is said to have loved the kosmos, but not the aion. The kosmos is said to have been founded; but the aions disposed, arranged, or constituted. The phrase "foundation of the world," occurs ten times, and always kosmos. But wherever mere time or continuance is implied, it is always aion, and not kosmos.

As we have given all the places where aion is translated world, the English reader can easily ascertain where kosmos occurs. This data will afford him matter for reflection.

AMBASSADORS of Christ, Πρεσβευς, (from presbeuo, to go upon, or perform an embassy.) The verb occurs only twice in the writings of the Apostles, 2 Cor. v. 20; Eph. vi. 20; and is exclusively applied to the Apostles, who alone, of all Christian teachers, carried a message from the person of the Great King to his rebellious subjects. Presbeuo occurs twice in Luke in this sense, chap. xiv. 32; xix. 14. To hold a commission and carry a message immediately from the person of the Prince.

ANALOGY OF FAITH, Αναλογιαν της πιστεως, analogian tes pisteos, literally the analogy

APPENDIX.

of faith. This phrase, indeed the word *analogia,* occurs but once in the Christian Scriptures. We have in the same connection, the phrase μετρον τες πιστεως, *metron tes pisteos,* the measure or portion of faith, Rom. xii. 3, 6. This phrase also occurs but once, and naturally means the portion of belief, or of the truth believed, which the speaker is supposed to possess. Let him not transcend his knowledge of the truth, but speak in accordance with his own consciousness of what he understands and believes. But "the analogy of faith," or *proportion* of faith, is not so easily decided. Analogy, in the classic import of the term, means resemblance, or in accordance with something. The analogy of faith, in speculative theology, means, "according to the scope or system of revealed truth," which is so arbitrary, that every one's own system is his analogy of faith. Yet the Apostle might mean, let him interpret, preach, or speak, according to the general scope of the ancient revelations. But there is a meaning more in accordance with the context, which we prefer, which is well expressed by Professor Stuart: "Let not the prophets exceed what is intrusted to them. Let them keep within the bounds of their reason and consciousness, and not, like the heathen, (*manteis,*) rave, or speak they know not what." To this agree the interpretations of Chrysostom, Theodoret, Oecumenius, Pelagius, Calvin, Flat, Tholuck, and many others, says Mr. Stuart. To these I will add Locke, Dr. G. Campbell, and Whitby, who learnedly contend that *analogia* here imports proportion, measure, rate, and is the same with " measure of faith," verse 3. The analogy of faith, in popular import, is every one's own creed; but the proportion of faith is every one's measure of knowledge of the Christian religion.

ANGEL, Αγγελλος, *angellos,* messenger, occurs one hundred and eighty-three times in the Christian Scriptures, and is applied to celestial spirits, to men, good and bad; to the agents of Satan; to the winds, fire, pestilence, and every creature which God employs as his special agent. It is the name of office, and not of nature. The nature of the celestial spirits is not revealed to us, but they are known as messengers of God, of great intellectual and moral endowments, and as excelling in wisdom and power. See note on Angel of the Lord, Matthew ii.

ANIMAL MAN, *natural man,* Ψυχικος ανθροπος, *psuchicos anthropos.* This term is first found in 1 Corinthians ii. 14, and by the King's translators is rendered the *natural* man, contrasted with the *spiritual* man. It occurs only six times in the Christian Scriptures, and is translated in the common version by the following words: 1 Cor. ii. 14, *natural;* 1 Cor. xv. 44, twice in this verse, and once in verse 46, in connection with *body,* translated *natural;* James iii. 15, translated *sensual;* Jude, 19th verse, applied to persons, *sensual.* It is three times applied to the body, which is certainly animal; once to wisdom, which is not natural wisdom; and twice to the whole person. Parkhurst defines it as signifying animal or sensual, as opposed to spiritual, and cites 1 Cor. ii. 14; James iii. 15, and Jude 19th verse, in proof of this. His second and last meaning of it is *animal,* opposed to *spiritual* or *glorified,* and quotes 1 Cor. xv. 44, 46, as proof. We prefer *animal* in the passage first quoted; for the animal man there spoken of is supposed to be destitute of all knowledge which comes by revelation, and withal so sensual as to despise it. Locke also prefers animal to natural in this passage, and defines the animal and spiritual man in the following terms: "The *animal* is opposed to the *spiritual* man—the one signifying a man who has no higher principles to build on than those of natural reason; the other, a man that founds his faith and religion on divine revelation."

ANSWER OF A GOOD CONSCIENCE. The word translated answer, is επερωτεμα, *eperotema,* which is found but once in the whole volume. The verb *eperotao,* which occurs fifty-nine times, from which it is derived, signifies to ask, interrogate, question, inquire. Parkhurst says, that "the Apostle very probably alludes to the question and answers which we learn from Tertullian were used at baptism. The Bishop asked, Dost thou renounce Satan? Dost thou believe in Christ? The candidate answered, I renounce—I believe." [Carr, in his Antiquities, details these matters more fully.] "This, Tertullian, De Baptismo, chap. xviii., calls *sponsionem salutis,* an engagement of salvation." Grotius, Mill, and Wolfius concur in interpreting *eperotema,* 1 Peter iii. 3, *the response or answer.*

We have little or no confidence in the many comments and criticisms we have read on this word, and the whole construction of this passage, and we have examined not a few. The common French render it *the response;* Beza, *the stipulation;* Sir Norton Knatchbull, *the covenant;* others, *the engagement* of a good conscience. Macknight is in doubt, though he prefers *answer,* which can not be the meaning of a word naturally descended from a verb more than fifty times rendered *to ask, to seek, to desire, to beseech,* in the common version. After much examination of all the alleged difficulties, both in the punctuation, the relative *ho,* and the word *eperotema,* we adopt the following punctuation and translation of this passage; which is the most natural, and, we think, obviously the most defensible:

" In the days of Noah when the Ark was preparing, wherein few (that is eight) souls were saved through water. Immersion, which is the antitype, does also now save us— not the putting away the filth of the flesh, but the seeking of a good conscience toward God, by the resurrection of Jesus Christ.'

ANTICHRIST, Αντιχριστος, *Antichristos*, against Christ, occurs only five times—1 John ii. 18, twice, 22; iv. 5; 2 John, 7th verse. Antichrist is defined by John to be any individual who denies the Father and the Son. Such were apostate Christians, who renounced the hope, and denied the Father and the Son. Compare 1 John ii. 18, and 22. Every spirit that confesses not that Jesus Christ has actually come in the flesh, literally and truly, profess what he may, has the spirit of Antichrist, and does deny both the Father and the Son. Paul's *Man of Sin*, and John's *Antichrist*, are not two names for the same personage.

APOSTLE, Αποστολος, *Apostolos*, one sent by another. It occurs more than eighty times in the Christian Scriptures. It is applied to Jesus, to the Twelve, to Barnabas, Sylvanus, Timothy, Epaphras, and some others. There are three orders mentioned in the sacred writings. Jesus Christ was the Apostle of God, and is the Apostle of the Christian profession. Heb. iii. 1, compared with John xvii. 18. It is applied to the twelve personal companions of Jesus, who are called *his* Apostles; and it is applied to persons sent out by the congregations. 2 Cor. viii. 23; Phil. ii. 25.

ATONEMENT, Καταλλαγη, *Katallage*, from *katallasso*, reconciliation. It occurs, Rom. v. 11; xi. 15; 2 Cor. v. 18, 19; In all four times: in the first instance translated *atonement* in the common version; and in the other three, *reconciling, reconciliation*. The verb occurs, Rom. v. 10, twice; 1 Cor. vii. 11; 2 Cor. v. 18, 19, 20; in all six times; and always rendered *reconcile*. Reconciliation is the coming together of parties at variance. We see no good reason why it should not always be translated *reconciliation*.

BAPTIZE, Βαττω, Βαπτιζω, *bapto, baptizo*. These words are never translated *sprinkle* or *pour*, either in the common version, or in any other, ancient or modern. *Bapto* occurs three times; Luke xvi. 24; John xiii. 26; Rev. xix. 13; and is always translated *dip* by the authority of King James. *Baptizo* occurs seventy-nine times: of these, seventy-seven times it is not translated at all, but adopted into the language; and twice, viz: Mark vii. 4; Luke xi. 38, it is translated *wash*, without regard to the manner in which this washing was performed. Dr. Campbell explains the manner of this washing in his note on Mark vii. 4, which he renders, "Wash their hands by dipping them." All lexicographers translate it by the words *immerse, dip*, or *plunge*—not one, by *sprinkle* or *pour;* metonomically, some translate it *wash*, and *dye* (to color).

In the Greek version of the Old Testament, *bapto* frequently occurs in the law, and is contrasted with *sprinkling* and *pouring* in the performance of certain rites, where every thing depended on the manner of doing them. Thus we have *sprinkle, pour* and *dip*, in the same institution, occurring in Leviticus xiv. 15, 16, "He shall pour the blood, he shall dip his finger in it, and he shall sprinkle the blood." Here we have *cheo*, to pour; *raino*, to sprinkle; *bapto*, to dip, contradistinguished in the same institution. No word in the Greek language is more definite.

BAPTISM, Βαπτισμα, Βαπτισμος, *baptisma, baptismos*. These words are neither in the common version, nor in any other, translated *sprinkling* or *pouring*. *Baptismos* occurs four times, once translated *washing;* and *baptisma*, twenty-two times, never translated at all by the King's authority; but by Campbell and Macknight sometimes translated *immersion*, and in other places retained in the original form; but never by them rendered *sprinkling* or *pouring*.

BAPTISM IN FIRE.—Compare Malachi iv. and Matthew iii. 10, 11, 12; from which it appears that to be "immersed in fire" is the emblem of destruction, as the "burning up of chaff," and "turning of dry trees into fuel," were the emblems of this visitation. In the day of vengeance all who would not submit to Jesus would be immersed in fire, as Malachi foretold, and as the Baptist preached to the Pharisees and Sadducees.

BAPTISM IN THE HOLY SPIRIT, as promised by Jesus, Acts i. 5, and explained on Pentecost, Acts ii., and in the house of Cornelius, Acts x. 16, 17, indicates those supernatural gifts of the Holy Spirit bestowed, for the confirmation of the testimony, upon the Apostles and first converts from among the Jews and Gentiles. This immersion of the Jews and Gentiles was only once, as in the case of private or personal immersion. So Peter explains it, Acts xi. 15, compared with verses 16, 17. These gifts appearing externally and internally of the persons on the Apostles and the first fruits of both people, were so overwhelming as to be figuratively called an immersion in the Holy Spirit.

BISHOP, Επισκοπος, *Episcopos*, overseer, occurs five times: Acts xx. 28, translated *overseer;* Phil. i. 1, *bishops;* 1 Tim. iii. 2, *bishop;* Titus i. 7, *bishop;* 1 Peter ii. 25, *bishop*. Other versions have it sometimes *overseer*, and sometimes *bishop*. The verb occurs twice, *episcopeo*, Hebrews xii. 15, "*looking diligently;*" and 1 Peter v. 2, "*takin the oversight*." *Episcope* also occurs four times: Luke xix. 44, translated *visitation;* Acts i. 20, *bishopric*, *overseer's office*, and simply *office;* 1 Tim. iii. 1, *the office of a bishop;* and 1 Peter ii. 12, *visitation*. From all the usages of this word, it plainly denotes one who has the oversight of Christians, a plurality of such was in many of the ancient congregations.

BLASPHEMY, Βλασφημια, *blasphemia*—speaking against. It is found nineteen times, applied to men, to God, and the Holy Spirit. Matt. xii. 31; xv. 19; xxvi. 65; Mark ii. 7; iii. 28; vii. 22; xiv. 64; John x. 33; Eph. iv. 31; Coll. iii. 8; 1 Tim. vi. 4; Jude, *th verse; Rev. ii. 9; xiii. 1, 5, 6; xvii. 3—from an examination of which its meaning may be clearly discerned.

BODY OF CHRIST—*Mystical Body*.—In speculative theology a name given to the Christian community, equivalent to the metaphorical body of Christ, distinguished from his natural body. There is but one *metaphorical*, as there is but one *literal* body of Christ. Of this body all Christians are members in particular. To it belong all the Apostles, Prophets, Evangelists, Teachers, gifts, miracles, and honors bestowed by its Head after his glorification. This body is the temple of the Holy Spirit. Jesus is the head, and the Holy Spirit is the soul of this body, from which all the members receive life, health, and joy. As the Head is glorified, so will all the members be glorified with him.

CALL, Καλεω, *kaleo*, and Προσκαλεω, *proskaleo*, to call, to invite, occur often in the Christian Scriptures, the latter about thirty times, and the former about one hundred and fifty times. The latter is literally to call to one, and the former to call in every import of that word. In the following very important passages it is *proskaleo*: Acts ii. 39; xiii. 2; xvi. 10. In the last passage it is used to denote a call to preach the gospel. In more than twenty of the places where it is found, it denotes the most ordinary calls given to persons on all sorts of occasions.

CALLED, Κλητος, *kletos*, from *kaleo*, to call. *Kletos* is found eleven times in the sacred books—always translated *called*. In the sacred writings it appears to have always the same meaning in which our Lord used it. He introduced it, Matt. xx. 16, and repeated it, chap. xxii. 14, "Many are *called*, but few chosen." The *called* are all who professedly obey Christ; but the approved or chosen are that class of these who honor their profession. It occurs eight times in the Epistles: Rom. i. 1, 6, 7; viii. 28; 1 Cor. i. 1, 2, 24; Jude, 1st verse. In the Revelation, chap. xvii. 14, it is used as descriptive of character. Those that are with the Lamb are "*called*, chosen, and faithful." The *called*, indeed, are now very many; but the choice spirits, or the chosen, are still few.

CALLING, Κλησις, *klesis*, profession; so the word is used in common intercourse. Every trade is termed *a calling*. The Christian's calling is from God, and leads to God. It is found Rom. xi. 29; 1 Cor. i. 26; vii. 20; Eph. i. 18; iv. 1, 4; Phil. iii. 14; 2 Thess. i. 11; 2 Tim. i. 9; Heb. iii. 1; 2 Peter i. 10, in all eleven times. 1 Cor. vii. 20, it is used to designate a common trade. Eph. i. 18, it is translated *vocation*. In all other places, *calling*; and refers to the Christian profession. "You see your *calling*, brethren," says Paul. You see those of your profession. "Amongst them are not many noble," etc. So one would speak to any fraternity, if he desired the addressed to form a just estimate of the whole profession.

CHARITY, χαρις, *charis*, charity, free gift, favor. This word is often confounded with αγαπη, *agape*, love. 1 Cor. xiii. αγαπη, love, is found nine times, and χαρις, not once. *Charis* is not once translated *charity* by the authors of the common version; and *agape*, love, is rendered *charity* twenty-five times. We have never rendered αγαπη, *charity;* but have sometimes rendered χαρις, *charity*, when the connection seemed to require it.

CHRISTIAN, χριστιανος, *Christianos*. It is found only three times in the book: Acts xi. 26; xxvi. 28; and 1 Pet. iv. 16, and was a name given to the disciples of Christ. A Christian is one who believes what Jesus says, and does what he bids him.

CHOSEN, Εκλεκτος, *eklektos*,—elect, chosen. This word is found twenty-three times; seven times translated *chosen*, common version, Matthew xx. 16; xxii. 14; Luke xxiii. 35; Romans xvi. 13; 1 Peter ii. 4, 9; Rev. xvii. 14; and sixteen times *elect*. It is unquestionably used sometimes as descriptive of character, as we use the word *chosen* or *choice*—"He is a *choice* or *chosen* General," not regarding the manner in which he obtained the office, but the manner in which he performs the duty. Paul calls Rufus an *elect* or *chosen* person in the Lord, and as such salutes him. He salutes Appelles in the same sense; but chooses another word, *dokimos*, approved in the Lord. Matthew xx. 16; and xxii. 14, it seems to be used in the same sense. The *approved* are few. Thus Paul speaks of a few in Corinth as *chosen* or *approved*, in comparison of the many *called*. 1 Cor. xi. 19. The *called* here were many, (for he says they were all called,) but the *chosen*, the *approved*, were few.

CHURCH, Εκκλεσια, *Ecclesia*, congregation, assembly, occurs one hundred and twenty times in the sacred books. It is derived from εκκλεω, I call out, *the called out*. Such was the assembly in the wilderness, first designated the congregation. It is an assembly of *the called*, or those who are brought together by one leader, or profession. The whole community of professing Christians make the one body or congregation of the Lord; and those meeting in one place, constitute the Christian congregation in that place. This word is applied to those in Jerusalem, Rome, Corinth, Ephesus; and, in the plural form, to the churches in Galatia, Judea, Asia, etc. Gal. i. 2, 22; 2 Cor. viii. 1, 18, 23; xi. 28; 1 Cor. vii. 17; xvi. 19; 1 Thess. i. 4. It is also very often applied to the whole body or aggregate of the faithful: 1 Cor. xv. 9; Eph. i. 22; v. 23, 24, 25, 27, 29, 32; Gal. i. 13; Phil. iii. 6; Col. i. 24.

COMFORTER, Παρακλητος, *paracletos*, advocate, monitor, comforter. Advocate, or one who pleads the cause of another, is the most current signification of this word. Parkhurst, Greenfield, Robertson, and Stokius, give it as the most general meaning of the word. Dr. Campbell in some places prefers *monitor* or *guide*. Comforter is the most remote meaning of the word, either in sacred or classic use. It is rendered *advocate* once only by the King's translators, (1 John ii. 1,) and four times, *comforter*. Dr. Campbell renders it *monitor* four times in John xiv. 16, 26; xv. 26; xvi. 7. These five places are all the places in which it is found in the sacred writings of the New Institution. We uniformly render it *advocate*—because, in our judgment, the work of advocating the pretensions of Jesus being assigned to the Holy Spirit, was the reason why he was called the *Paracletos*—and because it is only as the pleader of our cause Jesus is called our Παρακλητος, (advocate,) 1 John ii. 1.

COMING OF THE SON OF MAN *on the clouds of heaven.* Matt. xxiv. 27, 37, 39, 30; xxvi. 64; Mark xiii. 26; xiv. 62; Luke xxi. 27. Whether this *"Coming of the Son of Man"* denotes a literal, or a figurative coming, is a question which has, recently, been much agitated. Since the days of President Edwards' History of Redemption till now, it has been a commonly received opinion, that there are four comings of the Son of Man spoken of: Of these, two are literal, and two figurative—his coming in the flesh; his coming to destroy Jerusalem; his coming to destroy the works of the Man of Sin, and to reign with his saints a thousand years on earth; and his coming to judge the world at the last day. The first and the last are said to be literal and personal comings; the others, figurative.

The question before us is purely a literary one; and for the following reasons it would seem to us that, however we may talk of a figurative coming, either at the destruction of Jerusalem, or of the apostasy, the phrase, as it is found in Matthew and Luke, must denote a personal and literal coming of the Son of Man:

1. On leaving the temple for the last time, Matt. xxiii. 39, he told the representative of the Jewish nation that their house, or temple, was soon to be deserted, and that they should not again *see* him, till the day they would say, "Blessed be he that comes in the name of the Lord." After going out of the temple, this *coming* is made the subject of conversation between him and his disciples in private, chap. xxiv., and of course must be explained to them in the sense in which it was expressed in the temple; and there we learn it was such a coming, or return of the Saviour, as could be *seen* by the Jews— "You shall not *see* me" till a particular day.

2. The Apostles ask, "What shall be the sign of thy coming?" and as they must have understood him in the sense he delivered himself in the temple, he would answer them in the same sense; for had they misunderstood him, he would have corrected them, as his manner was. The conversation was then about a personal, and not a figurative coming of the Son of Man.

3. As his going away, or his absence, was not figurative, but literal and personal, so must his return, or coming, be literal and personal, else there is an application of words in a double sense in one and the same period; and if so, rules of interpretation are wholly unavailing.

4. But the coming of the Son of Man introduced Matt. xxiv. could not apply to Jerusalem's ruin; for the Jews did not then *see* him, nor say to him, "Blessed be he that comes in the name of the Lord," which he declared would be the case when he would next come. As they have not yet thus addressed him, we are assured that he has not come in the sense of Matt. xxiii. and xxiv.

5. As the Lord addressed the Scribes and Pharisees as representing the nation, so he addresses his disciples as representing his body, the congregation of saints; and after telling them, in order, the things that must happen them, and the nations, before the coming of the Son of Man, he places that event (Luke xxi. 27, and Matt. xxiv. 27) after the destruction of Jerusalem, the dispersion of the nation, and the long persecutions and sufferings of the real followers of the Lord.

6. When they should see these signs, they were taught to rejoice, inferring that their deliverance, or redemption, drew nigh. But this deliverance has not yet arrived; consequently, the Son of Man has not yet come on the clouds of heaven.

7. But this *coming* can not be secret, or figurative, for it is to be as visible and striking as the lightning which, breaking forth from the east, shines even to the setting sun—"so shall the coming of the Son of Man be."

8. Neither is it spoken of as if there were a plurality of events called "comings of the Lord," but as one and singular—*The* coming of the Son of Man.

9. Again, as Daniel the prophet is quoted in reference to the desolations coming upon the city and sanctuary, it is natural to suppose that the disciples would also remember that Daniel had placed the coming of the Son of Man at the destruction of the little horn, when the "thrones were cast down," and "the beast was slain, and his body destroyed and given to the burning flame," and therefore could not be led to think that "the coming of the Son of Man" was either figurative, or to be at the desolations which came on Judea.

10. But as seven parables are introduced, in this discourse, to explain the coming of the Son of Man, or the Saviour's return; and as the last of them is on all hands agreed

APPENDIX. 79

to denote a personal, and not a figurative coming, we are compelled to the conclusion, that the coming so often mentioned and so fully explained, must always be one and the same, which the last of the seven parables certainly makes literal and personal. These seven parables, or comparisons, all found in one and the same discourse, relative to one and the same coming of the Lord, are first, the parable of the fig-tree: from this he teaches them to know when his coming is near—second, the days of Noah and the deluge, sudden and unexpected by the world; "So shall the coming of the Son of Man be"—third, the parable of the thief; "Be you also ready; for in such an hour as you think not, the Son of Man *comes*"—fourth, the parable of the faithful and unfaithful servant; "The master of that servant shall *come* in a day when he looks not for him"—fifth, the parable of the marriage, or of the wise and the foolish virgins; "Behold the Bridegroom *comes*: go out and meet him"—sixth, the parable of the talents; "After a long time, the lord of those servants *comes*, and reckons with them"—seventh, the parable of the sheep and the goats; "When the Son of Man shall *come* in his glory," or in the clouds, he will gather the Gentiles, all *the nations*, before him, and separate the good from the bad. The coming of the Son of Man is always kept in view, in these seven comparisons; and if we regard any one of them as literal, we must so regard them all.

These are a few, and but a few, of the reasons which incline us to regard this coming of the Son of Man as not figurative, but literal: and not at the time of the destruction of Jerusalem, but at the close of the times of the Gentiles.

To this import of the phrase, the most plausible objection is drawn from the saying, This generation shall not pass, or fail, till all these things be fulfilled. But, as it will be seen under the word "generation," in the judgment of lexicographers, and some able biblical critics, the word *genea* signifies not only the race of living men on the earth at one time, but nation, people, or race, as a distinct and peculiar stock or family. Indeed, the word *generation*, at the time of the King's version, signified nation, or people, very frequently, as will be seen by examining the following passages: Prov. xxx. 11, 12, 13, 14; Ps. xxiv. 4–6; xiv. 5; xxvii. 30; cxii. 2; 1 Peter ii. 9: compare Jer. ii. 28, 31; vii. 28, 30; Deut. xxxi. 29; xxxii. 5. "A nation void of counsel," is at another time called "a froward generation;" a peculiar people is also called a chosen generation. To this it may be added, that the word translated *kindred* is often, in the Septuagint, this same *genea*, at other times translated *generation*. From all which it appears that our Lord meant no less than that the nation, or race of people among whom, and in reference to whom, these things were spoken, should continue to exist, notwithstanding all their desolations and dispersions, till he came again, and then they should hail him as blessed, coming in the name of Jehovah.

CONFESSION TO SALVATION, Ομολογεω, *homologeo*, I confess, or profess; whence comes *ομολογια*, *homologia*, confession, profession. The verb occurs, translated, common version, to confess, in Matt. x. 32, twice; Luke xii. 8, twice; John i. 20, twice; ix. 22; xii. 42; Acts xxiii. 8; xxiv. 14; Rom. x. 9, 10; 1 Tim. vi. 12; Heb. xi. 13; 1 John i. 9; iv. 2, 3, 15; 2 John, 7th verse. It is only twice translated *profess*, (Matt. vii. 23; Titus i. 16;) once, *to promise with an oath*, (Matt. xiv. 7;) and once, *to give thanks*, (Heb. xiii. 15)—in all twenty-four times.

Homologia, *confession* or *profession*, occurs six times; translated *profession*, 2 Cor. ix. 13; Heb. iii. 1; iv. 14; x. 23; translated *confession*, 1 Tim. vi. 12, 13. Macknight has it *confession* twice in the Hebrews. Excepting 2 Cor. ix. 13, where the phrase required a change, we have it always *confession*. "Confession of the faith" is a public avowal of it at the time of putting on Christ, to which salvation is annexed. Romans x. 9, 10.

Exomologeo occurs eleven times, and is equivalent to acknowledging publicly, or confessing from the heart, and is the word generally used for confessing sins. In this sense it is found in Matt. iii. 6; Mark i. 5; Acts xix. 18; Rom. xiv. 11; James v. 16. It is also translated (common version) once by *promise*, Luke xxii. 6; and twice by *giving thanks*, Luke x. 21; Matt. xi. 25.

CONSCIENCE occurs in the common version thirty times, and once in the plural form, 2 Cor. v. 11; for which we have in the original, Συνειδησις, *suneidesis*, compounded of *sun*, together, and *eideo*, to see or know—in Latin *con scio;* whence comes *conscience*, the power of judging ourselves, which is always in accordance with the knowledge of ourselves, and the relations in which we stand to our Creator and fellow creatures. The conscience is said to be *weak*, when knowledge is limited; *pure*, when free from accusation; and *evil*, when polluted with guilt.

COVENANT, Διαθηκη, *diatheke*—institution, arrangement, constitution, covenant, and sometimes dispensation—occurs in the Christian Scriptures thirty-three times; translated sometimes testament, will. See note on Covenant and Testament, p. 72.

The New *Diatheke* is spoken of, Matt. xxvi. 28; Mark. iv. 24; Luke xxii. 20; 1 Cor. xi. 25; 2 Cor. iii. 6; Gal. iv. 24; Hebrews vii. 22; viii. 6, 8, 10; ix. 15; x. 16; xii. 24; xiii. 20.

DEACON, Διακονος, *diakonos*, minister, servant, deacon, (translated sometimes *almoner*, because they ministered to the poor,) occurs, Matt. xx. 26; xxii. 13; xxiii. 11; Mark ix 35; x. 43; John ii. 5, 9; xii. 26; Rom. xiv. 4; xv. 8; xvi. 1; 1 Cor. iii. 5; 2 Cor. iii.

6; vi. 4; xi. 15, 23; Gal. ii. 17; Eph. iii. 7; vi. 21; Phil. i. 1; Col. i. 7, 23, 25; iv. 7 1 Thess. iii. 2; 1 Tim. iii. 8, 12; iv. 6—thirty-one times, applied to males and females, whose business it was to serve the whole congregation in any capacity.

DEAD—" Let the dead bury their dead." Metaphorically, they who are not alive to God, may bury those who are literally dead. "She that *lives* in pleasure is *dead* while she *lives*." Thus we have the *dead* and *alive* literally and metaphorically used in the sacred writings.

DEMON, Δαιμων, *daimon*, supposed to be the ministers of Satan; though the spirit of a *dead* man is called *demon*, without respect to his character; but generally they are understood to be unclean spirits. See note on the words *diabolos*, *daimon*, *and daimonion*.

DEVIL, Satan, Διαβολος Ὁ Σατανας, Diabolos Satanas. See note above referred to.

ECONOMY, Οικονομια, *Oikonomia*, economy, administration of affairs—from *oikos*, a house, *nemos*, from *nemo*, to administer—economy, the management of a family; hence arrangement, dispensation, or *administration*, in a more general sense—occurs, Luke xvi. 2, 3, 4, *stewardship*, management of affairs; 1 Cor. ix. 17, *dispensation* " of the gospel ;" common version, Eph. i. 10, *dispensation* " of the fullness of times ;" iii. 2, 9; Col. i. 25; 1 Tim. i. 4, common version, "godly edifying"—in all nineteen times. The Christian economy and the Christian dispensation, are, therefore, two versions of the same phrase. The *economy of the gospel*, the economy of God, or of Heaven, is an adoption rather than a translation of the phrase. The *stewardship* of the gospel house belonged to the Apostles; therefore, they called themselves, " stewards of the secrets of God."

ELDER, Πρεσβυτερος, *presbyter;* whence the word *presbytery*. This word was in the antecedent dispensation applied to those who presided over the congregation of Israel. Thus it was appropriated to a certain class of officers among the Jews centuries before the Christian era. The elders or *eldership* of one synagogue, or particular congregation, were denominated the *presbuterion, presbytery*.

Presbuterion, presbytery, occurs, Luke xxii. 66, and is applied to the council of elders which presided over the Jews, whose office was chiefly *political*. In Acts xxii. 5, it is (common version) translated " *the estate of the elders*," the presbytery or sanhedrim, the senate which governed the nation. It is found applied to the eldership of the Christian congregation, 1 Tim. iv. 14, "The laying on of the hands of the presbytery"—or estate of the elders—*eldership.—Macknight*. These are the only occurrences of the word *presbytery* in the Christian Scriptures.

Presbuteros, an elder, occurs sixty-seven times. It is applied often in the historical books to the elders among the Jews. In the Acts of the Apostles it begins to be applied to the elders of the Christian communities. We have the phrase, " apostles and elders " contradistinguished several times. In Acts xv. 2, 4, 6, 22, we find them four times in the same sentence.

Apostles were sometimes called elders; for the word is used to designate a *senior*, an old man, 1 Tim. v. 1, 2. All old men in this sense are called elders. John calls himself an elder in the year 70 of his life, when he wrote his second and third epistles, verse 1; and Peter called himself an elder, 1 Pet. v. 1. Paul calls himself *presbutes*, an *aged man*, Phil. 9th verse—though he may have had an allusion to the office of an ambassador, as this word *presbutes* sometimes indicates.

The word *Priest*, from the Saxon *Preostor*, contracted *Preste* and *Priest*, is a corruption of *Presbyter*. The High and Low Dutch have *Priester;* the French, *Prestre;* the Italian, *Prete;* and the Spanish, *Presbytero*.

Elder, as the name of an officer in the Christian Church, is defined Acts xx. 17, 28; Titus i. 5, 7; 1 Peter v. 1, 5—from all which it appears that the same duties—oversight, ruling, teaching, etc., which the term *Bishop* imported, were discharged by the elders. Some, however, devoted themselves especially to presiding; while others labored in the word and teaching. 1 Tim. v. 17.

ELECTION, Εκλογη, *ekloge*—election, choice, chosen, approved, beloved; metonomically used for the persons chosen, approved, or beloved. It occurs only seven times: Acts ix. 15, *chosen*. Rom. ix. 11; xi. 5; vii. 28; 1 Thess. i. 4, *election*. 2 Peter i. 10, *Make your election sure*. See *chosen*.

ETERNAL, Αιωνιος, *aionios*, eternal, everlasting, forever, occurs seventy-five times in the Christian Scriptures. Wherever we have the words " eternal," and " everlasting" in the common version, or this, it is *aionios* in the original. It is thrice applied to fire; Matt. xviii. 8, 25, 41; Jude, 7th verse. Thrice to glory: 2 Cor. iv. 17; 2 Tim. ii. 10; 1 Pet. v. 10. Once to the following: Punishment, Matt. xxv. 46; Destruction, 2 Thess. i. 9; Damnation, Mark iii. 29; Habitation, Luke xvi. 19; Chains, Jude, 6th verse; Covenant, Heb. xiii. 30; Gospel, Rev. xiv. 6; Kingdom, 2 Pet. i. 11; Power, 1 Tim. vi 16; Purpose, Eph. iii. 11; House, 2 Cor. v. 1; Spirit, Heb. ix. 14; Inheritance, Heb. ix. 15; Judgment, Heb. vi. 2; Redemption, Heb. ix. 12; Salvation, Heb. v. 9; Consolation, 2 Thess. ii. 16; Unseen things, 2 Cor. iv. 18. It is three times applied to the ages. [see *age*,] once in Philemon translated *forever*, 15th verse. It is applied to life, Com. Ver. eternal life, thirty-one times; everlasting life, fourteen times. We have eternal life forty-five times, *aionion zoe;* once, the eternal King, 1 Tim. i. 17; and once "the everlasting God," Rom. xvi. 26.

ETERNAL LIFE. *The phrase,* ETERNAL LIFE, *the burden of the New Testament, occurs not once in all the Jewish Scriptures.* But the Christian religion proposes an everlasting constitution, administered by an eternal King, who, having achieved an eternal redemption, was crowned with eternal glory, to bestow an eternal inheritance, in an everlasting kingdom, with everlasting consolations, according to an eternal purpose, to make eternal life a free gift to all the heirs of an everlasting salvation. If this word implies not duration without end, there is no life without end.

EVANGELIST, Ευαγγελιστης, *euangelistes,* evangelist, occurs three times: Acts xxi. 8; Eph. iv. 11; 2 Tim. iv. 5. The work of an evangelist was to preach the gospel and plant churches.

EXHORTATION, Παρακλησις, *paraklesis,* exhortation, consolation, comfort, occurs twenty-nine times—translated by all interpreters both consolation and exhortation. When connected with speaking, exhortation is the most appropriate, because consolation is the end proposed, and exhortation the means. He that consoles or comforts does it by exhortation. Thus Barnabas was a son of exhortation, and a consolation to many, because eminent in this gift. Acts xi. 23; xiii. 43; xxiv. 22.

FAITH, Πιστις, *pistis*—faith, belief, trust, confidence. When a person confides in testimony, he believes it, or has faith in it. When a person has confidence in a man, he trusts in him, or has faith in him. It always presupposes testimony; for where there is nothing said, reported, or testified, there can be nothing believed or disbelieved. The verb *pisteuo* [I believe] occurs two hundred and forty-six times; and the noun *pistis* [faith] occurs two hundred and forty-four times. We have the phrases, "believe on him," "believe in him," and "believe him." When any one receives testimony as true, he believes it; and when he regards the promises of any person as true and certain, he believes on him, or in him. The simple definition of this term, of so frequent occurrence, is, *the assurance or conviction that testimony is true.* When regarded as a *principle of action,* Paul defines it, "the confidence of things hoped for; the conviction, evidence, or demonstration, of things not seen." Heb. xi. 1.

FOREKNOWLEDGE, Προγνωσις, *prognosis.* Foreknowledge occurs twice: Acts ii. 23; 1 Pet. i. 2—*proginosko* [I foreknow] occurs five times: Acts xxvi. 5; Romans viii. 29; xi. 2; 1 Pet. i. 20; 2 Pet. iii. 17. It is, in the common version, translated *foreordained,* 1 Pet. i. 20, and in 2 Pet. iii. 17, "you knew before;" in the other places, in the same manner. *Know,* in the Hebrew idiom, signifies sometimes to approve, to acknowledge, and to make known, "The Lord knows them that are his"—approves them. "The world knows us not"—acknowledges, approves us not. "I will know nothing among you"—make known nothing among you: 1 Cor. ii. 2.—*Macknight.*

FULLNESS OF TIME, Πληρομα του χρονου, *Pleroma tou chronou.* The fullness of time, the completion of any period of time, Gal. iv. 4; Eph. i. 10. The completion of the period which was to precede the Messiah.

FULLNESS OF THE GENTILES—The completion of the salvation of the Gentiles, or the bringing of all the Gentiles into the kingdom of Jesus.

The *pleroma* of times of the Gentiles, and of the Jews, are topics of much interest in the apostolic writings. Rom. xi. 12, 25. The fullness of the times of the Jews, of the times of the Gentiles, and of all the great epochs is spoken of, Eph. i. 10, where *kairon,* seasons or epochs, instead of *chronon,* is used. The Jews had their time of being God's people; the Gentiles will soon have had their time; and then God will bring in the Jews under a new arrangement. The word *pleroma* occurs sixteen times. The church is called the fullness of Christ, or "the fullness of him who fills all in all." Eph. i. 23.

GENERATION, Γενεα, *genea*—generation, race, or age of men, occurs forty times; and in the King's version is frequently rendered "generation," and once, "nation," Phil. ii. 15. Campbell sometimes renders it *race* and *generation.* Much depends on the preference given to its meaning in understanding Matt. xxiv. 34. It is enough for us to say, that either *race* or *generation* is the current meaning of the word. Beza has translated it about twenty times, *gens,* nation.

GIFT OF THE HOLY SPIRIT.—This phrase occurs but twice: Acts ii. 38; x. 45; and in both places designates the splendid miraculous influences of the Holy Spirit. Δορεα, *dorea,* and not χαρις, *charis,* is the word used here. This same miraculous display is called "the gift of God," Acts viii. 20, and "the same gift," Acts xi. 17, in both of which *dorea* is found. Besides these, this word *dorea* is found, John iv. 10; Rom. v. 15, 17; 2 Cor. ix 15; Eph. iii. 7; iv. 7; Heb. vi. 4—in all eleven times. See "Baptism of the Holy Spirit."

GOSPEL, Ευαγγελλιον, *euangelium*—good news, glad tidings. The promise of blessing all nations in the seed of Abraham, is called *gospel,* Gal. iii. 8. The promise of a rest in Canaan, is called *gospel,* Heb. iv. 2. The announciation of the birth of the Messiah, is called *gospel* by the angels, Luke ii. 10. But that which is emphatically called THE GOSPEL, is what was first promulged in Jerusalem, including the facts of the death, burial and resurrection of Jesus; from which arose the proclamation of remission, adoption, and eternal glory. *Euangelizo*, to proclaim good news; and *euangelium*, good news, occur frequently—the former fifty-seven times; and the latter seventy-six times.

GRACE, χαρις, *charis*, occurs one hundred and fifty-six times. rendered *favor* and *grace*. It is found in numerous acceptations in the volume. Parkhurst and Greenfield give some fifteen meanings to it; such as acceptance, benefit, liberality, contributions, thanks, gratitude, graciousness, kindness, grace, a gift, etc. On the last Parkhurst observes. "While the miraculous influences of the Spirit are called gifts, or separately, a gift; and though I firmly believe his blessed operations or influences in the hearts of ordinary believers in general; yet, that χαρις, *charis*, is ever in the New Testament particularly used for these, is more than I dare, after attentive examination, assert. On the passages where *charis* may seem to have this meaning, the reader may do well to consult Whitby, and especially his Notes on 2 Cor. vi. 1; Gal. vi. 1, 18; Heb. xiii. 9."—*Parkhurst*. With this statement we must concur from all the evidence before us.

HADES, Αδης, *hades*—The state of spirits while separated from their bodies. The separate state of human existence, which intervenes between death and the resurrection, occurs, Matt. xi. 25; xvi. 18; Luke x. 15; xvi. 23; Acts ii. 27, 31; 1 Cor. xv. 55; Rev. i. 18; vi. 8; xx. 13, 14—eleven times. See Note on Acts ii. 27, p. 57.

HEAVEN, Ουρανος, *ouranos*—the air, the expanse in which the sun, moon, and stars, appear; but specially the residence of God, and the high and holy intelligences of the Universe. The Jews have three heavens; that in which the birds fly; that in which the sun, moon, and stars appeared; that in which the throne of God is placed, called by them "the heaven of heavens"—the palace of the Almighty. It is used figuratively; see "Prophetic Symbols" under this word. It is found in the apostolic writings more than three hundred times.

HELL, Γεεννα, *gehenna*, hell, occurs Matt. v. 22, 29, 30; x. 28; xviii. 9; xxiii. 15, 33; Mark ix. 43, 45, 47; Luke xii. 5; James iii. 6—in all twelve times. See Note on Acts ii. 27, p. 57.

HERESY, Αιρεσις, *hairesis*, occurs Acts v. 17; xv. 5; xxiv. 5, 14; xxvi. 5; xxviii. 22; 1 Cor. xi. 19; Gal. v. 20; 2 Pet. ii. 1. It is found nine times, translated both *sect* and *heresy*, in the common and other versions. Sect of the Pharisees, sect of the Sadducees, and sect of the Nazarenes, are all called *hairesis*. It imports in profane writers, *choice;* but in the Christian Scriptures and Josephus, it is used to denote such a form of *religious opinions as any one chooses to follow*, by which he is distinguished and separated from others. A sect, a party under a human leader: 1 Cor. xi. 19; Gal. v. 20; 2 Pet. ii. 1. Its ecclesiastical import is different; for an erroneous doctrine is, by ecclesiastics, called a *heresy*. In scripture usage it generally means a sect, or a schism, rather than the opinions embraced by the sect.

HERETIC, Αιρετικος, *airetikos*, factionist, sectarian, occurs but once, Tit. iii. 10. One who makes a party or faction.

HONOR, Τιμη, *time*, honor. Many instances can be adduced from Greek writers, showing that *time* [honor] is used to represent reward, stipend, maintenance, as well as from the New Testament. To honor one's parents is not merely to reverence them, but to maintain them when they need it. *Double honor*, compared with that bestowed upon widows, indicates greater liberality or support. It is, Matt. xxvii. 6, used for price, reward, also, verse 9; Acts iv. 34; v. 2, 3; vii. 10; xix. 19; 1 Cor. vi. 20; vii. 23, etc. Thus it is often found for price, reward, maintenance. In all it is found forty-three times.

IMPUTED, Λογιζομαι, *logizomai*, occurs forty-one times. It is translated, "I reckon," "impute," "conclude," "reason," "discourse." It is a word used in arithmetical calculation, and its primary and radical import is to reckon or account: Rom. iv. 6; 2 Cor. v. 19. In the passive sense: Rom. iv. 3, 4, 5, 8, 9, 10; 2 Tim. iv. 16, etc.

IMPOSITION OF HANDS, or *laying on of hands*. This phrase, denoting the communication of some gift, benefit, power, or office, (for an office is a gift,) occurs, Matt. xix. 15; Mark vi. 5; Luke iv. 10; xiii. 13; Acts vi. 6; viii. 17; xiii. 3; xix. 6; xxviii. 8. The phrase, "laying on of hands," occurs 1 Tim. iv. 14; Heb. vi. 2. The persons who laid on hands were Jesus, the Apostles, Prophets, Teachers, Elders, or the Presbytery. The persons on whom hands were laid, were the sick, and such as desired to receive spiritual gifts, and those designated for public trusts or offices in, or for, the congregation.

JUSTIFICATION. We have this word but three times in the common version: Rom. iv. 24; v. 16, 18. Justify occurs in reference to God: Rom. iii. 30; Ga iii. 8. Christians are said to be justified by *Christ*, Acts xiii. 39; by *grace* or *favor*, Rom. iii. 24; by *faith*, Rom. iii. 28; by *his blood*, Rom. v. 9; by *the name of the Lord Jesus*, 1 Cor. vi. 11; by *works*, James ii. 24. See Note 35, p. 64. The words translated "justification" in the common version, are δικαιοσις and δικαιωμα.

KINGDOM OF HEAVEN, Βασιλεια των Ουρανων, *Basileia ton Ouranon*, Reign or Kingdom of Heaven. *Basileia*, with the Greeks, denoted either Reign or Kingdom. "The Kingdom of Heaven is at hand," by Dr. Campbell is rendered "the Reign of Heaven approaches." While the reign of a king may advance or recede, the kingdom with us

APPENDIX. 83

is as stationary as the ground upon which the people live. The burden of the testimonies of Matthew, Mark, and Luke, is this "Reign of Heaven." The nigh approach of it is announced by John, Jesus, the *Twelve*, and the *Seventy*, during the public ministry of Jesus in Judea and Galilee. The near approach of this Reign, and the peculiarities of this Kingdom of Heaven, or of God, is spoken of more than forty times in Matthew alone, and about one hundred times in the historic books. Dr. Campbell's rule of translating this phrase is a good one. Whenever the approach or progress of *Basileia* is spoken of, he renders it *Reign;* but it is a matter of discretion, in other places, whether to prefer the one or the other.

The Reign of Heaven could not commence before the King ascended to his throne—before Jesus was glorified. Such were the ancient prophecies, and such are the facts stated by the Apostles. "The Spirit was not given till Jesus was glorified;" "the Reign or Kingdom of God is not meat and drink, but righteousness, and peace, and joy in the Holy Spirit."

LETTER AND SPIRIT occurs 2 Cor. iii. *Letter* is contrasted with the New Institution. Paul was a minister not of the Law, but of the Gospel—here called " Letter and Spirit." The Law kills, but the Spirit gives life." The ministry of Moses was a ministration of condemnation; but that of Christ is a ministration of justification. The glory of the first ministry was continually fading, like that of Moses' face; but the glory of the Christian ministration is an increasing glory, from glory to glory. *The Lord is the Spirit* of which Paul was a minister; for Adam the second is a quickening Spirit. The Messiah is not the Lord of the Spirit; but is himself the Lord the Spirit.

LIFE AND DEATH. Life, though in common usage it denotes existence, animal or rational, is used in a great variety of meaning. In the sacred scriptures its most current meaning is a mode of existence which we call happiness. Death, which is always contrary to life, is found in exactly the same number of acceptations; for in whatever sense we use the word life, the loss of that is denominated *death*. Hence we have natural life, natural death; moral life, moral death; the spiritual life, and the spiritual death; the present and future life and death; happiness and misery, temporal and eternal; second life, and second death, etc. Death is mere privation; therefore, whatever is called life, the privation of that is called death, as the Hebrew term *muth*, first used for death, indicates.

THE LORD THE SPIRIT occurs twice; 2 Cor. iii. 17, common version. The Lord is that Spirit; literally, The Lord is the Spirit, verse 18. *The Spirit of the Lord*, common version. It is literally, The Lord the Spirit—not *of the Spirit*. See "Letter and Spirit."

MAN OF SIN, Ανϑροπος της Αμαρτιας, *anthropos tes amartias*, 2 Thess. ii. 3, occurs but once; the son of perdition. The revelation of this man of sin was subsequent to the revelation of Jesus Christ: for even in the apostolic age it was a *mystery* of iniquity of which this man of sin was to be the minister. In the temple, or church of God, he erected his throne; and after mystifying the revelation of Christ, and corrupting his institutions, has become the Father of Apostates, and as such goes into perdition. His destruction draws near.

MEDIATOR, Μεσιτης, *mesites*, occurs, Gal. iii. 19, 20, applied to *Moses*. Jesus is called the One Mediator, viz: of the Christian Institution, 1 Tim. ii. 5, and the Mediator of a new and better institution, Heb. viii. 6; ix. 15; xii. 24. It occurs six times. One that negotiates between two parties—God and Man. Therefore Jesus unites both in his own person. He mediates a new institution between God and Man; and is *Emanuel*, God with us.

MIND OF THE FLESH, φρονημα του σαρκος, *phronema tou sarkos;* common version, "carnally minded," occurs only Rom. viii. 6 and 7. It is the offspring of yielding to the desires of the flesh, and is enmity against God. See Note on Rom. viii. 6, 7, 27, p. 69. This is to be *in the flesh*, and under the curse.

MIND OF THE SPIRIT, φρονημα του πνευματος, *phronema tou pneumatos*, occurs also twice: Rom. viii. 6, 27. It is the offspring of yielding to the Spirit of God, and is life and peace. See Note on Rom. viii. 6, 7, 27, p. 69.

MINISTER, Διικονος, *diakonos*. See *Deacon*. A minister is a voluntary servant, whose service is called "ministry."

MIRACLE—that which is above the regular operation of the established laws of nature. Every institution of God began with miracles, or works beyond the power of natural law. The first man was an adult, and never an infant, as reason, experience, and revelation assert. The Jewish institution began in miracle. So did the Christian commence with a glorious display of miraculous powers. This was "the demonstration of the Spirit," and this " the power of God," on which the faith of Christians rest.

MYSTERY, Μυστεριον, *mysterion*, secret, hidden meaning, occurs twenty-eight times. The secrets of the kingdom of Jesus are so called, Matt. xiii. 11; Mark iv. 11; Luke viii. 10. The calling of the Gentiles is called a mystery, Col. i. 26, 27. Besides these passages, the reader, curious to know the meaning of this word, will consult Rom. xi. 25; xvi. 25; 1 Cor. ii. 7; iv. 1; xiii. 2; xiv. 2; xv. 51; Eph. i. 9; iii. 3, 4, 9, v. 32; vi. 19;

Col. ii. 2; iv. 3; 2 Thess. ii 7; 1 Tim. iii. 9, 16; Rev. i. 2(; x. 7; xvii. 5, 7. See Note on Rom. xvi. 25, 26, 27. p 70.

ORDAIN, Ορίζω, horizo, to limit, to bound; hence the word *horizon* which bounds our view. This word, so much controverted, we shall lay before the reader in all its occurrences and translations in the common version: Luke xxii. 22, "determined;" Acts ii. 23, "determinate;" x. 42, "ordained;" xi. 29, "the disciples determined;" xvii. 26, "determined the bounds of their habitation," or "marked out;" xvii. 31, "ordained." Luke is the only sacred historian who uses this word. Paul uses it, Rom. i. 4, "declared;" and Heb. iv. 7, "he limits," or marks out a certain day. These are all the occurrences of this word and its versions in the common Testament.

We have *pro orizo*, to foreordain, or previously declare, or mark out, in the following passages: Acts iv. 28, "determined before," "thy hand determined or marked out before," "had written in the book to be done;" Rom. viii. 29, 30, "predestinate;" 1 Cor. ii. 7, "ordained before:" Eph. i. 5, 11, "predestinated." Thus we have *orizo* eight times, and *pro orizo* six times—the former translated by ordain, determine, declare, limit, in the common version; and the latter, by determine before, predestinate, and ordain before.

We have also another compound word, from the same root, (*aphorizo*,) which occurs ten times: Matt. xiii. 49; xxv. 32, twice; Luke vi. 22; Acts xiii. 2; xix. 9; Rom. i. 1; 2 Cor. vi. 17; Gal. i. 15; ii. 12—always translated *separate* or *separated*.

We have the word *ordain* often in the English Testament, when it is not *orizo* in the original; such as to ordain Apostles, Elders, and to institute observances, etc. For this word we have *poieo*, to make, or appoint; and we have *kathistemi*, to constitute. *Poieo* occurs, Mark iii. 14, "Jesus ordained twelve." *Kathistemi* occurs, Tit. i. 5, "Ordain elders." *Ginomai* is also used to make or ordain an Apostle, Acts i. 22.

ORDAIN TO ETERNAL LIFE, Acts xiii. 48. *Tasso*, the word here used, occurs, Acts xv. 2, the brethren *determined;* xxii. 10, *appointed;* xxviii. 23, when they had *appointed* him a day: also found, Matt. xxviii. 16; Luke vii. 8; Rom. xiii. 1; 1 Cor. xvi. 15.

ORDAINED TO CONDEMNATION, before, of old, Jude 4. The word thus rendered is προγραφομαι, *prographomai*, before written. It occurs, and is translated, Rom. xv. 4, twice, *written aforetime*, were before *written;* Gal. iii. 1, Jesus Christ evidently *set forth:* Eph. iii. 3, I wrote afore. These are all its occurrences in the Apostles' doctrine, and certainly ought in Jude, as in other places, to be "*before written.*" These persons were long ago written of as worthy of condemnation.

PASTOR, Ποιμεν, *poimen*, shepherd, pastor. By a very natural figure of speech, the term *shepherd* became, among the Jews, the name of one who takes care of souls. Jesus called himself the Good Shepherd, and Peter called him the Chief Shepherd: under him there are many shepherds, else he could not be the chief. Isaiah speaks thus of him: "He shall feed his flock like a shepherd, and gather the lambs in his bosom, and gently lead those that are with young." "Peter, feed my lambs." The shepherds of Israel called *pastors*, were those who taught the *people* knowledge, Jer. iii. 15; xxiii. 1, 2; Ezek. xxxiv. 2, 8, 10, etc. Though we have the word *pastor* but once in the common English, we have the original word, *poimen*, seventeen times; translated in the historical books fourteen times, and twice in the Epistles, shepherd, Heb. xiii. 20; 1 Pet. ii. 25; and once, *pastors*, Eph. iv. 11. The shepherds here mentioned were those who fed the flock of God, as Peter was commanded to tend the sheep and lambs of Christ. As the *shepherd* and *bishop* of souls are the same, 1 Pet. ii. 25, so are the pastors and teachers, Eph. iv. 11; for they are expressed as one class in the original, contradistinguished from the *tous men*—Apostles—the *tous* prophets, the *tous* evangelists, and the *tous* pastors and teachers.

PILLAR AND SUPPORT OF THE TRUTH. Such, in the judgment of the best critics, is one of the characters given to the Christian church. It is an allusion to the ancient Roman pillars on which were inscribed or hung up the laws of the state; on the church is inscribed, not in letters made by hands, but in the behavior of Christians, the law of the Lord, and thus the church becomes a pillar and support of the truth. Hence we learn that the best support of truth in the world, is the character or behavior of Christians.

PREACH. Κηρυσσω, *kerusso*, from *kerux*, a herald, or public crier. This is the word used, Mark xvi. 15, 20, and is found in the sacred writings sixty-two times. It always indicates to publish facts, to make proclamation as a herald. See Note 23, page 60.

PRIEST. For the origin and meaning of this word, see *Elder*.

The *office* of a priest is that of an intercessor, one who officiates in things pertaining to God in behalf of men, by offerings and prayers. See Heb. v. 1, 4.

PREDESTINATE. See the word *Ordain*. It occurs four times only in the English Testament, and has *pro orizo*, before defined, answering to it in the original.

PROPHET. This word, and the word *prophecy*, have two meanings in the sacred writings; the one is the foretelling of events yet future—the other is uttering the meaning of ancient oracles, or speaking, from the impulse of the Spirit, to the edification and comfort of Christians: 1 Cor. xiv; Rom. xiii.

RECONCILIATION. See *Atonement*.

APPENDIX.

REDEMPTION. Λυτρωσις, *lutrosis*, deliverance, occurs Luke i. 68; ii. 38; Heb. ix. 12. We have also, Acts vii. 35, the word *lutrotis* translated a *deliverer;* and *lutroo*, Luke xxiv 21, I redeem; Tit. ii. 14, to redeem us; 1 Pet. i. 18, redeemed. *Apolutrosis*, deliverance from, or redemption from, occurs ten times: Luke xxi. 28; Rom. iii. 24; viii. 23; 1 Cor. i. 30; Eph. i. 7, 14; Col. i. 14; iv. 30; Heb. ix. 15; xi. 35. The dismissing of a person after a ransom has been paid, is called by the Greeks, *apolutrosis*.

REFORM. Μετανοεω, *metanoeo*, occurs thirty-four times; and *metanoia*, reformation, twenty-four times. See Note on Romans ii. 4, page 66.

It may be added, that *metanoeo* etymologically signifies to think *after* the fact, or to change one's mind so as to influence the behavior. But no change of mind which does not result in a change of life, fills up the measure of the imperative of *metanoeo*.

To give *reformation*, or to give repentance, common version, *dounai metanoian*, Acts v. 31. Doddridge makes Josephus explain this phrase. He quotes from Josephus the phrase, "Dounai metanoian epi tois pepragmenois," to publish a pardon to those who lay down their arms. To give repentance, is to afford scope for it, or to make a proclamation offering inducements to it.

REGENERATION. Παλιγγενεσια, *palingenesia*, occurs twice: Matt. xix. 28, the renovation, or change of state or condition; and Tit. iii. 5, the washing, or bath of regeneration, connected with the renewing of the mind by the Holy Spirit. "Born again" is a figurative expression, and in figurative language there must be a correspondence in the figures used.

As the figure of a gate requires an inclosure; or of a door, a house: as the figure of a branch presupposes a tree, or a vine: as the figure of a net corresponds with fish and fishermen; or as the figure of a marriage requires a bride and bridegroom; so does the figure of a new birth, or *being born again*, require a kingdom. Hence, when Jesus first spoke of being born again, he had a kingdom in his eye. As a person can not be married without a bride, or a child born without father and mother; so no one can be born again without father and mother, and a family or state to be born *into*. Unless a man be born of water and Spirit, he can not enter into the kingdom of God. The phrase "born again," *gennethe, anothen*, occurs John iii. 5, 7; 1 Pet. i. 23.

REMISSION. Αφεσις, *aphesis*, remission. The noun occurs seventeen times, and the verb, *aphiemi*, used in the Lord's Prayer for *forgive*, occurs one hundred and forty-six times; rendered to forgive, remit, set free from, dismiss, in all versions. No word more fully expresses deliverance from sin, than the verb and noun above interpreted.

REPENT. Μεταμελομαι, *metamelomai*, Matt. xxi. 29, 32; xxvii. 3; 2 Cor. vii. 8; Heb. vii. 21, I repent, or am concerned for the past. The word is always translated repent, in the common version and the new. See Note on Rom. ii. 4, page 66.

REPENT AND BELIEVE THE GOSPEL. This arrangement of reformation and belief occurs but once, and is addressed to Jews: for the Jews, who had the knowledge of God in the oracles, could reform without the Christian faith; and unless they first reformed, they could not believe the gospel. Paul preached to Jews and Gentiles, reformation in relation to God, and faith in relation to Jesus Christ.

REPROBATE—*not approved*. This word occurs eight times in the sacred writings; Rom. i. 28; 1 Cor. ix. 27; 2 Cor. xiii. 5, 6, 7; 2 Tim. iii. 8; Tit. i. 16; Heb. vi. 8; translated undiscerning, unapproved, rejected, once a cast-away, 1 Cor. x. 27, and several times reprobate, in the King's version. "Not approved" is its most natural meaning, and will make good sense in every place where it is found in the New Testament.

SALVATION. Σωτερια, *soteria*, deliverance from evil. We have the present salvation of the body from physical dangers; also the salvation of the soul from the guilt, pollution, and dominion of sin; and the future andieternal salvation of the whole person consummated at the resurrection and glorification of all who die in the Lord. It is found in the first sense, Acts xxvii. 34, translated health; Heb. xi. 7, to the saving of Noah's house; 1 Tim. ii. 15; Acts xxvii. 20; vii. 25. In this sense, God is the Saviour of all men. Of the second salvation, Acts ii. 47; Mark xvi. 16; 1 Cor. i. 18; 2 Cor. ii. 15; 1 Peter iii. 21; James i. 21; Eph. ii. 5, 8, and in most places in the Epistles. In relation to the ultimate and complete salvation, it is found 1 Cor. vi. 5; Rom. v. 9; xiii. 11; Phil. ii. 12; Heb. v. 9; 2 Tim. ii. 10.

SANCTIFY. Αγιαζο, *hagaizo*, to separate any thing to God. *Agiazo* occurs twenty-eight times, translated to sanctify, to make holy; *agiasmos*, sanctification, holiness, occurs ten times. The meaning of *agiazo* will be found, John xvii. 17, 19; x. 36. Jesus was said to be sanctified, made holy, *i. e.* set apart and devoted to God. The setting apart or consecrating of the body, soul, and spirit, to God, through Jesus Christ, is the holiness of Christianity.

SIN-OFFERING. Αμαρτια, *amartia*, sin, and sin-offering. From comparing Lev. iv. 4, 15, 21, 25; i. 4; xvi. 21, it will appear that in the Septuagint, this word was frequently used to denote sin-offering, and so it appears to be used 2 Cor. v. 21; Heb. ix. 28. In Hebrew, both the sin and sin-offering are also denoted by the same word.

SPIRIT, πνευμα. This word frequently occurs in the Septuagint of the Old Testament, as well as in the New. In the former, it means sometimes *wind* and sometimes *spirit*:

but in the latter, where it occurs three hundred and thirty-nine times, it means **spirit**; and is uniformly so translated by the King's translators, except in John iii. 8; see Note on John iii. 5, 6, 8, page 56. Πνευματα, Heb. i. 7, common version, *spirits*, in this is rendered *winds:* "He makes winds his angels." We are authorized to render πνευματα winds in this place, only because it is here a quotation from the Septuagint, (Psalm civ. 4,) and the connection shows that such was its meaning both here and there.

SPIRITS IN PRISON. These are explained by Peter to mean, the spirits of those who died under condemnation when the flood came upon the world of the ungodly in the days of Noah. They, like the angels that sinned, are reserved under sentence to the resurrection of the unjust, when the devil and all his angels shall go away into everlasting destruction, from the presence of the Lord and the glory of his power.

SPIRITUAL MAN. Πνευματικος, *pneumatikos*. One who possessed some spiritual gift, 1 Cor. ii. 13, contrasted with the animal man. Persons under the influence of the teachings of the Holy Spirit, may be called spiritual men; but in the Epistles it appears to be applied to those who possessed some of the peculiar gifts of that age. The word spiritual is applied to food, drink, body, and gifts: 1 Cor. x. 3, 4; xii. 1; xv. 44, 46. It occurs twenty-five times.

SURETY. Εγγυος, *enguos*, sponsor, pledge, Heb. vii. 22. This word occurs but once in the sacred writings: It is found in the Apocrypha, Eccles. xxix. 15, 16; 2 Mac. x. 28; and its conjugates are found in Proverbs. The Greek interpreters explain it by *mesites*, mediator. Upon the care and faithfulness of our High Priest, constituted by an oath, Christians can rely, as upon a surety, that his sacrifice is accepted, and we permitted by it to come to God. The high priests went alone into the holiest of all; so did ours. We, then, can only have his word for what was done in the heavens, and that is sufficient for our drawing *enguos* near.

WIND—Aνεμος is the New Testament word for *wind;* and occurs twenty-nine times viz: Matt. vii. 25, 27; viii. 26; xi. 7, 14; xxiv. 30, 32; xxiv. 31; Mark iv. 37, 39, 41; vi. 48, 51; xiii. 27; Luke vii. 24; viii. 23, 24, 25; John vi. 18; Acts xxvii. 4, 7, 14, 15; Eph. iv. 14; James iii. 4; Jude, 12th verse; Rev. vi. 13; vii. 1—never translated *spirit.*

WORD—Λογος, ρεμα—the first of these, *logos*, is chosen by the Holy Spirit in John i. 1, as the proper name of the DIVINE character of our Lord Jesus Christ; or, of HIM "who was in the beginning with God, and was God;" and in Rev. xix. 13, it is given to the Messiah in his glorified state—"and his name is called THE WORD OF GOD."

WORLD TO COME. Οικουμενη, *oikoumene*, world, occurs Mark xxiv. 14; Luke ii. 1; iv. 5; xxi. 26; Acts xi. 28; xvii. 6, 31; xix. 27; xxiv. 25; Rom. x. 18; Heb. i. 6; ii. 5; Rev. iii. 10; xii. 9; xvi. 14—fifteen times in all; literally, the inhabited earth.

As this is the only occurrence of this phrase rendered, (Heb. ii. 5,) the world to come, and because it is one of the greatest and most sublime topics in the Christian Scriptures, we beg leave to add the following remarks:

If the first four verses of Heb. ii. are regarded as a parenthesis, then the 5th verse naturally follows the 14th verse of the first chapter, which appears to be its proper connection. "The world to come," then, is the world which Christ entered after he rose from the dead; in which he obtained by inheritance a more excellent name than the angels after he had by himself purged our sins. It was then, when he was brought again into the world, verse 6, that the government of angels ceased; for they were subjected to him; and it was then he was anointed Lord of the Universe, and his throne established forever. It was then that he made *all* the angels ministers to the heirs of that kingdom. This then, is "the world to come," of which Jesus was the first-born, of which Paul here speaks, and into which, in its earthly dispensation, called the *mellon aion*, (but, in its heavenly, the *mellon oikoumene*,) all Christians come; and this is the consummation of which Paul speaks, Eph. i. 10, "That in the economy, or dispensation, or fullness of the times or epochs, he would gather together under one head, all things—under Christ—all things in heaven and earth—even under him."

www.ingramcontent.com/pod-product-compliance
Lightning Source LLC
Chambersburg PA
CBHW032029150426
43194CB00006B/207